ROSECRANS' CAMPAIGN

WITH THE

Fourteenth Army Corps,

OR THE

ARMY OF THE CUMBERLAND:

A NARRATIVE OF PERSONAL OBSERVATIONS, WITH AN APPENDIX, CONSISTING OF OFFICIAL REPORTS OF THE

BATTLE OF STONE RIVER.

By "W. D. B.,"

CORRESPONDENT OF THE CINCINNATI COMMERCIAL.

CINCINNATI:
MOORE, WILSTACH, KEYS & CO.,
25 WEST FOURTH STREET.
1863.

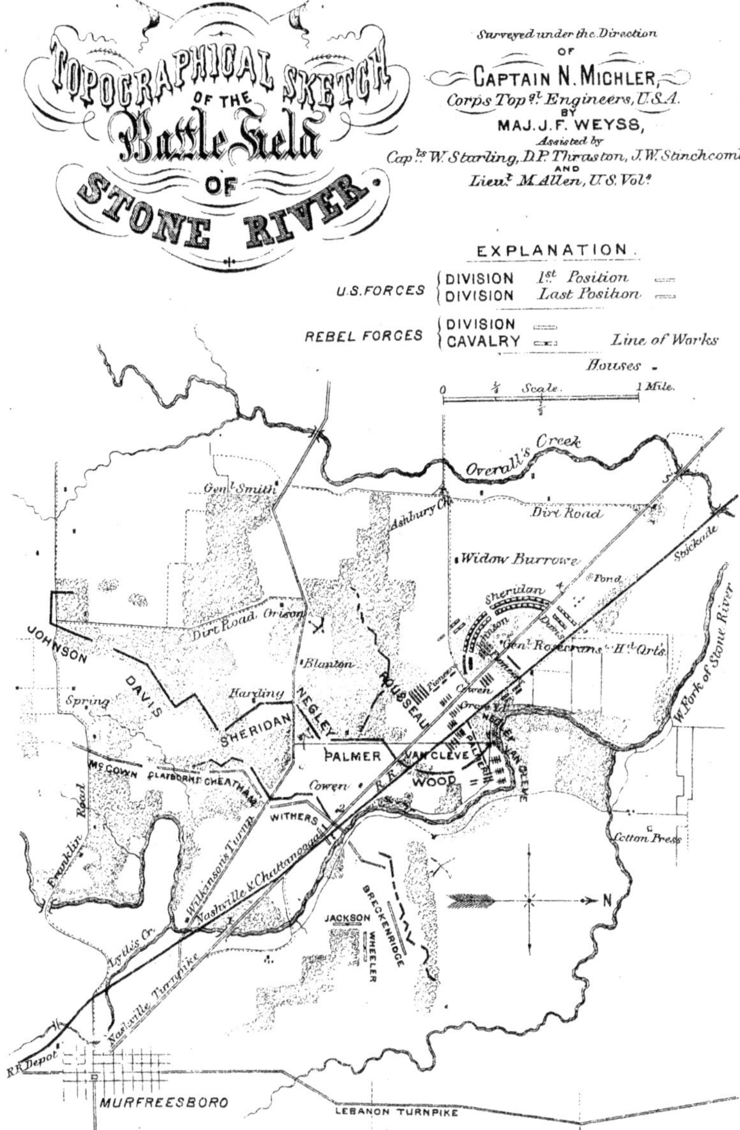

Explanatory.—The rebel line of battle and their line of attack on the first day (as represented in the map), do not correspond. It was impossible for the Topographer to represent both. He therefore chose the line of battle of the rebels until they moved to the attack. The divisions of McCown and Withers then obliqued to the left until the left of their line projected beyond the right of Johnson's right, flanking him. The reader will bear in mind that the attack first fell upon the left of Johnson's division, then his right brigade, then Davis and Sherridan. The position occupied on the first day of January, is not fully represented; the entire line of the Left Wing not appearing in the map. This was omitted by the Topographer to avoid confusion in a reduced map. Otherwise the diagram is very perfect.

PREFACE.

THIS volume presents a narrative of the personal observations of the author during the three months' campaign of Major General Rosecrans, commanding the original Fourteenth Army Corps—popularly designated the Army of the Cumberland. It embraces a period beginning with the 30th day of October, 1862, when General Rosecrans assumed command of the Department of the Cumberland, and the Fourteenth Army Corps, and concludes with the occupation of Murfreesboro, Tennessee, immediately after the memorable battle of Stone River. Doubtless it contains some statements which might have been wisely omitted. Certainly many very interesting facts which could have been profitably introduced, were excluded. But it is purely narrative. It aspires to nothing but to record the truth candidly and clearly. No ill-natured flings or *ex parte* criticisms are indulged. An earnest effort is made to deal fairly with all the actors in the great drama which culminated in the victory on Stone River.

The description of the Battle of Stone River, which concludes the narrative, was written partially from personal observation, and partially with the assistance of the official reports. The successive action of brigades is followed as nearly as possible. Biographies of regiments, obviously, could not be included without unduly expanding the proportions of the volume. The plan adopted by the author, of generally describing the disaster to the Right Wing, and the concurrent preparations of the General-in-Chief to retrieve the misfortunes of Wednesday morning, up to the period of the first repulse of the enemy, and then returning to follow the tide of battle as it flowed tumultuously from Right to Left, until it had involved the entire army, was conceived to be the best for the development of the whole series of involved engagements. Time and circumstances were elusive. Distinct actions were convulsing the field simultaneously, and to bring out each clearly, required some sacrifice of the important elements of time and continuity. To write a summary description of the battle, and compensate for omission of the special engagements of brigades and divisions by the ultimate introduction of rhetoric, would be comparatively easy. As the author wrote this volume more particularly for the Army of the Cumberland and its friends, he preferred, at the sacrifice of some proprieties of descriptive writing, to exhibit the action of each division or brigade, as far as possible. If any are slurred it is the misfortune of the author. It certainly was not his purpose to overlook or unjustly disparage any of the worthy soldiers who, by their valor and conduct, are entitled to a nation's gratitude.

The Appendix embraces the Official Reports of the Commander-in-Chief of the Army, of the three Corps Commanders, of all the Division Commanders, of the Chief of Cavalry and some of his subordinates. The author desires to express his obligations to Corporal Thomas Worthington, of the One Hundred and Sixth Ohio Volunteers—a gentleman who merits a much higher position in the army than he now holds—for appreciated services in assisting him to collect the official documents in the Appendix.

The author is also sincerely obliged to the accomplished Major J. F. Weyss, of the Topographical Engineers, Department of the Cumberland, for the beautiful reduced map of the battle-field of Stone River, which precedes the title page.

Cincinnati, April 20, 1863.

CONTENTS.

CHAPTER XXVI.

CHAPTER XXVII.

CHAPTER XXVIII.

CHAPTER XXIX.

CHAPTER XXX.

CHAPTER XXXI.

CHAPTER XXXII.

CHAPTER XXXIII.

APPENDIX.

ROSECRANS' CAMPAIGN

WITH THE

FOURTEENTH ARMY CORPS.

CHAPTER I.

THE Army of the Ohio—Discontent of the Soldiers—Major General Buell Retires from Command—The Army Countermarches Again—Assumption of Command by Major General W. S. Rosecrans—Popular Fallacies—Embarrassments of the New Commander—His Communications—Cumberland River Innavigable, the Louisville and Nashville Railroad a Wreck—Condition of the Army—Its Partial Demoralization—The Cavalry Arm.

GENERAL BRAGG and his army had just escaped from Kentucky. The federal army was discouraged, and the nation profoundly disappointed. A twelve month had been spent in fruitless campaigning; millions of money had been lavished without compensation; and the bones of thousands of brave men were moldering among the hills and valleys of the South, sad monuments of unrequited toil, and uncomplaining sacrifice. It was no fault of the gallant soldiers who carried muskets and manned our cannon. They still rallied around the old flag, but sternly and bitterly, while they clamored for a chieftain to lead them to victory. The powerful Army of the Ohio, which had been renowned for discipline and steady valor, was now much wasted by tedious marches and distressing vicissitudes, and partially demoralized by the dissatisfaction of the troops and their officers with their commander. Their discontent, and the popular distrust of Major General Buell, engendered by his failure to achieve results adequate to the means within his control, rendered his removal imperative. Wheeling his columns in the direction which they had so eagerly pursued at the heels of the fugitive battalions of Albert Sidney Johnson but a few months before, he left them in charge of Major General Thomas, and repairing to Louisville, met orders requiring him to relinquish his command to Major General William S. Rosecrans, then freshly crowned with the laurels of brilliant victories in Mississippi.

Prior to the assignment of General Rosecrans to the command of this army, it had been designated the "Army of the Ohio." The War Department, which had frequently displayed a knack for cutting up the territory of the United States into military departments—more, it seems, for the purpose of providing commands for superfluous chieftains, with which it had embarrassed itself, than for any other appreciable reason—now carved out another slice of military territory, denominated it the Department of the Cumberland, changed the designation of the Army to "Fourteenth Army Corps," and nominated Major General Rosecrans to the command. The department consisted of all that portion of Tennessee, east of the Tennessee River, and so much of the States of Alabama and Georgia as General Rosecrans might occupy. Fort Henry and Fort Donelson were subsequently included, inasmuch as they were essential to the water line of communication with the department, and had no intimate relationship with the contiguous departments of Major General Grant, and Major General Wright.

General Rosecrans assumed command under peculiarly embarrassing circumstances. His uniform success as department commander and field officer, had inspired the nation with confidence in him, and the popular imagination was inflated with visions of victories which were only probable under the brightest auspices. The people, informed that his army was one of the largest in the nation, and inaccurately impressed that it was perhaps the best disciplined and best appointed, and smarting under recent and trying disappointments, were clamorous for achievements which would swiftly wipe out the stains upon the national escutcheon, and revive their flagging hopes. They presumed and assumed that the instruments of success were already prepared to the hand of the commander, and that nothing remained for him to do but to move upon the enemy and destroy him.

Strange that the costly lessons of experience should have been so quickly forgotten. Strange that the disasters of the Peninsula, and the fruitless Siege of Corinth, should have so soon escaped their memory. It would seem that a people possessing facilities such as we enjoy for acquiring information, scarcely needed a reminder of the tedious delays and serious obstructions which must now protract decisive operations.

To say that General Rosecrans was profoundly impressed with the gravity of the responsibilities he assumed is almost a pointless phrase. He encountered formidable discouragements from the moment he assumed command. We can but glance at some of the most conspicuous. He had relieved General Buell at the expiration of a year of almost barren campaigning. The army had marched through Kentucky and Tennessee into the borders of Alabama and Mississippi, toiled through weary months in the mountains and swamps of the South without victory, and had vainly countermarched again in pursuit of an inferior enemy which had twice eluded their commander. Its shattered columns were at right about toiling listlessly and dispirited toward the desolated and hostile territory which they had twice traversed within a single year, and which, ravaged and exhausted by war, promised but little forage and no subsistence. The season was pressing sharply upon winter—and winter in Tennessee means cold, and snow, and rain, and boundless mud; and these mean hospitals thronged with suffering soldiers, and valleys crowded with the bodies of the dead. The only water line of communication with the seat of hostilities was a thin ribbon which would barely buoy a shallop, and the capricious season, now provokingly constant, offered no prospect of navigation before the dissolution of winter. A single thread of railroad from Louisville to Nashville, insufficient without hostile interruption—even if managed by an enterprising and zealous directory—to properly meet the requisitions of the service, was wrecked and obstructed from Green River to Nashville—more than three-fifths of the length of the line of communication from the primary to the immediate base of operations at Nashville. It was evident that it would require a month of incessant labor to repair it, and it was liable to continuous irruptions of hostile cavalry organized to destroy it, requiring the detail of large detachments of the effective force of the army for its protection. These, among other equally serious and protracting embarrassments were to be overcome, before a decisive movement could be ventured.

General Rosecrans was unacquainted with his army —a matter of no trifling moment—but happily his previous career had prepared it to confide in him. The nation had been taught to consider it a standard of discipline. History, when she lingers tearfully at the little green graves of Chaplin Hills, will attest the valor of its trusty soldiers. But it was no longer the proud army which had swept the frightened foe from the heart of Kentucky into the far distant cotton fields of Mississippi. It had not been bruited that the solidity of those once splendid legions had been well nigh dissolved by repression of their fiery ardor in retreat, by the vicissitudes of painful marches, and confidence destroyed. It had not been told by lightning tongues that nearly ten thousand of those heroes, heart-sick with barren efforts and unrequited trials had deserted when the columns countermarched to Louisville, nor that it required the highest exercise of patriotism on the part of those veterans, and the sternest vigilance of their officers to prevent the regiments from melting to skeletons—a result almost to have been feared had not the spirits of those wearied and discouraged troops been revived by the substitution of a new commander whom they had learned to admire, for one, who, by his coldness and apathy had alienated the confidence they had reposed in him.

General Rosecrans hardly dreamed that almost one-third of his army was in hospitals ; or scattered over the great West, fugitives from duty to the flag. Moreover, many of his regiments were raw levies without drill or discipline, and were often inefficiently commanded. Ages of experience had attested the inability of an armed mob to withstand veteran battalions like those of the rebel armies in shock of battle. Besides, the army was barely half equipped, and its cavalry arm was so inadequate in numbers, and so deficient in equipment and discipline, as to excite astonishment and alarm. A few weeks later the General Commanding wrote officially that "the enormous superiority of the rebel cavalry, kept our little cavalry force almost within the infantry lines, and gave the enemy control of the entire country around us."

CHAPTER II.

Popular Expectations—General Order No. 1—The Temporary Staff—Their Qualifications—Lieutenant Colonel Ducat—The Chief Commissary—Position of the Fourteenth Army Corps—Bragg's Movements—Nashville Invested by Rebel Cavalry—Five Millions of Rations—Railway Annoyances—Military Superintendent of Transportation.

It is well to consider the degree of success, and the period of its accomplishment that a just and discriminating people could expect of an officer under the circumstances which domineered over General Rosecrans. Had the nation guaged its expectations by the achievements of commanders of other great armies during the war, and upon these demanded but moderate improvement, it had more accurately conformed to the logic which had been established for reflection. "We shall expect much of you," said authority. The people had been so often disappointed by results immeasurably inadequate to the instrumentalities employed in conducting the war, and had grown so restive and impatient, that they were now inclined to require too much. Though grateful to General Rosecrans for his past and invariable success, they were disposed to be more patient with him than they would have been with any other commander who might have been assigned to the department.

Nevertheless General Rosecrans assumed his responsibilities cheerfully, and begun his labors with characteristic earnestness and vigor. The summons from the War Department had reached him at the head of his command in Mississippi, and he promptly repaired to his new department, tarrying but sixty hours with his family and friends in Ohio. On the 30th October, 1862, he relieved General Buell, and assumed command by virtue of the following order:

HEADQUARTERS 14TH ARMY CORPS,
Department of the Cumberland,
Louisville, Ky., Oct. 30, 1862.

GENERAL ORDERS NO. 1.

I. By direction of the General-in-Chief, the undersigned assumes the command of the Department of the Cumberland, and the troops under General Buell's command, which will hereafter constitute the Fourteenth Army Corps.

II. The following officers are announced and will act until a permanent organization of Staff is effected:

Lieutenant Colonel ARTHUR C. DUCAT, Twelfth Infantry, Illinois Volunteers, Acting Assistant Inspector General and Chief of Staff.

Major C. GODDARD, Senior Aiddecamp, Acting Assistant Adjutant General.

Major W. P. HEPBURN, Second Iowa Cavalry, Acting Judge Advocate.

Captain SAMUEL SIMMONS, A. C. S., Acting Chief Commissary.

Captain T. G. CHANDLER, A. Q. M., Acting Chief Quartermaster.

Captain N. MICHLER, Chief Topographical Engineer.

Captain J. H. GILMAN, Nineteenth Infantry United States Army, Inspector of Artillery.

Captain J. T. PETERSON, Fifteenth Infantry, United States Army, Acting Assistant Inspector General.

First Lieutenant T. EDSON, Ordnance Corps, Ordnance Officer.

First Lieutenant CHAS. R. THOMPSON, Engineer Regiment of the West, Aiddecamp.

Second Lieutenant BYRON KIRBY, Sixth Infantry United States Army, Aiddecamp.

Surgeon ROBERT MURRAY, U. S. A., Medical Director.

Surgeon A. H. THURSTON, United States Volunteers, Medical Inspector.

Reports will be made and business transacted in accordance with existing orders and regulations.

Official: W. S. ROSECRANS,
C. GODDARD, *Major General.*
Major and A. A. A. G.

The majority of the executive members of this staff accompanied the General from Mississippi. They had proved themselves capable and trustworthy, no meaningless phrase with an officer whose personal staff are all confidential aids, and who are speedily instructed to acquaint themselves with all the duties necessary to qualify them to meet the requisitions of a commander who holds that "a staff officer should know all that his General does."

Lieutenant Colonel Ducat, an Irishman by nativity, and a soldier by nature and habit, had been detailed for Acting Inspector General for qualifications pre-eminently fitting him for that office. "I regard him an extraordinary man," said the General subsequently, alluding to the admirable system of inspections which had been perfected and put into complete working order by himself and his assistants, Captains Peterson and Curtis of the regular army. For the present, he was Chief of Staff, but it was understood that position was reserved for the brilliant Garesche.

Major Goddard, for zealous and intelligent service

in the Adjutant General's office of the Army of the Mississippi, and for gallantry as Aiddecamp at Iuka and Corinth, had been promoted from a Lieutenancy in the Twelfth Ohio Volunteer Infantry, to a Majority, and the Senior Aidship.

Captain Chas. R. Thompson, Aiddecamp, for gallantry at Iuka and Corinth, had been promoted from a Lieutenancy in the Engineer regiment of the West, to a Captaincy on the Staff, a proud position for a youth of less than twenty-three years. Lieutenant Byron Kirby had faithfully served on the staff in Western Virginia, and through the campaign in Tennessee and Mississippi. Major Hepburn had exhibited marked capacity as Judge Advocate, but later in the campaign, being promoted to the Lieutenant Colonelcy of his regiment, he was announced Inspector of Cavalry, and was succeeded by Major Ralston Skinner, appointed Judge Advocate by the President, and assigned to General Rosecran's Staff, at the personal request of the Commanding General.

Captain Samuel Simmons, Commissary of Subsistence—promoted a few weeks later to Lieutenant Colonel, had displayed unusual, it may be justly said, extraordinary foresight, comprehensiveness of judgment, and energy, in the administration of the Subsistence Department of the Army of the Mississippi. Such qualifications were peculiarly demanded in the new field.

Captain Chandler, an Assistant Quartermaster of large experience, had served General Rosecrans in the Department of Western Virginia, and had been Chief Quartermaster in the Department of the Ohio. His present assignment, however, was but temporary—

Lieutenant Colonel J. W. Taylor, by his ability in Mississippi, having merited the approbation of his commander, had been previously designated Chief Quartermaster of the Department. The additional members of the temporary staff, had been in General Buell's command, and their merits at this time had not been demonstrated to the new commander.

General Rosecrans remained but another day at Louisville. The railroad bridge across Green River being now reconstructed, he repaired to Bowling Green, on the 1st of November, and established headquarters temporarily at that point. His army had concentrated at Bowling Green and Glasgow, but the divisions at the latter post were presently ordered forward. Bragg's army was still painfully toiling over the rude mountains of East Tennessee, heading by a wide detour via Chattanooga, toward Murfreesboro. Information touching his designs was scant. General Breckinridge was posted at Murfreesboro with a strong division, and Nashville was invested by swarms of active and enterprising rebel cavalry. It was held by a splendid division of troops, under General Negley, and although communication between the garrison and headquarters of the army was irregular, it was not in jeopardy. The rebels could not now concentrate to assault it before General Rosecrans could move to its relief, so that it was not a subject of embarrassment to him.

Bowling Green was the present southern terminus of the railroad, and the temporary supply depot. The army could not profitably advance two marches beyond until the railroad was repaired to Mitchellsville, on the northern line of Tennessee, nearly forty miles from Nashville, but from which point, after arriving at Nashville, it might, with great labor and trouble, be subsisted from day to day. The Chief Commissary at once displayed his grasp by ordering forward the extraordinary supply of five millions of rations, to be renewed as rapidly as the tedious operation of the railroad would permit. Had the energy of the Commissary met a fair response from the managers of the railroad, the General Commanding would have been relieved of serious vexations. The policy of taking entire military control of the line was carefully considered, and finally dismissed. In the sense of occupation, it was monopolized by the government, but it was managed by the corporation which owned it. Colonel J. B. Anderson, of Louisville, was announced Military Superintendent of Railroad Transportation, but eventually his administration was not warmly approved.

CHAPTER III.

INTRODUCTION of Headquarters to the Female Rebel Element—Madam applies Soft Soap—The Result thereof—Business at Headquarters—Red-tape Defended—Resignations and Furloughs—Improvement of the Cavalry—Colt's Revolving Rifles—Brigadier General David S. Stanley—Mounted Infantry—Pack Mules—East Tennessee—Discipline.

THE General Commanding had arrived at Bowling Green in advance of his camp equipage. Although habitually preferring camp, he was constrained to appropriate a dwelling for headquarters. It is not customary in war to quarter upon friends where virulent enemies are accessible to instruction in the rights of arms. Some high caste families in Bowling Green had endeavored to indoctrinate loyal men and women into the virtues of rebel rights. The General proposed to vindicate his appreciation of the example, and required accommodations at the mansion of a prominent officer of the bogus goverment of Kentucky. He was enjoying the amenities of a retreat with Bragg's army, and his wife remained in possession of the homestead. She was not cordial according to the traditionary style of Kentucky hospitality, but submitted frigidly to the "exigencies of the service." She requested privilege to retain part of the premises for her own occupation, a favor which was graciously granted. During some eight or nine days, the General and his military household perseveringly squeezed themselves into the parlor and two chambers, dining in the hall, for the accommodation of her ladyship. But madam was ungrateful. She seized the earliest opportunity to exhibit her temper and quality by a high-toned act of gentility which signally demonstrated privileged breeding, and fortified her claims to federal favor. It was a season of drought, and such periods in Bowling Green subject the people to inconvenience. They are obliged to cart water for family consumption from Barren River. In any northern town the citizens would make haste to provide themselves with cisterns, but where labor is not compensated, the people do not learn to make themselves comfortable so easily. But this is irrelevant. Madam's chattels had accumulated several barrels of water, and headquarter servants inconsiderately began to use it. Madam's rights were invaded, and she vindicated them by dissolving a quantity of soft soap in the barrels. Not long afterward she was fretted by the seeming misuse of her parlor carpet, and applied to remove it, whereupon the General gave her a counter-emollient in the amiable form of a disquisition upon soft soap and water. This was the introduction of headquarters to the female element of rebellion. It was afterward more elaborately developed, though not at Bowling Green. The rebel women of that city were generally recluse, and did not often come in contact with the "Yankees." The few Union ladies remaining there, sustained the ancient fame of Kentucky hospitality; but their social life was stifled by rebellion.

General Rosecrans continued to apply himself to business unremittingly. No member of the staff found an idle hour. The vast machinery of the department was put in motion. Lines of couriers, connecting with Nashville and the various camps, were immediately established, Captain Elmer Otis, an active, enterprising officer, assuming charge of them. Military maps were collected from every source; friendly people were required to furnish all possible information concerning the topography and geography of the country; and business of every character affecting the campaign, was rapidly systematized and dispatched. The amount of business which had accumulated in the Adjutant General's office was formidable, and it required nearly a regiment of clerks to reduce it. Everything touching the organization of the army, the hundreds of applications for the acceptance of resignations, the almost thousands of appeals for discharges from service; pleas for furloughs, or relief from duty; the million and one items of minutiæ which no thorough General can safely overlook in a volunteer army, formed an almost discouraging aggregation of business. How feebly do they who read the results of a campaign, comprehend the prodigious amount of physical toil that is supported by a commanding general, not to consider the incalculable intellectual labor and moral exasperations which harrass him. Brief observation would invincibly persuade the most inveterate enemy of much calumniated red-tape, that no human skill or industry, without the aid of system, would be equal to the disposition of the mountains of details which roll up in sucessive billows at headquarters.

It was found necessary in the beginning to curb the disposition of officers to apply for leave of absence or to resign. An invalid might obtain temporary respite in the hospitals, or resign. A hale man, unless recommended by his superior to resign, "for the good of the service," was summarily notified to return to duty. The rule was inexorable. But the General was swift to relieve the army of incompetents. He declined to listen to personal appeals. "I don't care for any individual. Everything *for the service;* nothing to individuals." Although an ardent friend, he would not permit the claims of friendship to interpose against the interests of his country.

"THE EYES OF THE ARMY."

The improvement of his cavalry was a primary consideration in his system of reorganization. "Cavalry," he was wont to say, "are the eyes of the army. They can be made its hands and feet." It was his object to elevate them to that excellence. Lee's Kansas Cavalry in the Army of the Mississippi, under his encouragement were renowned in all that country for their efficiency. He wanted whole divisions like them. When he assumed command of the Fourteenth Army Corps, he supposed he had twelve or fifteen thousand veteran cavalry troops. He was surprised and chagrined that he could not muster half that number. A portion of these were chiefly valuable for their capacity to evade danger and good service. A troop of jockeys with riding whips were quite as effective as some of the squadrons. No fault of theirs, but of neglect, lack of capable officers, and deficiences of equipment.

He applied for Brigadier General David S. Stanley, an officer of great spirit, and superior military skill, for Chief of Cavalry, and that General was relieved of the command of perhaps the best division of volunteer infantry in the federal army, to regenerate the cavalry arm of the Fourteenth Corps. There was no reserve from which to draw reinforcements, and the General Commanding applied to the War Department for five thousand Colt's revolving rifles as a substitute for men. About three thousand were received, when the arsenals were exhausted. His mind was so impressed with the conviction that revolving arms would give best assurance of success, that if he had been offered the option of raw men or improved arms, it is probable he would have preferred the latter. It needs no argument to satisfy the public that five charges are superior to one, but the War Department has not yet discovered it. The moral ascendency, which such arms impart to troopers who know how to use them, is of more value to the service than their relative physical strength. They have a double force, inspiring with confidence the men who are supplied with them, and terrifying the enemy.

General Rosecrans desired to make the cavalry arm perfect by combining with it an organization of mounted light infantry with light batteries for rapid movement, but the government had no such troops. The rebels had adopted it with brilliant success. It finally became so indispensable that infantry brigades were mounted and disciplined for the service.

The physical contour of his department also required a pack mule train to mutually adjust the parts of his projected system of warfare. It was almost impossible to penetrate the mountains of East Tennessee with ordinary transportation. It was a paramount object with him to relieve that Switzerland of America from oppression. It was crushed with the most accursed tyranny on the face of the earth. Its quiet citizens had been murdered for loyalty to their government. Its helpless women and children had been driven to the mountain caves, and their dwellings were eaten up by incendiary flames. Thousands of its patriotic men were fugitives, or were toiling and fighting to reach their homes once more. Their hearts were stricken, and they might well exclaim in agony of hope deferred: "How long, oh Lord, how long!" It never will cease to be astonishing that the deliverance of the mountaineers of Tennessee was so long delayed. General Rosecrans from sympathy and for important military reasons determined to accomplish it. But there was delay here too. A train of five thousand pack mules, which were indispensable to the enterprise was ordered, and months elapsed without satisfaction of the requisition.

DISCIPLINE.

The discipline of the corps in all its departments was an object of unremitting effort. There was no sound reason why the discipline of veteran volunteers should not be equal to that of regulars. It was not the fault of the soldiers, who exhibited a ready acquiescence to orders when officers showed capacity and nerve. There were a few regiments in the army fully equal to those in the regular service. These had zealous officers of large capacity. There was one mode especially by which neglect of duty, carelessness and incompetency, would be eliminated and the army purified. General Rosecrans solicited authority to dismiss officers from the service for satisfactory military reasons. The reply of the Secretary of War expresses the character of the application, to wit:

"*Washington, Nov.* 3, 1862.

"MAJOR GENERAL ROSECRANS:

"The authority you ask, promptly to muster out or dismiss from the service officers for flagrant misdemeanors and crimes, such as pillaging, drunkenness and misbehavior before the enemy, or on guard duty *is essential to discipline, and you are authorized to use it.* Report of the facts in each case should be immediately forwarded to the War Department, in order to prevent improvident restoration.

"[Signed,] E. M. STANTON,
Secretary of War."

A general order (No. 4) embodying the foregoing was promptly published, directing that officers disgracefully dismissed, should be divested of the insignia of rank in the presence of their respective commands, and be escorted by soldiers outside of the camps. It was severe but it had a most salutary influence.

CHAPTER IV.

WORKING Habits of the General Commanding—His fancy for Young Men—His Aidesdecamp—Reviews—His Searching Inspections—His Injunctions to Careless or Neglected Soldiers—Major General George H. Thomas—His Person and Characteristics—His Popularity.

INDUSTRY was one of the most valuable qualities of General Rosecrans. Labor was a constitutional necessity with him. And he enjoyed a fine faculty for the disposition of military business—a faculty which rapidly improved with experience. He neither spared himself nor his subordinates. He insisted upon being surrounded by active, rapid workers. He "liked sandy fellows," because they were so "quick and sharp." He rarely found staff officers who could endure with him. Ambition prompted all of them to remain steadfastly with him until nature would sustain no more. Often they confessed with some exhibition of selfish reluctance that he was endowed with extraordinary vital force, and a persistency which defied fatigue. Those who served upon his staff in Western Virginia or Mississippi predicted a severe future. They were not deceived. He was habitually prepared for labor in quarters at ten o'clock in the morning. On Sundays and Wednesdays he rose early and attended Mass. He never retired before two o'clock in the morning, very often not until four, and sometimes not until broad daylight. He often mounted in the afternoons and rode out to inspect or review the troops. It was not extraordinary that his Aids sometimes dropped asleep in their chairs, while he was writing vehemently or glancing eagerly over his maps, which he studied almost incessantly. Sometimes he glanced at his "youngsters" compassionately, and pinching their ears or rubbing their heads paternally until he roused them, would send them to bed. Captain Thompson, and Captain Robert S. Thoms—the latter a Volunteer Aiddecamp of superior merit—were favorites, deservedly. They were his amanuenses, had custody of all the ciphers, and necessarily were confidential Aids. Lieutenant Frank S. Bond was attached to the staff subsequently. in a similar capacity, and soon won the respect of his commander. When in the field, General Rosecrans was apt to be the first officer in camp to spring from his blankets, and the last to dismount at night.

REVIEWS.

During the few days he remained at Bowling Green, he reviewed most of the divisions which had reached that vicinity. Night labor compensated for hours thus stolen from his maps, reports, and schemes for the improvement of the army. At the reviews, the satisfaction of the troops with the change of commanders, was manifested by their enthusiastic reception of him. The manner of his inspections at once engendered a cordiality toward him which promised happy results. The soldiers were satisfied that their commander took an interest in their welfare—a moralizing agency which no capable General of volunteers can safely neglect. He examined the equipments of the men with exacting scrutiny. No trifling minutiæ escaped him. Everything to which the soldier was entitled was important. A private without his canteen instantly evoked a volley of searching inquiries. "Where is your canteen?" "How did you lose it—when—where?" "Why don't you get another?" To others, "you need shoes, and you a knapsack." Soldiers thus addressed were apt to reply frankly, sometimes a whole company laughing at the novelty of such keen inquisition. "Can't get shoes," said one; "required a canteen and couldn't get it," rejoined another. "Why?" quoth the General. "Go to your Captain and demand what you need! Go to him every day till you get it. Bore him for it! Bore him in his quarters! Bore him at meal time! Bore him in bed! Bore him; bore him; bore him! Don't let him rest!" And to Captains, "You bore your Colonels; let Colonels bore their Brigadiers; Brigadiers bore their Division Generals; Division Commanders bore their Corps Commanders, and let them bore *me*. I'll see, then, if you don't get what you want. Bore, bore, bore! until you get everything you are entitled to;" and so on through an entire division.

"That's the talk, boys," quoth a brawny fellow. "He'll do," said another—and the soldiers returned to their camp-fires and talked about "Rosy," just as those who knew him best in Mississippi had talked.

The confidence which such deportment inspired was pregnant with future good. And it was soon observed that he was careful to acknowledge a private's salute—a trifling act of good breeding and military etiquette, costing nothing, but too frequently neglected by officers who have much rank and little generous sympathy with soldiers who win them glory.

This is a wise "regulation," but it reaches far deeper than mere discipline.

Shortly after headquarters were established at Bowling Green, Major General George H. Thomas reported himself. The military family of the Commanding General quickly recognized the real Chief of Staff. It had been observed that General Rosecrans did not "consult" habitually upon the principles and policy of the campaign with other commanding officers. The keen eyes of those familiar with his customs, however, discovered an unusual degree of respect and confidence exhibited toward General Thomas. Confidential interviews with him were frequent and protracted. It soon got to be understood in the camps, that "Pap" Thomas was chief counsellor at headquarters, and confidence in "Rosy" grew apace.

General Thomas had been with the army a twelve month or more. The veterans knew him, and revered him to a man. His old Mill Spring division loved him. He had the confidence and esteem of the officers. The old troops filially spoke of him as "Pap" Thomas. In facetious moods he was "Old Slow Trot." The former was a soubriquet of affection; the latter a merry nick-name quickened of one of those trifles that tickle an idle soldier's fancy. Habitually, a veteran acquires a habit of boiling a man down into an expression. General Thomas' steadiness rather attracted the lads. He was as deliberate on the march as at quarters. His escort, more impatient than their commander, sometimes took advantage of a temporary aberration and pushed him into unusual speed. Directly his revery ended, he was apt to order "slow trot!" It caught popular fancy, and the General was fixed in a soubriquet. General Rosecrans himself expressed an almost reverential respect for him. Alluding to him, one day, he said, with a glow of enthusiasm, "George H. Thomas is a man of extraordinary character. Years ago, at the Military Academy, I conceived there were points of strong resemblance between his character and that of Washington. I was in the habit of calling him General Washington." His grave aspect, dignified deportment, and imposing presence justified this conceit.

Most men diminish as you approach them. A few magnify, and you feel their greatness. General Thomas grows upon you. Even his physique has this peculiarity. He has a massive, full rounded, powerful form, which seems at first to absorb several inches of his six feet of stature, but it gradually expands upon you, as a mountain which you approach. His features are heavy but well carved, with a strong, thin, combative nose, cleanly cut lips, and great square jaws and chin, indicating that firmness which he develops so grandly in battle. It needs but a glance under his bushy brows, set like a luxuriant hedge upon the edge of his broad white forehead, to discover the strength and warmth of his deep, steady, blue eyes, which seem of fathomless depth. A ruddy, weather-stippled complexion indicating robust health, and light brown, curly hair, impart a glow of cheerfulness to his fine countenance which irresistibly inspires your confidence. A short, thick-set, sandy beard, a little silvered since the war began, and closely trimmed habitually, completes an *ensemble* of unusual personal comeliness and vigor in a man struggling among the unrelenting fifties.

He looks like a sanguine man, but the sanguineous is balanced by the lymph in his composition. His aspect is peculiar, grave but not stern, with a benignant expression which warms your heart while it commands respect. He is a close observer, but a better thinker, and he matures his opinions deliberately—usually reflecting twice before he speaks once, in carefully measured language. You can not doubt his firmness. He has an appearance of heaviness, but it is more corporeal than intellectual. He is altogether a soldier, simple in deportment and unaffected, without a soldier's vanity. Without his uniform you might easily mistake him for a substantial western farmer. He was a Brigadier General some months before he thought of permitting the star to supplant the eagle which he wore by virtue of his rank in the regular cavalry; and for months after he was promoted to Major General, he continued to shoulder the single star. The twin stars were mounted soon after the battle of Stone River, but it is suspected they found their way to his broad shoulders surreptitiously. No perfect history of the war of the rebellion in which Major General George H. Thomas, of Virginia, does not figure conspicuously, can be written.

CHAPTER V.

REGIMENTAL Pioneer Corps—General Gilbert—General R. S. Granger and Colonel S. D. Bruce—Major General McCook's Corps moves to Nashville—Attack upon Nashville—Morgan's Dishonorable Ruse—The Attack Foiled—Breckinridge concludes the Mortgage upon Nashville can not be Lifted—The Fifty-First Illinois Volunteers.

ADOPTING Napoleon's dictum, that "to command an army well a General must think of nothing else," the General Commanding applied his restless and vigorous mind in studying and correcting the deficiencies of his own corps. It needed discipline, and he held the officers, not the privates, responsible. The new regiments were relentlessly drilled. Pioneer corps were organized in each regiment of the army to repair roads and construct bridges, and contraband negroes were either organized into gangs of laborers or employed as teamsters—a service in which they excelled. The General was not content with ordinary formal reports; he insisted upon statements of minutiæ, and in important matters the officers in charge were personally examined and instructed.

At this period, the guard for the protection of the railroad north of Bowling Green was detailed, and Brigadier General Gilbert was assigned to command, with headquarters at Munfordville. Colonel Sanders D. Bruce, of the Twentieth Kentucky Volunteers, who had recently distinguished himself by zeal and energy, was relieved from command of the post of Bowling

Green by Brigadier General Robert S. Granger, and assigned to command a cavalry force to drive the rebels out of South-western Kentucky. Besides these arrangements, there were innumerable matters of routine necessary to the success of the military administration of the Department rapidly disposed of, but the details would swell this narrative into a tedious volume. Allusion is made to them merely to convey a feeble intimation of the amount of business which necessarily harrasses the mind of the commander of a great department.

Major General McCook's corps had already arrived at Bowling Green. In consequence of information that the enemy were menacing Nashville, General McCook was directed, on the 4th November, to move his corps to that city, pressing forward briskly so as to reach there by 10 o'clock a. m., on the 7th. He marched accordingly at dawn of the 4th. On the morning of Thursday, officers at Bowling Green reported that they had heard the mutter of heavy guns in the direction of Nashville—a distance of perhaps fifty miles, as the crow flies. It was incredible that the detonation of artillery could be carried so far overland. But the succeeding day the report was seemingly verified by the arrival of couriers with official dispatches, announcing that the enemy had been baffled in an attempt to destroy the railroad bridge which spans the Cumberland river at Nashville. But they had succeeded in unmasking the great batteries of Fort Negley, Fort Confiscation, and the Casino. It is barely possible that the mumbling of their guns was heard at Bowling Green.

The attack upon Nashville was a mere dash, but the

design of the enemy was almost accomplished. It was afterward apparent that they had but little confidence in the enterprise, otherwise their efforts would have been sustained more persistently. They actually pushed within easy musket range of the bridge before they were driven away. They attacked General Negley's pickets simultaneously soon after midnight on the 6th, while a column of mounted infantry under John Morgan forded the Cumberland and moved upon Edgefield. A bickering picket fire was sustained on the south front of Nashville until daybreak, our pickets falling back gradually to their reserves. As soon as it was light enough, the enemy opened a field battery from the crest of a ridge on the left of the Murfreesboro pike, the only effect of which was to unmask our siege batteries in the forts.

Part of the Fifty-First Illinois Volunteer Infantry, on picket on that road, were sharply attacked by rebel infantry, but they resisted gallantly until the remainder of the regiment came up in support, when the enemy were handsomely repulsed, with severe loss. Our loss was three severely and four slightly wounded, and two missing.

Morgan, meantime, was preparing to dash upon the bridge. In order to gain time, it was reported that he had resorted to a dishonorable stratagem. A flag of truce was sent to our lines, asking an exchange of prisoners. The ruse was too flimsy to deceive, but it gave Morgan time to form his line advantageously. As soon as his flag returned, he swept suddenly upon our pickets and skirmishers, and drove them in upon the main body. Taking advantage of hollows and the railway embankment, he moved swiftly upon the bridge without exposure, but as the head of his column raised to a level with the road, it was met by a biting fire from the well-poised rifles of the Sixteenth Illinois Infantry, under Colonel Smith. Discovering the futility of further effort, Morgan quickly withdrew with a loss of a half dozen men, and revenged himself by destroying an old frame freight house and a few platform cars. The Sixteenth Illinois had three slightly and three severely wounded, including Captain Rowe, but the enemy were satisfied to retire.

General Negley, deceived by the maneuvers of the enemy, supposed the main attack would be made in the direction of the Franklin pike, because Nashville was most vulnerable on that side. Proceeding upon that belief, he pushed out that road with an escort of forty men from the Seventh Pennsylvania Cavalry, Stokes' First Tennessee Cavalry, one section of Battery G, Marshall's Fourth Ohio Artillery, and one section of Houghtaling's Illinois Battery, supported by the Fourteenth Michigan, Sixty-Ninth Ohio, and Seventy-Eighth Pennsylvania Infantry. Quite a warm artillery fight was sustained for several hours, and both parties tried to gain advantage by maneuvering, but the enemy finally withdrew with considerable loss of men and horses. Our loss was four wounded. The enemy did not afford our infantry an opportunity to take a decisive part in this brush. Prisoners reported that Breckinridge in person commanded the rebel forces. He fell back that night to his position in front of Murfreesboro, satisfied that the "Yankee" mortgage on Nashville could not be lifted by his command.

CHAPTER VI.

The Right Wing at Nashville—Railway Communication with Mitchellsville Resumed—Organization of the Army—Sketches of McCook, Crittenden, Rousseau, Negley, and other Division Generals.

Brigadier General Sill's Division, of McCook's command, was the first to arrive at Nashville. The General Commanding promptly made acknowledgements to General McCook for his activity and energy in arriving two hours in advance of the time designated. He had opened and secured regular communication between that city and General Headquarters, and it was now safe beyond peradventure. This was equally gratifying to its trusty garrison, who had been so closely beleagured that they were suffering for ration-al comforts. Tidings from the enemy were equally reassuring. They were moving around from Chattanooga, but with difficulty. The railway bridge across the Tennessee River at Bridgeport had been destroyed—which involved the necessity of transhipment and laborious ferriage of troops and armament at that crossing. It was clear they were not ready to advance.

On the 6th railroad communication to Mitchellsville was re-established, and heavy trains of subsistence were forwarded to that depot. General McCook was directed to supply himself by wagons thence, and the other corps were moved forward. The three grand divisions of the army were now designated the

Right Wing, Center, and Left Wing, although the general order to that effect was not issued until some days later. The Right Wing, commanded by Major General McCook, consisted of three divisions, under Brigadier General J. W. Sill, Brigadier General Philip H. Sherridan, and Colonel W. E. Woodruff, who temporarily commanded the old division of Brigadier General R. B. Mitchell. Major General Thomas commanded the Center, consisting of the divisions of Major General Lovell H. Rousseau, Brigadier Generals Dumont, Fry, Palmer, and Negley. Dumont and Fry were subsequently relieved, and Palmer was transferred to the Left Wing. The Left Wing, commanded by Major General Thomas L. Crittenden, consisted of the divisions of Brigadier Generals Thomas Jefferson Wood, H. P. Van Cleve, and W. L. Smith. The Headquarters Staff was increased by the announcement of Captain Elmer Otis, commanding the Fourth regiment of United States Cavalry, as Chief of Courier Lines, and R. S. Thoms, of Cincinnati, Volunteer Aiddecamp, with rank of Captain.

MAJOR GENERAL M'COOK.

Major General McCook was considered a good soldier. He was prompt, energetic, and enterprising, with ambition to excel. His command was always in fine condition, and, apparently, was attached to him. He was fortunate in division commanders of military knowledge, experience, and ability, and his brigade officers—such as Sill, Willich, Kirk, Carlin, Roberts, and Shaeffer, and Gibson, later, were of the elite of the army. His troops had fought, some of them in Missouri, a portion at Pea Ridge, others at Shiloh, and all at Chaplin Hills. Three-fourths of them were veterans, and the raw levies were required to drill incessantly. General McCook himself was in the prime of youthful vigor—not exceeding thirty-three years of age, and free from vicious habits which tend to impair the constitution. He had graduated at the National Military Academy, in 1851, and entered service immediately as Brevet Second Lieutenant of the Third United States Infantry. After promotion to a First Lieutenancy, he was Professor of Tactics at West Point, and was First Lieutenant of the line when the rebellion declared itself at Sumter. Governor Dennison at once commissioned him Colonel of the first three months' regiment organized in his native State, and the first organized in the West under the President's requisition for volunteers. After serving three months on the Potomac with distinction, as tactician and disciplinarian, he was recommissioned by Governor Dennison for three years. While reorganizing his regiment, the President promoted him to the position of Brigadier General, and he was assigned to the Department of the Ohio. At Shiloh he commanded a division, and distinguished himself. The President promoted him to the grade he now enjoys, and General Buell assigned to him a corps of three divisions, with which he fought the sanguinary but indecisive battle of Chaplin Hills. General Rosecrans continued him in the same command.

MAJOR GENERAL CRITTENDEN.

Major General Crittenden was considered, in army circles, an officer of popular manners, and an earnest, zealous soldier. In his youth he had served as Aiddecamp in Mexico, on the staff of General Taylor. Otherwise he had no military experience. He never vascillated in his devotion to the Union, while his most intimate friends in Kentucky were proclaiming themselves traitors. Exercising great influence in his native State, the President commissioned him a Brigadier General. He applied himself to his duties, and the division to which he was assigned as commander, soon took rank among the effective forces of the Army of the Ohio. He had now served a year or more, and for his good conduct and valor at Shiloh had been promoted to Major General. Later, three divisions, which constituted his present corps, were assigned to him. There was no cooler or more thoroughly self-possessed soldier in the Fourteenth Army Corps. He is the second son of Hon. John J. Crittenden—his elder brother, George, being in the rebel army. He is about forty years old, of medium stature, spare figure, and straight as a ramrod—with swarthy complexion, long straight black hair, with strong, prominent features, and a proud, stately bearing. He is rather reticent, but "Old Kentucky" asserts herself in his deportment.

He was fortunate in commanding a corps of veterans, some of whom had learned the rudiments of grim visaged war in Western Virginia. Only nine regiments of them were unseasoned. Two divisions had fought at Shiloh, and won laurels with their commander. Nelson's famous "man-of-war" division, afterward commanded by Palmer, was one of them. Brigadier Generals Wood and Van Cleve, regular officers, ranked high for skill and enterprise—Wood especially, who was regarded second to none in experience and cultured intellect. Palmer afterward made his mark. These were ably sustained by Brigadier Generals Hascall and Cruft, Colonels Hazen, Harker, Stanley Matthews, Wagner, Grose, Samuel Beatty, and Fyffe, whose testimony is a rubric of rebel blood.

MAJOR GENERAL ROUSSEAU.

Major General Rousseau, commanding the reserve division of the Center, was molded for a hero. Nature had infused into him a spirit of fiery enthusiasm, which blazed in his features, spouted from his beaming eyes, and declared itself in a voice which rung in battle like a clarion. It was impossible to resist his captivating influence, and no man could so inflame the ardor of troops in the shock of conflict. His soldiers roared at his presence, hailing his magnificent port with joyful acclamations. Soaring above the heroic stature and swelling out in grand physical proportions, with a countenance glowing with frankness, generosity, and courage, and manners irresistibly seductive, you perceive in him the representative and model of true chivalry. Mounted upon his thoroughbred chestnut, and careering before his embattled host, you recognize your beau ideal of a gallant soldier. He is thoroughly a Kentuckian, and thoroughly a patriot, who loves his country and the government of the people with unconquerable affection. Lovell H. Rousseau is one of the true men of Kentucky and of the nation, and when the scroll of honor is complete, his name will glow with the noblest. He is a volunteer soldier, promoted from the Colonelcy of the Louisville Legion—the first regiment enlisted in Kentucky, and by himself—first to a Brigadier General, and afterward to a Major General, for distinguished gallantry and services at Shiloh and Chaplin Hills.

BRIGADIER GENERAL NEGLEY.

Brigadier General James S. Negley, of Pennsylvania, commanding the second division of the Center, was not popular with a certain clique of officers, but thoroughly enjoyed the confidence of the General Commanding, of his immediate commander, and of his splendid division. At this period he was not with the main army. He had been left by General Buell in command of the garrison at Nashville, where, by his energy and activity, and by his patriotic civico-military administration he had won the respect of the Government. He was yet in command at Nashville, and had but recently repulsed an attack of the enemy. He was destined to win further honor. He was a volunteer officer, but ever proved himself a trusty soldier. After all the divisions had been reviewed by the General Commanding, there was no dispute in the staff that his was among the best divisions of the Fourteenth Corps. Dumont and Fry soon afterward disappeared, and Palmer took a division in the Left Wing. After the Hartsville affair, Dumont's Division was merged in others, and Brigadier General James B. Steadman, a soldier and a zealous patriot, succeeded General Fry. The brigade commanders of the first and second divisions, Scribner, John Beatty, Starkweather, "Black Jack" Shepherd, Miller, R. T. Stanley, and sturdy old Spears, were all distinguished men. The other brigadiers do not fall within the scope of this narrative.

CHAPTER VII.

SABBATH in the Army—Review of Ten Days—The Military Situation—The Army Moving—Outlines of the Campaign—Its Relations to Other Departments—Bragg's Advantages—Rosecrans' Difficulties—His Numerical Force.

ON the 8th it was announced that headquarters would be transferred to Nashville on the morrow. Subsequently remembering that the succeeding day was Sunday, the General Commanding suspended the order twenty-four hours. This is worthy of notice simply as an indication of the principle by which he was governed. He entertained an aversion to movements upon the Sabbath, unless they were indispensable. The troops soon understood this, and they approved it from motives which seemed a curious combination of superstition and conscientious scruples. But the impression that Sunday military enterprises could not prosper was fixed in their minds, and they commended the example of their commander.

Ten days had now expired since General Rosecrans had assumed command. We may regard this as the introductory period of preparation. It will clear the record to glance at the situation. Every available hour had been devoted to the preparation of his forces and the maturation of his plans for future operations. The railroad had been repaired to Mitchellsville. Supply trains were rushing over the road as rapidly as steam and energy could press them. Measures had been taken for the perfection of the cavalry; an immense pack-mule train had been ordered; garrisons had been established to protect communications; pioneer corps had been organized; the army itself had been reorganized, and was displaying its old spirit; horses, arms, equipments, subsistence, were coming forward, and vast quantities of uncatalogued but indispensable routine business had been cleaned out of official pigeon holes. The army was sweeping like a great torrent toward Nashville, overflowing the country with its legions and innumerable trains. Intense activity was visible in every quarter of the department, and the campaign was opening auspiciously. How much labor, how many harrassing vexations were in the womb of the future! The season of drought was not yet at its zenith. Cumberland River continued a feeble rivulet, threading its way limpidly through the clefts of the mountains, and the Military Chief of the nation, unmindful of the lessons of experience, was disposed to exact more than he himself had genius to accomplish under far happier conditions.

The outline of the campaign was part of a vast system devised—it must be finally confessed with great sagacity—at Washington. This system extended from the Potomac to the western borders of Missouri, and from the Potomac and the Ohio to the Gulf of Mexico. The part assigned to General Rosecrans was a carving from the general scheme. His success depended as much upon that of the commanders of other departments as upon his own genius. Either one of them failing, jeopardized him, and would necessarily compel him to suspend aggressive operations, if it did not throw him upon the defensive. Major General Grant, commanding the Department of Western Tennessee, was on his right, pressing sharply into Mississippi. If he met with disaster, it would uncover Rosecrans' right flank, and expose him to superior numbers. If Grant held his own, Rosecrans' right was safe against any project from Pemberton's Army of the Mississippi; and the distance from Pemberton to Bragg, and the vital necessity to hold the Mississippi Valley for the rebel government, insured him against the sudden concentration of any material portion of Pemberton's with Bragg's forces against him.

Major General Wright, commanding the Department of the Ohio, which included Kentucky and Western Virginia, covered the left and rear of Rosecrans. With his formidable army, there was little danger to be apprehended on that flank unless there was misfortune elsewhere. If the Army of the Potomac met with disaster, it involved each army of the Republic, but the Fourteenth Army Corps most directly and seriously. It would enable the rebels to detach heavy reinforcements for the relief of other departments, and Bragg was likely to receive assistance earliest. Fortunately, the Army of the Potomac promised to afford employment for all of Lee's forces. If federal operations on the coast were successful, they would occupy all the rebel troops in the South-Eastern States. If otherwise, Bragg would draw accessions thence. But the signs were all hopeful, and it seemed morally certain that Bragg could not get reinforcements enough to give him a decided numerical superiority. Still he enjoyed the formidable advantage of operating upon comparatively short interior lines in a friendly mountainous territory, which afforded him fair supplies of forage and subsistence, while Rosecrans waged offensive warfare in a hostile and desolated country, in which almost every white inhabitant was a spy and bitter enemy—a country which had been gleaned of supplies, and which is remarkable for the defensive military positions it affords. He, therefore, was compelled to transport his supplies over two hundred miles before he could hope to reach the enemy; and his difficulties would increase as he progressed, according to the length of his line of communication. The feebleness of his cavalry secured rebel communications, and the superiority of their's constantly endangered his communications, so that each day's march depleted his already greatly diminished effective force, which, after deducting the sick, and heavy details for garrison duty, did not exceed sixty-five thousand men. The number of absentees on November 15, as exhibited by the consolidated semi-monthly report on file in the Adjutant General's Office, exhibits something of the condition of affairs when General Rosecrans assumed command, to wit:

Commissioned Officers absent by authority,	1,188
Enlisted Men " " "	25,294
Total absent by authority,	26,482
Commissioned Officers absent without authority,	123
Enlisted Men, ' " "	6,361
Total,	6,484

Grand total, *thirty-two thousand nine hundred and sixty-*

six. Those absent without authority were deserters. Those absent by authority embraced details and the sick. But nearly one-fourth of the number of soldiers belonging to the Department did not muster for duty. It is worth while to remember this fact, because it is often inquired, What became of the great Army of the Cumberland?

CHAPTER VIII.

MOUNTED—A Sharp Trot through Rebel Ruins—Picture of the Abomination of Desolation—Fire in the Forest—Copy of Blue Grass—Bivouac Fires and Tattoo—To Board and to Blankets.

BUT to return to narrative. At dawn on the morning of November 10, General Rosecrans and the staff took passage on a special railway train at Bowling Green, and were whirled swiftly to Mitchellsville. Horses were in waiting, and five minutes after the cars stopped, the General, escorted by a squadron of the Fourth Regular Cavalry under Captain Otis, mounted and trotted briskly to the right upon a country road connecting with the old Louisville and Nashville turnpike. There was a distance of little less than forty miles before him. The country was infested by roving bands of hostile guerrillas, and the route was rather hazardous, but it was thronged by long transportation trains strongly guarded, which was deemed sufficient protection. Nevertheless the staff were cautioned to remain with the escort.

The route was interesting as the early highway of rebellion. The first camp of instruction of the insurgents (Camp Trousdale), was passed a mile or two after crossing the Kentucky and Tennessee line. It was from this point that South-Western Kentucky was impregnated with the virus of active rebellion. We were then trifling with Kentucky neutrality, and covert treachery, while Simon Bolivar Buckner was

5

sending the State Guard of Kentucky into this camp, and amusing General McClellan and the Administration with hypocritical professions of loyalty.

The first acre of Tennessee soil betrayed the ruthless track of war. Fallow fields were spread out before the vision, and the voice of the planter was not needed to prove that the peaceful plowshare had been transformed into the biting sword. Fences had been absorbed in camp-fires; the click of the old mill wheel had ceased; broken windows and shattered frames stared from deserted homesteads; and charred chimneys begrimed with smoke stains, stood in stark solitude in the bosom of deflowered gardens and blistered groves—painful monuments of rebellion and grim pictures of its bitter fruits. Ravage and desolation everywhere. There were no little children gamboling on cabin thresholds. Hardly a dog barked at the rattling cavalcade. Now and then a woe-stricken woman peered sadly through a shivered window-pane. Yonder, a rugged and ragged and wretched man in butternut jeans, clinging with the resolution of desperation to the last rafter of the dear old homestead, scowled ferociously at the passing strangers in his country's uniform. But, as if deliberate purpose had not afflicted the land with fell visitation, carelessness and chance were now aggravating havoc. Idle soldiers or heedless teamsters kindling bivouac fires among the dry leaves of autumn, had communicated flames to the forests, and consuming conflagrations were streaming like whirlwinds through their brittle branches. Fences far outside of the beaten war-path, obscure fields of corn covered by friendly distance, dwellings, once homes of innocence and rustic joy, but pleasant homes no more, farm tenements and standing grain, were now licked up by the scathing fury as the sand of the desert is swallowed by simoon. A gloomy pall of smoke, fit emblem of the mournful pestilence which desolated that sad land, hovered over the scotched and blistered face of nature in dismal clouds, through which the Southern sun, like an angry globe of fire, but dimly scattered its enfeebled blaze—the abomination of desolation, but fitting retribution for parricidal war.

The face of the country pretty much all the way to Nashville is rudely rumpled. About midway it is intersected with rugged irregular ridges spurring out from the Cumberland Mountains, until they sink insensibly into the lowlands of Western Tennessee. But the surface of the whole territory is diversified with cross ridges and bluff hills—many of them too rude for profitable cultivation, though the intervening valleys and the frequent plateaus are fertile and tillable lands. Compensated labor and a liberal interspersion of schoolhouses would make it an attractive and desirable country. The sword is carving through its stingy barbarism toward its industrial millennium.

Ten or more miles north of Nashville the prospect opens into a vista of beauty and high cultivation. You fall upon a wide wavy landscape decorated with stately and tasteful mansions, seducing sense by pleasant prospects of lofty ceilings and spacious porches. They are war-scarred now, but even the wrecks report their former comeliness. Neat stone fences which circumvallate the rich plantations; substantial stock and chattel tenements—both empty now; noble groves of oak and maple, casting their friendly misletoe shadows upon rich carpetings of thick-set turf, remind you much of the sumptuous Blue Grass region of Central Kentucky; all, the possessions of traitors who have rushed to the tumult of war, leaving wives and little ones behind them to weather the withering storm alone.

Night had ensabled the prospect long before the cavalcade discovered the feeble glimmer of the distant city. The groves and hill-sides were blazing with cheerful bivouac fires. The merry to-bed tattoo rataplanned cheerily in the deep valleys of the Cumberland, and the good-night taps of great drums rolled up their solemn diapason ere the horse-hoof-clatter of the coming chief echoed in the dismal streets of desolate Nashville. It was a wearisome, dusty march, and the smothering smoke of smoldering forest fires had well nigh suffocated jaded steeds and their shattered riders. A generous feast at the hospitable board of General McCook—and the memories of the day, for the nonce, were soon buried in the oblivion of soldiers' blankets.

The recollection of such marchings usually are invested with a restricted interest. But the future historian will not complain when he searches among the dusty pages of these stirring times to find the feeblest pictures which may illustrate the character of his heroes. Occasions like this disenthralled the mind of the Commanding General, and it sought recreation in wandering over the field of thought and speculation—nevertheless pursuing persistently the great object of his contemplation as the helm which governed his reflections. But he found relaxation from the tread-mill of office. Riding along the highway, he was careful to observe the configuration of the country and its military characteristics, requiring the inscription upon the note-book of his Topographical Engineer of intersecting roads, as often as such roads rambled off into the forests along the line of march. Habitually cheerful, in a remarkable degree, on such expeditions the mercury of his spirits rises into playfulness, which develops itself in merry familiar quips and jests with his subordinates, and none laugh more pleasantly than he. Fine scenery excites his poetic temperament, and he dwells eloquently upon the picturesqueness of nature, exhibiting at once the keenest appreciation of the "kind mother of us all," and the niceties of landscape art. But the grandeur of nature more frequently carries his mind into the realms of religion, when he is wont to burst into adoration of his Maker, or launch into vehement and impatient rebuke of scoffers. All of nature to him is admonition of God. Such is his abhorrence of infidelity, that he would banish his best loved officers from his military household, should any presume to intrude it upon him. He is wont to say he has no security for the morality of any man who refuses to recognize the Supreme Being. Religion is his favorite theme, and Roman Catholicism to him is infallible. In his general discussions of religion, he betrays surprising acquaintance with the multifarious theologies which have vexed the world, and condemns them all as corruptions of the true doctrines of the Mother Church. His social conversations of this character are seldom indulged with his cherished guest, Rev. Father Trecy, with whom he is always *en rapport*, but he is ever ready to wage controversy with any other disputant. But argument with him on his faith, had as well be ended with the beginning, save for the interest with which he invests his subject, and the ingenious skill with which he supports it. Ambling along the highway in a day's journey, unless some single theme of business absorbs him, he will range through science, art, and literature with happy freedom and ability. You do not listen long before you are persuaded that you hear one who aspires ambitiously beyond the mere soldier. The originality and shrewdness of his criticisms, the comprehensiveness of his generalizations, and his erudition, assures you that you talk with no ordinary man. Ten hours' trotting with him, though a sore trial of flesh, is richly repaid by instruction received, and the happy recollections which his companions afterward find stored in their memories.

CHAPTER IX.

CUNNINGHAM HOUSE—Nashville in Military Dress—Fort Negley—Unhappiness of the Rich—Misery of the Poor—Heartlessness of the Master Class—A Picture of Wretchedness—The Male Population—Social Tyranny—The Unwritten Law of Female Despotism—Non-Intercourse with Yankees—The Pass System—The Ruined Suburbs of Nashville.

HEADQUARTERS were established in the Cunningham mansion, a spacious and elegant edifice well adapted to the patriotic uses to which it was appropriated. The staff enjoyed it, but the elite of rebellious Nashville did not seem to appreciate their comfort. Cunningham was a Quartermaster in the rebel service and a Federal Quartermaster was now occupying the dwelling of his neighbor, Colonel Stevenson, also a rebel Quartermaster. A little later the Provost Marshal General was elbowed out of the Cunningham house, and occupied the former residence of General Zollicoffer. Many other private and public buildings were also appropriated to federal uses, and they were found quite convenient. This will interest the rebels hereafter, and it is desirable likewise to designate objects of historical interest for the future entertainment of residents of Nashville who are now involuntarily absent.

Nashville was now a military city. It exhibited many of the features of a conquered city which had been recently relieved from a long investment. It was girdled with a waist of formidable fortifications and encircled by a zone of warlike camps. Its proud capitol, graceful and beautiful, upon the crown of a rocky hill which commanded a charming prospect of splendid suburbs, and a rich mosaic of forests and fields lining the shores of the picturesque Cumberland, was a castle frowning with great guns on its battlements and bristling with glittering bayonets. The streets were barricaded with cotton, and earthen parapets. St. Cloud Hill, once the cynosure of the Rock City, when it was decorated with stately oaks which might have excited the pagan fervor of Druid High Priest, was a menacing fortress grinning at traitors in the rear and scowling at armed rebels in front. The Casino and Fort Confiscation beyond, confirmed the hopelessness of relief to the prisoned malcontents within their range. The tramp of hated soldiery, and the ominous rumble of cannon wheels echoed in the stony streets.

THE RICH AND POOR.

A sad mixture of luxury and desolation excited generous commiseration. The dwellings were full of rich furniture but the markets were bare and money scant. Once opulent families secretly sought charity that they might live. Thousands of wretched poor women and children existed in squalid want. Labor was scarce and the "poor white trash" were often too spiritless to work when offered—a fact abundantly attested. They suffered their children to chatter with cold, and shivered through the dreary nights of winter themselves, rather than çut and carry home the wood in the adjacent forest, which the authorities had condemned for their use. And they awaited in wretchedness and listless apathy for the tardy collection and distribution of the charity tax which the Governor levied upon the wealthy classes of traitors for their relief. The latter were heartless, but sensible to the strong arm of power. The appeals of misery among their own poor was sound to them, and nothing but a sound. In November, a miserable tenement in the edge of town was burned. An emaciated women dying with slow fever, was dragged out of the fire by her almost equally wretched sister, and laid helpless upon the bed in the commons. Scores of citizens passed her with scarce a word and no deed of sympathy. The prostrate sick woman lay there two days with no canopy but the clouds, and the penniless sister stirring a little pile of smoking chips waited for her to die. Nobody took them in. Three federal officers dashing across the commons were horror-stricken at the woe-begotten, and woe-begone spectacle, and the sick woman and poverty-stricken sister suffered no more. This was one visible picture of scores like it. There were hundreds invisible to public eyes.

FEMALE DESPOTISM.

Most of the able-bodied male population had gone to war. Very few fought under "the banner of beauty and glory." Scarcely a score of hale young men remained in the city. No matter about their inclination. They dared not resist rebel power where it governed them. The women who governed the master class scorned them if they remained at home, after the army was driven out. The social influence of the domineering caste was a more relentless tyranny than the sword. Some loyal men remained, but for the most part the men were either very poor or rich who exceeded the military age. These remained to plot treason and communicate tidings to their confederates in arms. Many families had removed far South, but most of the women and children were left in Nashville. The former were cold and unsocial, but generally when necessarily thrown in contact with federal officers they were courteous. Often, the exceptions occupied dubious positions in society. If otherwise, it was fair to infer that their husbands had gone to war for the sake of peace which they were denied at home. Occasionally there was pleasant social intercourse between the women and federal officers, but it required unusual daring to violate the unwritten law of female despotism. The front window shutters of dwellings—which during balmy peace were wont to be flung glaringly open habitually—were now as habitually closed as if there were a funeral in every house. There had been mourning in almost every leading family, and there was woe in store which they had not drawn.

THE PASS SYSTEM.

The rebel blockade of Nashville, and the necessity of severe military restrictions had kept marketers away from the city. Even the few supplies which were ventured in from the country were mostly appropriated for the military hospitals, so that there was a sort of necessity for people to go foraging. But all were forbidden to pass the military lines without written permit. It was hazardous to pass any persons because, with an exception now and then, they were mostly self-avowed rebels. Nothing was clearer than that a majority of them would avail themselves of all opportunities to convey information or smuggle articles contraband of war through the lines to the enemy. Experience had taught the authorities to doubt the veracity of all, and especially the fair portion of community—whom men are ever willing enough to trust. General Negley, commandant of the post, had tested the question thoroughly and although a gallant man himself, he admonished the Provost Marshal General to beware of the women—a very necessary admonition. There was more need of it, however, at the outposts, since soldiers all over the world, ever susceptible to beauty, insisted that a pretty face is a valid countersign.

But the unanimous testimony of the various commandants of the city, had been cast in the balance against the women. The burthen of proof touching their veracity was laid upon them heavily. Whatever they may have been at the time of the first Yankee irruption, there was no disputing now that they were generally very courteous. But whether it was frailty of memory, or an assurance that they were not in honor bound to keep faith with Yankees, too many were accustomed to violate their most sacred pledge, so that often truthful and excellent women suffered the consequences of the turpitude of their friends. Many who resided in the suburbs but outside of our lines found it necessary to visit the city, and hundreds who resided within the lines either had good reasons for desiring to pass outside, or feigned them. Consequently there was an incessant clamor for passes until General Negley interdicted them entirely. After the embargo was raised the demand increased, and the General Commanding arrived at Nashville in the midst of the pass epidemic. We have had the diagnosis of the humor; we shall hereafter observe the treatment of the (im)patients.

The exquisite suburbs of Nashville, renowned all over the Union for their tasteful elegance, were more war-stricken than the once fair city. Splendid seats, garnished with all the appliances of wealth, and lustrous with the polish of art and graces of munificent nature, were now bleak, lonely, and ruined—sad monuments of rebellion. Their graceful porches were scotched by flames, their stately columns carved and hewn with rude inscriptions, their noble groves scattered in chips, and broken branches, and ashes, over the dark green turf. The rich furniture of lordly dwellings, their treasures of art and literature were mutilated, scattered, or destroyed, and charming gardens were trampled in the dust. Ruin glared at you with baleful visage. Now and then a dwelling was dismally tenanted, but there were no external signs of animation. You would say "somebody is dead." The men were exiles, but lone women remained in woeful gloom. Those palaces were more dreary than a monastery. The fronts frowned in loneliness; the wide doors were sealed to the frames like the gates of a dungeon. Scarce a glimmer of light, a furtive gleam perhaps, sometimes flashed through the latticed shutters and violated the shrouded sanctity of the somber occupants. Those mournful women not long ago were gay and graceful queens of brilliant *salons*, shedding their luster upon society whose equal in the social art could hardly be found in all the sunny South. They mope there now in hopeless solitude, brooding bitterly through the weary months upon the miseries of war, which was born of their pride, and weeping unquenchable tears over the fall of those they loved. So let them cherish their self-created sorrow. It is the penalty of rebellion.

CHAPTER X.

Administration of the Department—Civico-Military Policy—The Provost Marshal General—Female Diplomacy—Persistence of Rebel Women—Female Smugglers—The Petticoat System finally Adjusted—The Chief of Army Police—His Signal Services—Trade Matters—The Non-combatant Policy.

The concentration of the army at Nashville having been ordered, General Rosecrans directed his attention to the general administration of the department while he tediously awaited the accumulation of supplies. The duties of the department of the Provost Marshal General were the most vexatious. They involved questions of both individual and general policy; of trade and of political administration. Captain Wm. M. Wiles, of the Twenty-Second Indiana Volunteer Infantry, a young officer of energy and capacity, who had discharged similar functions on the staff of the General Commanding in Mississippi, was announced Provost Marshal General. He was at once involved in the meshes of rebel female diplomacy. He had hardly eaten his first breakfast in Nashville before he was enveloped by swarms of bewildering beauties—some of them not so pretty—pleading, beseeching, coaxing and plying the seductive arts of their sex to secure permits to pass through the military lines; or soliciting guards to protect their premises against pillagers; or begging for safe-guards, which would secure them against the visitation of foragers. During a little while, Wiles found playful gossip with sprightly women a very nice thing, but a dozen, a score, a room full at once, sapped his philosophy speedily; he summarily denied all applications. The pouting petitioners clamored for the General. He was inaccessible. They lingered willfully in the hall waiting for him to emerge from his apartment. A cordon of pathetic women blockaded the staircase, and fired whole volleys of touching petitions at him. One "had a baby at home, outside the lines. She must have a pass to return. It would cry its eyes out. If it did'nt, she would." She learned that she had no business to come inside the lines. Another was obliged to have a pass to go to the country for provisions. The General excused himself. "It's not my business," he said, "to give but to refuse passes." A third had a "poor sick uncle," whom she "must see." Quoth the General, "I have a sick uncle. When my Uncle Sam recovers from his severe indisposition, I may consider the propriety of granting passes to rebel women."

CUNNING LADIES.

This species of vexation did not cease while headquarters were in Nashville. A rigid rule governing the issue of passes was established, but necessarily there were exceptions. Sometimes two hundred women applied in a day. A certain class of marketers and poor people were liberally indulged. It was indiscreet to grant a permit to any of the aspiring classes without rigidly catechising each, and requiring a moral guarantee against imposition. The artfulness of some of the more accomplished women was diverting. Such were too cunning, if not too well bred, to offend an officer. If unsuccessful in their application to the Provost Marshal, they devised schemes to gain an interview with the General. They rarely failed to see him, but they often regretted it. Army officers interceded for them; influential loyal citizens, whose petitions it was not politic to refuse, became their advocates and guarantors. Finally, a number of women were permitted to pass to the rebel lines under flags of truce, conditioned to return no more within federal lines, and solemnly pledged to convey neither military information or articles contraband of war to the enemy.

THE PETTICOAT SYSTEM.

The perfidy which has so prominently characterized the rebels from the beginning of the war, was frequently exhibited by ladies whose social position should have elevated them above the crimes of perjury and larceny. It seemed impossible for them to resist temptation. They were often detected in smuggling both contraband goods and information, after having entered into sacred obligations to respect the conditions upon which passes were issued. They were mean spirited enough afterward to boast that they had perfidiously outwitted the "Yankees." A female detective entrapped one honorable dame, enveloped in an enormous grey cassimere pettyskirt, which was intended for a rebel uniform. An immense pocket, spacious as a market basket, was crammed with quinine. Another was politely denuded by the female detective, and a quantity of letters directed to rebel officers was found under her chemise. Another, who had a permit to remove her household goods South, was arrested at the outposts, and escorted back to the Army Police Office. A prodigious quantity of quinine, blue mass, morphine, men's brogans and boots for army use, with grey uniforms, clothing, needles, threads, buttons, *et cetera*, were found concealed inside of her feather beds. Two pairs of long-legged heavy cavalry boots, which madam had attached to her own skirts, fell from their delicate hiding place, when she sprung from her vehicle at command of the officer who arrested her. It was shrewdly suspected that the "Southern Ladies' Aid Society," which had a flourishing branch at Nashville, was not entirely innocent in the premises, and its members finally exhibited anxiety to avoid the keen espionage of the Army Vidocq.

COLONEL WILLIAM TRUESDAIL.

The adjustment of the petticoat system was finally perfected by Colonel William Truesdail, Chief of Army Police—an officer who has rendered most signal services to the Government, but whose operations can not be described until there shall be peace in all our borders. His department, though intimately associated with the office of the Provost Marshal, rapidly developed into the proportions of a great bureau. He gathered about him an army of spies and scouts, and for local administration devised a system of surveillance, which pursued declared and secret enemies into their most secluded haunts. His faculty for acquiring satisfactory information from the enemy was wonderful. He was accustomed to make daily written reports to the General Commanding of the forces, location and movements of the rebel army, and subsequent development established the integrity of his information. There was no species of evil affecting the prosperity of the campaign that escaped his observation. Mischievous sutlers were watched; the trade in counterfeit confederate notes was broken up; smugglers were detected; Knights of the Golden Circle in the army and out of it were circumvented; the Southern Ladies' Aid Society—organized to promote the comfort of rebel officers—was embarrassed, compelled to operate more secretly, and was often defeated in its enterprises. In short, the system was a vast net-work, extending its meshes far and wide, and enveloping the shrewdest conspiracies of declared enemies or falsely-professing neutrals.

Colonel Truesdail is remarkably adapted for this peculiar service. He is a gentleman by nature and habit, with large experience among men, and a searching, penetrating cast of mind, which, united with untiring vigilance, secures him against the deceptions which his profession requires him to exercise. He first entered the service with General Pope, and it is often said that "Truesdail made Pope"—the value of the creation being a subject not under consideration. But there are not a few military men of sound judgment who entertain an opinion that if General Pope had taken Truesdail with him to the Potomac, his rear never would have been successfully assailed by the enemy. In Nashville his first business was to prepare a directory of rebels and loyal people, which was a valuable guide in the issue of passes. The list of professedly innocuous persons was large. These were regarded suspicious characters until they had proved their fidelity. The catalogue of thoroughly loyal people did not occupy many sheets of foolscap, but there was a surprising number of men and women who were in favor of the "Union *as it was*" — the meanest and most treacherous description of traitors, since their cowardly energies were secretly directed against the Government. The conspicuous rebels were too adroit to thrust themselves upon the attention of authority. Nevertheless they were dangerous, because they shrewdly used the professing non-combatant class. After a few days' experience in Nashville, Truesdail adopted a bitter police maxim, which he incessantly enjoined upon the Provost Marshal— "Don't trust women"—a biting commentary upon the virtue of high-toned chivalry; the more severe, since Colonel Truesdail himself was a Missourian, who comprehended the influence of the "institution." There were some, however, to whom the rule was not applicable.

TRADE MATTERS.

The justification of trade matters was one of the most perplexing subjects of internal police. The merchants who remained in business were anxious to resume trade. Most of them were rebels. It was morally certain that all of them, unless deterred by sharp restrictions, would sell to all purchasers, regardless of the requisitions of patriotism. The malcontents claimed trade privileges on the score of non-combatancy, but they were unwilling to enter into bonds to assure their neutrality. The loyal men resisted the applications of this class, and resented the encroachment of numerous speculators from abroad. Their trade was purely local to the military occupation. They could not hope to extend it beyond the outposts. After consultation with Governor Johnson and prominent loyal citizens, General Rosecrans ordered all army sutlers out of Nashville, requiring them to rejoin their regiments, closed the doors against foreign speculative enterprise, and announced, in orders, to people of all classes, that the government would afford them protection and trade privileges, conditioned that they would enter into penal bonds, with security, and upon taking an oath to remain non-combatants until the close of the war. In its simplest form, it said to secessionists, who were not disposed to take arms, "If you will not hurt us in any way, we will not hurt you; but we require security for your pledges. We have the right and the power to prevent you from injuring us, by exiling you. We will not exercise either, if you guarantee neutrality, and we will protect you as citizens entitled to certain rights." A Board of Trade, composed of several loyal citizens of Nashville, was also appointed, to whom all applications for the importation of merchandise was referred; and upon their written approval, permits were granted by the Provost Marshal General.

A form of parole bond for non-combatants, secured by two sureties, in an amount according to the property ability of each, was issued for the subscription of all who desired to accept the terms. The subscriber gave his penal bond, and bound himself by oath to "keep the peace, and afford neither aid nor comfort to the enemies of the Government of the United States; that he will be a true and steadfast citizen of the United States, and that during the present rebellion he will not go beyond the lines of the federal armies, nor into any section of the country in possession of the enemy, without permission of the authorities of the United States." Whereupon he was entitled to the benefits of the following

GUARANTEES OF PROTECTION.

This is to certify, that the citizen named in the within bond, having properly executed the same with approved surety, he is entitled from henceforth, to the full protection and support of the Government of the United States, and which is hereby pledged to him. All persons, military as well as civil, are hereby commanded to respect him as a good and loyal citizen, in the full enjoyment of his property, both real and personal. All foraging is hereby forbidden upon his premises, unless actually necessary for the support and well-being of the federal armies, in which case all possible care shall be exercised, and full receipt be given by the officer in charge, which shall be duly recognized, and the property paid for by the United States Government. Officers in command of foraging expeditions will be held to the strictest accountability for the protection herein guaranteed.

W. S. ROSECRANS,
Major General Commanding Department of the Cumberland.

ANDREW JOHNSON,
Military Governor of the State of Tennessee.

The execution of these bonds was entrusted to Provost Judge Fitch, who had been instrumental in adjusting the system, and whose services in the Police Department entitle him to honorable recognition. The new policy embraced all persons within the military lines. Many accepted it with alacrity, especially the middle class; but the master class resented it.

During a few day it excited general discussion, and was so variously misinterpreted that General Rosecrans finally issued the following explanatory paper, viz.:

HEADQUARTERS FOURTEENTH ARMY CORPS,
Department of the Cumberland,
Nashville, *Nov*. 30, 1862.

Questions have arisen as to the nature of the Parole Oath, why and how far it is binding. In answering them, I shall assume that to be true which is *not* so, viz.: That the Southern Confederacy is a lawful established government. Whence it would follow that males of Tennessee capable of bearing arms, who are within the control of the federal lines, are lawful subjects of that [the Confederate] Government, and liable to be put into its army.

According to the laws of war, it is at the option of the Federal Government to dispose of them and all their effects as it sees fit, subject to the laws and usages of civilized nations.

If, by those laws, an invading army may depopulate a country, and take captive its inhabitants, with greater reason, as a lesser evil, it may take prisoners and confine, whenever and wherever it may be necessary to prevent mischief, those of them who are liable and likely to bear arms against it.

When it says to them, "Out of humanity I will not do so; I will allow you now to follow your peaceful avocations, if you will pledge me, and keep your promises, that you will do me no military mischief," it is a great mitigation of its rights in favor of humanity.

The parole of a soldier not to take up arms until lawfully exchanged, overrides all his obligations as a citizen and his oath of enlistment, and as a relaxation of the rigors of war is held sacred by civilized nations.

The parole of harmless inhabitants is a still greater mitigation of the rights of war, because it does more good, and he is under but the single obligation of a citizen. For still stronger reasons, it must therefore be held sacred by all who pretend to civilization, or even to humanity.

Its justice is obvious. It is humane, and promotes the welfare of the country, which is for the benefit of the people, as well as of whoever ultimately holds it.

The motto of our Government is not that of the Confederate Revolutionists—"Rule or Ruin;" but "Government is instituted for the good of the people."

The end to be attained, and the justice of the means being thus pointed out, I have only to say that the non-combatant's oath is justly, and will be held, binding during the war; and those who take it, unless exchanged, like prisoners of war, will be absolved from its obligations only when the war is ended.

W. S. ROSECRANS,
Major General Commanding.

Whatever may prove the result of this policy ultimately, it unquestionably had a good effect at that time. It imparted a healthy and cheerful tone to trade circles, and palliated the discontent of many who were sour because they were afflicted, and had not intelligence to attribute their grievances to the system of social and political tyranny which forced Tennessee into the rebellion.

CHAPTER XI.

THE Army in Front of Nashville—Changes in Commands—Brigadier General J. J. Reynolds — Operations of the Enemy — General Orders—The Night-cap Order—The Permanent Staff—Garesché—"Gay Old Stanley"—St. Clair Morton—Other Staff Characters.

THE garrison of Nashville, constituting General Negley's command, was reviewed by the General Commanding on the 11th of November, and the other divisions of the army successively, as they arrived in front of the city. Major General McCook's corps soon took up a line on the south-eastern front of Nashville, covering the Murfreesboro turnpike, and extending to the right, covering the Nolensville road. Some days later Major General Crittenden's corps arrived, when McCook's line withdrew further to the right, Crittenden's right flank connecting with his left, and covering the Murfreesboro pike, his left extending across Stone River, with Millcreek in front, and outposts about nine miles from the city. Subsequently the divisions of Major General Rousseau, and Brigadier General Negley of the Center, moved to the front and connected with McCook's right, covering the Franklin turnpike. The other divisions of the Center remained at Gallatin to protect communications, but General Thomas repaired to Nashville. Meantime, Colonel W. E. Woodruff, commanding the first division of the Right Wing, was relieved by Brigadier

General Jeff. C. Davis, and Brigadier General R. W. Johnson, senior officer, relieved Brigadier General J. W. Sill of the command of the second division. General Sill was assigned to command the first brigade of General Sherridan's division, and Colonel Woodruff took command of General Davis' third brigade. Other changes were also made. Brigadier General Joseph J. Reynolds, who greatly distinguished himself in Western Virginia, and who was esteemed one of the ablest officers in the service, reported for duty, and a division was organized for him. The changes consequent upon the merger of Dumont's division threw Reynolds into the Center, and he was now at Gallatin. Brigadier General J. M. Palmer relieved Brigadier General William L. Smith, who was in command of Nelson's famous division, and Smith was ordered to Bowling Green to organize a cavalry command. Brigadier General Manson relieved Brigadier General Robert S. Granger at Bowling Green, and the latter was ordered to report at Nashville. Brigadier General Robert B. Mitchell, an officer of fine ability, who had conspicuously distinguished himself in the battles of Wilson Creek and Chaplin Hills, relieved General Negley, commandant of the post of Nashville, and the latter went to the front.

The line in front of Nashville described a wide expanded arc trending in a south-easterly direction, girdling the city with a broad zone of fleecy camps, which wound over the evergreen and russet hills like a belt of snow. Millcreek, a small and sinuous stream, with bluffy banks, and skirted with thin canebrakes, formed a good natural fosse in front. The troops rested upon a range of commanding cross ridges and bounding hills, which upheaved the surface in great round billows, and culminated in crests of oak and cedar forests, which subserved the triple purposes of landscape beauty, cover for the army, and powerful natural fortifications.

THE SITUATION.

The situation was not yet clearly announced. The enemy masked his operations carefully with a formidable shield of cavalry, which were untiringly vigilant. It was reported that Bragg was reconstructing the railroad bridge across the Tennessee River, and fortifying the banks of that stream, but the principal energies of the enemy seemed to be directed to the collection of able-bodied negroes and supplies from the surrounding country, and to the enforcement of the conscript act. Squads of refugees found their way into our camps daily, complaining that they were compelled to fly to us for protection or take up arms against the government. They reported camps of the enemy all the way from the Tennessee River to Murfreesboro, and at towns on either side of the railroad. Federal spies had not been able to ascertain satisfactorily whether Bragg intended to stand north of the Tennessee, or to fall back upon Chattanooga. Rebel residents at Nashville bitterly insisted that our advance would be resisted in force in Middle Tennessee, and that Nashville itself would be attacked. But this seemed to be contradicted by the wives of rebel officers, who betrayed anxiety to see their friends "before they moved further south." Altogether the attitude of the enemy was so uncertain that it was concluded they would not stand north of the Tennessee River, but would adopt the wiser course of drawing General Rosecrans as far as possible from his base.

The line which had been taken up by General Rosecrans was thin and extended, and rather invited the enemy to attempt the left, but they could not be induced to try the experiment. It was credibly stated that Kirby Smith was moving to Lebanon with a view to striking a blow, but with the strong display of federal force at Gallatin, it was not a hopeful enterprise. The enemy had no foothold whatever on the north side of the Cumberland, the cavalry division, under Colonel John Kennett, having driven them south, while Colonel Bruce was giving Woodward's gangs, in south-western Kentucky, their *coup dé grace.*

BUSINESS.

Routine business, correspondence, the adjustment of a new system of inspections, devised by Lieutenant Colonel Ducat and Captain Peterson, the organization of a signal corps, by the same officers, and innumerable items of official detail now absorbed the time of the Commanding General and his rapidly-increasing staff. A flood of general orders, correcting evils which had fastened themselves upon the army, were published and enforced. The performance of guard duty—more difficult than any other to enforce in volunteer armies—was rigidly required of officers. The abuses of sutlers were corrected. General Order No. 4, threatening disgraceful dismissal from the service, was sharply executed upon dozens of drunken, incompetent, or deserting officers. Cowardly soldiers who had been disaffected, doubtless, by Knights of the Golden Circle, and who were practically deserting by willfully surrendering to the enemy in order to be paroled, were menaced with an order threatening to garnish their heads with night-caps and march them through the streets of Northern cities in this humiliating disguise.

THE PERMANENT STAFF.

The following permanent staff was also announced, viz.:

Lieutenant Colonel Julius P. Garesche, Assistant Adjutant General and Chief of Staff.

Major W. H. Sidell, Fifteenth United States Infantry, Acting Assistant Adjutant General and Chief Mustering and Disbursing Officer.

Major C. Goddard, Senior Aiddecamp, Acting Assistant Adjutant General.

Captain J. Bates Dickson, Assistant Adjutant General.

First Lieutenant Henry Stone, First Wisconsin Volunteer Infantry, Acting Assistant Adjutant General.

Major Ralston Skinner, Judge Advocate.

Captain Charles R. Thompson, Aiddecamp.

First Lieutenant Frank S. Bond, Tenth Connecticut Volunteers, Aiddecamp.

Second Lieutenant Byron Kirby, Sixth United States Infantry, Aiddecamp.

Captain Robert S. Thoms, Volunteer Aiddecamp.

Captain William D. Bickham, Volunteer Aiddecamp.

Lieutenant Colonel A. C. Ducat, of Illinois, Assistant Inspector General.

Captain J. C. PETERSON, Fifteenth United States Infantry, Acting Assistant Inspector General.

Captain JAMES CURTIS, Fifteenth United States Infantry, Acting Assistant Inspector General.

Lieutenant Colonel J. W. TAYLOR, Quartermaster's Department, Chief Quartermaster.

Lieutenant Colonel SAMUEL SIMMONS, Commissary of Subsistence, Chief Commissary.

Surgeon EBEN SWIFT, United States Army, Medical Director.

Surgeon —— WEED, Medical Inspector.

Captain JAMES ST. CLAIR MORTON, Corps of Engineers, Chief Engineer.

Second Lieutenant GEORGE BURROUGHS, Corps of Engineers.

Second Lieutenant H. C. WHARTON, Corps of Engineers.

Captain N. MICHLER, of Topographical Engineers, Chief of Topographical Engineers.

First Lieutenant T. EDSON, Ordnance Corps, Ordinance Officer.

Brigadier General D. S. STANLEY, United States Volunteers, Chief of Cavalry.

Colonel JAMES BARNETT, First Ohio Artillery, Chief of Artillery.

Captain J. H. GILMAN, Nineteenth United States Infantry, Inspector of Artillery.

Lieutenant Colonel W. P. HEPBURN, Second Iowa Cavalry, Inspector of Cavalry.

Captain W. M. WILES, Twenty-Second Indiana Volunteer Infantry, Provost Marshal General.

Captain ELMER OTIS, Fourth United States Cavalry, Chief of Courier Lines.

Captain J. H. YOUNG, Fifteenth United States Infantry, Assistant Mustering Officer.

Captain JESSE MERRILL, Volunteers, Signal Officer.

The gallant and accomplished Lieutenant Colonel Garesché reported for duty on the 14th of November, and at once assumed position as Chief of Staff. He was a man of remarkable character, distinguished for the delicacy and strength of his intellect, his moral purity, his refined and exquisitely cultured manners, and his systematic business habits and capacity. Such qualities, with disinterestedness and entire absence of ostentation endeared him to all with whom he was associated. He proved a treasure to the Commanding General, who had long esteemed and admired him. There was hardly a more polished and universally respected officer in the regular service. He was devoted to his profession, and his military judgment carried conviction whenever his advice was sought. And that which his countrymen admired most in him was his pure and exalted patriotism. It is now known that he joined the Fourteenth Army Corps with the presentiment firmly fixed in his mind that he would fall in his first battle.

Garesché was a native of Cuba—born of French parents. When quite young he removed to Delaware. He spent a few months at Georgetown College in the District of Columbia, where the brilliancy of his intellect caused him to be regarded the most promising student in his classes. In 1837 he entered the Military Academy at West Point, and graduated June 30th, 1841, well up in a numerous class, which embraced Major Generals Buell, Schuyler Hamilton, Reynolds, and Richardson, Brigadier Generals Lyon,

Totten, Plummer, Brannan, and others of the federal army, who have distinguished themselves in this war. On the 1st of July, of that year, he was commissioned Second Lieutenant of the Fourth Artillery, and was promoted to a First Lieutenancy, June 18th, 1846. He served in the war with Mexico, on General Taylor's line of operations. After declaration of peace he remained on the frontiers of Texas, about a year, when he was recalled to Washington and was assigned to the Adjutant General's office, with the rank of Captain. He proved so peculiarly competent that he was permanently transferred to that department. The desertion of officers of this corps to the rebels, made room for his promotion, first to a Majority, and later to the rank of Lieutenant Colonel. The business of the office was now enormous, but as Chief Assistant he proved himself fully equal to the responsibilities which devolved upon him. He carried the same system which had characterized his department in Washington into the Department of the Cumberland, and he relieved the General Commanding of vast labor which otherwise would have oppressed him. The general orders of which he was the author, were remarkable for their clearness and precision. As specimens of military literature they were unsurpassed. Until the instant of his fall upon the battle field he was the constant and cherished personal friend and adviser of his General.

GENERAL D. S. STANLEY.

The Chief of Cavalry is also a marked man, but of another stamp. He is an active, enterprising soldier, familiar alike with the abstract science, and the practical art of war. He stood high in the regular army before the rebellion, and later, by his skill and courage, won distinction in various severe battles. It was his good fortune to be loved by all whom he commanded. The soldiers had faith in his zeal and skill, and his fiery courage inspired them with confident enthusiam. They compared him not inaptly with Murat, and airily applied to him the *soubriquet* of "gay old Stanley"—singing merrily at festive board or cheerful bivouac fire

> "Here's to gay old Stanley
> Pass him round, pass him round."

His associates in the regular army think there are no better field officers than Brigadier General (now Major General) David S. Stanley, and many esteem him the best cavalry officer in the service. He had distinguished himself under the eye of General Rosecrans in the brillant battle of Corinth, in command of the best division in Major General Grant's Department—a division which he had disciplined—and had been invited by Rosecrans to his present distinguished position.

He is a native of Ohio, aged about thirty-six years. He entered the Military Academy, at West Point, in 1848, and graduated with honor 1852; entering the service as Brevet Second Lieutenant of the Second United States Dragoons, on the 1st of July, 1852, and at the commencement of the rebellion he ranked as Captain. At that time his sympathies were erroneously assumed to be with the rebellion, because he had come into the possession of slave property by marriage, but he soon and decidedly silenced that calumny. He first served with distinction in Missouri, and was appointed Brigadier General of Volunteers, in consideration of his services and abilities. He is a man of sanguine nervous temperament, of vehement and fiery spirit, with blazing blue eyes and a lithe figure somewhat above medium stature. Notwithstanding his disappointment he cheerfully assumed command of his small cavalry command, and was not long in promoting it to a state of discipline which made it formidable to the enemy.

JAMES ST. CLAIR MORTON.

The staff also embraced a military genius. Garesché was a peculiar man, but St. Clair Morton, Chief of Engineers, is a most striking character. His fertility of resource baffles all obstacles. The mastery of his profession was not singular, but his mastery of all obstacles which obstruct his designs; the domineering confidence with which he assails difficulties in his path, and the success which invariably crowns his exertions are remarkable. He never admits that he can not accomplish an enterprise intrusted to him, but he enters upon it, no matter how difficult, with determined and assuring alacrity. Be sure he never fails. Fort Negley, a star and bastion fort of great strength and beauty, which frowns upon Nashville from the oval crown of St. Cloud Hill, will long remain to illustrate his skill in the legitimate line of his profession. The moral influence of his cheerful deportment innoculates all with whom he comes in contact. It inspires his subordinates with unconquerable ardor and inflames a spirit of enterprise which defies opposition. His commander and he were soon *en rapport.* The former has ever delighted in the expression of admiration for his Chief of Engineers, and the latter—though not insensible to the partiality of his Chief—as modest as he is worthy, betrays his appreciation of such distinguishing praise by ever increasing zeal for the service he loves.

Morton's spirit and his person happily accord. As one aspires so is the other imposing. The former would assert a proud place in any arena, and his commanding figure and striking face would win attention among chosen men. In spite of the few years against him — (he is thirty-six) — his countenance recalls the image of

> "A youth, who bore, 'mid snow and ice
> A banner with the strange device."

He is a Saxon, with Norman fire gleaming in his strong steadfast blue eyes, vivifying his fair, boldly chiseled and expressive features. His long, wavy, almost flaxen hair brushed back from his broad, compact brows, as if to give his faculties unobstructed play, crowns an *ensemble* which romance might happily borrow for a hero. St. Clair Morton, still a Captain of Engineers, though promised a Brigadier's commission by the President, entered the Military Academy at West Point, in September, 1847. On the 1st of July, 1851, he entered the service as Brevet Second Lieutenant in the Corps of Engineers—having graduated second in a numerous and talented class.

There were no other brilliant names in the staff when it was organized, though all subsequently won honorable distinction. Excepting Garesché and Taylor, all were under fifty years of age—young and zealous patriots, energetic and brainy. Lieutenant Colonel Taylor, a native of New York, but now a citizen of the great West, had established his reputation as a Quartermaster in the Army of the Mississippi, capable to administer a great department. There was no more gallant man in the field, or a more graceful gentleman in the army. The superior qualifications of the Chief Commissary have been remarked. Colonel Barnet, Chief of Artillery, had acquired deserved professional reputation in an active arduous career dating from the first operations of the federal army in Western Virginia, when at Phillippi, he fired the first field piece which had been heard among those mountains. He had displayed his coolness and courage in various fields and was regarded one of the best volunteer artillerists in the service. Major Skinner was a novice in military life, but he entered the service with distinguished recommendations for large capacity, incorruptible integrity, and enthusiastic zeal for his country. Goddard, Wiles, and Thompson, had each fought under the eye of the General, and were approved good soldiers. The youthfulness of the staff was characteristic of the General. He ever insisted upon being surrounded by young men. "Young men without experience," he said, "are better than experienced old men. Young men will learn; old men fixed in their habits and opinions will not learn." In short he "liked youngsters. They are full of snap, think rapidly and execute quickly. They will do what I require of them."

CHAPTER XII.

Governor Andrew Johnson—Municipal Affairs of Nashville—The Contraband Question—The Railroad Repaired—The Enemy Takes up a Line in Front—His Cavalry Enterprises—Colonel John Kennett strikes Back—Reconnoissances and Skirmishes—The Night-Cap Battalion.

Hon. Andrew Johnson, the Military Governor of Tennessee, appeared, to the eyes of superficial observers, to be busy enough, but it was difficult to define his functions. His authority could not extend beyond the military lines, which were then rather contracted. The civil and military administration of Tennessee, on the other hand, were so intimately blended that it was quite impossible to separate them, so that the responsibility of civil government really devolved on General Rosecrans. Rebels who had business with the government declined generally to hold intercourse with the Governor, and loyal men sought the attention of the military chief. Excepting the issuance of commissions to officers of Tennessee volunteers, and to a magistrate now and then; the collection and distribution of taxes levied upon wealthy rebels for charitable purposes; and correspondence with the State Department at Washington, there was really nothing else for the Governor to do. Hon. Hugh Smith was Mayor of Nashville, but his office was almost a sinecure, the municipal government being reduced to petty police business and the hebdomadal meetings of Aldermen.

The customary annoyances of the contraband question had not involved the Commander of the Department. Efforts were made to elicit his views upon slavery in the rebel States, but he declined to embarrass himself. He had adopted the only wise course that an officer could safely pursue. The Proclamation was then a paper promise of the President. The General replying to suggestive inquiries upon this point was wont to say emphatically, "I am bound to obey the orders of the government, not to inquire why they are issued. I shall obey." He did not hesitate to appropriate the services of the slaves of rebels for public purposes, and he was not at all squeamish in denouncing slavery as a vital element of military strength, of which a wise government was bound to take advantage. Numerous gangs of fugitive negroes had been already organized, and were constructing fortifications around Nashville—and this was a competition in the labor market against which free white soldiers raised no objections. Indeed, they seemed to approve it. The practice of General Rosecrans in this connection is illustrated in the following extracts from one of his general orders, viz.:

I. Negroes may be employed and paid, in conformity with the Act of Congress, as follows:

1. As teamsters on Quartermasters' trains, provided a sufficient number of white teamsters and wagon-masters are retained to preserve order.

2. As laborers in the Quartermaster and Engineer Departments.

3. As cooks, nurses, and attendants in hospital.

4. As company cooks, two to a company.

5. As officers' servants, according to number allowed by law.

Commanders of corps, divisions, brigades, and independent posts are authorized to procure and employ negroes, as above:

1. From those found free and roaming at large.

2. From those belonging to masters serving in the rebel army, or who have been employed, in any manner, in the rebel service.

3. From those belonging to persons who, though not now serving in the rebel cause, are disloyal, or have children or other near relatives in the rebel army, who are benefited or maintained by the labor of such slaves.

Lastly, when it becomes an absolute necessity, from among those belonging to loyal men. In this case, a copy of the order directing their employment, and a descriptive list of persons so employed, shall be given to the owner, duly authenticated by the commanding officer of the troops in whose service they are employed.

The Commanding General enjoins great caution in the employment of women, in any case where it might lead to immorality.

II. All persons so employed in each regiment, except those employed as officers' servants, will be entered on Quartermasters' rolls as laborers or teamsters, stating their age, sex, name of master or claimant, date of employment, and the length of time employed; and in the column of "remarks" will be noted on what duty and by whom employed. Those employed by the Engineer, Quartermaster, or Medical departments, will be entered on their appropriate rolls. They will be provided with clothing, to be deducted from their pay, the balance to be paid to the person employed, unless he belongs to a loyal master, in which case payment will be made to the master.

Every negro thus employed will receive a certificate from his employer, setting forth the fact and nature of his employment, and no male or female negro will remain in camp, or be subsisted therein, without such certificate.

A few loyal persons complained of the abduction of their slaves by the troops. General Rosecrans promptly ordered the ejection of such from camp, according to orders from the War Office, but refused to exercise the power of the government to apprehend and deliver the fugitives.

On the 26th of November railroad communication with Louisville was resumed. Up to this period the army had been subsisted, and two or three days' rations had accumulated in the public warehouses. The railroad managers were urged to push their carrying capacity to the utmost. They had agreed to run through one hundred car-loads a day, but they hardly averaged one-fourth of that number. There was no alternative. The drought continued, and Cumberland River still remained at its lowest ebb.

The enemy had latterly developed strongly in our immediate front. Bragg had taken up a line in the rear of Stewart's Creek, nineteen miles from Nashville, extending from the Lebanon pike on his right to the Franklin pike on his left. Strong lines of cavalry videttes with heavy reserves covered his front from Lebanon pike to a point on the left of Nolensville, intersecting the Murfreesboro pike eleven miles in front of Nashville, and separated from our outposts about two miles. Strong bodies of cavalry and mounted infantry were posted on the flanks, and at Lavergne and Nolensville—Morgan on the right, Forrest on the left, General Wheeler at Lavergne, General Wharton at Nolensville. The right wing of the enemy was then commanded by Kirby Smith, the left by Hardee, the center by Polk. Colonel Truesdail estimated their effective infantry force at not exceeding forty thousand men, and not long afterward reported the completion of the railroad bridge across the Tennessee River.

SKIRMISHES.

In the meantime the enemy's cavalry had been constantly harrassing our outposts. Scarcely a day elapsed that they did not disturb our pickets with spiteful musketry, and occasionally they flung a few shells by way of diversion. Innumerable efforts were made to punish them, but they uniformly fled from attack. Our forage trains, usually guarded by a brigade of infantry and a section of artillery, industriously collected forage from the debatable belt of territory between the camps, but they hardly gathered a nubbin of corn without fighting for it. Several vigorous dashes had been made at our trains from Mitchellsville to Nashville, and in the course of a fortnight we lost probably one hundred and fifty men and a few wagons by capture. But our own expeditions captured as many from them. On the morning of the 13th of November, Lieutenant Beals and his command of twenty men from the Fourth Michigan Cavalry were sharply picked up on Stone River by a superior force of Morgan's troopers.

The veteran and enterprising Colonel John Kennett, acting Chief of Cavalry until General Stanley reported for duty, gave the enemy sharp counterstrokes in the vicinity of Hartsville, pouncing suddenly upon large depots, and capturing large quantities of stores, with some men. Following up his success energetically, he soon drove Morgan's gangs to the south side of the Cumberland, and reported back at Nashville for further orders. Lieutenant Colonel Stewart of the Second Indiana Cavalry, also made a spirited dash in front with five hundred men, riding down some Texas troopers. On the 27th, Colonel Kennett made a reconnoissance on our right front and drove a strong body of the enemy pell mell some fifteen miles down the Franklin pike. The same day Brigadier General Kirk, one of the best soldiers in the volunteer army, with part of his brigade consisting of a squadron of the Third Indiana Cavalry under Major Kline, Seventy-Seventh Pennsylvania, Twenty-Ninth and Thirtieth Indiana, Thirty-Fourth and Seventy-Ninth Illinois Infantry, made a successful reconnoissance against sharp resistance, and drove General Wheeler's force out of Lavergne, where he destroyed a few public storehouses which had been occupied by the rebels. In that brisk little affair we had eleven wounded, including Lieutenant Colonel Hurd of the Thirtieth Indiana—none missing or killed. The enemy's loss was not ascertained, but General Wheeler was among the wounded. That afternoon Brigadier General Sherridan also reconnoitered in front of Nolensville, driving the enemy back to that village without loss. Colonel Roberts, of the Forty-Second Illinois Infantry, commanding brigade, moved out the Charlotte pike the same evening, and surprised Captain Portch and a few men of Morgan's command, capturing the whole party with their arms, equipment and horses.

General Stanley had reported for duty about the middle of November, and upon assuming command of the cavalry organized it in two divisions, taking the first under his own direction, and assigning the

8

second to Colonel John Kennett. The latter organized his command into brigades, the first consisting of the Fourth Michigan regiment, Colonel Minty, the Third Kentucky, Colonel Murray, Seventh Pennsylvania, Major Wynkoop, and First Tennessee, Colonel W. B. Stokes, which was commanded by Colonel Minty. The second brigade, under Colonel Lewis Zahn, consisted of the First Ohio, Colonel Millikin, Third Ohio, Lieutenant Colonel Murray, and Fourth Ohio, Lieutenant Colonel Pugh. The Fifth Kentucky, Lieutenant Colonel Scott, was posted in Nashville; the Fourth, Colonel Bayless, at Bowling Green; and the First, Colonel Woolford, was detained on scouting service in Kentucky. The remaining regiments constituted a reserve under General Stanley's immediate direction. General Stanley kept the enemy agitated on the right and in front, and Kennett was posted on the left, where he did excellent service.

Among the encouraging little affairs of this period, a dashing exploit by Major Hill with a squadron of the Second Indiana met the approbation of the Chief. The enemy had made a sudden dash across the Cumberland near Hartsville, capturing a forage train and some men. Hill pursued vigorously some eighteen miles, recapturing the train and prisoners, besides killing seme eighteen or twenty rebels. The General Commanding promptly complimented him and his command for their "good conduct and energy." He regarded "this little affair as very creditable to the cavalry."

The night-cap order of the General Commanding had been regarded as a humorous menace. On the

28th of November, however, all doubts upon the subject were settled. Fifty straggling cowards who had voluntarily surrendered to the enemy without resistance and had been paroled, were crowned with white cotton night-caps of a ridiculous pattern and decorated with fiery red trimmings. In this humiliating plight they were paraded grotesquely through Nashville with fifes and drums to the tune of Rogue's March, and were then forwarded to a camp for paroled prisoners in Indiana. The example was severe but salutary.

CHAPTER XIII.

MORAL Influence of Success—The Hartsville Disgrace—Colonel John Morgan Surprises and Captures a Federal Brigade—The Fight—Vain Gallantry of the Soldiers—Imbecility of the Commander—Casualties.

BRISK and successful skirmishes occurring frequently had a happy effect. The cavalry especially, begun to exhibit encouraging confidence in themselves. The enemy, who had professed contempt for "Yankee cavalry," were exhibiting wholesome dread of it. General Stanley vainly endeavored to coax an equal fight out of them. Their unsleeping vigilance foiled him. But they watched their opportunity to strike unguarded points. On Sunday morning, the 7th of December, they found one, and struck successfully at Hartsville. The blow was squarely in the face of the army.

Brigadier General Dumont's division was posted at Castillian Springs, in front of Gallatin. Complying with orders, he had thrown forward a brigade some eight or nine miles to Hartsville, to guard a ford at that point, and to observe the Lebanon road. Under direction of General Thomas, they took up a strong position upon high ground, which, by good management and strong fighting, it was presumed they could hold against a division. They were at first commanded by Colonel J. R. Scott, of the valiant Nineteenth Illinois Infantry, but he was subsequently relieved by Colonel A. B. Moore, of the One Hundred and Fourth Illinois Infantry, an officer without experience, and, it would seem, without moral determination. His brigade consisted of raw levies—the One Hundred and Fourth Illinois, the One Hundred and Sixth and One Hundred and Eighth Ohio Volunteers, together with a section of Knicklin's Indiana Battery, and three hundred men of the Second Indiana Cavalry, under Lieutenant Colonel Stewart, constituted a force of nineteen hundred and eighty-four men. The second brigade, under Colonel Harlan, and the Fortieth, under Colonel Miller, were at Castillian Springs, within good supporting distance.

THE WARNING.

Notwithstanding the repeated injunctions of General Thomas, to look well to his picket guards, the rebel Morgan, with a force of about fifteen hundred mounted infantry, surprised Moore at sunrise on the 7th of December, and captured him with fifteen hundred and five men, and most of their officers, together with their two field pieces, a large portion of their arms, equipment, ammunition, and transportation. It was a most shameful affair, without palliation. The skirmishing, combat, rout, and pursuit occupied less than an hour and a half. The cavalry was not efficient, the One Hundred and Sixth Ohio did some good fighting, and the One Hundred and Fourth Illinois acquitted itself gallantly. Knicklin's guns were also well handled. There was no reason, but the incompetency of the commander, why the rebels were not destroyed or captured. It was subsequently ascertained that Colonel Moore had been twice warned that he would be attacked on the 7th. A slave who had overheard his master—who was a member of Morgan's command—confide to his wife that the attack was contemplated, waded the Cumberland River after night, on the 4th, and notified Captain Lewis and Captain Bertassy of the contemplated surprise. They reported it to Colonel Moore, who dismissed the information with contemptuous indifference. On the night of the 6th, the same negro again crossed the river and notified Captain Lewis that the enemy were encamped within four miles of Hartsville, and would attack at daybreak next morning. The officer of the day and the Colonel Commanding, were promptly notified, but the warning was again unheeded.

SURPRISE OF THE GARRISON AT HARTSVILLE.

At sunrise Sunday morning, notice of the approach of the enemy in the rear was suddenly given by one of the camp guards, who discovered the gray jackets moving down the declivity of an opposite hill. His shout, "The rebels are coming!" was the first admonition the camp received. The posting of pickets on that side had been neglected. Captain Good, a brave officer, of the One Hundred and Sixth Ohio, swiftly moved, upon his own responsibility, to the right front with a company of skirmishers, and opened a sharp fire. The enemy, surprised at the hitherto quiet deportment of the camp, suspected stratagem, and were cautious in their approach. Time enough to form his line advantageously was thus afforded Colonel Moore, but he was too confused to take advantage of it. At the suggestion of Colonel Tafel of the One Hundred and Sixth Ohio, he occupied the crown of a bold bald hill to the right of the camps. The troops flung themselves along the crest and stood there silently, waiting orders, while the enemy were moving deliberately in column of fours down the declivity of the opposite hill, to form in the ravine which separated the hostile forces. Nobody seemed to think of the propriety of sending to Castillian Springs for reinforcements, but the enemy having approached in the rear, and clouds of mounted skirmishers beginning already to harrass Moore's flanks, efforts to send for aid probably would have been defeated. Nevertheless a prudent officer would have tried the experiment.

After descending into the hollow the rebels dismounted, moved forward in compact line, and under a scattering and ineffective fire from Moore's line, gained cover behind a fence at the foot of the hill below our troops. Moore's line was now thoroughly exposed, while the enemy fought with comparative security, and so effectively that our men soon begun to give way. Moore seemed thoroughly disconcerted, and it was clear that unless his troops fought their own way through the difficulty they would be hopelessly defeated. The Illinois troops and the One Hundred and Sixth Ohio stood up to the work well, the former especially, but the One Hundred and Eighth, indifferently officered, was the first to break and fall back. The field pieces, meantime, had opened from their park and were making some noise. One of them was soon brought to the center, and at the first fire exploded a rebel caisson. Colonel Moore now ordered the whole line to fall back to the *rear of the gun*, leaving it exposed to the enemy. In a few minutes its horses and many of its men were picked off by sharp-shooters, and it was dragged to the rear of the camps, taking position on a rocky hill, where the other gun was playing upon the rebel reserves on the opposite side of the river.

Moore's line, already badly confused, was ordered to fall back to the guns—a movement which was executed with more haste than skill. Colonel Tafel was carrying his regiment off on the right, on a skirt of timber, when the enemy made his appearance on his flank in strong force. Tafel engaged immediately, and a sharp fight ensued. The One Hundred and Sixth fought and fell back gradually, while the other regiments reformed on the hill. The rebels, however, finally pushed into the camps of the One Hundred and Fourth Illinois and One Hundred and Sixth Ohio, which compelled Tafel to retire to the main body. Before he reached that point, Colonel Moore surrendered. Squads of rebels dashed up toward Tafel's regiment and were fired on, but discovering that he was nearly surrounded, and that three-fourths of the command had been surrendered, Tafel at length succumbed. Captain Good and his skirmishers were still ignorant of the extent of the misfortune, and sustained a lively fight in the rear of the right flank, to prevent a squadron of cavalry from breaking into the camps. When notified of the condition of affairs, his gallant company scattered in the forests, and many saved themselves. After surrendering his sword, Captain Good himself managed to elude his captors and escaped.

MORGAN RETREATS.

Morgan, fully aware that fugitives would soon report at Castillian Springs, discovered necessity for haste. Gathering the cream of the spoils as rapidly as possible, he drove the captives across the river and moved swiftly in retreat. Before his rear guard had gotten out of the way, Colonel Harlan came up with his brigade, and enjoyed the melancholy satisfaction of flinging a few shells into the successful fugitives. The rebels had a right to be proud of their achievement, but it would have cost them dearly had Scott been in command of the post.

Our loss in this disgraceful affair, was fifty-five killed and one hundred wounded. The casualties of the enemy were about equal—the Second and Ninth Kentucky rebel regiments alone being sixty-four. Colonel Moore and the field officers of the three regiments of infantry, and Lieutenant Colonel Stewart, of the Second Indiana Cavalry, together with most of the line officers of the brigade, were captured. Major Hill, of the latter regiment, escaped after receiving a severe wound. Lieutenant W. Y. Gholson, Acting Assistant Adjutant General of the brigade, a young officer of superior merit, was killed while gallantly discharging his duty in the heat of conflict.

CHAPTER XIV.

Official Intercourse between General Rosecrans and General Bragg—An Effort to Meliorate the Severities of War—Mutual Reproaches—Violation of a Flag of Truce and Bragg's Apology—A Repetition of the Outrage under more Exasperating Circumstances—Correspondence finally Ended by General Rosecrans.

Prior to the 20th of November, intercourse between the Commanding Generals of the respective armies had been frequent. A high-toned courtesy generally had been observed. Flags of truce were interchanged almost daily. An effort was made by both General Rosecrans and General Bragg to mollify the asperities of war, and confine the exercise of martial power to its legitimate sphere. General Bragg complained of the ill treatment of certain of his cavalry who had been captured. After it was understood that he refused to acknowledge guerrillas as entitled to the rights of war, and upon his explanation that his recognized forces had all been mustered into rebel service as soldiers, the two leaders endeavored to adjust a system for the relief of non-combatants from arrest and imprisonment. General Rosecrans expressed his abhorrence of the practice of "harassing and arresting non-combatants, who are strictly so." He said, "I never authorize or permit the arrest of such persons unless there is a *prima facie* case of a forfeiture of their claims to non-combatants, by acts bearing the character of military mischief. * * *

Pillage, wanton destruction of private property, is strictly prohibited, and rigorously punished whenever detected. The burning of houses is only justified when they have been used as little fortifications." General Bragg concurred, but did not find it convenient to practice accordingly.

ROBBING UNION PRISONERS OF WAR.

The rebels continued to outrage the laws of war so grossly that General Rosecrans protested indignantly, sometimes provoking harsh replies. But as long as intercourse was maintained he continued to reproach the enemy with military crimes. Among others, their practice of plundering surgeons and other captives was most aggravating. A federal surgeon at Hartsville was robbed while he was dressing a wounded rebel. The Hartsville prisoners were deprived of part of their overcoats on the field of battle, and of the remainder by General Wheeler's order at Lavergne. The same evening they were marched to our outposts without previous notice to General Rosecrans, and offered in exchange—arriving in our front at nightfall.

General Rosecrans indignantly protested against it as a violation of the cartel for the exchange of prisoners which had been negotiated by the United States and rebel authorities. It had been agreed that all exchanges should take place at Aiken's landing, or Vicksburg, or some other place "to be previously agreed upon." Bragg's policy was transparent. He desired to avoid the expense and trouble of forwarding the prisoners to either of the foregoing places, and to impose corresponding cost and annoyance upon General Rosecrans. The sentiments of the latter were sharply expressed in the following note, which was forwarded immediately to the rebel general by flag of truce:

HEADQUARTERS DEPARTMENT OF THE CUMBERLAND,
Nashville, December 11, 1862.

GENERAL BRAXTON BRAGG:

General—Your letter, enclosing list of prisoners captured at Hartsville and paroled by you, has been received. It is reported to me that the flag of truce presented itself about dark and during a skirmish. As it will be impossible to verify the roll of prisoners to-night, or say anything of their condition, I have directed the prisoners to be receipted for, until the rolls can be verified, when they will be returned duly receipted. We take care of your prisoners, feed them, make them comfortable, and conduct them to the proper place of exchange. Ours were sufficiently clad, and I think ought to have been treated in a similar manner. Sending these prisoners here and imposing them on my humanity without a previous agreement is a violation of the spirit and letter of the cartel. I regret to notice this act of injustice and discourtesy, which is aggravated by their not being sent to us at a proper hour of the day, when all the business could have been conducted without inconvenience to either party. Paroled prisoners hereafter will only be received in accordance with the terms of the cartel.

I have the honor to be, General,

Yours, respectfully,

W. S. ROSECRANS,
Major General Commanding.

General Bragg attempted to wriggle himself out of the responsibility by virtuously assuming that he was moved by sentiments of enlightened humanity—conveniently forgetting how inhuman it was to rob the prisoners of their clothing. General Rosecrans determining to fix the mean record against him, responded to his paltry excuse in the following strain :

HEADQUARTERS FOURTEENTH ARMY CORPS,
Department of the Cumberland,
Nashville, December 11, 1862.

GENERAL BRAXTON BRAGG :

General—Your letter, enclosing list of prisoners captured at Hartsville and paroled by you, has been received. It is reported to me that the flag of truce presented itself about dark and during a skirmish.

The officer who conducted them to our lines insisted upon our receiving them, as I am informed, "upon the ground of humanity." We take care of your prisoners, feed them, make them as comfortable as we can, and conduct them to the proper place of exchange. That is our idea of humanity. Our prisoners were sufficiently clad when taken, and I think ought to have been similarly treated. Whether your idea of humanity consists in robbing them of their blankets and overcoats I know not, but such, they assure me, was the treatment they received from your troops.

Without entering further into that question, however, I must be permitted to observe that to send these prisoners to my lines without any previous agreement with me to receive them, is a violation both of the letter and spirit of the cartel.

I regret to notice that this act of injustice and discourtesy, which is aggravated by the fact of their not being sent to us at a proper hour of the day, when all the business could have been transacted without inconvenience to either party.

Paroled prisoners will hereafter only be received by me in accordance with the terms of the cartel. Herewith you will please receive receipts for the prisoners taken at Hartsville, conformed to the lists of them forwarded by you. Although purporting apparently to be original, these lists are evidently mere copies—not attested by the signature of any officer of either army. As it regards the third list sent by you, inasmuch as it contains the names of persons of whom I know nothing, it is impossible for me to say or do anything.

Very respectfully,

Your obedient servant,

W. S. ROSECRANS,

Major General Commanding.

"Upon the ground of humanity" was the identical expression used by General Bragg in his letter, but he subsequently said no special grounds for sending them to our lines was cited.

VIOLATION OF FLAGS OF TRUCE.

Throughout the correspondence Bragg had exhibited exasperating insincerity. And the spirit which animated him was illustrated by the evident care taken by him to publish his letters to General Rosecrans in the rebel newspapers. He was "firing the Southern heart," not seeking justice. His communications breathed that spirit of "high toned" assumption which will cause the Southern character to blaze in history with ridiculous glare. The element of truth was rarely a constituent. Truth itself crept in by mnemonical oversight. The abuse finally corrected itself rather abruptly. A detachment of his cavalry one day took advantage of a federal flag of truce, which was being entertained at his lines, to capture a post of three videttes, on the Murfreesboro pike. After a sharp correspondence, in which Bragg was evasive, he finally surrendered the prisoners, together with their horses and equipments—excepting their overcoats, of which they had been robbed by rebel troops—apologizing for the violation of the flag, but offering no excuse for pillaging the soldiers so wrongfully captured.

But on the 15th of November the flag of truce business received a paralytic shock. Bragg sent a flag to our lines, and while a detachment of some sixty of the Fourth Michigan Cavalry, under Captain Able, was entertaining the rebel flag officer at the outposts, a detachment of one hundred and fifty rebel horsemen suddenly charged upon the federal party, killed a half dozen, captured the remainder, and rode off with Bragg's flag officer. General Rosecrans immediately forwarded a formal demand to Bragg for an apology and the restitution of the prisoners, with their horses and equipments. He complained to Bragg that "another outrage of the grossest character has been perpetrated by your troops, in the presence of your own 'flag,' commanded by a Lieutenant Colonel in your service, who was courteously received. I can not believe you had authorized, or will permit to go unpunished or without prompt reparation such barbarous conduct — conduct hardly paralleled by savages. You can not restore life to my men who have been inhumanly murdered, but I shall leave to your own head and heart to devise such a reparation as is demanded by your own honor, and the honor of our common humanity."

It was a *prima facie* case, but Bragg evaded and finally sought to justify the outrage. General Rosecrans at once threatened to suspend further intercourse, writing that "after your (Bragg's) non-condemnation of the behavior of your men on a preceding occasion, under similar circumstances, and the return of three men thus captured—albeit minus overcoats and holsters, I will only most respectfully quote your own phrase. 'Words will not suffice—we must have deeds.' In short, my dear General, the *sine qua non* to our future correspondence or official intercourse is the prompt return of those men, with all their clothes, arms, and equipments. When you speak by such deeds of simple justice, I shall be able to understand you." Bragg had returned three men who had been wrongfully captured. Fifty were too great a temptation for his high toned virtue. He replied, at length, that having fully investigated the matter, he concluded not only that the action was fully warranted, but that General Rosecrans owed him an apology for the capture and detention of his flag twenty-four hours—both false pleas. General Rosecrans finally closed official intercourse with his perfidious enemy, in a sharp and comprehensive resume of the transaction.

He was "utterly amazed" at Bragg's impudent assertion that his flag had been detained. The rebel flag officer, Lieutenant Colonel Hawkins, had expressed his satisfaction with the generous courtesy with which he had been entertained. Hawkins was borne away by the rebel party who had shamefully violated the flag, "and did not," said General Rosecrans, "present himself again until next morning. The only detention of your flag that occurred took place the next day, when, having been dismissed, Hawkins halted by the way to feed his horse within two miles of our outposts, and that even this detention was but about half an hour, and was apologised for. It thus appearing that the statements contained in your letter, as to the occurrences connected with your flag, and the outrages perpetrated in its presence, utterly at variance with the actual facts reported to me by my officers, of the truth of which I have not the shadow of a doubt, have only to say, with profound disappointment and regret, that the sources of your information, or your own views, are such that until you shall redress that outrage, by returning my men, with everything they had when taken, so far as is possible, I shall not be able to hold any further official intercourse with you. Indeed, you render it impracticable, because I can not trust your messengers, or the statements made by them of occurrences patent as the sun. No flag will, therefore, be received from you, except the one conveying that reparation, or the statement that circumstances beyond your control render it impossible."

While this controversy was pending, Jeff. Davis, President of the Confederate States, arrived at Murfreesboro. It is fair to infer that he approved Bragg's perfidy. It is proper to observe, in this connection, that after the visit of President Davis in Tennessee, Bragg exhibited a more decided determination to resist the advance of the federal army.

CHAPTER XV.

THE Hartsville Affair Retrieved—Brilliant Repulse of the Enemy by Matthews' Brigade—Successful Foraging—Gallantry of the Soldiers—Good Conduct Publicly Approved by the General—A Brilliant Cavalry Exploit—General D. S. Stanley Routs the Rebels and Captures Franklin—Spirit of the Men.

ON the 9th of December the Hartsville disgrace was partially retrieved. A strong force of mounted rebel infantry and cavalry, with artillery, under Brigadier General Wheeler, attacked a brigade of infantry under Acting Brigadier General Stanley Matthews, of the Fifty-First Ohio Volunteer Infantry, and, after two sharp combats, were severely repulsed. Colonel Matthews moved into the debatable strip between the two lines with a large foraging train. His force consisted of the Fifty-First Ohio, Thirty-Fifth Indiana, the Eighth and Twenty-First Kentucky Infantry, and a section of Swallow's Seventh Indiana Battery. Diverging from the Murfreesboro pike, and striking to the left, he crossed Millcreek at Dobbin's Ferry, leaving a sergeant and ten men of the Twenty-First Kentucky to guard the rear. The Kentucky regiments, with skirmishers well out, were formed in front, the other two regiments loading the wagons and protecting the rear.

THE COMBAT.

The train was finally filled, and was about countermarching, when a smart rattle of musketry at the ford indicated an attack in the rear. Colonel Matthews immediately double-quicked the Fifty-First Ohio and Thirty-Fifth Indiana to the ford, arriving to the assistance of the gallant little picket guard in time to save them. The enemy were already charging through the woods. Matthews' inferior force was quickly deployed, and opened a sharp fire, which at once checked the rebels. Following up this success promptly, the gallant Buckeyes and Hoosiers speedily drove the enemy to cover, and finally compelled them to retire out of range.

The train had moved up during the combat. The situation was critical. Colonel Matthews anticipated another attack by increased numbers, and it was doubtful whether the train could be saved; but he determined to make the effort. The Kentucky troops were directed to protect the rear, while the Ohio and Indiana regiments took the advance, skirmishers being thrown out well on all sides. The spirited little force, now flushed by success, pushed homeward briskly, but anticipating attack. They had moved but a short distance when the pickets in the rear gave the alarm. The enemy pressed forward eagerly, evidently contemplating a charge. Wheeler himself was urging them by voice and example. The Kentuckians waited patiently until the enemy approached within direct range, and then gave them a volley which caused them to recoil.

They recovered in a moment, and again advanced, but less eagerly than before. The fight became general and sharp. Wheeler tried to press Matthews' flanks, but was driven back. Another strong effort was made to break the line, but being foiled, the rebels slacked fire, and in a short time disappeared altogether, leaving Colonel Matthews master of the field, though severely bruised by a fall from his horse. The brigade marched home triumphantly, and received the plaudits of the army for its brilliant conduct. Our loss was Adjutant B. R. Muller, of the Thirty-Fifth Indiana, and four enlisted men killed; two commissioned officers, including Lieutenant Colonel Balfe, and thirty-three enlisted men wounded, and four missing. The rebel newspapers announced that their casualties were one hundred. We captured but one prisoner. The skillful management and gallant bearing of Colonel Matthews was generously applauded by the General Commanding.

SPECIAL HONORABLE MENTION.

The conduct of the troops was scanned with interest because it was the beginning of the campaign, and it was desirable to measure the reliability of the army. Colonel Matthews reported that every man in the command behaved himself handsomely, and upon his official recommendation, General Rosecrans published a field order, of which the following is a copy, commending the heroism of the brave sergeant and ten men who held Dobbin's Ford so stoutly, viz.:

SPECIAL FIELD ORDER.

The General Commanding takes this method of complimenting the following non-commissioned officers and privates of the Twenty-First Kentucky Volunteer Infantry, for their gallant conduct in the skirmish near Dobbin's Ford, on the 9th inst.:

Sergeant J. F. Morton, Co. F, commanding squad.

Corporal Henry Stahel, Co. A.
" J. P. Hagan, Co. F.
Private Geo. P. Montjoy, Co. A.
" Cassius Kiger, Co. A.
" Edward Welch, Co. A.
" Wm. Murphy, Co. A.
" R. B. Clusin, Co. F.
" W. W. Oliver, Co. F.
" Jno. Morton, Co. F.
" B. S. Jones, Co. F.

By command of
MAJOR GENERAL ROSECRANS,
J. BATES DICKSON, *Captain and A. A. General.*

Such prompt recognition of good conduct in battle has vast influence upon the *morale* of an army. It is to be regretted that all commanders and the government have not yet learned to attach sufficient importance to the value of rewards to the brave soldiers of the Republic.

GENERAL STANLEY'S SPIRITED DASH ON FRANKLIN.

The revolving rifles were received four or five weeks after they were ordered. General Stanley distributed them immediately among his most reliable cavalry troops. The Fourth Ohio Cavalry, which was one of the best regiments in the field, was now properly armed for the first time since it had entered the army. Other regiments which had been neglected were also improved by the new arm. The men evinced anxiety to practice their five-shooters on the rebels. Stanley, nothing loth, proposed to gratify them. Massing a considerable force on the 11th of December, he pushed down the Franklin road for the purpose of making a reconnoissance and to surprise the rebel garrison at Franklin.

Soon after passing the outposts the twang of a carbine advertised the presence of the enemy. The advance guard pressed up sharply and evoked a sharp volley from a line of horsemen in a thicket. Dashing furiously forward a regiment of Wharton's Texas riders were driven out of their nests and scurried over the hills, our fellows after them at a slashing pace. It was an exciting hurdle race, over rocks and ridges, hedges and fences, while a merry ping of rifles and carbines rang through the woods in every direction. It was now rifle and spur; on, Stanley, on; run, rebels, run; until the last gray-back disappeared in the jungle. The bugles sang truce for the nonce, and the blue jacket clans gathered in to breathe a little.

Pushing out his scouts right and left, Stanley was not long in beating up more game. Again it was rifle and spur, and rattle of small arms, but the enemy refused to await the shock. The whole day was thus galloped away, Stanley losing not a man, the rebels keeping clean out of revolver range. At nightfall Stanley had chased the enemy beyond Triune, destroyed two camps, and had captured some prisoners and horses. The men were jaded, but flushed with success.

THE SURPRISE FOILED.

The command was now about west of, and only seven miles from Murfreesboro. There was a strong rebel force at Nolensville in front of them, the main body of Bragg's army was at Murfreesboro, and Buckner's division was behind them. Nevertheless Stanley determined to make a dash at Franklin. Accordingly the horses were fed, and the men rolled up in their blankets for a few hours' slumber. Unfortunately an hour or two before the time appointed to move a prowling rebel drew an ineffective shot from one of Stanley's videttes, a Tennessee sergeant. He returned the fire with fatal effect. Not long afterward another picket firing alarmed the rebels at Franklin so that a surprise was out of the question.

Determined not to be balked, Stanley prepared to move upon Franklin at all hazards, but he now waited until broad daylight. Gathering his force in hand, he advanced cautiously upon the town, drove in the rebel pickets, and then shot out the head of his column directly at the main street. The rebels fled to the houses and opened a brisk fire, but the Seventh Pennsylvania Cavalry under Major Wynkoop, charged into them, and drove them pell mell into the country. Stanley lost not a man. The enemy left a Captain and four privates dead in Franklin, and ten severely wounded, besides fifteen or twenty prisoners who were cut off. General Stanley occupied the town an hour or two, destroyed a valuable flouring mill, captured a considerable number of horses, and returned to receive the congratulations of the General Commanding for his spirit and enterprise. The conduct of the troops, especially that of the Seventh Pennsylvania and Fourth Ohio, was spirited and daring. The reconnoissance was perfectly successful. It had been reported that the enemy was shifting his forces to turn our right. General Stanley ascertained that no demonstrations of the kind were making.

CHAPTER XVI.

THE "Grapevine" Telegraph—A Southern Institution—Fabrication of False Intelligence—Southern Ladies' Aid Society—Its Policy—Social Life in Nashville—The Slaves and the Proclamation—The Year of Jubilee—The Slaveholders—Church-Going—Army Chaplains—Their Fidelity and Devotion.

THE false reports touching rebel movements, which incessantly circulated in Nashville, brings us to the consideration of the "grapevine telegraph"—a peculiar institution of rebel generation, devised for the duplex purpose of "firing the Southern heart," and to annoy the "Yankees." It is worthy of attention, as one of the signs of the times, expressing the spirit of lying which war engenders. But it is no more than just to say that there is often so little difference between the "grapevine" and the associated press telegraph, that they might as well be identical. But the "grapevine" was the favorite institution of Nashville—a purely Southern invention—furnishing entertainment, it was said—slanderously, no doubt—to gossipy females, who preferred the manipulation of this enchanting instrument to the less dainty exercise of their sewing machines—no, not sewing machines; labor-saving inventions are not apt to cross the Mason and Dixie line.

A PANDORA BOX.

A daily dish of alarming reports was served for Yankee entertainment by the inventive newsmongers.

Kirby Smith was moving here to-day; Hardee there to-morrow; Bragg had received great reinforcements; Grant was defeated, and so on for quantity. Inquiry for "grapevine" intelligence was as customary as sunset, and the solicitor of exciting reports was seldom disappointed. Any thorough-bred rebel was ever ready to open his budget on application, and it was usually a pandora of tidings evil to federal ears. An effort to devise a counter-irritation signally failed. The "Yankees," renowned the world over for their acuteness, were no match for the rebels in this species of invention. But it was extremely diverting to the malcontents, whose resources of enjoyment had been quite thoroughly excised.

BACK-PARLOR PROCEEDINGS.

The fabrication of false intelligence and smuggling goods contraband of war, was almost an absorbing business with the master-class of the Rock City. For a considerable period they enjoyed secret facilities of communication with the rebel camps, which puzzled even the ingenuity of Truesdail to detect. They received and forwarded letters constantly, and rebel newspapers were circulated by them when even our best spies failed to procure them. Meetings of men and women were held surreptitiously in dark back-parlors, where plans were concocted for the relief of their friends in the army. Women took the lead. They were best calculated to manage the Yankees. They were accomplished and beautiful. The Yankees were courteous and susceptible to women, but rough-handed with masculine rebels. This was the view the Southern Ladies' Aid Society took of it.

They condemned discourtesy to the federals. It was not good policy—certainly not lady-like. They "hated the Yankees," but it was wise to dissemble. These amiable conspiratrices were very adroit, and plied their cunning arts seductively. The leaders did not demonstrate themselves overtly. Their schemes were deeply masked under the innocent prattle of pathetic ladies who were "tired of the war," and anxious for "peace on any terms." Now and then a high-spirited dame of the "blue blood," permitted her temper to betray her; but such ebullitions were dangerous under the shadow of Truesdail. And yet they treated *him* with distinguished courtesy. He "was *so* kind."

SOCIAL FEATURES OF NASHVILLE.

Aside from those nocturnal seances, there was but little social enjoyment in Nashville. There were not gentlemen enough to make society, and truly there was a *skeleton* in every house—in every heart. The women got together to kiss each other, to cry together, to devise schemes to ameliorate the condition of their husbands, brothers, and so forth, but their glee was more mournful than their sorrow. A patriot could admire their constancy and courage, while he pitied their folly and condemned their malign influence. But God hardened Pharaoh's heart.

Public entertainment there was none. The theater was open, truly, but the drama was public tragedy—drums, banners, bayonets, cannon, a hearse rumbling a dirge over rude streets, at a dead rebel's funeral. Female forms on the stage were more attractive than the manager's programme. A lady in the proscenium boxes was a better card than a star glimmering at the foot-lights. Three-fourths of the audience were soldiers and officers—staff and commanders in stage-boxes, applauding to the echo, because there was now and then a spectral similitude of something they had seen when there was no popular frenzy. Here and there a gambling den, but few gamblers. They were mostly fighting under the bars sinister, and the absence of the paymaster from the federal army caused stagnation in the "chip" market. A few loyal residents, and the wives of Union officers, devised trifling schemes of enjoyment, but the baleful shadow of war interposed. The next battle might transmute ball costume into bombazine.

THE SLAVES AND THE PROCLAMATION.

The only jocund people were the negroes, and their's was pathetic joy. There was a cloud of doubt shading their happiness. Would their year of jubilee ever dawn? The modified proclamation was a death-warrant to them, and hope scarcely promised a reprieve. The shadow on the hearts of those creatures was darker than the skin which God gave them. More than anywhere else in the land of white and black bondage, the slaves of Nashville had hugged the delusive phantom of freedom to their breasts. To them it was "a thing of joy forever." With the usual exaggerative disposition of their race, they anticipated the dawn of January as if it were to be the Star of the East, to glow with stellar splendor.

Many were prematurely rattling their chains, and filing deep into the fibres of the shackles which had eaten into their marrows. Already they were independent of mastery, and foolishly boasted that their souls were their own. Some had rented shanties, which, prospectively, were their castles, and they lingered about the rattling doors with jealous fascination, waiting with throbbing hearts for the clangor of the midnight bell of the old year to proclaim their liberty. Never had there been such sounds of revelry in the house of bondage—balls, little dances, banjo flings in rickety cabins, concerts in which the touching pathos of the American negro race pealed in wild passion upon the resonant strings of homely violins, or swelled into melody upon the rich, full voices of the slaves. They sang *Io paeans* to liberty. They talked of the proclamation incessantly; celebrated their coming freedom in homely but happy refrains; dreamed of emancipation, and related their dreams with the eloquence of joy. They had borrowed the jewelry of the Egyptians prematurely. The word of promise was held to their ears, but broken to their hearts.

THEIR MISTRESSES.

Their haughty mistresses—for their masters were mostly self-exiled traitors—were as restive as their negroes. The proclamation was to them as a cloud surcharged with lightnings and thunders. Those whose humor was not so hot as to betray them into indiscreet bitterness, discussed the subject pitifully, but with a refinement of selfishness that stifled the sympathy which their sexual pathos had otherwise inspired. Invariably, " What will we do, if deprived of our servants? They are indispensable to us. We can not work. We were never taught to labor. We can not procure white servants. We will not endure to employ our emancipated slaves." Not a plea for the slave; no, not one, even from women, who, in all ages and in all nations, have plead more for liberty, sacrificed more for it, and contended more for it than men often dare. Now and then a visionary man, presuming on your ignorance, ventured that "the poor creatures could not take care of themselves," but they shunned an examination of their logic. Strange that a negro can support a whole family of white people by the labor of his hands, and yet be unable to subsist himself. A dog can do that.

CHURCH-GOING.

There was some church-going, but more at a traitor's funeral than at worship. A man of God preached on the corner, reading his petitions to the Throne of Grace from a prayer-book, and his flock echoed him as if mocking him, but they did not pray for their country. The passage was erased in all their missals—"Forgive them, Father, for they know not what they do." Opposite, sometimes, there was a generous, heartful voice of prayer which swelled and soared upward in grand volume, appealing to the God of battles fervently for the brave soldiers of the Republic. The preacher wielded the "sword of the Lord and of Gideon." *He* fought as well as prayed for his bleeding country, and his name is written Moody, among those of good men and heroes.

ARMY CHAPLAINS.

And now that we talk of the church militant, let indignant slander be silent. Who that has watched the man of God with the spirit of Christianity, dares libel the noble men who bear the cross of the Almighty into the field of blood? Will the soldiers of the Fourteenth Army Corps despise the office of the Christian chaplain, who was first by his side at the couch of suffering, and the last to desert him in his sorrow? Will any sneer at the office or curse the memory of Black, of John Poucher, of Layton, of Lozier, of Wilkins, of Gaddis, of Father O'Higgins, of Father Cooney, of noble and gallant Father Trecy, of Bradshaw, of Decker, and of scores of Christian heroes, who ventured health, happiness, life, in the camp and on the battle-field, to soothe the agony of the prostrate and dying soldier? The hand that wields the pen of calumny against the devoted chaplains of the armies of the Republic, should be forever palsied. Soldiers of the Union, cherish your worthy chaplains. Not many are unworthy. Citizens of the Republic, credit not the foul expressions of flippant and mischievous scoffers, who falsely tell you that the preachers of the army are recreant to their trust. Here and there is an apostate; now and then a hyppocrite; but they stand out like blasted trees upon some rude mountain, conspicuous because they are few in numbers. They are the by-word and the scorn of good and of evil men.

There is an unwritten history of the chaplains of your armies, but it is inscribed upon the scroll of the blessed. Is exile from the bliss of home nothing? Is privation, exposure, danger of sickness, of death by disease, or upon the battle-field, nothing? Are the trials, the heart-sickness, the toils, the weary marches, the night watches in the face of the foe, the hunger, the rain, the snow, the cold of winter, of trifling moment in the great record of wretched war? The preacher of the army writes to friends at home of the sorrows and hardships of the *soldier*. When he enjoys brief respite from his labors, he harrows your soul, from the pulpit, with descriptions of a soldier's trials; at your fireside your heart aches, and your eyes float in scalding tears, at his touching pictures of a soldier's last agony. He tells you of the soldier; glows with enthusiasm in recounting their deeds of heroism; the image of the dear old flag, which the preacher loves, floats before his vision, and you feel the silent benediction which swells in his heart, when his full, eloquent voice rings in enconium of the valor of *your* heroes—but the preacher says not one word of *himself;* no, not one word! And yet—and yet, the sorrows of the soldiers are his; the trials of the soldiers are his; the vigils of the soldiers are his—and more, for he stands by the wounded soldier's side in battle, as woman watches at the couch of those she loves.

Preachers have wielded the trenchant blade in the face of the foe. Preachers have spilled their blood on the battle-field under the old flag for which they fought and prayed. Preachers have died on the battle-field doing deeds of mercy and Christian charity. Preachers, worn and exhausted by the vicissitudes of a soldier's life, have eked their last sigh in soldiers' hospitals. Dozens of them, feeble and emaciated, the fountains of their life sapped by toil and exposure, have finally crawled home to linger out a few brief days of suffering, and to die—the victims of the scoffer, who never thinks of God, but to profane his name. It is their destiny to bear their cross patiently and bravely. There are hundreds to-day, in your armies, who labor and wait for the crown which compensates for all the bitter injustice of men.

CHAPTER XVII.

Exterior Pressure upon the Commander—He resists it—His View of War—His Situation—Number of Effectives—Organization—Muster Roll of the Regiments for an Advance—The Pioneer Brigade—The Tenth Ohio—States Represented in the Army—New Regiments—A Glance at Commanding Officers—Spirit of the Army—The Enemy Defiant.

Not long after the resumption of railroad communication with Nashville, General Rosecrans began to feel the influence of external pressure urging a forward movement. Said a very distinguished Tennessean, with some exhibition of bitter impatience, "Why does not Rosecrans move?" Perhaps the suggestion was insinuated from Nashville to Washington. It was believed such interference was resented. The General Commanding, concerning public impatience, said vehemently, "I will not move until I am ready! I will not move for popular effect! War is a business to be be conducted systematically. I believe I understand my business. If my views are not approved, let me be removed. I will not budge until I am ready. The next battle in this department is likely to be decisive of the war. There must be no failure." Why move? Supplies for five days had accumulated about the 5th of December. If the army moved from the immediate front of Nashville, a halt to await subsistence would be imperatively necessary at the expiration of three days. General

Rosecrans subsequently officially explained that under such circumstances "the evident difficulties and labors of an advance into this country, and against such a force, and at such distance from our base of operations, with which we are connected by a single precarious thread, made it manifest that our policy was to induce the enemy to travel over as much as possible of the space that separated us; thus avoiding for us the wear and tear and diminution of our forces, and subjecting the enemy to all these inconveniences, besides increasing for him, and diminishing for us, the dangerous consequences of a retreat."

But by Christmas rations enough had been collected at Nashville to supply the army until the 1st of February, by which period it was probable that navigation in the Cumberland River would be resumed. The army was therefore ready to advance, and prospects for the future were altogether favorable. The enemy had been induced to believe that Rosecrans had gone into winter quarters at Nashville, and had prepared his own at Murfreesboro, with some boastings of an intention to make them finally at Nashville, without, however, making any alarming demonstrations looking to that result.

Bragg having sent a large force of cavalry into West Tennessee to annoy General Grant, and another large force into Kentucky to break up railroad connection between Louisville and Nashville, it was deemed that the opportune moment for movement had arrived. Colonel Truesdail had definitely ascertained that Polk's and Kirby Smith's forces were at Murfreesboro, and that Hardee's corps was on the Shelbyville and Nolensville pike between Triune and

Eaglesville. Our own movable effective force was now collected in front of Nashville, stretching irregularly some ten miles or more across the country. Reynolds' and Steadman's divisions were now in pursuit of Morgan, or guarding the railroad. A strong garrison had been detailed for the protection of Nashville. Innumerable details and the large number of sick and deserters had reduced the effective offensive force to forty-six thousand nine hundred and ten men of all arms. Of these, forty-one thousand four hundred and twenty-one were infantry, two thousand two hundred and twenty-three artillery, and three thousand two hundred and sixty-six cavalry, and several regiments of the latter were raw and unreliable. The corps were organized as follows, viz.:

RIGHT WING—(Numbering 15,933 men.)

Major General Alex. McDowell McCook, Commanding.

FIRST DIVISION,

BRIGADIER GENERAL JEFF C. DAVIS COMMANDING.

First Brigade, Colonel P. Sidney Post Commanding.

Twenty-Second Indiana Regiment, Colonel Gooding.
Fifty-Ninth Illinois Regiment, Lieutenant Colonel Frederick.
Seventy-Fourth Illinois Regiment, Colonel Marsh.
Seventy-Fifth Illinois Regiment, Lieutenant Colonel Bennett.

Second Brigade, Colonel W. P. Carlin Commanding.

Twenty-First Illinois Regiment, Col. Alexander.
Thirty-Eighth Illinois Regiment, Major Gilmer.
Fifteenth Wisconsin Regiment, Colonel H. C. Heg.
One Hundred and First Ohio Regiment, Colonel Stem.

Third Brigade, Colonel W. E. Woodruff Commanding.

Twenty-Fifth Illinois Regiment, Major Norlin.
Thirty-Fifth Illinois Regiment, Lieutenant Colonel Chandler.
Eighty-First Indiana Regiment, Major Woodbury.

Artillery attached to First Division.

Fifth Wisconsin Battery, Captain Pinney.

Eighth Wisconsin Battery, Captain Carpenter.
Second Minnesota Battery, Captain Hotchkiss.

SECOND DIVISION,

BRIGADIER GENERAL R. W. JOHNSON COMMANDING.

First Brigade, Brigadier General A. Willich, Commanding.
Forty-Ninth Ohio Regiment, Colonel W. H. Gibson.
Thirty-Ninth Indiana Regiment, Colonel T. J. Harrison.
Thirty-Second Indiana Regiment, Colonel Von Trebra.
Fifteenth Ohio Regiment, Colonel W. H. Wallace.
Eighty-Ninth Illinois Regiment, Lieutenant Colonel Hotchkiss.
Second Brigade, Brigadier General Kirk Commanding.
Seventy-Seventh Pennsylvania Regiment, Colonel Stambaugh.
Twenty-Ninth Indiana Regiment, Lieutenant Colonel Dunn.
Thirtieth Indiana Regiment, Colonel J. B. Dodge.
Seventy-Ninth Illinois Regiment, Lieutenant Colonel Reed.
Thirty-Fourth Illinois Regiment, Lieutenant Colonel Bristol.
Third Brigade, Colonel P. P. Baldwin Commanding.
Sixth Indiana Regiment, Colonel Baldwin.
First Ohio Regiment, Colonel Ed. Parrott.
Ninety-Third Ohio Regiment, Colonel Charles Anderson.
Fifth Kentucky Regiment, Lieutenant Colonel W. W. Berry.
Artillery.
First Ohio Battery, Company —, Captain Goodspeed.
First Ohio Battery, Company E, Captain Edgarton.
Fifth Indiana Battery, Captain Simonson.

Four companies of the Third Indiana Regiment of Cavalry, commanded by Major Kline, were attached to the Second Division.

THIRD DIVISION,

BRIGADIER GENERAL PHILIP H. SHERRIDAN COMMANDING.

First Brigade, Brigadier General J. W. Sill Commanding.
Thirty-Sixth Illinois Regiment, Colonel Greusel.
Twenty-Fourth Wisconsin Regiment, Colonel Larrabee.
Twenty-First Michigan Regiment, Colonel R. R. Stephens.
Eighty-Eighth Illinois Regiment, Colonel T. T. Sherman.
Second Brigade, Colonel Shaeffer Commanding.
Second Missouri Regiment, Colonel Laiboldt.
Fifteenth Missouri Regiment, Major Webber.
Forty-Fourth Illinois Regiment, Colonel Reed.
Seventy-Third Illinois Regiment, Colonel Jacques.

Third Brigade, Colonel Roberts Commanding.

Twenty-Second Illinois Regiment, Lieutenant Colonel Swannick.
Twenty-Seventh Illinois Regiment, Colonel F. A. Harrington.
Forty-Second Illinois Regiment, Major N. H. Walworth.
Fifty-First Illinois Regiment, Colonel L. P. Bradley.

Artillery.

First Missouri Battery, Captain G. Hescack.
Fourteenth Illinois Battery, Captain Houghtaling.
Fourth Indiana Battery, Captain Bush.

CENTER—(Numbering 13,395 men).

Major General George H. Thomas Commanding.

FIRST DIVISION,

MAJOR GENERAL LOVELL H. ROUSSEAU COMMANDING.

First Brigade, Colonel B. P. Scribner Commanding.

Thirty-Eighth Indiana Regiment, Lieutenant Colonel D. F. Griffin.
Thirty-Third Ohio Regiment, Colonel O. F. Moore.
Second Ohio Regiment, Colonel John Kell.
Ninety-Fourth Ohio Regiment, Colonel John W. Frizell.
Tenth Wisconsin Regiment, Colonel A. R. Chapin.

Second Brigade, Colonel John Beatty Commanding.

Fifteenth Kentucky Regiment, Colonel Forman.
Third Ohio Regiment, Lieutenant Colonel J. H. Lawson.
Tenth Ohio Regiment, Lieutenant Colonel J. W. Burke, detached.
Forty-Second Indiana Regiment, Lieutenant Colonel Shanklin.
Eighty-Eighth Indiana Regiment, Colonel Humphreys.

Third Brigade, Colonel Starkweather Commanding.

First Wisconsin Regiment, Lieutenant Colonel Bingham.
Twenty-First Wisconsin Regiment, Colonel Hobart.
Twenty-Fourth Illinois Regiment, Colonel Mihatolzy.
Seventy-Ninth Pennsylvania Regiment, Colonel Hambright.

Fourth Brigade (Regulars), Lieutenant Colonel O. S. Shepard.

Fifteenth United States Infantry, Major J. H. King.
Sixteenth United States Infantry, Major Slemmer.
Eighteenth United States Infantry, First Battalion, Major Caldwell.
Eighteenth United States Infantry, Second Battalion, Major Fred. Townsend.
Nineteenth United States Infantry, Major Carpenter.

Artillery.

First Michigan Battery, Lieutenant Van Pelt (Loomis).
Fifth United States Artillery, Battery H, Lieutenant Guenther.
First Kentucky Battery, Captain Stone.

Colonel O. A Loomis, Chief of Artillery of the Corps.

SECOND DIVISION,

BRIGADIER GENERAL JAMES S. NEGLEY COMMANDING.

First Brigade, General J. G. Spears Commanding.

First East Tennessee Regiment, Colonel R. K. Byrd.
Second East Tennessee Regiment, Lieutenant Colonel Melton.

Second Brigade, Colonel T. R. Stanley Commanding.

Eighteenth Ohio Regiment, Lieutenant Colonel Given.
Sixty-Ninth Ohio Regiment, Colonel W. B. Cassilly.
Nineteenth Illinois Regiment, Colonel J. R. Scott.
Eleventh Michigan Regiment, Colonel Stoughton.

Third Brigade, Colonel John F. Miller Commanding.

Seventy-Eighth Pennsylvania Regiment, Colonel Sirwell.
Twenty-First Ohio Regiment, Colonel J. H. Neibling.
Seventy-Fourth Ohio Regiment, Colonel Granville Moody.
Thirty-Seventh Indiana Regiment, Colonel Hull.

Artillery.

First Ohio Battery G, Marshall's.
First Ohio Battery M, Schultz.
First Kentucky Battery M, Lieutenant Ellsworth.

Captain John Mendenhall, United States Army, Chief of Artillery of the Corps.

Other Tennessee regiments, which formed part of Spears' brigade, do not properly come within the scope of this narrative. Colonel Walker's brigade, which follows, had been temporarily detached from Steadman's division.

Colonel M. B. Walker's Brigade—(Detached.)

Seventeenth Ohio Regiment, Colonel J. M. Connell.
Thirty-First Ohio Regiment, Lieutenant Colonel P. W. Lister.
Thirty-Eighth Ohio Regiment, Colonel Phelps.
Eighty-Second Indiana Regiment, Colonel Hunter.
Ohio Battery, Captain Church.

LEFT WING—(Numbering 13,288 men).
Major General Thomas L. Crittenden Commanding.

FIRST DIVISION,

BRIGADIER GENERAL THOMAS J. WOOD COMMANDING.

First Brigade, Brigadier General Miles S. Hascall Commanding.
Twenty-Sixth Ohio Regiment, Colonel E. P. Fyffe.
Fifty-Eighth Indiana Regiment, Colonel Geo. P. Buell.
Third Kentucky Regiment, Colonel McKee.
One Hundredth Illinois Regiment, Colonel Bartleson.

Second Brigade, Colonel George D. Wagner Commanding.
Fifty-Seventh Indiana Regiment, Colonel C. C. Hines.
Fortieth Indiana Regiment, Colonel J. W. Blake.
Fifteenth Indiana Regiment, Lieutenant Colonel Wood.
Ninety-Seventh Ohio Regiment, Colonel Lane.

Third Brigade, Colonel C. G. Harker Commanding.
Fifty-First Indiana Regiment, Colonel Streight.
Sixty-Fourth Ohio Regiment, Lieutenant Colonel McIlvain.
Thirteenth Michigan Regiment, Colonel Shoemaker.
Sixty-Fifth Ohio Regiment, Lieutenant Colonel Cassil.
Seventy-Third Indiana Regiment, Lieutenant Colonel Hathaway.

Artillery.
Eighth Indiana Battery, Captain Estep.
Tenth Indiana Battery, Captain Cox.
Sixth Ohio Battery, Captain Bradley.

SECOND DIVISION,

BRIGADIER GENERAL J. M. PALMER, COMMANDING.

First Brigade, Brigadier General C. Cruft, Commanding.
First Kentucky Regiment, Colonel D. A. Enyart.
Second Kentucky Regiment, Colonel T. D. Sedgwick.
Thirty-First Indiana Regiment, Colonel John Osborne.
Ninetieth Ohio Regiment, Colonel Ross.

Second Brigade, Colonel W. B. Hazen, Commanding.
Forty-First Ohio Regiment, Lieutenant Colonel Aquila Wiley.
Sixth Kentucky Regiment, Colonel W. C. Whittaker.
Ninth Indiana Regiment, Colonel W. H. Blake.
One Hundred and Tenth Illinois Regiment, Colonel Thos. S. Casey.

Third Brigade, Colonel W. Grose Commanding.
Thirty-Sixth Indiana Regiment, Major Kinley.
Twenty-Fourth Ohio Regiment, Colonel Fred. Jones.

Sixth Ohio Regiment, Colonel N. L. Anderson.
Twenty-Third Kentucky Regiment, Major Hamrick.
Eighty-Fourth Illinois Regiment, Colonel Waters.

Artillery.

Fourth United States Artillery, Battery M, Lieutenant Parsons.
First Ohio Artillery, Battery B, Captain Standart.
Indiana Battery, Captain Cockerell

THIRD DIVISION,

BRIGADIER GENERAL H. P. VAN CLEVE COMMANDING.

First Brigade, Colonel Samuel Beatty Commanding.

Ninth Kentucky Regiment, Colonel Grider.
Eleventh Kentucky Regiment, Major E. S. Motley.
Nineteenth Ohio Regiment, Major C. F. Manderson.
Seventy-Ninth Indiana Regiment, Colonel Fred. Kneffler.

Second Brigade, Colonel J. P. Fyffe Commanding.

Forty-Fourth Indiana Regiment, Lieutenant Colonel Reed.
Thirteenth Ohio Regiment, Colonel J. G. Hawkins.
Eighty-Sixth Indiana Regiment, Lieutenant Colonel Dick.
Fifty-Ninth Ohio Regiment, Lieutenant Colonel Howard.

Third Brigade, Colonel Stanley Matthews Commanding.

Fifty-First Ohio Regiment, Lieutenant Colonel McLain.
Thirty-Fifth Indiana Regiment, Colonel B. R. Mullen.
Eighth Kentucky Regiment, Colonel S. W. Price.
Ninety-Ninth Ohio Regiment, Colonel P. T. Swaine.

Artillery.

Seventh Indiana Battery, Captain Swallow.
Third Wisconsin Battery, Lieutenant Livingston.
Twenty-Sixth Pennsylvania Battery, Lieutenant Stevens.

CAVALRY.

BRIGADIER GENERAL DAVID S. STANLEY COMMANDING.

First Ohio Volunteer Cavalry, Colonel Minor Millikin.
Third Ohio Volunteer Cavalry, Lieutenant Colonel Murray.
Fourth Ohio Volunteer Cavalry, Lieutenant Colonel J. L. Pugh.
Seventh Pennsylvania Volunteer Cavalry, Major Wynkoop.
Fourth Michigan Volunteer Cavalry, Colonel Minty.
Third Kentucky Volunteer Cavalry, Colonel Murray.
First Middle Tennessee Cavalry, Colonel W. B. Stokes.
Second East Tennessee Cavalry, Colonel Cook.
Third Indiana Cavalry (four companies only), Major Kline.

Fifteenth Pennsylvania (three hundred men), Major Rosengarten.
Fourth United States Cavalry, Captain Elmer Otis.

Colonel John Kennett, of the Fourth Ohio Cavalry, commanded the Second Cavalry Division on the left wing. Colonel Zahn, of the Third Ohio Cavalry, commanded a cavalry brigade on the right under General Stanley. Colonel Minty, of the Fourth Michigan, commanded a brigade under Colonel Kennett.

PIONEER BRIGADE.

Besides the foregoing, there was a brigade of Pioneers, which had been selected by Captain James St. Clair Morton, United States Engineers, from forty different regiments. It proved invaluable to the service. It numbered about seventeen hundred men, and was organized in three battalions, commanded respectively by Captain Bridges, of the Nineteenth Illinois; Captain Hood, of the Eleventh Michigan; and Captain Clements, of the Sixty-Ninth Ohio Infantry, the whole being under Captain Morton's command, and organized and disciplined by him. The Chicago Board of Trade Battery, Captain Stokes, was attached to it. But the members of this organization were included in the foregoing muster. The Michigan Engineers and Mechanics, Colonel Innis, numbering about four hundred men, was on detached duty, and it greatly distinguished itself. The immortal Tenth Ohio Regiment, Col. J. W. Burke, which had been proverbial for its splendid soldierly qualities, and distinguished for its brilliant gallantry at Carnifex Ferry and Chaplin Hills, had been detached from Colonel John Beatty's brigade, and as a token of honorable distinction was assigned to duty by General Rosecrans as General Headquarters' Guard.

Regiments were numerous enough, but many were reduced to two hundred and fifty fighting men each. The six battalions of regulars numbered only fourteen hundred men, and, as has been shown, there were only two thousand two hundred and twenty-three men to handle one hundred and fifty field pieces. Of the infantry regiments, thirty-two (including the First and Second Kentucky Infantry, which were enlisted and generally officered in Cincinnati), were from Ohio; twenty-five from Indiana; twenty-two from Illinois; three from Pennsylvania; five from Wisconsin; ten from Kentucky; two from Missouri; three from Michigan; and two from Tennessee. Three of the cavalry regiments were from Ohio, two from Tennessee, one from Kentucky, two from Pennsylvania, one from Michigan, and a detachment of four small companies from Indiana.

THE GENERALS.

The Right Wing and Center were commanded by educated soldiers of large experience. Major General Crittenden had not received a military education. He was essentially a volunteer, but was a vigilant and zealous officer. Brigadier Generals Johnson, Sherridan, Van Cleve, and Wood, commanding divisions, were graduates of the Military Academy at West Point, and were approved, good soldiers of experience. Brigadier General Davis was a regular officer of experience and skill. Major General Rousseau, Brigadier Generals Negley and Palmer, commanding divisions, were volunteers. General Negley, however, had served in the war with Mexico, and had devoted his attention to military matters during many years. Excepting Brigadier Generals Sill, Kirk, Willich, Cruft, Hascall, and Spears, the brigade commanders were Colonels. Sill and Hascall were graduates of West Point. Kirk, Willich, and Cruft were volunteers, but Willich had been a soldier in Europe. Lieutenant Colonel Shepherd, commanding the brigade of regular troops, Colonel W. P. Carlin, Colonel W. B. Hazen, and Colonel Charles G. Harker, were also graduates. All the remaining brigade commanders were volunteers. Excepting Colonel P. T. Swaine, commanding the Ninety-Ninth Ohio Regiment, all the regimental, field and line officers, excepting those in the brigade of regulars, were purely volunteers—many of them yet in the "School of the Soldier," but some were men of fine military capacity. Excepting the Chief of Cavalry, and the officers of the Fourth United States Cavalry, all the field, and staff, and line officers of the cavalry were volunteer soldiers. Mendenhall, Stokes, Guenther, and Parsons, were the only artillery officers, excepting several subordinates, who were regularly educated in gunnery; but few in any service were superior to Loomis, of Michigan, and Barnet, of Ohio. Bradley, Standart, Edgarton, Cox, Swallow, Bush, and Simonson, also ranked high in the art of gunnery.

THE SITUATION.

But the army, on December 25th, was generally in superb condition — well-appointed, spirited, and confident. They seemed animated with a conviction that with a fighting general they could redeem the blank record of the past months of barren toil. The General Commanding, relying upon Providence and trusting in the steadfast valor of his gallant legions, was sanguine and hopeful. The enemy were now facing us squarely and defiantly—separated from our line of outposts by a strip of territory two miles wide in our direct front, with a line of videttes posting upon an irregular front corresponding with our own, extending on their left from the front of Triune to Nolensville, thence to Baird's Mills, the line crossing the Murfreesboro pike four miles in front of Lavergne. It had been reported that Stevenson's division, of Kirby Smith's Corps, had been sent to reinforce Pemberton's Army of the Mississippi, and that Kirby Smith himself had gone to assume command of a new department. The remainder of his command, it was said, had been merged into the corps of Polk and Hardee. Hitherto, Kirby Smith had commanded the right, Polk the center, and Hardee the left of the rebel army. Their disposition of cavalry remained unchanged, save that Forrest, as already stated, was cutting up General Grant's communications, and Morgan was moving into Kentucky to cut railroad connections between Louisville and Nashville—General Reynolds' and General Steadman's forces pursuing him—Major General Wright, commanding the Department of the Ohio, endeavoring to head him off. But Morgan accomplished his enterprise—broke up the railroad at various points, destroyed much public property, captured many prisoners, and escaped without serious loss. Meantime, matters of great moment were culminating.

CHAPTER XVIII.

ORDERS to March—Preparation—Excitement in Nashville—Christmas Night—Consultation of Generals—Rosecrans, Thomas, McCook, Crittenden, Stanley, Johnson, Negley, Sherridan—"Fight them!"—The Plan of Movement—The Commanding General and his Military Household—Customs of Headquarters—Nocturnal Scenes—Lectures to Young Officers—Conversation—Politics, Literature, Science, War—Good Night.

THE opportune moment for aggressive movement was at hand. Orders for an advance of the Fourteenth Army Corps were issued Wednesday, the 24th of December. The columns would move at daylight Christmas morning. Presently the camps blazed with excitement. The sturdy troops greeted the announcement with shrill clamor, which swelled its cheerful volume far along the ridges and down into the valleys, as musket volleys roll along a line of battle. There was glorious assurance in that manful uproar. The populous hills blazed with sparkling fires. Thousands were cooking rations for the march. The commissariat labored under manifold requisitions. Muskets soon gleamed with fatal luster. Busy pens swiftly indited fond adieus, perhaps the last, to loved ones at home, and it was not long before the mails groaned under the weight of affectionate testimony from these brave hearts. The horseman carefully brushed his equipments, adjusted his last strap, looked well to his holsters, and patted his faithful charger kindly on his shining neck, as if soliciting his last proof of endurance and fidelity. The cannonier burnished his trusty piece until it glistened, then poised it again and again, sighting it at imaginary foes, so soon to assume stern substantial form. Aids and orderlies thundered over the highways and through the bustling camps, swiftly bearing messages. Here and there were tableaux of soldiers, earnest and animated, standing by the old flag at headquarters, talking of battle and of victory. Picturesque groups of officers in eager colloquy, clustered about brigade and division marquees, now and then one swiftly mounting and away with orders. And the surgeon, in his tent, drew from his case the glittering blade at which the bold heart shrinks in fear which no mortal enemy can inspire. The young soldier daintily fingers the probe, and shuddering, asks its use. The veteran of battles grimly jests at the knife, and stalks away soberly to his comrades. The surgeon, seemingly cold and unfeeling, but with warm and sensitive heart, covered, it seems to the soldiers, with a glare of ice, carefully wipes the last atom of moisture or dust from the gleaming steel, and his cruel preparation is done.

EXCITEMENT IN NASHVILLE.

The tidings wafted back to Nashville, and revolved upon a thousand busy tongues. Haughty dames of the capital stood upon their stately porticoes gossiping sagely with other dames, or hastily flitted from house to house wild with excitement—which flamed in their eyes and burned in their flushing cheeks. Had the eye of suspicion enjoyed power to peer into the mysteries of secluded apartments, it might have discovered nervous preparation for secret enterprise, that waited for execution only until darkness. Who can doubt that trusty messengers fled swiftly that night from ladies' chambers to the camps of the enemy, bearing great news? It was never explained, but before the hours of evening waned into midnight, other and countermanding orders went out, and the camps settled moodily to rest. But it was only a suspension for twenty-four hours. The General Commanding devoted Christmas morning to worshiping God.

CONSULTATION AT HEADQUARTERS.

Christmas night there was an assemblage of commanders at headquarters. There was consultation, but "council of war" none. The Chief likes them not. Decidedly, he indorses the martial maxim—"councils of war don't fight." Major General Thomas was there, certainly—"true and prudent, distinguished in council, and on many battle fields for his courage," could it be otherwise? McCook, "brave, faithful, and loyal soldier," standing with his elbow on the mantel, merry and confident, and boastful of his gallant corps—then heroes of two sanguinary battles; Crittenden, "whose heart is that of a true soldier and patriot," stately and reticent, believing in the justice of the "old Master" of us all, but assuring that "if the rebels stood at all there would be d——d hard fighting;" "gay old Stanley," hero of five battles, quick and comprehensive in suggestion, moving about restlessly, with saber rattling at his heels; Johnson, grave and saturnine, but earnest and thoughtful; Negley, prompt, decisive, and ready upon requisition, come when it might; and quiet

Phil. Sherridan, keen observer, but silent now, so unlike him in battle, where he shows a heart of oak. Others may have called between sunset and midnight.

ROSECRANS AND THOMAS.

There was swift interchange of thought, and two drew aside. The bed of the Chief occupied the space between two doors. The right hand door communicated with the military telegraph office. Between the bed and the front window near it was a narrow space. The topographical maps were tacked to the door and spread upon the bed. The aids' table set under the window-sill. The Chief sometimes used a corner of it, and sometimes a corner of Garesché's table, which was under the other front window, near the grate. When the Chief consulted the "true and prudent," the latter sidled and backed into the niche between the two tables, and his Commander seated himself directly in his front, looking into his eyes. General Thomas backed in there now, you would have said mechanically—it was a habit of a month's growth. The Chief was balanced upon the edge of a chair, leaning over vis-a-vis, almost in the embrace of Thomas. The conversation was animated, almost vehement, the consulted listening profoundly, the consulter talking rapidly and vehemently, with blazing eyes, the former nodding now and then, perhaps dropping a curt suggestion. All undertone, but there was destiny in it. Battle was flashing from the tips of nervous fingers which had base upon the edge of the chair. Those who know him can see the plan as he was manipulating it in his nervous way.

The others were chatting a little common-place

colloquy, or looking into the grate watching the cedar sticks curl into flame. How much of the past and of the future one may see in a blaze or a heap of glowing coals. Garesché, his head bowed over the corner of the table, which seemed part of him, until his broad, clear brow almost touched the tip of his pen—for he was near-sighted—was flinging off sheets of manuscript in his wonderful way—orders, correspondence, instructions—suspending now and then to respond pleasantly to some interpolated query. You supposed he was always sitting at that corner of his table—and indeed he was, from ten o'clock of morning till long after midnight, when not racing through a fresh newspaper, with a sort of impatience which indicated a jealousy that it was robbing him of precious time. Staff officers were tip-toeing in and out softly, or lounging about in easy chairs or upon a cot near the chimney-jam corner of the chamber, over against the back wall. Father Trecy slipped into the room in his gentlemanly way—everybody greeting him kindly—let fly his budget of "grapevines" which he had a faculty for picking up in the streets—and then slipped out again as softly. Ducat, a military Javert, devoted to duty, which he always discharged perfectly, stepped in promptly and stepped out promptly with instructions. The "old boy"—they addressed him so, and lovingly—looked in modestly, but when Kirby disappeared none could tell. He had a cat-like habit of getting away when there was nothing for him to do. Thoms and Thompson, at the foot of the cot, flanking a little deal table, dimly illumined by the feeble glimmer of a stearine dip, industriously worried out the pregnant ciphers. Tom fed the cheerful fire in the grate; the bright blaze was roaring pleasantly up the chimney; the telegraph fingers were clicking merrily in the little room, and Monsieur John produced his steaming toddy.

RESULT OF THE CONSULTATION.

Strange that nobody ever seemed jealous of Thomas. But he was so modest and unpretentious. When the command of the great Army of the Ohio was tendered him, you know he declined that glittering recognition of his worth. Monsieur Vault had instinctively timed the toddy. When the glasses got to the corner, there was an eager sentence or two, an acquiescing nod on either side, and history was made. The Chief was jocose an instant, but directly a glass went down upon Garesché's table with a clang. Garesché looked up, surprised a little, and lounged back in his chair. Suddenly the Chief—"We move to-morrow, gentlemen! We shall begin to skirmish, probably, as soon as we pass the outposts. Press them hard! Drive them out of their nests! Make them fight or run! Strike hard and fast! Give them no rest! Fight them! *Fight* them! FIGHT, I say," and his glittering blue eyes flashed like a gleam of lightning, and the nervous right hand dashed into the palm of the scarified left, ringing as if cymbals were clanging. Thomas looked up with a grim smile of approval; McCook's sharp eyes twinkled with internal enjoyment; and Crittenden straightened up his trim figure with a sort of swell, as if he had heard the programme exactly, and was prepared to execute it. It was then accepted as a probability that the enemy would make a stand at Stewart's Creek—

five miles in the rear of Lavergne, going by the Murfreesboro turnpike. General Rosecrans therefore directed the army to move in three columns, according to the following instructions, to-wit.:

PLAN OF MOVEMENT.

McCook, with three divisions, to advance by the Nolensville pike to Triune.

Thomas, with two divisions (Negley's and Rousseau's), to advance on his right, by the Franklin and Wilson pikes, threatening Hardee's right, and then to fall in by the cross-roads to Nolensville.

Crittenden, with Wood's, Palmer's, and Van Cleve's divisions, to advance by the Murfreesboro pike to Lavergne.

With Thomas' two divisions at Nolensville, McCook was to attack Hardee at Triune, and if the enemy reinforced Hardee, Thomas was to support McCook.

If McCook beat Hardee, or Hardee retreated, and the enemy met us at Stewart's Creek, five miles south of Lavergne, Crittenden was to attack him; Thomas was to come in on his left flank, and McCook, after detaching a division to pursue or observe Hardee, if retreating south, was to move, with the remainder of his force, on their rear.

Brigadier General Stanley was to cover the movement with his cavalry. He divided his corps into three columns, and directed the first brigade, commanded by Colonel Minty, of the Fourth Michigan Volunteer Cavalry, to move upon the Murfreesboro pike, in advance of the Left Wing. The second brigade, commanded by Colonel Zahn, of the Third

Ohio Volunteer Cavalry, was ordered to the Franklin road to dislodge the enemy's cavalry, and to move parallel to the Right Wing, protecting its right flank. The reserve cavalry, consisting of the new regiments—Anderson Troop, or Fifteenth Pennsylvania, the First Middle Tennessee, the Second East Tennessee Cavalry, and four companies of the Third Indiana Cavalry—General Stanley was himself to command, and precede General McCook's corps on the Nolensville turnpike. Colonel John Kennett, of the Fourth Ohio Cavalry, was to command the cavalry on the Left Wing. The Fourth United States Cavalry, Captain Elmer Otis, was reserved for escort and courier duty.

General Thomas was the first to say good night. It was full midnight before all the commanders had dispersed. As they rose to depart, the Chief took each by the hand, and to all gave his parting admonition: "Fight them! Spread out your skirmishers far and wide! Keep pushing ahead! Expose their nests! Fight! Keep fighting! They will not stand it. Good night!"

SOCIAL LIFE AT HEADQUARTERS.

This was the night preceding movement. It was, therefore, more interesting and exciting than other nights. Yet it was only an exaggerated copy of many. Ordinarily, officers of all departments, citizens, *et id omnia*, thronged the General's chamber during the day, and every hour was absorbed in business. The nights were busy, too, but there were pleasant episodes. Commanders were most apt to call socially there, and the Chief's military household assembled about him. Garesché, always present, was married to his papers, but never seemed oppressed. His faculty for disposing of business was marvelous. He never exhibited impatience or irritability, but was ever ready to oblige, and to respond to all questions with charming courtesy. On occasion he took cheerful part in conversation, displaying the charms of a richly cultivated intellect, and enjoying facetiæ with as keen relish as the most mercurial. Goddard and Dickson, for the most part, were swallowed up in the freshet which ever threatened to overflow the Adjutant General's Bureau. Bond, Thoms, and Thompson, were seldom absent. Thoms and Thompson had custody of the ciphers, but all the aids were thoroughly inducted into the mysteries and miseries of late hours and incessant labor. St. Clair Morton would flash in, state case, suggest, and flash out again, galloping away always as if everything he had to do was urgent, until it was accomplished. The General usually had a pleasant laugh at Morton after he was gone, narrating some happy anecdote illustrating his practical executive faculty. After a brief facetious episode, the Chief was apt to dictate three or four letters or dispatches simultaneously, setting Bond, Thompson and Thoms at work, while he chatted with somebody aside. Some of his most nervous letters and public papers were produced in this way. Bruner and Melarky meantime were incessantly manipulating the telegraph instrument in the adjoining chamber. Father Trecy—an exiled priest from Huntsville, Alabama, esteemed alike by the Commander and Staff for his worth—and the special guest of the former—usually dropped in about ten o'clock, entertained the circle with collections of "grapevine," enjoyed merriment with the gayest, talked eruditely with the learned, and then retired to his cot. Kirby ever slipped in and slipped out as he did Christmas night. The Quartermaster and Commissary were wont to report at night. Once in a while the army Vidocq surprised the staff by his meteoric blaze, but his commander usually went to see him. Wiles, the Provost Marshal, as admirable for his modesty as for zeal in the public service, ordinarily got in at midnight or later; an hour at which the General Commanding was ready to lecture him for following his own example by working too hard. But the General had such an affectionate, jovial way of reprimanding him, that the interview usually ended in general pleasantry. Ducat was always present when instructions were desirable. He hardly ever retired that his Chief did not say, "I like that man—he is a thorough soldier." "So say we all of us," ran the merry roundelay. Colonel Ducat had perfected a system of army inspections, by which the effective strength of the army, or any portion of it, could be determined in an instant, which, together with his high soldierly character, commended him to his Chief's regard. Skinner, high-minded and sympathetic, was keenly desirous to build up a system of army jurisprudence that would reflect credit upon the department, and was apt sometimes, by expressing his notions of equity rather generously, to run counter to the General's severer ideas of military justice and propriety, thus occasionally evoking sharp criticisms, which his sensitiveness caused him to misconstrue into censure—his staff companions rather enjoying his nervousness because they better understood the animus of their sometimes martial Rhodamanthus. Skinner understood it after awhile, and succeeded in so tempering justice with mercy that he seemed in a fair way to accomplish the object of his honorable ambition. The Chief esteemed no officer of his staff more thoroughly. Michler, of the "Topogs," often had a time of it. His was the nervous department. It was no bed of roses, but there were thorns enough. As map maker, he naturally touched sensitive points, and evoked searching criticisms from a commander who particularly insisted in having the exact location, range, direction, sinuosities, meanderings, elevations, depressions, and proportions of every river, rivulet, road, ridge, ravine, hill, hollow, forest, swamp, bridge, cornfield, cotton plantation, canebreak, or cedar thicket within the scope of the field of operations. He was very apt to conclude, after enveloping himself in his blankets at bed time, that his bureau was a sort of military Tophet. Edson, of the Ordnance Corps, worried through a similar experience, since powder and ball were as essential to war as maps and hard tack. But it was a matter of pride to all, at last, to meet the approval of a Chief who pertinaciously insisted upon knowing for himself that everything necessary to success had been done, and precisely how it was done. This course of Lectures to Young Officers interpolated in the course of a miscellaneous evening conversazione, was quite a treat to those who escaped fire, or had run the gauntlet successfully.

CONVERSATION.

When lectures were concluded, orders executed, correspondence all disposed of, somewhere about midnight—an hour earlier or an hour later was altogether immaterial — dull care was dismissed and pleasure assumed supremacy. Nobody then was more facetious or happy than the General. The temper of conversation, of course, depended altogether upon the direction given it in the beginning. If religious, it was apt to absorb the hours until they run almost into daylight. The Chief took the argument and carried it, often into the realms of Mother Church, where the vehemence of his intellect and his zealous temper developed themselves thoroughly. He had the Fathers of the Church at his tongue's end, and exhibited a familiarity with controversial theology that made him a formidable antagonist to the best read, even of the clerical profession. He would admit no fallibility whatever in any department of his own church, but he did not permit his strong reliance in the Church of Rome to warp his judgment in material things, especially in military matters. It has been recklessly said that he required the attendance of the Roman Catholics of his staff, escort, and attendants, at mass every Wednesday and Sunday. It is a gross calumny. He never interferes with the spiritual affairs of any subordinate, regarding those as sacred personal matters, to be governed by the convictions of each individual. Moreover, General Stanley and Garesché were the only Romanists on his staff.

He had no taste for party politics, having dismissed the subject until the rebellion should be crushed—a point upon which he expressed no doubts. And, indeed, he never had been a politician. Upon the general subject of slavery, he held the faith that had been proclaimed immemorially by his church and by all nations which have pretended to civilization—save the chivalrous portion of these United States. Touching slavery and the rebellion he was quite clear that there had grown up a necessity to emasculate that element of military power. The Proclamation was yet a promise. When it became an order he would obey.

Upon belle lettres he opened a mine of rich lore, and charmed you, as well by the felicity of his illustrations, as by the pungent and comprehensive character of his criticism. It was not a little amusing to the author to read in a leading Eastern journal, that in science and literature Rosecrans was probably the inferior of McClellan and Buell. Their respective mutual classmates, and later associates, are sure that either of the latter might learn from him in each department. His general knowledge of science is extensive. Geology and mineralogy are specialities, and in those sciences he ranks among the most accomplished in the country.

It was often a subject of curious speculation by members of the staff that a man so full of ideas, and who expressed himself so readily and forcibly without hesitating for language, and with such striking force, in the presence of his military family, should be an inferior public speaker. It was nevertheless true that he hesitated and stammered upon attempting to address even a line of soldiers at review. In those nocturnal scenes, and indeed habitually, his deportment toward his staff was extremely affable, often almost to affectionate familiarity. General McCook carelessly remarking of him to a friend, said, "The fact is, Rosecrans is too clever—he is too easy of access." It was singular that he rarely discussed his generals to their disparagement. If anybody knew anything of any commander, there was no relief for him until he had detailed the particulars. He was incessantly accumulating testimony by which he might guage his officers, that he might put them in their proper positions.

In professional matters he was exacting. The end of the night, and the lengthening hours of morning, often crept upon him and his coterie of the junior officers of staff, discoursing the art of war in all its practical ramifications, and it was not unfrequently suggested, that to a young man proposing to adopt the profession of arms, the Military Academy itself would hardly be so good a school for practical war, as an active position upon the staff of General Rosecrans. He considered war an exact science, admitting no carelessness or slovenliness. He often said—and when he said it irritably you might see it fly out of his eyes and off the ends of his fingers—"My staff should know everything I know;" "I don't allow any staff officer to forget anything." But if an unlucky wight knew anything imperfectly and attempted to report it, the Chief was apt, as the staff said, "to make the fur fly." "How do you know this?" "Who told you?" "How does he know?" "Why didn't you learn all the particulars?" "What are you an officer for?" "It's your business to know." "You *must* know." "War means killing," and so on to an end with a sharp sting in it. To one he would say, "You don't observe closely;" to another, "You don't state case clearly;" to a third, "You are deficient in geography—you must study." He took a great fancy to Thomas on account of his skill in mathematics and for his general intelligence. Thomas mastered the most difficult ciphers in a few hours, which was very unusual. Christmas had been gone several hours when the General Commanding said "good night!"

CHAPTER XIX.

THE Army Advances—Its Spirit in Gloomy Weather—Movements of the Center—Sharp Combats of the Right Wing—The Enemy Driven and Two Guns Captured—The Cavalry—Gallant Charges—The Left Wing—The Thirty-First Indiana and First Kentucky Infantry Charge and Rout the Enemy—Close of the First Day's Operations—The Commanding General Seeks the Right Wing—A Night's Adventures.

FRIDAY the 26th of December, dawned drearily. Daylight feebly struggled through an unbroken mass of black clouds and thick volumes of mist, which puffed up from the valleys. Rain was pouring down in streams which gathered into volumes in the gullies, and made foaming yellow torrents of the little brooks that lately stole so softly around the hills. Yet reveille rolled merrily along the line and through the drowsy camps. The stout soldiers sprung up gaily, and shook off the shackles of sleep, crowing like game-cocks, and roaring joyfully like giants refreshed. Yet a little while, and they were rushing along the highways in magnificent panoply, horsemen, infantry, cannon, cannoniers, and mighty trains. It needed but a blaze of sunshine to burnish their steel. The steady rain drenched their garments but did not quench their ardor. There were but few stragglers that exciting day. Strange, that when nature frowns so gloomily, soldiers should be so chery; nevertheless it is true, that when the barometer falls the mercury of their spirits rises until it culminates in hilarity. The veteran campaigner ever bears such testimony. The colossal columns overflowed the roads, and swept through the leafless forests like mighty waves. Brave hearts beat high, for the march had begun with glad augury for the future. There was battle in the breeze which now began to rise, but our soldiers felt that there was victory in their trusty steel.

"Gay old Stanley" and gallant John Kennett were on the right and left and in front, with their cavalry, to start the game and cover the flanks. General Thomas moved his column—thirteen thousand three hundred and ninety-five effective men—through the rich, rustic villas of the Franklin pike to Brentwood. Negley in front, diverging left to the Wilson pike, closely followed by Rousseau and Walker's brigade, Zahn's brigade of cavalry on the right. General McCook, with Stanley's cavalry reserve in front, pushed the first division of his corps, under General Davis, upon the Edmonson pike, with orders to move to Prim's blacksmith shop, whence it was to march direct, by a country road, to Nolensville and Triune. The Third Division, General Sherridan, moving upon the direct road to Nolensville, was followed by the reserve division under General Johnson. The Left Wing, under General Crittenden, moved in column upon the direct turnpike to Murfreesboro. General Palmer's division in front, covered by Minty's cavalry brigade, and followed by Wood's division, with Van Cleve's in reserve.

The country over which the army was sweeping, afforded peculiar advantages to the enemy. A small force could retard the advance of greatly superior numbers, and almost with impunity to themselves.

Considerable tracts of cultivated lands occur at intervals on either side of the turnpikes, but the intervening spaces are heavily wooded and interspersed with dense cedar ridges, which thoroughly masked the enemy. The country rolls up in great rude billows, ranging in successions of parallel cross ridges, now and then flanked by transverse crests, which served for observations. Cedar brakes, rugged defiles, and intersecting streams with rocky bluff banks, formed formidable natural barriers to the march of an aggressive army, and the enemy, perfectly familiar with the topography and geography of the field of operations, availed themselves skillfully of its defensive advantages. To dislodge them from these fortifications of nature, required careful, tedious and bold skirmishing, but our officers displayed skill and judgment, and the results inspired the army with renewed ardor.

THE CENTER.

General Thomas had directed his command to encamp that night at Owen's store, on the Wilson pike, but General Negley, hearing the sound of conflict in the direction of Nolensville, left his train with a guard to follow, and pushed forward across the country to support General Davis, who had uncovered the enemy, and was striking him hard in the face. Negley's aid was not needed, and his command bivouacked near Nolensville. Rousseau went into camp at Owen's store, and Walker's brigade, forming the rear guard, rested at Brentwood—the Center having failed that day to find the enemy.

THE RIGHT WING.

McCook had barely moved two miles when a sharp rattle of musketry, in front of both Davis and Sheridan warned him of the presence of the enemy. Moving laboriously out the Edmonson pike, which had been rendered almost impassable by the storm, General Davis had sent his escort, consisting of Company B, Thirty-Sixth Illinois Infantry, Captain Shirer, mounted for escort duty, to the front, directing them to drive in the enemy's pickets, and attack them incessantly on the flanks. The country was rude and broken, and embarrassed by cedar brakes, but Shiner did his duty so well that the Fifty-Ninth Illinois Infantry, thrown out on either flank of his little force, had hardly a chance to pull a trigger. The infantry, Post's brigade, in front, and the artillery, moved up, without hostile obstruction, to a point within a mile of Nolensville. General Davis now ascertained that the enemy occupied the village with cavalry and artillery in some force.

Post's brigade, consisting of the Twenty-Second Indiana, Seventy-Fourth, Seventy-Fifth and Fifty-Ninth Illinois Volunteer Infantry, with the Fifth Wisconsin Battery, Captain Pinney, was immediately deployed to advance upon the village, the left resting upon the pike, the right upon a hill which commanded the town, Pinney's battery posted on a knoll on the left of the pike. The enemy made show of resistance, flinging some shells, but Pinney soon made it too hot for them, and they evacuated the town. A large force of rebel cavalry was now discovered moving to the left and dismounting, apparently intending to attack our right and rear. The Twenty-Second Indiana Infantry moved to the right to repel the threatened attack. The Second Brigade, commanded by Colonel W. P. Carlin, and consisting of the Twenty-First and Thirty-Eighth Illinois, Fifteenth Wisconsin and One Hundred and First Ohio Regiments of Infantry, and the Second Minnesota Battery, Captain Hotchkiss, by this time had fomed in line of battle on Post's right. Moving rapidly forward, they soon engaged the enemy, the men deporting themselves splendidly. The Third Brigade, consisting of the Twenty-Fifth and Thirty-Fifth Illinois, and the Eighty-First Indiana Infantry, with the Eighth Wisconsin Battery, Captain Carpenter, and commanded by Colonel W. E. Woodruff, was deployed on the extreme right to check any flank movement that might be projected. It was now plain that the enemy were endeavoring to hold us in check to give their main body time to prepare for battle, but their strong exhibition of force, and the great advantage of position in their favor, required of General Davis the exercise of great caution. But the line was well formed, and Carlin pushed forward steadily, sustaining a sharp fire until the enemy were dislodged and driven from their position.

Day was waning, but the troops, although wearied by their heavy march and sharp skirmishing, exhibited splendid pluck. General Davis, eager as a game-cock, deemed it wise to follow up his advantage. The enemy retreated about two miles to a rugged hill, the road passing through a defile known as Knob's Gap. Deploying on either side of the road, with one section of their artillery in the defile, and other pieces on the crest of the hill, they waited another encounter. The line advanced in the order of battle of the first collision—Post's brigade moving up the road and to the left of it, Carlin on the right. The enemy opened upon Carlin with their artillery at long range. Hotchkiss and Pinney moved up, and went into action quickly, while Carlin charged up the hill, carried the crest in handsome style, and captured two bronze field pieces. Post had also carried the hights on the left, driving the enemy out of position, but they saved their guns. Woodruff on the right, had opportunity only to drive in the rebel skirmishers. The conduct of the troops during the entire day had been superb. The One Hundred and First Ohio, Colonel Stem, was particularly signalized because it was a new regiment—the men behaving like veterans. It had the honor to capture one of the guns, which was inscribed "Shiloh," and had belonged to Georgia troops. Our loss in the skirmishing and two combats was less than a dozen killed and wounded. The day had now closed, and Davis' gallant division went into bivouac.

STANLEY'S OPERATIONS.

At the crossing of Mill Creek, soon after leaving camp in front of Nashville, General Sherridan's division encountered the rebel cavalry, but his skirmishers routed them briskly, killing several and capturing a lieutenant and private. Stanley's cavalry reserve stirred up the enemy in considerable force a mile north of Balle Jack Pass, charged upon them sharply, and drove them at a slashing pace two miles to the left and rear of Lavergne, forcing them twice to hand to hand encounters, in which the individual as well as organized superiority of our gallant troopers was exhibited. The Fifteenth Pennsylvania Cavalry, commanded by Majors Rosengarten and Ward, and the four companies of the Third Indiana Cavalry, under Major Kline, conspicuously distinguished themselves. The Pennsylvanians were raw troops, but they displayed a spirit and courage which reflected great credit upon them. General Stanley, remarking their conduct that evening, said: "They went into the fight as if they liked it, and were unwilling to stop." Their gallant leader, Rosengarten, in the second charge, had an amusing single-handed combat with a stout rebel whom he overhauled. His pistol missed fire, and the rebel was equally unlucky. Their weapons being useless, they brought their fists into requisition. The rebel quickly put the Major's eye in mourning, but the latter, with a stout right-hander, sent his antagonist to grass, and left him a captive under guard. Stanley's work was done so neatly and effectually, that Sherridan moved up to Nolensville without further obstruction, and supported General Davis, while the latter was driving the enemy from Knob's Gap. General Johnson's division being in reserve, did not come in contact with the enemy. Colonel Lewis Zahn, with his cavalry command, moving down the Franklin pike, drove in the rebel pickets two miles in front of that town, charged gallantly, and drove the enemy two miles beyond town, killing four, capturing ten, including a lieutenant of General Bragg's escort, and destroyed a camp. Lieutenant Colonel E. H. Murray, with the Third Ohio Cavalry, also dismounted several rebels, and captured ten prisoners. The results of this day's operations were encouraging, and the impulse was felt all over the army. Ten men covered our casualties on the right, while the enemy had fifteen or twenty killed, many wounded, and lost nearly fifty prisoners. The Right Wing, numbering fifteen thousand nine hundeed and thirty-three effectives, went into camp at Nolensville and vicinity about dark, wearied, but hopeful and sanguine.

THE LEFT WING.

The Left Wing, Major General Crittenden, numbering thirteen thousand two hundred and eighty-eight effectives, moved down the main Nashville and Murfreesboro turnpike. Brigadier General J. M. Palmer's division had the advance, Brigadier General Charles Cruft's brigade of twelve hundred and seven effectives, comprising the First and Second Kentucky, Thirty-First Indiana and Ninetieth Ohio Infantry in front, covered by Colonel Minty's brigade of cavalry. Minty encountered the rebel videttes in a cedar thicket, about two miles from our late front, and drove them back upon their reserves. Pursuing them sharply under direction of Colonel Kennett, he found them constantly covered, but by dint of sharp riding and hard pushing, finally drove them back upon Lavergne, where they rallied in strong force with infantry and artillery. The afternoon was waning when General Cruft was directed to drive the enemy from the woods on the left, and take the village, if possible, before dark. The First Kentucky and Thirty-First Indiana Infantry, under Colonel D. A. Enyart, and the Third Kentucky Cavalry, Colonel Murray, covering their left, with a section of Standart's Ohio Battery, under Lieutenant Newall, were deployed for that purpose, and moved boldly upon the enemy. The Sixth Kentucky and Ninth Indiana Infantry, temporarily made the command of Colonel Walter Whittaker, were thrown out upon the right to cover that flank. The enemy opened sharply with artillery and musketry, but Colonel Enyart advanced steadily, and finally gave the order to "charge bayonets!" The gallant lads obeyed with a roar of enthusiasm, and the enemy fled to the opposite bank of Stony Creek. They never wait for bayonets. Colonel Whittaker, meantime, had suddenly fallen upon a force of the enemy in a thicket, and had one man of the Ninth Indiana killed, one wounded, and two of the Sixth Kentucky wounded. The enemy, however, declined to wait to give Whittaker revenge, and joined their comrades on the opposite side of the creek. In Colonel Enyart's affair, Lieutenant Newall gained credit by the skillful management of his guns. With one shell he killed three horses and dismounted seven men. Murray's Kentucky Cavalry kept the left flank clear, and captured five of the enemy. It was adjudged that night, however, that it would have been better policy, in that country, to have driven the enemy out of the defiles and cedar thickets with infantry — Colonel Kennett satisfactorily showing that it exhausted men and horses without compensatory advantages.

The divisions of General Wood followed Palmer in close supporting distance, but the work was so well done in front that their movements were unobstructed. But the resistance which the advance met prevented the left wing from gaining possession of the commanding hights south of Lavergne, and the affair at the village occupied so much time that no reconnoissance could be made. The enemy still occupied the hights in considerable force, admonishing our commanders to exercise vigilance. The mutual losses that day on the left were about equal. The troops settled to rest near Lavergne, fatigued but hopeful. It is now time to look at the movements of the Commander-in-Chief.

MOVEMENTS OF THE COMMANDER.

Mounting soon after eleven o'clock, in a drenching storm, General Rosecrans and the staff, with the original Anderson Troop, and a squadron of the Fourth United States Cavalry, detailed for escort, moved toward the Murfreesboro pike. The cavalcade was winding about the suburban highways of Nashville, when the sullen reverberation of cannon rolled up from the south-west. "Only shelling skirmishers," yet the thunder of hostile guns made the heart beat and the blood mount. Every rider straightened in his saddle, and struck impulsively into brisker speed. Mile upon mile was quickly left behind. The firing waxed sharper, and the trot of the troop stretched into a gallop. The uproar was on the right. McCook had started the game, and his pack was opening in full cry. But it was too far away for eager ears to catch the full swell of the sonorous music. A little while, and a whole tone bellowed from the direct front. Crittenden, too, had found something. The General spurred "Boney" gently, and the escort plunged headlong forward, up hill and down, on the side of the road or through the fields, it mattered little. The heavy trains lumbered onward, and the stalwart columns, thronging the highway, pushed ahead staunchly. Seven or eight miles from Nashville, the quick eye of the General caught glimpse of one of Merrill's signals, and called a halt. Riders dismounted, and panting steeds rested. There was silence again, now and then a gun booming far away to the south-west. "McCook must be near Nolensville now," quoth Garesché. "Yes," said the General; "he will find the enemy there in some force." The signal flag upon the distant ridge flared again. "What is it, Merrill?" "All right, sir." Somebody suggested, quietly, that the enemy might take advantage of the divided columns to strike the left. "That would be profitable to them," said the caustic General, "with the right swinging into their rear." A brisk breeze from the north-west had began to disperse the mist, and the clouds broke away. The sun shone out upon the cheerful landscape, and the General resumed the march.

SEARCHING FOR M'COOK'S QUARTERS.

Beyond Hamilton Church, just a half mile from the eleven-mile granite post, on the Murfreesboro pike, a rude country road, tracing the crest of a ridge, debouches into the main pike. The cross road, with divaricating branches ruder than itself, cuts a rugged country some ten miles across the waist, and after vexatious sinuosities, intersects the Nolensville pike several miles north of the village. There is a spacious dusty-hued frame house (in happier times it was a tavern) on the south-west corner of the Murfreesboro junction, with a cornfield and a pleasant maple grove in the rear. Upon arriving at this point, the General directed headquarters to be established in the field and grove, Kirby taking charge, Garesché dismounting and entering the house to forward orders to Crittenden. All was silent on the left, but there was uproar on the right, denoting sharp combat.

Halting but a moment, the General pushed onward briskly to reconnoiter and find the commander of the Right Wing. After crossing the railroad and examining the country until sunset, the cannonading on the right having now ceased, the Chief retraced his steps from the summit of a mountain, and drew up in a narrow lane in front of Smith's house. Smith said it was about five miles to Nolensville. Garesché, who had rejoined him, Goddard, Thompson, Barnet, Michler, Gilman, and one or two others, were detailed by the General to accompany him to McCook's headquarters, Lieutenant Royse commanding the escort. The rest were dismissed. Twilight, then darkness, and with darkness heavy clouds and rain, fell upon the cortege as it spurred briskly through the rugged narrow lanes and gloomy forests, upon unknown paths, which but an hour ago had rattled under the hoofs of rebel horsemen.

Later a barrier intercepted the march. A stone wall interfered. There was a dwelling on the left, and the tenant, an old woman, did not know the road to Nolensville. She "had never been three miles away from thar anywhar." There was another house on the right, where there was a man. It was quite agreeable to hear him announce that he occupied the premises of the notorious Dick McCann, a rebel colonel of cavalry, who had halted there but an hour or so before—perhaps he was then not far distant. But the fellow knew the way to Nolensville, and a guide was necessary. There was no alternative for him. Threading their way back through dismal forests and rocky roads (it seemed unnatural to find such wild country so near Nashville), the General and his attendants at last struck the main route. After a slashing pace of an hour or more over a highway from which the horses' iron hoofs struck fire at every leap, the Nolensville pike was gained. "General," interposed an officer of escort, "this way of going like —l over rocks will knock up the horses." "That's true," replied the General, rousing from his absorbing thought—"Walk!" It was dark as Erebus, and recognition without a voice was impossible. Directly the General called an orderly. "Go back," he said, "and tell that young man that he must not be profane."

THE BIVOUAC.

The General and his companions had now been in saddle nine hours. The latter were weary and hungry. Eager eyes had descried a vista of cheerful camps but a few moments before. As the column pushed out of a deep wooded vale, and wound laboriously up the curving ridge of a towering crest, a glare from innumerable bivouac fires, blazing meteor-like upon the opposite slope, partially dispelled the thick darkness. All hailed the flush of lights as a welcoming beacon, little dreaming that their indefatigable leader would be crashing back over the same dreary track before the noon of night.

As they pressed onward, the humid atmosphere became impregnated with pungent odor of burning cedar, which shivering soldiers had heaped up in rude pyramids, and which now exuded grateful warmth and pleasant fragrance. The forests were glinting with incessant showers of glittering sparks flitting from the crackling fuel, and it seemed as if their barren boughs were emitting swarms of fire-flies. Here and there were cosy bivouacs under dense masses of evergreens, whose shadowy outlines, magnified into phantom forms by darkness, resembled vast convex thunder clouds hovering to the valleys and clinging to the hill sides, and sharp gleams of flame light flashing through the interstices of the branches which vibrated in the wind, rendered the illusion more perfect. Heaps of fragrant timber were glowing inside, and volumes of lack-luster smoke flowing up against the tangled twigs which formed almost impermeable ceilings—nature's inimitable groining—imparted a funereal aspect to those arboreal grottoes that might have enchanted the gloomy fancy of the weird's women—

"That look not like inhabitants o' the earth."

A shrill vocal murmuring roar, sounding like falling waters in the distance, ran through the camps, and now and then a cheery shout echoed afar off. The figures of restless soldiers, picturesquely grouped around the blazing piles, were eye-sketched through the dim crepusculaus haze against the black perspective of darkness behind the fires, and seemed in their dusky indistinctness like gigantic specters. But gradually the murmuring voices died away as an echo, the army settled softly to the grateful bosom of mother earth, and happy soldiers dreaming of home thought not of the morrow.

The escort picked its way carefully through a seemingly tangled mass of mules and wagons, and the Chief at last found the commander of the Right Wing at Nolensville, in the heart of a grove, just off the highway. The flames of a roaring fire were soaring high, and groups of officers were lounging about it, discussing the morrow. General McCook was the guest of General Johnson—that is to say, partook of his rations and enjoyed his cheerful brands. No tents were pitched, but the two Generals had established their quarters in the grove by the side of a rough moss-covered rock, which served for lounges and fire-place. A pair of roadmaster's cars, like ambulatory daguerreian establishments, were drawn up in front, and quarters for the night were provided within.

THE CHIEF AND GENERAL M'COOK.

It was evident that McCook expected his Commander. After brief greeting they drew aside with Garesché and Goddard into one of the cars, and entered upon the business of the succeeding day. It was a curious group; the two Generals squatted upon the floor vis-a-vis to Garesché and Goddard, a feeble candle in the socket of a bayonet probed into the floor between them furnishing dim twilight. The Generals talked earnestly, the Chief of Staff and Senior Aid writing orders upon slips resting upon their knees. The General Commanding expressed his gratification with the gallant conduct of the troops, but was especially pleased with the ardor and firmness of the One Hundred and First Ohio, a raw regiment, under fire on the 26th of December for the first time. McCook reported Hardee in his front at Triune, some seven miles distant, and expected serious resistance next day. It was somewhere between ten and eleven o'clock when the consultation was ended. Many of the staff, overcome by fatigue, were drowsing in blankets upon the rocks around the fire. McCook was directed to move at daylight, and push the enemy hard. "We mount now, gentlemen," and a blast of the bugle rang through the valley. McCook followed a little way, and extending his hand, said, "Good night, General;" and then impressively, "with the blessing of God, General, I will whip my friend Hardee to-morrow!" "God bless you," echoed his Chieftain fervently, and a moment later he was sweeping rapidly down the pike. The darkness was now so dense that horses and riders in front would have seemed phantoms but for clattering hoofs and clanging scabbards. Occasionally horsemen were met on the highway. A curt "halt!" brought them to a stand. Explanation of business was required, and the column moved onward. Two aids of General Thomas were thus accosted, and a tedious ride was saved. After a trot of an hour or more, the column was suddenly checked by a fence beyond the edge of a forest. Lost, assuredly. A line of couriers had been stretched across the waist of the country, but even they were not now accessible. An hour or more was spent in retracing the route. The General was evidently provoked at the misadventure, and charged through the woods impatiently. A dozen voices hallooing and the twang of a bugle increased the confusion, during which the column was divided, the General and part of the staff pressing instinctively homeward, leaving Barnet, Gilman, Michler and the author with the Anderson Troop, to make their own way through the gloom. The Chief got back to camp soon after one o'clock in the morning, but the rear rambled obscurely through the forests an hour or more, pushing steadily toward the lines of the enemy until Michler advised a halt and glanced at his compass. Sure enough it was a hazardous adventure, and nothing remained but retrograde movement. The courier line was found at last, and a little after three o'clock in the morning camp was joyfully descried. The General was in saddle that day fourteen hours, riding forty-two miles; the deserted portion of his staff were mounted sixteen hours, riding forty-eight miles without partaking of food. But all that territory now is *terra incognita* to them.

CHAPTER XX.

OPERATIONS ON SATURDAY.

SUNRISE of Saturday was more dreary than the previous morning. Off the highways men and horses found deep mud. A glare of slush was dissolving the hard turnpike. It was very fatiguing to the infantry. The clouds which had broken at noon of yesterday had again massed heavily, and a dense pall of mist shrouded the horizon. Shaking his head with an air of disappointment, the Chief said ominously, "Not much progress to-day, I fear." It was not raining then, and the maps were spread upon a table in the grove. He ran his finger rapidly over the lines showing the various routes of march and the point of junction of the several columns. Suggesting that the enemy might stand on the south bank of Stewart's Creek, he yet expressed strong doubts of it, and was uncertain whether they would oppose his advance in force north of Duck River. The reasoning seemed against it. Why should Bragg fight him so near Nashville when he might do it more advantageously nearer his own base. Obviously it was Bragg's true policy to draw Rosecrans as far as possible from his base. Every mile traveled diminished the effective force of the latter and opened his communications to dangerous attack. And *e contra* the enemy by contracting his own lines concentrated his strength and protected his line of retreat in case of disaster. However, the General was sanguine and discoursed cheerfully of the future. At about nine o'clock the mist began to rise, and the sun shone out feebly. Meantime the Right Wing had been moving since daylight, and there was an occasional boom of cannon bounding from hill to hill.

THE CENTER.

General Negley's division waited at Nolensville until ten o'clock for his train to cross from the Wilson pike, where he left it the day before to move up in support of Davis. He now moved to the east over a rugged and difficult by-road with instructions to connect with Crittenden's right flank near Stewartsboro on the Murfreesboro pike. In consequence of the heavy rain of the previous night, Rousseau found the cross-roads from the Wilson pike nearly impassable, and consequently did not reach Nolensville with his troops and train until night. Walker's brigade, by order of General Thomas, retraced its steps from Brentwood and crossed over to the Nolensville pike. Negley's march was successfully executed but with great difficulty, though without obstruction from the enemy.

THE RIGHT WING.

General McCook was prepared to move at daylight. The Second Division, Brigadier General Johnson commanding, in advance, supported by the Third Division, Brigadier General Sherridan commanding; the First Division, Brigadier General Davis, in reserve; the Fifteenth Pennsylvania and the First and Second Tennessee regiments in front, under General Stanley,

The fog was so dense that it was impossible to distinguish objects a hundred and fifty yards distant. Movement was therefore greatly retarded. About two miles from camp, General Johnson's vanguard—Brigadier General Kirk's brigade in advance—encountered the enemy in strong force of cavalry, infantry, and artillery. A sharp fire was opened upon Johnson, but the fog was so dense that it was impossible to distinguish friend from foe. Our own flank skirmishers had fired upon Stanley's cavalry, and General McCook being unfamiliar with the ground, and having ascertained that Hardee had been in line of battle all night waiting for him, deemed it prudent to delay further operations until the fog lifted.

At one o'clock the mist being partially dissipated the columns moved forward, the Thirty-Fourth Illinois and Twenty-Ninth Indiana Infantry in advance as skirmishers, supported by Edgarton's Ohio Battery and the Thirtieth Indiana Infantry; the Seventy-Seventh Pennsylvania and Seventy-Ninth Illinois following in line of battle in reserve. Baldwin's brigade deployed on the right of the road. Upon approaching Triune, General McCook ascertained that the main body of rebels had retired, leaving a force of cavalry with a full battery to contest the crossing of Wilson's Creek on the edge of the village, the bridge having been destroyed by the enemy. Driving the rebel skirmishers before him, General Johnson, by sharp fighting, finally gained the crest of an elevation overlooking Triune, and the enemy were descried in line of battle, with their center in the village. Edgarton's Battery was immediately put in position, and opened with such effect that the rebels were quickly thrown into confusion, and retreated rapidly down the Eaglesville road, Johnson's skirmishers following as speedily as possible. It had now began to rain, and thick fog again obscured the country. The ground was also very heavy and movement was seriously retarded. General McCook therefore determined to halt. General Johnson crossed Wilson's Creek with much labor, rebuilt the bridge, and encamped on the opposite side. Throughout the day the men had displayed the steadiness and pluck of veteran soldiers, and notwithstanding the stubborn resistance they met, they did not lose a man, the enemy losing several. Sherridan's division also went into camp near the village, and General Davis took position at the junction of the Balle Jack road with the Nolensville pike. Thus far all was well, but the designs of the enemy were not yet divined.

THE LEFT WING.

The troops of the Left Wing had been ordered to be roused an hour and a half before dawn of the 27th, to breakfast as speedily as possible, and form under arms in line of battle before daylight. General Wood, an officer who enjoys a peculiar reputation in the army for his vigor and his vigilance, and his precision in regulating guard duty, having the lead upon this day, superintended the exact execution of this order. An occasional shell from the opposing hights shortly after morning dawned, showed that these precautions were not lost. The Left Wing being further advanced than the Right, the former did not move forward until eleven o'clock, when Wood's division, Brigadier General Hascall's brigade in front, took the lead. The entire cavalry on the Left Wing had been directed to report to General Wood, and that officer, satisfied from the nature of the country that its position in front would be injudicious, and retard rather than aid the progress of the infantry, directed it to take position in the rear of the flanks of the leading brigade.

General Hascall moved forward in two lines with skirmishers well out upon the front and flanks. Harker's and Wagner's brigades advanced on either side of the turnpike road prepared to sustain the advance, and especially to protect its flanks. General Wood also directed the supporting brigades to protect their outward flanks by flankers, so that the advance of the column was entirely insured against any flanking operation the enemy might project. Possession of Lavergne, a mile from our front, was the first object to be attained. The approach was through open fields over fallow grounds. The enemy was strongly posted in the houses of the village, and upon the wooded hights in the rear, from whence he was enabled to oppose our advance by a direct and cross-fire of musketry. Hascall's brigade advanced gallantly across the field under a galling fire, and with a line of steel quickly routed the enemy from his positions, the two leading regiments, Twenty-Sixth Ohio, Major Squires, and Fifty-Eighth Indiana, Colonel Buell, losing some twenty men, all of whom were wounded, one of them mortally.

Hascall's brigade, supported by Estep's Eighth Indiana Battery pressed forward vigorously, encountering the enemy constantly in the numerous cedar brakes which afforded them cover, but the enthusiasm of our troops was irresistible. The rebels found but little time to rest before they were driven in confusion to new positions. General Wood, constantly on the alert, was watching every movement with jealous eye, permitting nothing to escape him, and the troops, confident in their able leader, pressed on rapidly under a drenching storm toward Stewart's Creek. It was a matter of cardinal importance to save the bridge at the crossing of the Murfreesboro road, and General Wood strained every nerve to accomplish that object. The creek is narrow and deep, flowing between rugged and precipitous banks. The destruction of the bridge would retard progress, and involve the necessity of constructing a new one. The advance pressed so hotly upon the heels of the enemy that they saw them cross the stream at double-quick, the artillery horses under whip and spur. It was afterward ascertained that this rapid maneuver was executed by Brigadier General Maney's brigade. The enemy, however, took time to kindle a fire upon the bridge, expecting from the opposite side to repel any effort to extinguish it, but the line of skirmishers and Colonel McKee's Third Kentucky Infantry, which had now been sent to the front, dashed gallantly forward under a sharp fire of musketry and extinguished the flames. While the skirmishers were performing this brilliant exploit, Hascall's left flank was attacked by cavalry. The line immediately changed front to the left, repulsed the attack quickly, and a company of the One Hundredth Illinois Infantry succeeded in cutting off and capturing twenty-five prisoners with their arms, and twelve horses with their accouterments. The enemy now fell back some distance from the creek, leaving strong pickets upon the crest of the hill near the bridge. General Wood had pressed them so sharply that they left tents standing upon the southern side of the creek, and the encampment was strewn with arms.

A STEEPLE CHASE.

Meantime, after passing Lavergne, the Nineteenth Brigade, Colonel W. B. Hazen commanding, was directed to proceed via the Jefferson pike to Stewart's Creek to save the bridge at that crossing if possible. Ninety cavalry of the Fourth Michigan, under command of Captain Maxey, reported to Colonel Hazen, and they were placed under charge of his Acting Assistant Inspector General, Captain James McCleery, Forty-First Ohio Infantry, with directions to clap spurs to the troop as soon as the enemy were started, and not slack rein until the bridge was crossed. The distance did not exceed five miles. Flankers were thrown out, and the infantry and artillery were urged forward at a speed that kept them within supporting distance of the cavalry. The enemy were less than three miles from the bridge. McCleery and Maxey, by following Hazen's nervy directions to the letter, made an exciting steeple chase of the whole affair. The rebels outnumbered our gallant little detachment fully five to one, but they went over the bridge at a slashing pace, Maxey's troopers charging at their heels. After crossing they formed upon the opposite side of the creek, but were soon dispersed by our artillery. In this brilliant affair we lost one trooper killed and two were captured. We captured ten prisoners, killed one commissioned officer and several men.

Colonel Kennett had been slashing at the rebel cavalry all day, and by a gallant dash succeeded in cutting off and capturing a detachment of thirty-six men of Colonel John T. Morgan's Alabama regiment. The field was now clear to the line of Stewart's Creek on the left. Negley's division closed up on General Crittenden's right, and General McCook was quietly encamped in the mud at Triune. The General Commanding remained at his quarters until noon receiving reports, and in the evening rode to the left front to inspect the position. He expressed great satisfaction with the results of the day's operations, especially commending the vigor and skill exhibited by General Wood and Colonel Hazen.

CHAPTER XXI.

OPERATIONS on Sunday and Monday—General Rosecrans at the Front—Picket Skirmishing—Prospects for Monday—Headquarters at Lavergne—Rousseau joins the Center—McCook's Reconnoissance—Willich's Brigade Captures Prisoners—Operations on Monday—Hardee Retires to Murfreesboro—Battle Indicated—The Left Wing in front of Murfreesboro—Crittenden Ordered to Occupy the Town—Exploit of Harker's Brigade—Monday Night.

GENERAL ROSECRANS had frequently expressed his opposition to military operations upon the Sabbath, unless they were indispensible. It was, therefore, a foregone conclusion that Sunday, December 28th, would be a day of comparative rest. There was both principle and policy in halting. The troops needed rest, Rousseau's division was still at Nolensville, and it was desirable that he should join the Center; it was essential, also, to ascertain the object of Hardee's movements. If he had retired to Shelbyville, it indicated a withdrawal of Bragg's army from Murfreesboro. If he had merely fallen back to Murfreesboro, it justified conclusion that the enemy had determined to meet us in a general engagement in that vicinity.

The General Commanding rose early, as usual, on Sunday morning, and devoted an hour to religious exercises, Rev. Father Trecy officiating at Mass. Garesché, and a few soldiers of the Tenth Ohio Volunteers, knelt at the same altar. Providence smiled that morning, too, for the mist was swept away by a strong western breeze, and the sun broke through the clouds, shining with genial luster. About noon, General Rosecrans, attended by his entire staff, cantered down the Murfreesboro pike to the extreme front, and observed the enemy from the north bank of Stewart's creek. A battery, supported by a considerable force of mounted rebels, was distinctly visible upon a commanding elevation of the road a mile south of the stream. The woods on the opposite side of the creek were swarming with pickets of the enemy, and noisy firing, at long musket range, was going on at various points above and below the road, but without casualties of serious consequence on either side—a very interesting but an unprofitable exercise. There was a general concurrence among the numerous officers upon the ground that the opposite side of the stream was so admirably adapted for defense that the enemy would be apt to resist our crossing in force. Many supposed that they were then contemplating the great battle-ground which was to decide the fate of Middle Tennessee. Appropriate dispositions were made to meet the anticipated engagement. After a brief visit to General Crittenden's quarters, in the forest on the right of the road, a mile from the creek, General Rosecrans returned to headquarters, which had been advanced to Lavergne.

Meantime Rousseau's division was laboriously winding through the rude defiles from Nolensville toward the Murfreesboro pike to take its proper position in column. Night had fallen before his jaded men, and weary teams finished their severe march.

The Right Wing, excepting Brigadier General August Willich's brigade, which had been sent in pursuit of Hardee's column, remained over Sunday in the position in which it halted Saturday night. General Willich followed the enemy to Rigg's cross-roads, about seven miles below Triune, capturing forty-one rebels of his rear guard, and ascertaining that Hardee had withdrawn his corps to Murfreesboro. It was therefore certain that Bragg intended to accept battle. The troops sunk to rest that night, anticipating a sanguinary conflict on the morrow.

THE RIGHT WING ON MONDAY.

It was expected that sunrise of Monday, the 29th, would be saluted by roar of artillery. The troops were under arms before daybreak, and as soon as it was light, the columns marched toward Murfreesboro—seven miles from Stewartsboro. General McCook detached Baldwin's brigade, of Johnson's division, to remain as a corps of observation at Triune, and moved toward Murfreesboro on the Balle Jack road, Gen. Davis' division in advance, Woodruff's brigade in front, supported by Sherridan's division, the Second Division, General Johnson, in reserve, Stanley's cavalry in the front. In consequence of the mud and the ruggedness of the road, marching was extremely difficult. Upon arriving at Stewart's Creek, it was reported that the enemy had shown in strong force on the opposite side, but General Stanley soon contradicted it, reporting the road clear; and the column moved with but little obstruction to the Wilkinson pike, on Overall's Creek, within three and a half miles of Murfreesboro, at which point the advance division went into bivouac in line of battle, the left brigade resting on the Wilkinson pike.

THE CENTER.

General Negley's division of the Center crossed Stewart's Creek two miles south-west and above the bridge on the Murfreesboro pike, supporting the head and right flank of Crittenden's corps, which moved on the turnpike. The cavalry rear guard of the enemy contested the advance obstinately, but with only trifling casualties on either side. Rousseau remained in camp at Stewartsboro, detaching Starkweather's brigade, with a section of artillery, to the Jefferson pike crossing of Stone River to observe the movements of the enemy in that direction. Walker's brigade moved over from the Nolensville pike, and encamped at Stewartsboro about dark.

THE LEFT WING.

Grose's brigade, of Palmer's division, with a regiment of skirmishers in front, took the advance of the Left Wing, on the west side of the Murfreesboro pike, Parson's Fourth United States Artillery shelling the forests in front; Wagner's brigade, of Wood's division, in front on the eastern side of the pike, with Harker's brigade covering his left, Cruft's and Hascall's brigades in reserve, in column, Van Cleve's division in the rear. Hazen's brigade was marching to the front from the bridge over Stewart's Creek, at the Jefferson pike crossing. The leading brigades moved at ten o'clock across Stewart's Creek, and advanced in line of battle, skirmishing with the enemy, who fell back rapidly, but resisting. The Left Wing continued to advance steadily in this manner, driving the enemy from cover constantly, until at about three o'clock in the afternoon, it reached Stone River. The enemy were now discovered in great force in front of Murfreesboro, in line of battle, and it was evident that they were prepared to resist further progress in general engagement.

THE ENEMY IN FRONT.

General Rosecrans meantime had moved forward to Stewartsboro, and established field quarters at Bridge's house, where he was joined by Major General Thomas, who remained with him nearly all day. Generals Wood and Palmer had halted for orders, in consequence of the formidable front of the enemy, the supporting columns being too far in the rear to justify a continuous advance. General Crittenden approved the halt, and reported to General Rosecrans.

Wood's division on the left and Palmer's on the right were immediately disposed in order of battle in two lines, the front securely guarded by a continuous line of skirmishers well out in advance of their reserves. Wagner's brigade rested on the pike occupying a piece of wooded ground with an open field in front. Harker's brigade in the center occupied the same woods and extended toward the left into an open field, covered in front by a wave in the surface, and Hascall's brigade was posted on the extreme left, its left resting upon Stone River—the latter running obliquely in front of the position, leaving a triangular field some hundreds of yards in breadth in front of the right, and narrowing almost to a point in front of the left. Palmer's brigade was formed in a similar manner, Cruft's left connecting with Wagner's right, with a fallow field in front; Grose on the extreme right, Negley and Van Cleve moving up in support some distance in the rear, their movements having been retarded by serious natural obstructions.

MARCH ON MURFREESBORO.

A signal message about three o'clock in the afternoon from the front from General Palmer, said that he was in sight of Murfreesboro, and the enemy were running. Whereon an order was sent by General Rosecrans to General Crittenden directing him to send a division to occupy Murfreesboro. General Wood, and subsequently General Palmer, deemed such a movement injudicious under the circumstances, but prepared with alacrity to obey, though representing its hazards. Harker's brigade took the advance, throwing out a strong line of skirmishers in front, and directing the Fifty-First and Seventy-Third Indiana, and Thirteenth Michigan regiments to cross the river simultaneously, press forward, and seize the commanding hights beyond; the Sixty-Fourth and Sixty-Fifth Ohio Infantry and Bradley's Battery to follow in support; Hascall's brigade to follow on the left. The troops gallantly dashed forward, and as the line of skirmishers debouched from the stream on the opposite side, they were met by a crash of musketry from a regiment in front covered by thickets and a fence. Our lads held their fire until within short range, then let drive, and charged enthusiastically. The rebels fell back in confusion upon their main body about five hundred yards distant, which was subsequently ascertained to be Breckinridge's division. The movement of the entire brigade was handsomely executed, and Harker gained his position. But the enemy, though evidently disconcerted by the boldness and spirit of the attack, were obviously too strong for the little force in front. Harker, therefore, reported for orders.

In the meantime, General Crittenden consenting to suspend further movement in consequence of the obvious strength of the enemy until he could report to the General Commanding, Colonel Harker was recalled in pursuance of orders received by General Crittenden countermanding the movement. To obey the order to fall back was almost as hazardous as to advance, but it was skillfully executed, Colonel Harker losing but two men killed and three wounded in the whole affair. The order for the occupation of Murfreesboro having been based upon erroneous information, the General Commanding approved the course of General Crittenden in suspending its execution. The Left Wing with Negley's division bivouacked in order of battle without fires, seven hundred yards distant from the enemy's entrenchments, our left extending some five hundred yards down the river.

CAVALRY OPERATIONS.

Before dark General McCook had also reported that his advance was in sight of Murfreesboro. The enemy were in his front drawn up in line of battle, and reinforcements were coming up from Shelbyville by railroad. In this day's operations the cavalry were signally conspicuous on the right flank. Colonel Zahn, with part of his brigade, consisting of the First Ohio Cavalry, commanded by Colonel Minor Millikin, and part of the Fourth Ohio Cavalry, Lieutenant Colonel Pugh, marched upon Murfreesboro by the Franklin road, but coming upon the enemy's artillery they thought it advisable to retire, after a sharp encounter, in which they captured six prisoners. General Stanley moving on the Balle Jack road with the reserve cavalry, encountered the enemy at Wilkinson's cross-roads, and after a series of charges and running fights drove them across Overall's Creek, and to a point within a half mile of the enemy's line of battle. The conduct of the Anderson Cavalry this day elicited the generous approval of their commander, who reported officially that they "behaved most gallantly, pushing at full charge upon the enemy for six miles. Unfortunately their advance fronted too recklessly; having dispersed their cavalry, the troops fell upon two regiments of rebel infantry in ambush, and after a gallant struggle were compelled to retire, with the loss of Major Rosengarten and six men killed, and the brave Major Ward and five men desperately wounded." Unhappily the loss of their two gallant Majors demoralized them, and a spirit of jealousy and strife, which was subsequently engendered in the regiment, destroyed its usefulness.

On the left flank, Colonel Minty was skirmishing lightly with the enemy all day. The Seventh Pennsylvania, Major Wynkoop, on the extreme left, the Third Kentucky, Colonel Murray, on the right, the Fourth Michigan, Lieutenant Colonel Dickinson, in reserve, the Second Indiana Cavalry on courier duty.

THE GENERAL COMMANDING AT THE FRONT.

The General Commanding remained at Bridge's house during the entire day receiving reports and giving orders. His mind was absorbed in his business to the exclusion of all other themes. He seemed more anxious about the situation on the right, and was much gratified when General McCook's successful progress was reported. The mutually confirmatory reports from the commanders of the Right and Left Wings, removed all shadow of doubt concerning the disposition of the enemy. Orders were sent to the former to form two of his divisions in two lines, with one division in reserve, sending a reconnoitering force down toward Salem on his right. Negley would form in two lines in front in the center, Rousseau supporting him. Crittenden's corps was to form like McCook's. Stanley and Kennett were again enjoined to guard well the flanks with their cavalry.

Some time after dark, headquarters were established on the south bank of Stewart's Creek. After supper, the General Commanding, attended by Lieutenant Colonel Garesché, Lieutenant Kirby, Lieutenant Bond, Colonel Barnet, Major Skinner, and Father Trecy, who never deserted him, proceeded to the front, and after observing the situation, he took quarters in a little wood hard by the Murfreesboro pike. General Crittenden and the respective staffs of the two Generals, enveloped in blankets, squeezed themselves into a little rickety log-cabin and lay down to sleep. The Pioneer Brigade, under Captain St. Clair Morton, had arrived at Stewart's Creek that afternoon, and by four o'clock next morning, when they were ordered to the front, had constructed two bridges across the stream. The clangor of their axes was heard all night echoing in the dreary forests. The darkness seemed to bear upon its wings strange, ominous sounds. Thousands thought it the night before battle, and put up their prayers to God.

CHAPTER XXII.

TUESDAY, December 30—The First Shot at the General Commanding—An Orderly Decapitated—Skirmishing on the Left—Field Quarters Established—Military Groupings—A Growl on the Right—Music—Garesché and his Missal—An Old Woman's Dream—Stone River—The Rebel Position—Orders to General McCook—Reports—Obstinate Resistance of the Enemy—Ominous Sounds on the Left—Starkweather's Combat—Rebel Cavalry in the Rear—The Tenth Ohio Distinguishing Itself—Rosecrans Orders McCook to Prepare for Battle—Better Prospects—Operations of the Day.

TUESDAY, the 30th of December, dawned drearily. It had rained heavily during the night. The surface of the earth was a heavy muck—such a soil as caused Napoleon to delay attack from six o'clock until eleven. The sun was shut out by heavy masses of clouds, and thick mist was floating in the atmosphere, obscuring vision and oppressing the senses. The soldiers, who had lain all night in the mud without fires, stood to their arms shivering in saturated garments long before daylight. They had plenty to eat, but that was their only comfort. But as they fared, so fared their officers, save when they slept their officers were vigilant.

The Leader was among the earliest to start from his blankets—as he had been among the last who had slept at all to seek rest. At half-past three o'clock that morning, Major General McCook reported to him in person, and was instructed to rest the left of his line upon the right of General Negley's line, and to throw his right forward until it was parallel, or nearly so, with Stone River, the extreme right to rest on or near the Franklin road—General McCook describing the field which furnished the base for this order. The order of the Center and Left Wing were to remain as already described—Negley's two brigades in the center, Palmer on his left, Wood on the extreme left, Van Cleve on the left in reserve.

HEADQUARTERS IN THE FIELD.

About seven o'clock, Crittenden's lines moved up a little, and the enemy opened a brisk but ineffective fire. Negley pushed laboriously forward through the heavy cedar thickets, the pioneers cutting roads through the timber for the passage of his trains. The General Commanding, not yet mounted, stood in front of his quarters watching the progress of affairs when the fire opened upon Crittenden. Presently an officer who had been wounded was borne to the rear on a stretcher. Directly the enemy trained a gun at headquarters. The first compliment whizzed over a little crest and ricochetted in the road. The next cannon ball was in better range, striking nearer the General. The third whizzed almost in a line with him, and carried away the head of McDonald, of the Fourth Regular Cavalry, one of the orderlies. It was deemed prudent to remove, and the General and staff rode up the slope to a less exposed position, halting at a solitary panel of fence under three vigorous young trees, perhaps a hundred yards from the pike on the left—a point from whence movements were observed during the day. It had begun to rain again, and the prospect was dismal.

A canopy of rails, supported by a rider upon crotchets, was constructed, and several gutta-percha blankets spread over them, enabled the staff to write orders under shelter. Every member of the staff proper was now with the Chief. General Crittenden and his staff swelled the group. Colonel John Kennett and his Adjutant, Chamberlain, had reported in obedience to orders. Otis was there superintending the transmission of orders by couriers. The escorts of Rosecrans and Crittenden, with orderlies, were drawn up in the rear holding horses. The Fourth Regular Cavalry were in line behind a crest, perhaps three or four hundred yards in the rear. After a while a petulant bicker of musketry in Negley's front, occasionally a growl of cannon away over on the right, indicated that the enemy were finding cause of quarrel. Thousands of troops, forming the second line, were visible as far as the eye could reach, stalking about the mucky fallow grounds near their posts, or lounging upon their blankets, their bayonets fixed and sunk into the soil, with butts of muskets uppermost, as if this was a field of fire-arms ripening for a harvest. As the muttering in the distance grew more ominous, the superb band of the Fourth Cavalry soothed the growing discord with noble harmony; and as the "Star Spangled Banner" swelled and rolled in spirit-stirring volume over the somber plains, stout-hearted fellows greeted the welcome music with joyful clamor.

A fire had been kindled in front of field quarters, and a fence was constructed around it for seats. Officers, enveloped in uncouth rubber pouchos, with gutta-percha covers on their heads, reminders of chivalrous knights around cap-a-pie, clustered around the roaring flames, and while battle waged in the forest they eked comfort from the blaze and waxed jolly. Why not? Doubtless they had made their peace with God. Perhaps to-day or to-morrow they might die. Men learn to toy with the grim majesty of death. There is often a gay *insousiance* in the midst of horrors that thrills you when reflection seizes you in solitude. "Who of us will go up to-morrow?" quoth one. "Not I," "Nor I," say each. When all enter the iminent deadly breach, who may survive? Yet who thinks it will be himself?

THE FOLLOWING OF CHRIST.

There was one in that assemblage who felt not thus. He was sitting alone, aside, at the foot of one of the trees, leaning against it. In his hands, partially concealed by the flowing folds of his overcoat, there was a little book — a *Missal* — "*De Imitatione Christe.*" He carried it in his pocket habitually. A few had observed his custom. Yet he was as stealthy as a woman with a sweet missive from a lover. Had he dreamed that he appeared in the least ostentatious, he would have blushed to his temples. He bowed meekly over his book; his lips uttered inaudibly; the index finger of his right hand described the imaginary cross with which men of his faith symbolize their faith. He was no more conscious that he was observed by mortal man than a little child is capable of crime. He communed upon the battle-field with God. The witness shuddered with indescribable emotion. Garesché felt that he was a doomed man. On the morrow the comrade who shuddered, shuddered the more when the scene premonished under that tree became a horrible reality. It was very curious. An old woman at St. Louis—a poor distraught creature, who fancied she had inspirations superior to mortal gifts—dreamed that Garesché would be killed in his first battle. She warned him, and he smiled with amiable contempt. He was at Washington—she on the Mississippi. A year later, and he was in front of Murfreesboro. But a presentiment had possessed his mind. He left Washington to join Rosecrans, fixed in the somber belief that he would fall in his first battle. This was confided to a near relative. He never spoke of it to others. We shall see how cheerfully he devoted himself.

GROUPINGS IN THE FIELD.

There were various groupings that may yet elicit the skill of a graceful limner. The Chief, Garesché, Goddard, Thompson, Thoms, Bond, in the center—pencil and paper, orders—couriers flying away, couriers swiftly approaching, aids galloping over the field, officers reporting; the Chief grave, anxious, absorbed. Crittenden and his staff waiting orders. Officers with glasses scanning the line, which to-morrow will be a line of blood. A troop, a squadron, a regiment of horse skirring over the plain; columns moving through the forest; great trains lumbering in the highway; cannon rumbling on the stony road. Cold winds blew from the north-west about noon and swept the mist and the smoke from camp-fires in the thickets over the enemy, and the cheerful sun gleamed out strongly but fitful through clefts between clouds, which looked like gaps separating mountains. The enemy were visible in front, anxious, and observant in groups with glasses, as we were.

FIGHTING FOR POSITION.

According to descriptions of the geography of the rebel position and of the topography of the country in their front, furnished by General McCook, orders had been given him which consumed the day in execution. His extreme right refused to the enemy was to rest on or near the Franklin pike, tracing a wooded ridge along the front of the enemy until his left connected with the Center. Early in the morning, Negley had obliqued to the right in order to bring him into position. Stanley's brigade on the right, Miller's on the left, joining Cruft's brigade of Palmer's division left wing. Rousseau's three brigades had been ordered forward early, and they got into position in reserve about four o'clock—Starkweather's being on the Jefferson pike.

The reports which reached the General Commanding, were not reassuring. The energies of the Center and Right Wing were engaged in fighting for position. Negley, under Thomas, was meeting resistance which amounted almost to battle. Thunder of cannon and rattle of musketry swelling upon the right was still more ominous. McCook was instructed to feel his way cautiously but firmly. Before noon artillery was heard away off on our left. It was unexpected, and therefore menacing. Colonel Kennett was directed to inquire into it, and the facts were subsequently reported. A train of sixty wagons, proceeding toward the bridge on the Jefferson pike, was attacked while the head of the train was going into park at Starkweather's camp, near the bridge. His brigade, numbering seventeen hundred men, was quickly deployed, the Twenty-First Wisconsin, Colonel Hobart, dividing to the front and rear of the train, the First Wisconsin, Lieutenant Colonel Bingham, on the flanks as skirmishers, the Twenty-Fourth Illinois, Colonel Mihalotzy, at the bridge crossing with a section of Stone's First Kentucky Battery, the Seventy-Ninth Pennsylvania, Colonel Hambright, and two sections of Stone's Battery, going to the front under Colonel Starkweather. A detachment of fifty of the Second Kentucky Cavalry, Captain Craddock, was sent to the front to feel the enemy and were at once engaged. The enemy, three thousand five hundred strong, under Brigadier General Wheeler, and Colonel Allen, advanced on foot supported by two howitzers. A sharp combat lasting two hours and a half ensued. Starkweather's gallant brigade, however, finally repulsed the enemy with severe loss, his own casualties being one killed, eight wounded, one hundred and four missing, and nine captured. Eighty-three of the enemy, including a Lieutenant Colonel, were killed outright, and eight were captured—two of whom were mortally wounded. Their wounded were numerous, but the enemy removed them. Wheeler, however, succeeded in destroying twenty wagons in the rear of the train. The troops of the brigade behaved gallantly.

EXCITING REPORTS.

At noon, General McCook reported that Colonel Zahn had discovered a brigade of rebel cavalry with three pieces of artillery on the Franklin pike, evidently menacing our communications. Later in the day they made a dash on the Murfreesboro pike, directly in our rear, cutting off a train of wagons. Rousseau's division having moved to the front, Colonel J. W. Burke's Tenth Ohio Infantry, which had been left to guard Headquarters' camp, at Stewartsbore, immediately moved in pursuit under that gallant officer and recaptured the train. Harrassing reports were constantly arriving, indicating a general effort on the part of the enemy to cut off our trains in the rear, and sever communications with Nashville, causing anxiety to the General Commanding. General McCook reported strong resistance, with Hardee in his front. At a quarter before four o'clcok, Captain H. N. Fisher, Volunteer Aid to General McCook, reported to the General Commanding that Kirby Smith's corps and Breckinridge's division had concentrated in front of the Left Wing. "Tell General McCook," said the Chief, that "if he is assured that such is the fact he may drive Hardee sharply if he is ready. At all events tell him to prepare for battle to-morrow morning. Tell him to fight as if the fate of a great battle depended upon him. While he holds Hardee, the Left, under Crittenden, will swing round and take Murfreesboro. Let Hardee attack if he wants to. It will suit us exactly." "It is looking better," said the Chief, moving around to the fire.

Soon after it was reported that the enemy had captured Lavergne, with thirty troops and the telegraph operator, besides interrupting the line of couriers. Not much later General Thomas reported successful progress in front of the Center, and was directed to press the enemy at his discretion. General McCook reported Sherridan's division moving steadily into the position assigned him. Davis on his right, fighting vigorously but gaining ground. "Things look bright, gentlemen—brighter than they did this morning," said the Chief cheerfully, and for the first time during the day he indulged in pleasantry. All this time there was an angry chatter of musketry in the center and on the right, while great guns roared incessantly—very much resembling battle. It is now time to follow the respective movements of the columns.

THE LEFT WING.

Was already in position in order of battle in two lines, Cruft's, Grose's, Wagner's, and Harker's brigades in front, with Hazen's and Hascall's brigades, and Van Cleve's division, in reserve. The rebel sharpshooters kept up a harrassing fire all day, and at four o'clock in the afternoon General Palmer was ordered to advance and make a demonstration with all his artillery. The enemy retaliated, and there was a grand fusilade, but nothing serious grew out of it.

THE CENTER.

Negley had obliqued to the right, and with the Seventy-Eighth Pennsylvania and Nineteenth Illinois in front skirmishing, he fought his way into position over rugged ground, beset with cedar-brakes, and against obstinate resistance. He was also formed in two lines, with Rousseau's division in reserve.

THE RIGHT WING.

At half past nine o'clock in the morning, General McCook moved his column down the Wilkinson pike toward Murfreesboro. Sherridan's division had the lead, Roberts' brigade in advance, with a regiment of cavalry in front. Not long after crossing Overall's Creek, the infantry pickets of the rebels were encountered. Sherridan had thrown a regiment of skirmishers to the front, but when they reached a point within two miles and three-quarters of Murfreesboro, the enemy showed so strongly in front that two regiments—the Twenty-Second and Forty-Second Illinois—were required to drive them. They resisted obstinately, bringing batteries into play occasionally.

Complying with orders from General McCook, General Sherridan now formed in line of battle and placed his artillery in position—on the right of and obliquely to the pike—four regiments to the front, four in close support, and Shaeffer's brigade in reserve in columns of regiments in rear of the center. General Davis formed upon his right in similar manner, with Carlin's brigade on the right to direct the movements of the division. In consequence of a demonstration of the enemy toward Davis' right, Kirk's brigade, of Johnson's division, was formed still further to the right, with his own right refused to protect that flank. Edgarton's Battery took position upon an elevation on the right flank and opened his full battery with splendid effect, driving the enemy back in confusion, disabling pieces, killing horses and men. A second battery in Post's front was also silenced in a few moments.

The enemy, covered by a heavy bolt of timber in Sherridan's and Davis' front, had succeeded in retarding their progress, but Davis' division and Sherridan's right brigade were now ordered to swing by the right, so as to face nearly east, but in effecting this movement Davis met with severe loss. Carlin found his right within one hundred and eighty yards of a rebel battery at Smith's house. He had intended to halt here for Post's and Woodruff's brigades to come up, but Colonel Alexander, commanding the Twenty-First Illinois, acting upon his own responsibility, charged gallantly at the battery, and upon obtaining a point within eighty yards of it, the enemy abandoned their guns. The regiment continued its career, but directly it recoiled before a furious fire opened suddenly by infantry concealed behind fences and outhouses. The battery which Edgarton silenced soon after was also harrassing them, and Colonel Alexander, seeing no alternative, was constrained to retire. The conduct of his regiment, however, was admirable.

The two divisions, with one of Johnson's brigades, had now been quite sharply engaged, losing about two hundred men, and it was verging upon sunset. The maneuver which had been directed was successfully executed, and McCook soon saw his command in the position for which it had struggled so inflexibly. Sherridan's left, resting upon the Wilkinson pike, connected with Negley's right, his right resting in the timber, his reserve brigade in the rear of his center. Davis' left was closed in upon Sherridan's right, with his own right deflected so that it formed nearly a right angle with Sherridan's. Subsequently Brigadier General Kirk's left joined Davis' right; and General Willich's brigade, with his right at the Franklin road, refused so as to protect the flank, was posted upon the extreme right of the entire line of battle. Meantime, Baldwin's brigade, which had been ordered forward from Triune, had joined General Johnson early in the afternoon (of the 30th), and went into camp in reserve, about eight hundred yards in the rear.

The entire cavalry force of the army, excepting details for courier and escort duty, were engaged protecting the flanks that day, skirmishing a little. General Stanley, with a small force, went back to Lavergne, to watch the rebel operations in the rear.

CHAPTER XXIII.

THE Line of Battle—Right, Left, and Center—The Field—Picket Guards—Vigilance of Commanders—Position of the Enemy—Headquarters of the General Commanding the Night before Battle—McCook's Information from the Enemy—Instructions to McCook—The Plan of Battle—Explanations—The Order of Battle by Brigades—Address to the Army—The Army on the Eve of Battle.

THERE was now a continuous line of battle in two lines, with reserves, in position, describing an irregular figure about three miles in length, and tracing in a general direction north-east and south-west. It was nearly parallel with that of the enemy. The left rested on Stone River, the right stretching rather south-westerly, and resting on high wooded ground, south of and near the Franklin pike. The right brigade (Willich's) flanked in a line nearly perpendicular to the main line, forming a crotchet to the rear to guard against a flank movement. The Right Wing generally occupied a wooded ridge, with open ground in front. A valley, narrowing from right to left, say from four hundred to two hundred and fifty yards, separated it from the enemy, who were covered by dense cedar thickets, oak forests, and, as was subsequently discovered, rude breastworks of loose stones, rails, and brush.

The Center was posted on a rolling slope in advance, but joining Crittenden's right and McCook's left. In front, a heavy growth of oak timber extended toward the river, which was about a mile distant. A narrow thicket diagonally crossed Negley's left, and skirted the base of a cultivated slope, expanding to the width of a mile as it approached the Murfreesboro pike. The enemy were posted on the crest of this slope, behind intrenchments, which extended with intervals from the oak timber in Negley's front to Stone River, on our left, obliquing to our left front, with a battery of six guns in position near the woods, about eight hundred yards from Negley's front. The enemy's columns were massed behind this timber on the river bank.

The right brigade of the Left Wing rested upon a wood, the next stretched across an open cotton field into a thin grove, and the left brigades were also partially covered by timber, with open ground in front. The enemy occupied a commanding crest in the open field, perhaps eight hundred yards distant from our line. The railroad on high ground, to the left of the pike, the turnpike on low ground, intersected the Left Wing on Palmer's left, and crossed each other near the rebel line in a depression, forming a sharp triangle, the base of which, a half mile in the rear, was about five hundred yards wide. About half way between the two lines were the scarified walls of a brick dwelling, now famous as "Cowan's Burnt House," occupying a knoll, with a peach orchard on the north side. The great struggle for mastery finally took place in this front, behind the apex of the triangle.

In rear of our line the country was undulating and rough, excepting on the left. Behind the Right Wing and Center, there were alternate fallow fields, fences, and dense cedar thickets and ridges. The left moved into line over an undulating cornfield, which had one distinct trace ranging south-westerly from Stone River until it abruptly fell off into a broad bluff on the right of the pike on the west, and sloped southerly from a crest which fronted the enemy. On the rump of this trace there was a small grove of saplings. Behind it a hundred yards distant, perhaps, and near the railroad, a family cemetery, shaded by a clump of stunted cedars. This graveyard is now populous with dead patriots.

On the right of the pike, going south, there was an irregular triangular cottonfield swelling to a crest, a hundred and fifty yards on the right of the pike, when it fell off into thicket-skirted swamps at the northern angle, and sloped almost imperceptibly in a southerly direction into an open marsh, skirted on its opposite side behind Cruft's brigade, by dense cedar-brakes. Its southern base opened clearly in front of the enemy's right center. Behind this field, on the north side, was an oak forest, with cedar underskirting, verging upon the highway, the ground swelling with a rocky surface in a north-westerly direction. All this is historical ground, sacred to the memory of thousands of gallant soldiers who fought over it and lavished their blood upon it—a frank offering to their country. Their moldering bones are monuments of their sacrifice.

PRECAUTIONS.

A strong continuous line of pickets stretched from the extreme right to the extreme left in front of the entire line of battle, and cavalry was posted on either flank. General Willich, ever vigilant and careful, posted his pickets seven hundred yards in his front, and patroled six hundred yards beyond. In consequence of the propinquity of his line to the rebel front, General Kirk was not able to post his picket line so far in advance, but he pushed it to the utmost limit; and he complained that he was obliged to extend his line unduly to cover a gap between his left and the right of General Davis. The necessary precautions were taken by all the other commanders. General Wood, however, exercising his characteristic caution and care, had also caused three days' subsistence, and twenty rounds of cartridges additional to be issued to his men. His artillery horses were kept attached to their pieces, and extraordinary vigilance was enjoined upon his commanders and troops, in order to be prepared for all emergencies. In these respects, as in the field, the soldierly qualities of General Wood shone conspicuously. His vigor and skill in pushing the enemy from Lavergne to Stewart's Creek and Stone River had before elicited the earnest approval of the General Commanding.

POSITION OF THE ENEMY.

Stone River, a summer stream—a ribbon in dog-days, but a wild torrent in spring-time, sweeping bridges and the debris of forests before its volume—is a cleft between high bluffy banks, tracing in a general direction from south to north, with many sinuosities. It curves abruptly toward Murfreesboro on the western side of the town, and the enemy availed themselves of the horse-shoe. Their right intersected Stone River, nearly parallel with our left front, and rested upon hights on the east side of the river, their extreme right obliqued to correspond with the course of the river, toward our left. The left of their Right Wing and their Center were posted behind intrenchments on the crest of a cottonfield, which sloped gradually toward our front, rather abruptly in their rear. Their left was prolonged upon the trace of a bluffy, rocky ridge, south of the Franklin road, and covered the roads going southward toward Shelbyville. Their Center was an obtuse angle, trending north-westerly, their right and left somewhat retired. The slopes toward the river covered their columns. At this period the river was at its lowest ebb, fordable at any point where roads could be cut to it, so that the enemy could retire across it without obstruction, if necessary, while it formed a natural fosse against us, difficult to cross in the face of opposition.

HEADQUARTERS THE NIGHT BEFORE BATTLE.

At sunset the marquee of the General Commanding, and a few tents for his staff, were pitched on the knoll hard by the little graveyard, in the most exposed position on the field. The railroad was the toss of a penny in the rear. He remained until dark at his field quarters under the three trees, when he repaired to camp. General Crittenden's quarters were a stone's throw to the north; those of General Thomas and General Rousseau in a rickety cabin further in the rear; and General McCook's in a Mr. Harding's house, in the rear of the center of his own line.

Meantime, McCook had sent a captured citizen, under guard to General Rosecrans, with the information that the enemy were massing their forces upon his right. The citizen said to McCook, "I was up to the enemy's line of battle twice yesterday, and once this morning, to get some stock taken from me. The enemy's troops are posted in the following manner: The right of Cheatham's division rests on the Wilkinson pike. Withers is on Cheatham's left, with his left resting on the Franklin road. Hardee's corps is entirely beyond that road, his right resting on that road, and his left extending toward the Salem pike." General McCook also reported that his right rested directly in front of the rebel Center, which gave him some anxiety. He therefore posted Kirk's and Willich's brigades on the right of Davis, extending his line south of the Franklin road. Upon receiving this information, General Rosecrans directed McCook to build large and extensive camp fires beyond his right, to induce the enemy to believe he was massing troops there, and the order was executed by Major Nodine, of McCook's staff. When General McCook informed the General Commanding that his corps was facing strongly toward the east, the latter told him that "such a direction to his line did not appear to him a proper one, but that it ought, with the exception of his left, to face much more nearly south, with Johnson's division in reserve; but that this matter must be confided to him, who knew the ground over which he had fought."

INSTRUCTIONS TO M'COOK.

At about six o'clock in the evening, General Rosecrans dictated the following instructions to General McCook for the following day. They were written by Captain R. S. Thoms, Volunteer Aiddecamp, and by him they were forwarded to McCook, to wit:

"Take strong position. If the enemy attack you, fall back slowly, refusing your right, contesting the ground inch by inch. If the enemy does not attack you, you will attack them, not vigorously, but warmly. The time of attack by you to be designated by the General Commanding."

At nine o'clock the corps commanders met at headquarters, and the following plan of battle for the morrow was presented and explained:

PLAN OF THE BATTLE.

McCook was to occupy the most advantageous position, refusing his right as much as practicable and necessary to secure it; to receive the attack of the enemy, or, if that did not come, to attack himself, sufficient to hold all the force on his front.

Thomas and Palmer to open with skirmishing, and gain the enemy's center and left as far as the river.

Crittenden to cross Van Cleve's division at the lower ford, covered and supported by the Sappers and Miners, and to advance on Breckinridge.

Wood's division to follow by brigades, crossing at the upper ford, and moving on Van Cleve's right, to carry everything into Murfreesboro.

"This," said General Rosecrans subsequently in his official reports, "would have given us two divisions against one, and as soon as Breckinridge had been dislodged from his position, the batteries of Wood's division, taking position on the hights east of Stone River, in advance, would see the enemy's works in reverse, would dislodge them, and enable Palmer's division to press them back and drive them westward across the river, or through the woods, while Thomas, sustaining the movement on the center, would advance on the right of Palmer, crushing their right; and Crittenden's corps, advancing, would take Murfreesboro, and then moving westward, on the Franklin road, get in their flanks and rear, and drive them into the country, toward Salem, with the prospect of cutting off their retreat, and probably destroying their army.

"It was explained to them that this combination, ensuring us a vast superiority on our left, required for its success that General McCook should be able to hold his position for three hours; that if necessary to recede at all, he should recede as he had advanced on the preceding day, slowly, as steadily, refusing his right, thereby rendering our success certain."

Having thus explained the plan, the General Commanding addressed General McCook as follows:

"To-morrow there will be battle. You know the ground; you have fought over its difficulties. Can you hold your present position for three hours?"

To which General McCook responded: "Yes, I think I can."

The General Commanding then said: "I don't like the facing so much to the east, but must confide that to you, who know the ground. If you don't think your present the best position, change it;" and the officers then returned to their commands.

THE ORDER OF BATTLE IN BRIGADE FRONTS.

The order of battle by divisions, as already described, remained unchanged, but several of the front brigades were relieved, and fell back in reserve. (To designate the transposition of regiments is impossible.) The final order of battle, by brigades from right to left, was as follows:

On the extreme right, Second Division (Right Wing), Willich's brigade, and Kirk's in front, Colonel Baldwin's in reserve. First Division — First Brigade, Colonel P. Sydney Post; Second Brigade, Colonel W. P. Carlin; Third Brigade, Colonel W. E. Woodruff. Third Division—First Brigade, Brigadier General Sill; Second Brigade, Colonel F. Shaefer; Third Brigade, Colonel G. W. Roberts.

Center.—Second Division—Second Brigade, Colonel T. R. Stanley; Third Brigade, Colonel J. F. Miller.

Left Wing.—Second Division—First Brigade, Brigadier General Cruft; Second Brigade, Colonel W. B. Hazen; Third Brigade, Colonel W. Grose (in reserve). First Division—Second Brigade, Colonel George D. Wagner; Third Brigade, Colonel Charles G. Harker; Fourth Brigade, Brigadier General Miles S. Hascall. The First Division, General Van Cleve, in reserve. The artillery, generally, was posted upon the brigade flanks, with a strong reserve in the Center. Rousseau's division was in reserve; Walker's brigade was posted at Stewartsboro to protect communications, and Starkweather's brigade remained on the Jefferson pike. The cavalry were posted on either flank of the army, with a reserve in the rear of the Center. The Pioneer Brigade was preparing fords in Stone River on the left.

ADDRESS TO THE ARMY.

Before seeking repose to prepare him for the great duties of the morrow, General Rosecrans directed the following address to the soldiers of the Army of the Cumberland:

HEADQUARTERS DEPARTMENT OF THE CUMBERLAND,
In Front of Murfreesboro, *December* 31, 1862.

ORDERS.

The General Commanding desires to say to the soldiers of the Army of the Cumberland, that he was well pleased with their conduct yesterday. It was all that he could have wished for. He neither saw nor heard of any skulking. They behaved with the coolness and gallantry of veterans. He now feels perfectly confident, with God's grace and their help, of striking this day a blow for the country the most crushing, perhaps, which the rebellion has yet sustained. Soldiers! the eyes of the whole nation are upon you; the very fate of the nation may be said to hang on the issues of this day's battle. Be true, then, to yourselves, true to your own manly character and soldierly reputation; true to the love of your dear ones at home, whose prayers ascend this day to God for your success. Be cool. I need not ask you to be brave. Keep ranks. Do not throw away your fire. Fire slowly, deliberately—above all, fire low, and be always sure of your aim. Close readily in upon the enemy, and when you get within charging distance, rush upon him with the bayonet. Do this, and victory will certainly be your's. Recollect that there are hardly any troops in the world that will stand a bayonet charge, and that those who make it, therefore, are sure to win. By command of

MAJOR GENERAL ROSECRANS.

J. P. GARESCHE, *A. A. G. and Chief of Staff.*

But four brigades of that splendid host had opportunity to hear it. The shock of battle was felt before the ink with which it was penned was fairly dry.

THE EVE OF BATTLE.

The eve of battle was dreary. It had rained nearly all day, and the atmosphere was humid. A blustering wind swept coldly from the North, whistling dismally through the forests. Our brave soldiers, saturated to the skin, lay upon the bleak wet soil enveloped in damp blankets, unprotected by canopy save the mottled sky. They were weary with marching, and fighting, and standing at arms, and notwithstanding their comfortless couches, the multitudes who were not on guard fell easily to sleep. But few bivouac fires blazed through the darkness, and only a solitary bugle broke night's stillness at tattoo. Alas, too many slept that night who slumber no more in life. The sad soil upon which they reposed was made sadder before the morrow night by the warm blood which swelled from their bounding hearts. Battle would thunder upon that field at sunrise of the last day of the departing year.

The General and staff were crowded into less than one-third the usual allowance of tents. All superfluous bedding and baggage had been left behind. Most of the staff had blankets, and those not on duty rolled up in them early, and sought repose. Garesché Goddard, Thompson, Thoms, and Bond remained faithfully with the General most of the night. Garesché was always at his elbow, faithful as a shadow, until death chose him for his own. The General's mind—active, vigorous, and restless—inquired into every detail. In the absence of exact information from any quarter, couriers were instantly dispatched to satisfy inquiry. Each General in command was required to observe closely, and report explicitly, the most minute information. The deportment of the General Commanding, all that day and that night, was an absorbing study.

CHAPTER XXIV.

THE 31st of December, 1862—Prayer before Battle—The Left Ordered to Swing—"It is, it is the Cannon's Opening Roar!"—Din of Battle on the Right—Evil Tidings—Panic—Anxiety at Headquarters—Incredible Reports—Firmness of General Rosecrans—The Plan of Battle Defeated—The General Mounts and Gallops to the Front—Batteries Open upon Him—They are Silenced by Barnet—The Field—Sherridan Debouches from the Forest—The Day going against us—New Line Formed—Batteries Massed in the Center—The General Commanding leads a Charge—The Enemy Repulsed—The Tide of Battle turns—St. Clair Morton and the Pioneer Brigade—Night.

MORNING of the last day of the old year dawned brightly. A thin mist floated along the channel of Stone River, but otherwise the horizon was clear. When the outlines of a familiar face were but barely recognizable in the uncertain haze of early morning, the General Commanding, cheerful and refreshed, appeared at the eye of each tent and roused the still slumbering members of the staff. But long before, the soldiers stood at arms and waited the opening of battle. Every charger was equipped for mounting. Minutes rolled away and there was yet no uproar.

PRAYER BEFORE BATTLE.

A little later the dauntless leader of that army knelt at the altar and prayed to the God of battles. High Mass was celebrated in a little tent opposite his marquee. Rev. Father Cooney, the zealous Chaplain of the Thirty-Fifth regiment of Indiana Volunteers, officiated, assisted by Rev. Father Trecy, the constant spiritual companion of the General, and whose fidelity to his Chief was second only to his devotion to the faith he preached. General Rosecrans knelt humbly in the corner of his tent, Garesché, no less devout, by his side; a trio of humble soldiers meekly knelt in front of the tent; groups of officers, booted and spurred for battle, with heads reverentially uncovered, stood outside and mutely muttered their prayers. What grave anxieties, what exquisite emotions, what deep thoughts moved the hearts and minds of those pious soldiers, into whose keeping God and their country had delivered, not merely the lives of thousands of men who must die at last, but the vitality of a principle—the cause of self-government and of human liberty!

THE LEFT ORDERED TO SWING.

Breakfast was hurried. General Crittenden reported in person. The General Commanding walked with him to his quarters where General Wood, suffering from indisposition, was resting briefly before battle. Wood was really unfit for duty, but refused to quit the field. General Van Cleve's division, in pursuance of the plan of battle, was already moving to cross Stone River to sweep into Murfreesboro, while McCook held the enemy on the left. Part of it had already crossed. General Rosecrans directed Wood to cross Stone River in front of his division by brigades. Harker was to move in front, Hascall to follow, Wagner's brigade last. Wood himself rode to the front to examine the ground. Before him, on the southern and eastern side, there was a long timbered ridge within a few hundred yards of the stream, and the enemy seemed posted there in force. Some firing had then been heard on the right, but not enough to indicate battle.

"IT IS, IT IS THE CANNON'S OPENING ROAR."

Officers of the staff were grouped about little fires in the avenue between the tents. They were clad in overcoats, for it was chill. The General Commanding, Garesché, and General Crittenden stood near the marquee conversing eagerly. It was nearly seven o'clock. Suddenly all hearts were thrilled by a sound sweeping from the right like a strong wind soughing through a forest. Now a deep reverberation like thunder rolling in a distant cloud. Directly a prolonged, fierce, crepitating noise, like a cane-brake on fire. Ears that once hear that appalling sound never forget it. Days afterward the rattle and rumble of a wagon will startle and thrill you.

PANIC.

The din of battle swelled rapidly. Its volume increased, and it seemed sweeping "nearer, clearer, deadlier than before." It could not be! This must be hallucination! It can not be disaster! No tidings yet! Wiles and a comrade were sent to the right to observe and report. They galloped across the field and plunged into the forests. Directly a tide of fugitives poured out of the thickets—negroes, teamsters, and some soldiers. You have seen cinders from burning buildings flying when the conflagration was invisible. You could hear the roaring flames and crackling beams. Seeing the cinders you would say, "there is a fire." You have observed broken twigs and leaves whirling in the air when there was a roar of mighty winds in the forests. You had not yet felt the blast, but its avant couriers were unmistakable. You said, "a tornado is coming." There was a conflagration, a tornado, now rushing through the forests in front, raging forward with vengeful fury. These teamsters, negroes, soldiers, flying before it were cinders, twigs, leaves, fugitives from the flames and tornado of battle.

"What is the matter? Why do you run?" Many push on heedless of stern questioning. A cocked pistol brings a squad to a halt. "We are beaten! The Right Wing is broken! The rebel cavalry is charging the rear! The enemy is sweeping everything before them! General Sill is killed! Edgarton's Battery and part of Goodspeed's are captured!" Incredible! But few soldiers, thank God! in that panic-stricken mob, and most of them cling to their muskets. The negroes, poor souls, had cause for fright. The enemy murdered them as if they were beasts of prey. Wiles gallops back to report. His comrade moves on further, and meets straggling multitudes. The awful uproar increases and stretches swiftly now to the left. Bullets are clipping the twigs overhead and chipping the bark from trees. Heavy drops which precede a thunder storm seem to be dropping on the dead leaves.

ANXIETY AT HEADQUARTERS.

At headquarters the groups have gathered into a cluster. They are talking in low, eager tones; their eyes searchingly peering into the mysteries of the dreadful forest. The Chief stalks through the avenue, disturbed, obviously. It does not seem to him nor to any that McCook is contesting that ground "inch by inch." But sound is elusive. Minutes that seemed hours rolled away. Suspense was horrible. As yet only reports that the woods are swarming with fugitives. Who will credit stragglers against the reliance men have in good soldiers? McCook is an approved good soldier. The army has no better Generals than his—Johnson, Davis, Sherridan, Willich, Kirk, Carlin, Sill, Shaeffer, Roberts. The soldiers of the Right Wing are veterans of Shiloh and Chaplin Hills; some had met the enemy in Western Virginia, some at bloody Pea Ridge, and had never turned their faces from foe.

Garesché had sent Otis to the right to watch rebel cavalry, concerning which there had been rumors. Lieutenant Baker gallops back from Otis with tidings. "The Right Wing is broken, and the enemy is driving it back." Incredible! McCook is surely falling back with an object. "All right—never mind—we will rectify it," said the General cheerfully. Stragglers were overflowing the plain and the Murfreesboro pike like a freshet, within an hour—oh, horrible hour—from the opening of battle. A staff officer from McCook confirms evil rumors. McCook needs assistance. "Tell General McCook," said the Chief vehemently, "to contest every inch of ground. If he holds them we will swing into Murfreesboro with our left, and cut them off." Then to his staff, "It is working right." Alas, it was not "working right." "Every inch of ground" was not contested. He was not yet advised of the rout of Willich's and Kirk's brigades, nor of the rapid withdrawal of Davis' division, necessitated thereby. "Moreover," he said, "having supposed McCook's Wing posted more compactly and his right more refused than it really was, the direction of the noise of battle did not indicate to me the true state of affairs."

The reported death of Sill was confirmed. "We can not help it; brave men must be killed in battle," said the General impatiently. "General Kirk is wounded and disabled; Willich killed or captured." "Never mind," persisted the inflexible leader, "we must win this battle."

Battle was flowing along the line, communicating first with the Center, then the Left. The frightful delusion was dissipated. The enemy were pressing McCook swiftly and in disorder clean back upon the Center. Negley was already engaged. An aid from McCook advises that Rousseau had better be held in hand. What! Reserves so soon! "Tell General McCook I will help him," was the instant reply, and Rousseau marched at double-quick into the cedar-brakes on Negley's right, to brace up Sherridan, and stand as a break-water before the torrent that was engulfing the army. It was full time.

The plan of battle is crippled. The Right Wing fails to hold Hardee "three hours"—nay, an hour, on its right. Therefore the Left Wing can not swing into Murfreesboro and cut them off. A third of the Left Wing is absolutely necessary to save the Right from annihilation. Van Cleve is already crossing the river to swing the left into Murfreesboro. Harker is moving in the same direction; Hascall and Wagner ready to follow. Wood bears an order to halt. Said Hascall, "the most terrible state of suspense pervaded the entire Left as it became more and more evident that the Right Wing was being driven rapidly back upon us." Wagner is on the extreme left of the army. Harker finds cover on a little crest behind some shocks of corn in the open field. Hascall waits developments. Wood directs Wagner to "hold his position to the last." Everything depends upon it. Wagner is reliable. No danger there. An order goes to Van Cleve to double-quick a brigade to the right. Rich Mountain Beatty thunders across the field and forms west of the turnpike. Fyffe follows rapidly to form on his right. It is not yet eight o'clock. The battle is all against us.

GENERAL ROSECRANS TO THE FIELD.

The General Commanding comprehended the dire extent of the calamity. He gathers about him all his faculties, and threw his own weighty sword into the scale of battle. Henceforth he consulted no one, asked no man's opinion, trusted in God, and relied upon himself. It was now a series of commands too often delivered in person to superior or subaltern, it mattered not, while his staff galloped at his heels in mute anxiety lest he should fall. Dispatching an order to McCook, he moved suddenly to horse, and curtly commanded, "Mount, gentlemen!"

A battery had already opened in range with headquarters at one of Mendenhall's Batteries, which was in position in front of the grove on the cemetery knoll. The ordnance train endangered was rumbling from right to left, balking upon the railroad. Hastening its movement, the General pressed through the obstruction and leaped across the railroad, halting briefly for observation. The enemy's shells were crashing among our own batteries a few feet to the right, and they were thundering in reply. Wood was discovered on the left of the railroad near a clump of trees waiting orders. Harker was descried down in the cornfield.

Just now a flight of bullets pict-pict-pict-pict slipped through the staff and escort. A poor orderly toppled gently from his saddle, reeled over the side, and plunged headlong to the earth. One convulsive shudder and he was dead. The General might have reached the dead soldier with his sword. The fatal missile made no premonitory sign. You simply heard "thud," and saw a soldier die. The dead man's bridle fingers still clung to the rein. A comrade dismounted and loosed his grasp rudely with his foot. His faithful grey stood quietly waiting for the corpse to mount. Another bullet stung Benton's beautiful chestnut. The spirited colt, smarting with agony, struck violently with his feet at his invisible tormentor. Benton dismounted to see him die, but soon remounted and galloped his gay chestnut all through that fiery day. Hubbard's horse was struck in the neck, and several others of the escort wounded. A blue haze of smoke had now spread all over the field. The valleys were enveloped in battle clouds, and the woods seemed consuming with invisible fire. Indeed,

"There's a cloud in the sky,
A cloud in the glen,
But one is of nature,
The other's of men."

A shell struck near and spattered the mud in a shower over a dozen horsemen. The Chief dashed toward Wood, who rode out eagerly and saluted. He was to send Harker across the pike to Beatty's right. Seeing Hascall soon, he ordered him to the right of Harker to readjust the line of battle. Then he thundered down across Harker's left, and wheeled to the right, to ride up the front line of battle. He gave Harker orders in person. Harker was already moving in column by the right flank at double-quick. There was serious business in hand, but the gallant fellow really seemed desirous to show the Chief how compactly he could move his noble brigade under fire. Every member of the General Staff, a troop of horse, and a dozen orderlies, followed the Chief—a conspicuous target on such a field. Taylor, Simmons, Skinner, Wiles, Father Trecy, Chief Quartermaster, Chief Commissary, Judge Advocate, Provost Marshal General, and Priest respectively—what should they do there, galloping madly through the wild revels of a battlefield? Did they not seem out of place? But it was so all day long. Kniffin, Chief Commissary to Crittenden, also made a risky dash with them before he joined his own Chief. As they galloped across Harker's late front, a terrific tempest of solid shot and shell danced around their heels, whizzed over their heads, bounded under their horses, flushed in front of them, and a few wicked missiles sped through the midst of them. Every man, save the leader, ducked his head clean to the saddle bow. One shot gutted a gap through Harker's column. The hideous rent was visible an instant; then it was healed; but the column was shorn of four men. It was not even shaken. A frantic horse galloped riderless over the field, leaving his master mangled. In the rage of conflict the human heart expresses little sympathy for human woe. Your best friend is lifted from his saddle by the fatal shaft, and plunges wildly to the earth—a corpse. One convulsive leap of your heart, you dash onward over the stormy field, and the dead is forgotten until the furious frenzy of battle is spent. After battle! O, reader! the mind furnishes no language befitting the anguish of the soul when we drag from the bloody mass the mutilated and disfigured forms of those we love. Battle is then frightful delirium—a superlative horror!

But the tumult raged fiercely. "Barnet," shouted the General to his Chief of Artillery, "silence that battery." "Yes, sir." Barnet, cool and imperturbable, brought up the first battery he found. The commander of the pieces was wheeling into an unfavorable position. "On the crest! on the crest!" shouted the General, pointing to the best position in view, and on the crest went the guns. Then the General dashed along the front of the left under the fire of musketry and artillery, until he halted on the turnpike within full view of the "Burnt House." A storm of musket balls and shells spattered and whizzed about the column, but marvelously, not a man was hit. The flocks of shells sounded like the flutter of quails' wings. A round shot flew over the staff, struck a horse a hundred yards beyond, and tore him to pieces. It must have knocked him a rod. Strange to say, his rider escaped. He gathered himself out of the mud and limped to cover. A little further onward, a shell struck a soldier and splashed him out of battle. The rattle of musketry and thunder of cannon was deafening. But the General charged through the deathly storm as if it had been no more than hail. It was wonderful that he escaped.

Pursuing his swift career toward the right, and directly behind the line of battle, while bullets and artillery charges hurtled in the atmosphere, his eye gathered the features of the field rapidly, and his mind directed dispositions to stop the torrent which was well nigh overwhelming. No complaint escaped him. That was no moment for reproach. But it was obvious that he was profoundly moved. His florid face had paled and lost its ruddy luster, but his eyes blazed with sullen fire. His lips were firmly compressed, and his stern manner disclosed that his heart was undaunted. One moment's hesitation or vascillation now, and all were lost. Human tongue nor pen can describe the yearning anxiety of those who rode with him in that mad maelstrom of death. Thank God, he was firm as iron and fixed as fate. Clearly, he did not deem the battle lost. Now he was on the verge of the forest filled with friends and foes—friends unavailingly fighting, foes rushing onward with fierce yells of triumph. Gallant and quiet Sherridan debouched from the tangled forest at the head of his compact column, out of ammunition, but unbroken. Negley was in the thick darkness with the noble Eighth Division, beating back the relentless tide. Johnson appeared, too, with the remnant of his crumbled command. Rousseau was sent into the fiery cauldron to extricate his struggling division comrade. The Regulars—trusty and heroic, were contending stoutly, but receding slowly before the infernal torrent, until they could brace themselves upon Guenther's and Loomis' guns. Pointing to his solid column sadly, but with true soldier's pride, said faithful Sherridan, "Here is all that are left, General." The General Commanding, himself directed Sherridan where to find ammunition. The Second and Fifteenth Missouri had already replenished their cartridge-boxes, and now they plunged to the front again under brave Shaeffer, and fought the enemy with unflinching firmness.

The day was going against us. The enemy were streaming through the woods a few hundred yards on the right front. They were swarming in savage multitudes at every point. Our batteries were thundering across the plains with frightful vehemence, wheeling into position and firing at the populous forests with terrific rapidity. The enemy poured shot and shell into our receding columns with remorseless vigor, and there appeared to be clusters of sharpshooters in almost every tree. Racing swiftly back now, the General and staff again became a conspicuous target. A flight of Minie balls slitted through the troop. One of them struck Garesché's gay black in the nose. The spirited animal flung his head scornfully at the sting, scattering blood upon his rider. "Ah, hit! Garesché?" quoth the General—his mind for the first instant, and only that instant, relieved from its painful tension. "My horse," was the laconic response, and the gallant rider, whose proud deportment had excited the admiration of the army, spurred onward at the side of his Chief. A drop of blood, fiercely flung away by the wounded horse, crimsoned the cheek of the General, and an hour later it gave rise to exquisite apprehensions.

Some who saw it, fancied it was his own blood, and spread the report that he was wounded. The rumor reached officers of the staff who were away executing orders. They ransacked the field and the hospitals to find him. After an hour's torment, they discovered him, unscathed and inflexible, in the forefront of battle. Expostulation with him was vain. He sternly replied, "This battle must be won."

The Right Wing was broken and driven back. It was almost doubled backward upon the left. Johnson's line had crumbled, but his soldiers had fought desperately. Davis had withdrawn, bearing back his banners. Sherridan had swung back, contesting his ground "inch by inch," until relieved by Rousseau, and until his ammunition was exhausted, then marched out in close column, with colors flying. Eleven guns of the Second Division of the right—all of Edgarton's, three of Goodspeed's, and two of Simonson's—after the horses were killed, had been captured, with Houghtaling's six from the Third Division—eighty horses of which were killed. Hundreds of men were slain or wounded, and nearly two thousand were captured. Negley, unprotected on his right, was fighting an overwhelming enemy on three sides of him, and he was holding them stubbornly. Rousseau was receding; and still the great Chieftain of that battle, with sublime defiance of disaster, said: "We shall beat them yet."

THE BATTERIES ARE MASSED IN THE CENTER.

Now galloping to the crest of the hill (for there was but one elevation like a hill on the left), the General Commanding, still in the flame of conflict (for on that field there was no security but in God's providence), massed his batteries on its crown, and swept the forests with an awful volume of shell and cannister. Soldiers of the Right Wing were streaming back through the forests in disorder. The gleaming steel of the hotly pursuing foe flashed in the glowing sunlight through vistas of the woods. Through a gap of timber opening into a cornfield beyond, masses of somber-looking foes moving down hill, long lines of heads and glittering musket tubes, rising one above another in terraces, were rolling onward in seemingly resistless force. But a new line had been formed to meet them. The right *had* faced eastwardly. Part of the left had been hurled across the plain from Stone River. Van Cleve's division and Harker's brigade, with Rousseau's reserves, had formed the new line, which faced westward. It was almost "about face" from the original position.

"NOW LET THE WHOLE LINE CHARGE."

The new change in the order of battle was executed by the General Commanding at incessant personal hazard. There was not a private soldier in the army so much exposed. There was hardly a point in the front of battle which he had not inspected—Wood's line, perhaps, excepted. Some five or six batteries, posted upon the bluff under his personal direction, now thundered in direful accord. Solid shot, shell, grape, cannister, were crashing through the brittle timber in destructive tumult. A thick canopy of smoke hovered over the field. Clouds of smoke enveloped the gunners. They seemed like demons reveling in infernal orgies. With his staff gathered about him, the Chief halted briefly upon the cemetery knoll, watching the play of the batteries and the hot fury of Sam Beatty's infantry. Now, without a word, he plunged headlong into the tempest, his staff and orderlies following with wild enthusiasm. The enemy had tipped over the crest of the last ridge in front, and were bearing down fiercely. Spurring up to the very heels of Beatty's men, until his steed almost trampled them, he shouted cheerily, "Now let the whole line charge! Shoot low! Be *sure!* Then charge home!" Bitterly whistled the leaden hail. The chips and twigs flew from the trees as if thousands were hacking them. A soldier falls, with a shudder, under the feet of the General's horse. The staff and orderlies fling themselves along the line, hats in hand and swords drawn, cheering the men, who respond with a shrill clamor that leaps like lightning from rank to rank, and thrills along the lines until lost in distance. O! it was a wild, passionate moment. The troops spring to their feet and push up the slope; the forests are riven with the tempest; bayonets gleam; lurid flames spout from the long line of muskets. Yon savage line of gray and steel, which but a moment since plunged so madly over the hill, halts! It wavers! Another tempest from the blue line in front—they reel, they stagger—"There they go!" shouted the gallant leader; "there they go! Now drive them home!" Away they fly over the hill, shattered, disordered, broken, struggling to escape. Great God, what tumult in the brain! Sense reels with the intoxicating frenzy. Shot and shell pursue the frightened fugitives, shrieking through the forests, crashing the flimsy branches, scattering death and dismay wherever they strike. There was a line of dead blue-coats where that charge was so gallantly made, but the forms of mangled foes were thickly strewn upon that bloody slope.

THE SPECTACLE.

The glory of the shout that now went up, is a recollection to be treasured forever. Hearts that thrilled with its rapture, will ever throb tumultuously when memory recalls it. And such a spectacle! That gallant leader, dauntless, and upright in saddle, with countenance inspired—such light of battle in his features as fairly blazed—unmoved by the death terror around him, pursuing, with calm determination, the one thought of success. The ardor of that gallant line which so splendidly turned the sweeping tide of battle; the lurid, malicious blaze and furious stream of sparkling fire viciously emitting from thousands of trusty muskets; the blue haze of smoke eddying in circling currents, and spreading an azure shade among the thick branches of those funereal cedars; the fierce rattle of rifle volleys; the deafening uproar of more than fifty cannons working, with awful destructiveness, in a canopy of smoke which obscured the batteries and magnified the gunners into great shadows—O! who that was in it can ever forget?

When the pale faces which came out of that furious storm flushed again, and when hearts had ceased their wild flutter, it almost seemed as if men had been born again. "Oh, wasn't that glorious, old fellow?" quoth gallant Skinner, laying his palm affectionately upon the shoulder of his equally youthful friend Kirby—as brave and staunch a soldier as ever carried bullet and shattered arm from a battle-field. Reader, no human language can describe the convulsing charms of a charge in battle. It is a frightful ecstacy.

The fiery valor of Garesché, in that dread carnival, would have inspired a coward with courage. Gay as a youth of twenty, with hat jauntily cocked on his fine head, he seemed, upon his lithe and spirited black steed, a perfect transformation. Usually grave and saturnine, with an habitual calmness almost provoking, he looked in the fury of the fray as if his soul had broken into a new stream of existence. When he dashed into the charge, his sword flew from the scabbard and glittered in the sunlight. When the enemy fled over the hill, he glanced at them with a smile of triumph, and rammed his blade back into its scabbard with a force that made the steel ring again. Yesterday some had felt a thrill of anxiety for him. He deported himself like one who had premonition of sudden death. Always deeply pious, conscientious in attention to religious duties, prayerful, there was something peculiarly striking in the absorbing attention with which he poured himself into his little prayer-book, as he sat in a quiet fence corner on Tuesday, awaiting the culmination of martial events. All this day of battle, through a hundred death currents, he had swept gaily over the field. But his General's charge was his climax. Alas, an hour or two more of life, and he was a victim for the little graveyard upon which he had slept but the night before. Always by his General's side in life, death struck him there at last.

Further upon the right, too, there was a struggle. The shock of collision thrilled along the whole line.

Fyffe, then Harker, were standing up stoutly—now receding, now charging the foe; but at last, when the "General Commanding led a charge in person, and drove the foe pell-mell into the forest," Fyffe and Harker, with mighty effort, rolled back the avalanche from their front, and joined in the pæan of victory.

ST. CLAIR MORTON'S PIONEERS.

But the foe was not yet gone. He was advancing from the Right to the junction of the Left and Center. He was yet driven only from the extreme right. There was a valley to the left of Beatty's line, partly open, through which one of our broken columns was retiring disordered before the enemy. The new Right was advancing steadily. The batteries were ordered forward. Stokes' Chicago Board of Trade Battery was on a knoll nearest the critical point of danger. At a gesture from the General, it thundered down the slope and struggled manfully across a heavy field to another little crest, from whence another battery had been driven. Three mangled horses struggled there under a shattered caisson—tangled in harness, with broken limbs, bleeding, and one of them moaning with agony piteous as that of a human being. Bullets were whistling fiercely, but the spirit of that battle was pulsating for victory. General Rosecrans again plunged into the breach, urging the battery to follow, and by his own dauntless example checked the disorder of the retiring brigade. Garesché and St. Clair Morton were by his side. Morton commanded a picked battalion of pioneers. It was necessary to bring even them into the fight, as every soldier on that field was carried in that desperate day.

"Support the battery, Morton." "Aye, aye, sir;" and the pioneers deployed right and left, and opened a vicious fire. Morton's fine face glowed with excitement. The battery got into position, and opened with telling effect, but the pioneers had already sent the rebels howling back up the valley and into the woods. Morton looked as if he was delighted all over. "We're doing it about right now, General, ain't we? Can't I do something more, General?" said he, with a charming simplicity. It was a mystery that all were not torn to pieces.

During this furious encounter, Colonel Garesché, accompanied by Lieutenant Byron Kirby, Aid to General Rosecrans, galloped through a withering fire to carry an order to General Van Cleve, who, though wounded, was resisting a renewed attack. While riding across the field, there occurred one of those chivalric episodes which are sometimes celebrated in romance. A ball disabled Garesché's horse. Kirby dismounted, and insisted that Garesché should mount his horse. Mutually forgetful of the storm of battle, they disputed a point of controversy. Kirby finally prevailed on the score of duty, and walked back over the field until he found the staff. Not much later a Minie ball struck the brave soldier's left arm, and shot him clean out of his saddle. The bone was shattered, and he was compelled to quit the field. No bolder or more modest soldier ever drew bright blade. He nobly earned promotion. But Kirby belongs to the Regular Army—that step-child of the nation, which, though smarting at the injustice that pursues it, says, with splendid eloquence, "If we can't win honors, we'll do more—we'll deserve them;" and Kirby remembers that the country sometimes forgets its step-children.

Rousseau's division had also moved into the woods on the left and struggled out. Negley, after Sherridan had withdrawn, subjected to murderous cross-fire of artillery and musketry, had also fallen back, and was replenishing his ammunition. Grose was fighting vehemently to protect the rear of Palmer from masses swarming around his right, while troops in his other brigades were falling by hundreds in front. Wagner had repelled an assault upon his position, and Hascall went to the assistance of devoted Hazen. Crittenden was in front, watching his steady Left. Thomas calmly directed the Center, and their omnipresent Chief, now directing the Right, then glancing at the Left, was gathering together his legions for the trial which would determine victory.

Perhaps it was now eleven o'clock—a little earlier, a little later, no matter—when the first act of the sanguinary drama was concluded. There was a lull in the storm. Where would it break next? Certainly the enemy were preparing for a new assault. Rosecrans could not now take the initiative. The Right had not yet recovered from its shock. The enemy were feinting away off on the Right. General Rosecrans divined that the onset would fall upon the Left, and he was preparing for it.

The reader will now return to the opening of the battle, and follow the disaster through its unbroken series, until the rainbow of hope was clearly visible.

CHAPTER XXV.

PRAGUE upon Austerlitz—The Onset of the Rebels—The columns of Attack—Gallant Kirk Overpowered—Edgarton's Battery Swallowed up—Willich Unhorsed and Captured—His Brigade Pulverized—Noble Struggle of General Davis' Division—Woodruff Retires, then Post, and then Carlin—Splendid Resistance of Sherridan—Death of General Sill—Reported Repulse of the Enemy—Roberts Charges and Falls—The Missourians at Bay with Empty Muskets—The Right Wing Reaches Support.

IT was never said by him, but Rosecrans' plan of battle was the plan of Austerlitz. Bragg hurled Prague upon Austerlitz and defeated it. Rosecrans recoiled upon Prague with his own trusty sword and was victorious. But Austerlitz was simple, and should have been crushingly successful. Could not fifteen thousand veterans resist double their number "three hours?" How was it?

"At six o'clock and twenty-two minutes on the morning of the 31st," said General Johnson, "the outposts in front of my division were driven in by an overwhelming force of infantry." "The enemy," said General Rosecrans, "advanced in heavy columns, regimental front, his left attacking Willich's and Kirk's brigades, of Johnson's division, which, being disposed—thin and light, without support—were, after a sharp but fruitless contest, crumbled to pieces and driven back, leaving Edgarton's and part of Goodspeed's battery in the hands of the enemy.

"The enemy following up, attacked Davis' division, and speedily dislodged Post's brigade. Carlin's brigade was compelled to follow, as Woodruff's brigade, from the weight of testimony, had previously left its position on his left. Johnson's brigade, in retiring, inclined too far to the west, and were too much scattered to make a combined resistance, though they fought bravely at one or two points before reaching Wilkinson's pike. The reserve brigade of Johnson's division, advancing from its bivouac near Wilkinson's pike toward the right, took a good position and made a gallant but ineffectual stand, as the whole rebel Left was moving up on the ground abandoned by our troops.

"Within an hour from the time of the opening of the battle, a staff officer from General McCook arrived, announcing to me that the Right Wing was heavily pressed, and needed assistance; but I was not advised of the rout of Willich's and Kirby's brigades, nor of the rapid withdrawal of Davis' division, necessitated thereby."

The Right Wing was flung back upon the Left with a violence which shattered it into fragments. Part of it withdrew into the open ground near the Murfreesboro pike behind the Center; part escaped to the pike a half mile further in the rear; another fraction had flared away off to the right, and made a wide detour to get back into line.

KIRK AND WILLICH.

Kirk first felt the shock. Willich's brigade recoiled under it almost immediately, and Baldwin in reserve came up under Johnson's own eye to brace the staggering front. Willich was on the extreme right, refused to protect the flank, and forming a crotchet. Kirk's brigade joined Willich's on the left, fronting the enemy's line of battle, and facing east. Baldwin's reserve brigade was eight hundred yards in the rear, near the headquarters of McCook and Johnson. Edgarton's Battery was posted near the angle formed by the junction of Kirk's right and Willich's left, with a narrow cleared field in front.

Kirk's line covered the Franklin road, which runs due east and west, and there was a lane behind him tracing north and south, intersecting the road. The ground behind him was undulating, open, and obstructed by fences. The enemy's left overlapped the right division, and was almost oblique to it. Their flank was covered by a powerful force of cavalry. Willich's brigade had rolling, partially open ground, and fences in its rear.

At three o'clock in the morning, by order of General Willich, Colonel Jones, of the Thirty-Ninth Indiana, patroled six hundred yards in front of the picket line, and reported that there were no indications of movement in front. General Kirk inspected his own picket lines at the same hour, and found all quiet in front. General Sill, at two o'clock in the morning, reported to General Sherridan that there was great activity immediately in *his* front. This was the narrowest part of the valley, and General Sherridan, fearing an attack at that point, posted two regiments of the reserve within short supporting distance of Sill. But at five o'clock in the morning the whole Right Wing was under arms, and were prepared for the enemy. They stood there over an hour and discovered no signs of movement in front. Captain Edgarton, however, imprudently permitted some of his battery horses to go to water. At dawn the right brigade received orders to build fires and make coffee. General Willich soon afterward turned over the command temporarily to Colonel W. H. Gibson, of the Forty-Ninth Ohio Volunteers, while he repaired to General Johnson's headquarters, giving directions respecting the troops in case of an attack during his temporary absence. He had been gone but a few moments when firing was heard in front of Kirk's right, at the angle of the crotchet. Willich's brigade seized their arms instantly. The enemy appeared in enormous masses. Colonel Gibson sent for Willich, who galloped back to his command. His horse was killed, and he was a captive before he gave an order! The calamity was swift.

THE ATTACK UPON KIRK.

The enemy were descried in the fields by General Kirk a half mile from his front. They advanced in four columns, regimental front, with powerful reserves in mass. "They moved up steadily," said Kirk, "in good order, without music or noise of any kind. They had no artillery in sight." They poured across the valley in mighty force, swept away the strong lines of skirmishers as if they had been cobwebs, and fell upon Kirk's lines like wild beasts. The Thirty-Fourth Illinois, which had been sent forward to check them, closed with a crash in almost hand to hand conflict with them, fighting with magnificent fury.

> "Alas, in vain, ye gallant few,
> From rank to rank your vollied thunder flew."

The contest was hopeless; the gallant regiment sternly resisting, fell away, and the storm struck the line and shook it from center to its flanks. The rebels recoiled under the first terrific volley, but gathering head, they rolled onward again with resistless momentum. Edgarton's Battery was swallowed up; he down under his guns wounded, his men fighting with their swabs until they were bayoneted or captured. Brave Edgarton had fired but three rounds, says one report; eight guns says another.

It matters not which brigade first gave way. Both were soon broken. Lightning struck the crotchet they formed, ran along both fronts, and involved them in common ruin. Kirk was soon flanked. His four brave regiments were well nigh cut to pieces. He had sent to Willich for support. Willich was gone. His brigade was struggling for self-preservation. The rebel cavalry was careering and surging upon their right. Servants and teamsters were flying over the field. Colonel Baldwin had quickly taken arms, and General Johnson threw the regiments into line of battle supporting the struggling front. The First Ohio, commanded by Major Stafford, Sixth Indiana, Lieutenant Colonel Tripp, Thirtieth Indiana, Colonel Dodge and Lieutenant Colonel Hurd, and the Louisville Legion, Colonel Berry, made a good, strong, bracing front. The Ninety-Third Ohio, Colonel Charles Anderson, was retained in reserve in a wood. As Kirk and Willich were driven back they flared off to the right, and left Davis' right exposed. Baldwin's reserve felt the shock speedily. Goodspeed's remaining four guns—for two had been taken—under Lieutenant Belding, and Simonson's Battery, fired sharply and quickly into the advancing masses. Baldwin opened a biting fire which eat deeply into the front rank of the undaunted rebels. But they spread over the field like a freshet, and gathered in clouds on the front and flanks. A minute more and Baldwin's command will be captives. They, too, withdraw, catching their heels a moment on a crest, turn to resist. The pursuit is too vigorous, and they again recede until they brace upon Rousseau, where they make another stand—all that remains of them.

McCook is cool but distressed. There is no hope for him now but to save all he can. O! that his line had been shorter and heavier. With Davis and Sheridan in front, and Johnson's heroes of Shiloh to support them, he could have "whipped my friend Hardee." Davis is now enveloped, but Kirk, wounded almost at the first fire, and dismounted twice, is yet in the field. He forms a new line in a skirt of woods at right angles with his original position. Gallant Reed races up from the wagon train with his Seventy-Ninth Illinois, and adds new vigor to Kirk's now almost nerveless arm. Kirk sinks at last, and is borne from the field. Colonel Dodge assumes command. Then Reed nobly falls, cheering his heroes. Houssam, of the Pennsylvania Seventy-Seventh, charges splendidly, recaptured Edgarton's guns, then, alas! he goes down, too, mortally hurt, and the enemy recovers the battery, and keep it. Van Tassel, Major of the splendid Illinois Thirty-Fourth, is sorely wounded. Captain Rose—there is no field officer remaining now—fights the Pennsylvania Seventy-Seventh most gallantly, but in vain. Soldiers and officers fighting desperately, fall by scores. A colonel commands a regiment at one instant, now a captain, at last an adjutant. Sergeants and corporals lead companies, until companies melt away with passing bullets. The brigadier is gone; two colonels are dead; other field officers are bleeding and exhausted; Dodge remains to command. Ten guns are gone now, another soon follows. The right division is routed. Melancholy satisfaction to know that the rebel General Rains was killed, and that more than man for man had fallen on the other sidė. Kirk was disabled, Willich a prisoner; that proud division is "scattered and peeled." The sting of defeat was more terrible than wounds and death. When Dodge retired the remnant to the Murfreesboro pike, he had "in all," he said, "about five hundred men." But the right brigade!

WILLICH'S BRIGADE.

Gibson, twice dismounted, sees disorder on all sides; gathers the battalions of captured Willich; flings them in pieces at the foe; falls back; careers again with all the fury of desperate courage, wards off the blow of circling cavalry striving to swoop upon him at every instant; gains brief respite; retires, and, Parthian-like, fights as he flies. Drake, Lieutenant Colonel commanding, and Porter, Major of the thrice approved Forty-Ninth Ohio, are prone on the field. The five regiments are almost orphaned—scarcely officers enough left to carry them to the rear—the regiments indeed are all fighting and flying together, with hardly a nominal distinction. Belding, by efforts of almost sublime energy, drags his four guns into position, with wounded and limping horses—his own gallant gunners placing their shoulders to the wheels. There is heroism worthy of history even in the midst of that dreadful carnival of carnage and defeat. At last Gibson and his little host reach a little creek in the rear, and make a final stand. The rebel infantry are beaten back, but Wheeler's cavalry sweep around their flanks. Barely three hundred are left. Destruction stares them in the face. The enemy, horse and foot, are in their midst. Gibson's sword is fiercely demanded. His rank is not apparent. His uniform is war-worn and tattered. But lo! a shout on the flank. With the shout there is a shock—with the shock, rescue. Gallant Otis and his cavalry has saved them.

THE RESERVE.

Early in the morning there were reports of cavalry demonstrations on our right. Garesché had said, "Otis, there is cavalry on our flank—go and look after them." Otis needed no second order. He was panting to show the mettle of his superb fellows—the Fourth Regulars. Gathering six companies in hand, he was soon thundering through the forest, and debouched upon a field. From the start he had been running across the track of straggling fugitives, and at length sent Lieutenant Baker to headquarters with the first confirmation of evil rumors from the Right. Forming his command in column by fours, led by their company commanders, the companies on parallel lines, company distance apart, himself leading the center, Otis looked about like a pugnacious Irishman for a head to hit. Directly, discovering a cloud of mounted gray-backs in the distance, he quickly directed his command to charge, pistol in hand. But said Otis, "Don't you fire a shot until you take each your man by the scalp. Forward—trot!" Away they go gallantly, the ground trembling beneath them. There is a heavy column of gray before them, but no cheek blanches. Each rider gathers his reins firmly. Their eyes flash lightning. The trot bears them swiftly; Otis rises in his saddle and thunders, "Charge!" Now they gallop—away they fly! It is an avalanche. The rebels vainly strive to disperse it by shot and shell. A storm of grape is scattered among those wild riders, but in vain. Their shock falls upon the enemy with terrific momentum. "Horse, rider, and all, in one red burial blent," go down together. Our gallant Long and some of his fellows went down in the tumult, but the glory of the charge made the noble fellows forget their pain. It was a thunderbolt, which rove the enemy from center to flank. A hundred threw up their arms in submission. Many had been killed. Gibson and his three hundred moved swiftly to the rear to fight another day. The gallant Fourth Regulars prepared to charge the battery which had fired upon them, but an order from superior authority called them to another field.

It requires hours to describe battle spasms of a minute's duration. A scattering clatter of musketry, a crash, the thunder of artillery, and it is done. The assault upon and pulverization of the Second Division was a paroxysm. It shocked the army and paralyzed the plan of battle. The tremor thrilled through the whole system, but thank God, it did not paralyze its heart. Return now to

GENERAL DAVIS.

The conflagration ran along Kirk's front, communicated with that of Davis, streamed along Sherridan's, enveloped Negley's, blazed in the face of Rousseau, rolled against Cruft and Hazen, and one of its forked tongues swooped around Cruft, and blistered the broad breast of stubborn Grose. The enemy advanced with four charging columns in echelon, in close supporting distance, Cleburne and McCown falling first upon Johnson, and then enveloping Davis' flank, while Withers made the onset in front. Then Cheatham precipitated his division upon Sherridan, the other divisions released by the withdrawal of Davis turning his flank, and the fourth column, consisting of various brigades, plunged headlong upon Negley and Palmer. Their columns moving over the field to attack, appeared like the diagonal squares of a chess board, each in succession shouldering upon the advance column. It was a martial spectacle of terrible grandeur.

Withers' column pushed forward utterly contemptuous of Davis' skirmishers, paying no more attention to them than an elephant would to a swarm of hornets. But his line of battle was a different thing. Davis, fully expecting an attack, waited in confidence, and was sanguine that he would hold his ground until he saw Kirk give way. This exposed his flank immediately. The enemy had been severely punished in front, and had recoiled; but with victorious hosts on his right flank, he had no alternative. The enemy saw their advantage, and rushed upon the obstinate division with savage ferocity. The men stood until the battle had almost become a tumult of personal encounters. Pinney, Hotchkiss, and Carpenter worked their guns with telling effect, but the enemy refused to be balked. Post's right, now in jeopardy, was withdrawn by Davis. Carlin, by a splendid burst, drove the enemy from his front, but they were surging back again. Both Pinney and Carpenter fell, the latter dead. Half the artillery horses are killed. The whole line retires, part of the guns being dragged back by the men. Several are abandoned. It is impossible to move all of them through the timber. The loss of the division is distressing. Stem and Wooster, Colonel and Lieutenant Colonel of the One Hundred and First Ohio, are weltering in their life-blood. Alexander, of the Twenty-First Illinois, still commands, with a boot full of blood; Lieutenant Colonel McKee, of the Fifteenth Wisconsin, is dead; Tanner, of the Twenty-Second Indiana, is a bleeding captive; Litson, of the same regiment, fighting heroically, is hurt, and falls into the hands of the enemy. Companies are without officers; regiments hold together by force of discipline. Davis watches with jealous eye to keep them together. Carlin's color guards are nearly all dead or dying, but when his noble remnant retires from the struggle, his banners are still flying. Heroic Williams, Colonel of the Twenty-Fifth Illinois, heart-sick at impending disaster, seizes the standard of the regiment from the nerveless grasp of its dying guardian, and shouting, "We will plant it here, boys, and rally the old Twenty-Fifth around it, and here we will die," the brave martyr falls under the flag. It was a hard struggle, but Davis finally worked through the woods, and gathered up his remnants to fight another battle. Carlin had seven hundred men left.

SHERRIDAN'S STRUGGLE.

When Davis was fully engaged, the enemy moved through an open cottonfield down across the valley, and spread up the face of the slope in front of Sill like a conflagration. Bush's Battery had a direct fire, and Hescock and Houghtaling thundered an oblique fire upon them, tearing fearful gaps in their front and sides, and shaking the mass to the center, but the disciplined legions of Cheatham with mighty effort shook off the effect, and struggled forward with admirable daring.

Sill, firm and patient, waits the onslaught. His men are covered. The enemy move toward them like a great gray cloud. Their muskets gleam like tubes of silver. They appear almost even with the crest. Now is the moment. Sill's trusty line seems to spring out of the ground. A long line of fire blazes in his front. It strikes full in the face of the foe. There are great gaps in his ranks. For an instant, they make manful efforts to close their ragged front. Sill's musketry is remorseless. Flesh and blood can not endure it. They stagger, recoil, catch a momentary foothold, slip backward, and at last plunge headlong into flight. Quick as thought, Sill orders a charge, leads it himself, and his gallant men shout with triumph. Alas! brave, noble Sill! That glorious charge was his last. The brightest and purest spirit among all the youth of that splendid army, beloved for his gentle manliness, admired for his lofty intellect, for his skill and dashing courage, thus to be cut down in victorious career, was most cruel sacrifice. A bullet struck him fairly in his handsome face, and he fell lifeless and disfigured upon the field. It was hideous that barbarians should have abused his remains. His body was plundered by the enemy.

The enemy rallied again, and renewed the attack with increased vehemence. Unhappily, the brigade on the right gave way. The enemy discovered it, and dashed forward impetuously to seize their advantage. One of the supporting regiments had also fallen back in disorder. It was soon rallied, but Sherridan's vigilant eye saw the mishap, and substituted a reserve regiment. But the retreat of the brigade on the flank was incorrigible. Hosts from the rebel divisions on the right, pressing in pursuit of the two retiring divisions of the Right Wing, flowed upon the right of Sill's brigade, and was about to envelop it. Sherridan instantly ordered Colonel Greusel, who succeeded Sill, to withdraw it. To relieve it of pressure, Roberts, on the left, fixed bayonets. Taking the Forty-Second and Fifty-First Illinois, the Twenty-Second supporting, he plunged into the woods. The enemy gave way before his glittering steel, and fled rapidly to the rear, abandoning one gun, which in turn was abandoned by Roberts.

This effective charge relieves the right until they are reformed in rear of the batteries upon a good position. Roberts retires from the woods and forms on the left. Sherridan vainly strives to rally retiring troops on his right, when, upon order from General McCook, he advances again and forms upon Negley's right, Roberts' brigade at right angles with Negley's right, and facing south, Shaeffer's and Greusel's brigades in the rear at right angles with Roberts, facing west, covering Negley's rear. Houghtaling's Battery, with a section of Hescock's under Lieutenant Tallia-ferro, and a section of Bush's Battery take position at the angle of these lines, the remainder of Hescock's and Bush's Batteries going to the angle formed by Negley's and Roberts' lines.

This maneuver—for it was a complete change of front under fire—is hardly perfected when the enemy strikes again with redoubled fury. None of Sherridan's regiments had broken, save one, and it had rallied under fire, and was now emulating its companions. Cheatham, enraged, seemed to have concentrated all his energies in the new attack. He appeared infuriated at his successive repulses. Sill had driven him back with cruel slaughter. Shaeffer, and his Missourians and Illinoisans, had caused his battalions to recoil under their galling fire, and gallant Roberts had repulsed him with steel. A rebel writer, whose history of the battle was published all over the South, said that "Cheatham stormed about the field gnashing his teeth at the slaughter of his braves." He was now reinforced by victorious hordes, flush in pursuit of the other broken brigades, and who gathered in clouds about Sherridan.

It was a final, but a gallant resistance. The enemy were coming at two hundred yards distant. Not a sign of faltering. Cheatham seemed concentrating his whole division on Roberts, but his men stood firmly as a mountain, and the rebels again recoiled. Again they advanced, and three times in succession they were compelled to give way under Sherridan's terrific infantry and artillery. But gallant Roberts was killed, and Harrington fell desperately wounded. It was a noble struggle, but the heroic fellows were compelled to retire. Shaeffer's ammunition was all expended. Already they had fired sixty rounds per man. He only remained of Sherridan's original commanders of brigade. The cartridge-boxes of Roberts' brigade were nearly empty, and Sill's staunch fellows were clamoring loudly for ammunition. Houghtaling had exhausted all of his, and there was no more accessible. The enemy had cut off the train! At Sherridan's command, Shaeffer's men grimly fixed bayonets, and waited their fate, holding the enemy in check with empty guns, while their comrades fell back. Roberts' brigade, now commanded by Colonel Bradley, and Greusel's, retired fighting. Houghtaling's Battery horses were nearly all dead. He strove manfully to drag away his pieces by hand, but the thickets were insurmountable, and the brave fellow reluctantly left them. Poor Talliaferro fell at his guns, and they were brought off by his sergeants. Two of Bush's guns were also left in consequence of the loss of horses, and the impossibility of dragging them by hand through the cedar-brakes.

The last division of the Right Wing, armed with empty muskets, fought at bay. They still preserved their compact order, with banners flying. The enemy, in awe of them, followed at a more respectful distance, but still galling them with heavy fire. Going through the woods, Shaeffer's Missourians—Germans—found a wagon with ammunition, and quickly swarming around it, gobbled up the precious cartridges and fell into line, manifesting bitter satisfaction. Sherridan instantly sent them to the front to beat back the enemy. At length Rousseau's division, having opportunely formed in his rear, in support of the struggling heroes, gallant Sherridan and the remnant of his command debouched from the thicket into the open field near the Murfreesboro pike.

But there was more work for Shaeffer and his sturdy Germans. Under the direction of General Rosecrans, Sherridan led them immediately to the front, on the right of Palmer's division, where they at once engaged, drove the enemy from the cedars and beyond, four of Hescock's guns going into action at the same time. These momentous conflicts, which require so much space for cold description, were the paroxysms of hardly three hours of horrific battle. The battle was not ended then, nor that day, nor the next, nor the next, but Sherridan's division, though losing elsewhere, did not afterward meet with serious loss. After the battle was over—"My loss, General," said Sherridan to his commander, "is seventeen hundred and ninety-six"—my three brigade commanders killed, and sixty-nine other officers; in all, seventy-two officers killed and wounded." Was it not Illiad of battle?—seventeen hundred and ninety-six brave soldiers out of an effective force of six thousand four hundred and ninety-five. Hearts of rock would melt in the presence of such touching tragedy. But these heroes repeat, with glow of honest pride, "*We came out of the battle with compact ranks and empty cartridge-boxes!*" That immortal boast should be inscribed on all their banners.

REMARKS.

For days after the battle, there was a wide-spread impression that the Right Wing was surprised. Such was the tenor of information which was constantly reported on the field. The swift capture of Edgarton's Battery, the sudden overwhelming of the Right Wing, the vehemence with which it was driven back to the Murfreesboro pike, where it, together with the whole army, was saved by the skill of the General Commanding, directing the valor of his trusty troops from the Left Wing and Center, seemed to confirm the erroneous statement. Such was the belief of the General Commanding, who, in his official report by telegraph to the General in Chief, denominated the misfortune a "surprise."

Subsequently upon sifting all the testimony, he decided that injustice had been done. It was adjudged that General Willich's picket lines were properly adjusted and diligently patrolled; that Kirk's were in front as far as they could be posted, and were inspected by the ever-vigilant Kirk himself, and that every regiment was under arms in line of battle before daylight. General Johnson, therefore, stands vindicated. The only point, it seems, in which there was remission of vigilance, was significantly reproached by Major General McCook, who, in his official report of the battle, said that "Captain Edgarton, commanding battery of Kirk's brigade, certainly was guilty of a great error, in taking even a part of his horses to water at such an hour." Edgarton was imprudent, but he desired that his horses should be well prepared for action.

The extent of the line, and its consequent thinness and lightness, together with the fact that it was attacked by greatly superior numbers, was the chief cause of disaster. There is, of course, some controversy whether the General Commanding or Major

General McCook was responsible. The respective official reports afford data for a clear decision. The official report of General Kirk, by omission, seems to imply that General Johnson was not on the field. It is not likely that General Kirk intended to insinuate that idea. General Johnson was there constantly, and exposed himself fearlessly—debouching from the forest with the remains of his reserve brigade, after his other brigades had been scattered. It has been said, likewise, that Willich's brigade was unprepared. The various commanders of the brigade dispute it staunchly, and the character of Willich, who is one of the most restlessly vigilant officers in the service, would go far to establish the claims of his subordinates.

The troops certainly fought with great obstinacy, but they were carried off their feet by simple momentum, and were kept rolling so rapidly by the swift-fighting enemy, that there was no opportunity for them to recover their equilibrium. "They were not whipped," said General Rosecrans; "they were routed." That they were not beaten, is attested by the fact that two-thirds of the survivors rallied, and subsequently redeemed themselves to the extent of the opportunities afforded. Had the line of battle on the Right been rolled up to half its length, McCook would have held Hardee "three hours." The firmness and steadiness of the men proves that conclusively. No troops ever displayed greater firmness and valor, and no officers ever devoted themselves more thoroughly. The conduct of General McCook was that of a cool, brave soldier. He exposed his person incessantly, and his horse was killed under him. His staff, in every way, showed themselves brave, faithful officers. But with his command shattered to pieces almost by the first shock, no opportunity to do otherwise than save all he could was afforded.

It is not the purpose of this volume to criticise or to censure any officer. The official reports may furnish sufficient data to critics. Yet it may be said of them, as of all official reports, that it is often difficult to sift true testimony from the abundance in official reports of that which is calculated to mislead. No officer will censure himself. All strive to tell the truth, but very few can avoid self-praise. And so many are apt to disparage or blame other officers, that it often requires information which the official reports do not embody, to adjust the truth of history. There is one point which no soldier can dispute. The General Commanding retrieved the fortunes of that day by his own skill and conduct, as he did the opening misfortune upon a subsequent day; and, in short, with his valiant soldiers, won the victory. It is now time to glance at the morning operations of

THE CAVALRY.

The rebel cavalry was swarming on the Right, on the Left, and in the rear. On the Left they attacked a train and slaughtered some stragglers. On the Right they charged upon McCook's ordnance train, but it was twice rescued through the gallantry and address of his Ordnance Officer, Captain Gates P. Thruston, who subsequently, for his good conduct in that sanguinary battle, was promoted to the conspicuous position of Chief of Staff of the Twentieth Army Corps, with the rank of Lieutenant Colonel. Directly in the rear, within two miles of the left front of battle, Wheeler and Wharton charged upon the General Hospital, and captured a large amount of stores, besides prisoners. Still further in the rear, they cut off and destroyed several subsistence trains. Once they impudently charged a battery in the pike, which, however, was unsupported, but they were quickly driven from their trophy by Colonel Kennett. The latter officer had been detained at headquarters by General Rosecrans, but when the flood-gates of evil opened that morning, he was directed to collect all the cavalry at his command, rally the Right Wing, and drive the rebel cavalry away. He found Colonel Murray, of the Third Kentucky Cavalry, with eighty men. Directing them to move to Wilkinson's cross-roads, he proceeded to collect more of his command. The woods were filled with stragglers. Murray soon found the enemy in possession of one of our trains, and two hundred and fifty federal prisoners. He sounded the "charge." In a moment the gallant little squadron were riding the rebels down in every direction. The prisoners were rescued and the train recaptured, together with portions of two batteries. The enemy also had possession of General Palmer's Division Hospital. Charging them with forty men, the rebel force fled, but Murray captured so many prisoners that almost his whole command was engaged guarding them. Twice more his little squadron overturned the enemy, and once dispersed Wharton's brigade. Altogether, they captured about sixty prisoners, rescued about eight hundred of our own men who had been captured, and saved a large part of the army train.

The Third Ohio, Lieutenant Colonel D. H. Murray, when the Right broke, also made a handsome dash, and drove the enemy from McCook's ammunition train. Subsequently they charged, saved the train of the Center, drove off the rebels, recaptured a hospital, and captured many prisoners under Colonel Kennett's eye. Two companies of this regiment were rallied by Colonel Kennett, who carried them into action, driving the enemy from the pike, recapturing a gun by a dashing charge, saving a train, and rescuing many of our men. Lieutenant Murray distinguished himself in this affair. Colonel Kennett himself had a hand to hand encounter with a rebel horseman. The result was doubtful. The rebel had leveled his carbine, the Colonel had his pistol leveled, and both were about to fire, when Farrish, an orderly of Kennett, threw his revolving rifle into the scale. The rebel delivered his arms and himself. In the charge of the Third Ohio, Farrish killed two rebels, and Jaggers, another orderly, rode down two gray-jackets, and released two of the Fourth Ohio Cavalry who had surrendered.

Colonel Zahn, of the Third Ohio Cavalry, commanding brigade, had been fighting incessantly from the beginning of the disaster up to this period. He was compelled to retire before the rebel infantry, but a charge of rebel cavalry was handsomely repulsed by the First Ohio Cavalry, Colonel Minor Millikin, and the Third Ohio Cavalry. Major A. B. Moore, of the former regiment, fell mortally wounded in this charge. The enemy charged Zahn twice in succession, and were again and again repelled. Zahn now went to the rescue of McCook's ammunition train, which was again in jeopardy. The enemy appeared in heavy force. After a gallant stand by the First, Third, and Fourth Ohio Cavalry, Zahn was compelled to retire, the dashing Colonel Millikin and his Adjutant, Lieutenant Condit, being fatally hurt. Millikin had been surrounded, but by his courage and his prowess with his saber, he cut his way through, and was escaping, when a rebel sharpshooter brought him down. There was no more gallant rider in that field. His sorrowing soldiers bore him to the rear, where he soon breathed his last, lamented by hosts of friends.

Later in the day, General Stanley moved up from Lavergne with the First Middle Tennessee, and a detachment of the Fifteenth Pennsylvania Cavalry, and assembled the rest of his available command to resist a movement of a strong force of rebel cavalry, under Brigadier Generals Wheeler, Wharton, and Buford, on the extreme right, north of Overall's Creek. Colonel Minty's brigade of nine hundred and fifty men, constituted by far the larger part of Stanley's command. After forming, a line of dismounted cavalry was thrown forward to skirmish. The enemy outnumbering our little force nearly three to one, of mounted and dismounted men and artillery, advanced rapidly, drove in the skirmishers and attacked the Seventh Pennsylvania. The Fifteenth Pennsylvania gave way and retreated rapidly, leaving the dismounted skirmishers and the Seventh Pennsylvania unsupported. They made a gallant resistance, but were forced to retire. Minty retreated across two fields, and formed again under cover of the enemy's artillery. The enemy followed sharply and confronted our line with three lines, one opposite the left flank, with skirmishers threatening the right. General Stanley ordered a charge, and in person at the head of two companies of the Fourth Michigan, and fifty men of the Fifteenth Pennsylvania, supported by the Seventh Pennsylvania, he dashed headlong into the rebels, scattered the line threatening his flank, and captured one stand of colors, which a sergeant of the Fifteenth Pennsylvania wrenched from the hands of its color-bearer. At the same time, Minty charged the first line in front with the remaining companies of the Fourth Michigan and the First Middle Tennessee, and drove the enemy from the field. The third line was formed on the opposite side of a lane with a partially-destroyed fence on each side. Minty now charged upon it, and put it to rout. The enemy disappeared from that vicinity. This affair concluded operations on the Right. The reader will now be carried back to the Center.

CHAPTER XXVI.

NEGLEY'S Division in the Cedar-brakes—Gallant Struggle of the "Old Eighth"—Staunch Fighting of Miller and Stanley—The "Twenty-Onesters"—"Father" Moody—Turchin's Regiment—The Pennsylvanians—Cutting their way out—Van Cleve, Beatty, Fyffe, Harker—The Charge—"They fly! They fly!"—Rousseau's Division—The Regulars.

IT was hardly ten o'clock when the Right Wing had been flung with such startling violence from a right line into an acute angle with the left, and in its rear. Exactness in the record of time in the tumult of conflict is impossible. In the midst of a hurricane when the good ship has sprung a leak, and the waves are breaking over her bulwarks, when all hands are piped to the pumps to save the sinking vessel, drowning men are not apt to be critical in marking minutes as the dial records them. All that has been described and much more, occurred in marvellous swiftness of succession—before eleven o'clock. The blood of thousands of men had saturated the field of Stone River.

General Rosecrans had hurled part of the Left across the field to save the Right; the lines had been readjusted, Rousseau had formed on Negley's right in his rear; St. Clair Morton's Pioneer Brigade had been flung into the gap between Rousseau's right and Van Cleve's left, Harker had fought victoriously on the extreme Right of the new line, Sherridan, Negley, and Rousseau had been driven out of the forest, Cruft, Hazen, and Grose had been fighting tremendously,

Wagner had repelled an assault, Mendenhall's and Loomis' various batteries had been distributed over the field, massed in the center, distributed again; Van Cleve, Harker, and the Pioneers had repulsed the enemy from the Right by eleven o'clock at latest. By that hour the enemy were rolling back again upon the new line of the Right. It seemed late. It was a day of almost endless extension. Some hours have a duration of years. They seem to embody the aggregate of a life-time of mortal agony. Every moment was a death-struggle. Every second was a period to a brave man's existence. The battle raged ten hours—thirty-six thousand seconds. Did not fresh blood flow every second? But to resume.

THE SECOND DIVISION OF THE CENTER.

While Sherridan was working out to the Murfreesboro pike, face to face, the storm of battle rushed across the front of Negley's division—the Second Division of the Center, but immortal as "the Eighth." When Sherridan carried his butchered column with his empty cartridge-boxes to the rear, it left Negley exposed to the swarms on his right. Sherridan held the key to the Center until he had nothing to hold it with but cold steel.

Negley was deep in the forest with two valiant brigades, almost surrounded by foes—stern old Stanley's and inflexible John F. Miller's. The one was proud to command Turchin's unconquerable Nineteenth Illinois, now gallant Scott's, Given's Eighteenth Ohio, Stoughton's Eleventh Michigan, and the Sixty-Ninth Ohio; the other to lead Sirwell's Seventy-Eighth Pennsylvania, Granville Moody's Seventy-

Fourth Ohio, Neibling's Twenty-First Ohio ("Twenty-Onesters"), and Hull's Thirty-Seventh Indiana—with Shultz's, Ellsworth's, and Marshall's batteries. Rough-handled Spear, with his East Tennesseeans, was there chafing in the rear, guarding trains.

Negley's troops, like all the rest, had shivered through the gloomy night without fires, cheerfully awaiting battle. With the onslaught upon the Right Wing, the enemy began to feint upon the Center and Left Wing. But the wave of battle soon flowed upon them. Again the rebels advanced, in strong, deep lines. This was the fourth thunderbolt which had been hurled. The batteries open upon them when they fall in range. They waver a little, but beat back the resistance. Stanley's and Miller's men are under cover waiting. Caustic Neibling's "Twenty-Onesters" (Twenty-First Ohio) had cuddled under a friendly fence. "Keep cool, boys! steady now! wait! When you fight, fight all over. Here they come! Now, 'Twenty-Onesters,' give 'em hell by the acre!" So, too, "Father" Moody, who wields "the sword of the Lord and of Gideon," glancing along his trusty Seventy-Fourth Ohio, shouted, in voice of thunder, "Now, my *boys*, fight for your country and your God—*aim low!*" So Hull, and Sirwell, and Scott, and Stoughton, and Given, each with stern encouragement, poised their regiments, and drove the yelling foe clean back to their cover. Moody, as enthusiastic as a boy, sets his line to shouting. They roar lustily for the Union. The old hero is wounded, and his clothes riddled with balls, but he will not leave his "boys." A drafted soldier in Neibling's regiment raised a whole battalion in laughter by shouting to a few drafted comrades, "Let's give 'em hell, boys—we 've only nine months to serve anyhow!"

The enemy gathered again. A furious conflict ensues. Negley keeps them at bay. They are loth to charge again. Cannon and musketry is doing the work at square stand-up fighting. The rebels do not like this. The Yankees will stand longer under it than they can. Rebels excel in onslaught. Sherridan now uncovers the right of the Center. The enemy flow upon it. A cruel cross-fire of musketry and artillery tears Negley's ranks to pieces. An aid reports that the enemy are in his rear. Veteran Thomas, who vigilantly watches and orders the battle in the Center, looks up surprised. Negley is alarmed, and cruelly disappointed. His soldierly pride revolts at a retrograde movement. There is no help for it. Thomas bitterly says, "Cut your way out." Negley desperately directs—"Men, we must cut our way out!" The men clutch their weapons with fatal determination. John Miller is wounded painfully, but he will cut his brigade through the foe. Stern Stanley gathers his stalwart battalions and prepares for desperate work. The enemy is advancing again in front. They are howling on the right and in the rear. Staunch Stoughton and young Scott dash out with the bayonets of the Eleventh Michigan and Nineteenth Illinois. The enemy fly from steel. The division is moving out of the woods. The foe roll back swiftly again. The "Twenty-Onesters" fix bayonets, the Nineteenth Illinois joins them on the right, and together they again clear the rear.

This relieved the whole division of serious embarrassment. It forced its way out steadily, and carried its batteries, save five guns, safely from the front. Moody's clothing had been riddled by balls, and his right leg and breast were bleeding with wounds. Colonel Miller received a shot in the neck, but, bleeding and smarting as he was, he remained at his post. Hull was badly hurt. Stanley (T. R.), though in the thickest of the fight from the opening until the close, was unhurt. The division lost heavily. The regiments composing it robed themselves with honor. When Negley came out the enemy followed him fiercely, but he turned at bay, and, together with Rousseau, gave them a bitter repulse. This was one of the most tremendous conflicts of the day, although where the whole field was so stubbornly and desperately contested, it is hard to determine which was the most appalling struggle. When the glorious Eighth retired from the forest, its ammunition was expended, a third of its original force were *hors du combat*, and most of the artillery horses were killed. Every inch of ground over which it retreated was strewn with the dead and mangled. Like Sherridan's, this division waded through the fire without breaking, and marched proudly among their companions-in-arms to take new position. "My men," said brave Miller, "did not run, but *marched* to the pike, carrying many of our wounded."

VAN CLEVE—BEATTY—FYFFE—HARKER.

When Harker went across from the left to the right and formed west of the Murfreesboro pike, and when staunch Van Cleve double-quicked with Sam. Beatty's and Fyffe's brigades to succor McCook, Price's brigade remained on the extreme left guarding the fords of

Stone River, and was not fairly engaged that day. Rousseau, almost simultaneously, was sent into the forest under the eye of Thomas, on the right of Negley. Leaving Harker on the crest of a hill, Wood, now guarding the left flank with his vigilant eye, held Hascall in hand to support Wagner, who, in the grove on the left, withstood a vigorous battering from the hights on the eastern bank of the river.

Beatty, with Fyffe and Harker on his right, was hardly in position, when the masses of the enemy in their gray surtouts, resembling a fog-bank in the distance, appeared rolling across the fields and through the timber in front—a throng of fugitives from the Right Wing flying before them. The lines opened for the passage of the retiring troops, and upon closing, a withering fire was opened upon the enemy, whose advance was suddenly checked. The latter availed themselves of the trees and ridges for cover, and during some twenty minutes a murderous fire was sustained. During this conflict, the General Commanding, having returned from the front, massed his batteries in the Center upon the cemetery knoll. While watching the cataract of shells and shot that was hurled into the forest, his eagle eye descried the mass of gray tipping over the hill in front of Beatty. "It was at this juncture," said brave Van Cleve, then suffering from his wound, "that the Commanding General led a charge in person, which drove the enemy pell-mell to their rear."

The terrific fire of the rebels had been sustained by the Ninth Kentucky and Nineteenth Ohio until their ammunition was almost expended. Beatty, unmoved by the tumult, effected a passage of lines, the Seventy-Ninth Indiana and Eleventh Kentucky going to the front, the former regiments retiring and forming the second line, in support. It was they who, under the eye, and at the command of the Chief, had the honor to make that glorious charge. It was along their lines that Garesché flamed like a meteor. It was here that Gilman, with drawn sword, Michler in top-boots, Taylor on his superb bay, Skinner, and truly brave Thoms, the first time in battle, devoted and gallant Father Trecy, Goddard, Simmons, Wiles, Kirby, Bond, Thompson, young Willie Porter, and Reynolds, Hubbard, Curtis, cool Barnet, and the brave orderlies of headquarters, first saw the backs of the enemy on that woeful morning.

As the gray-backs went over the hill, a streaming line of steel, reaching from Beatty's left to Fyffe and Harker, gleamed in swift pursuit, and dead men marked the progress of slaughter. The chase ended only when the fugitive rebels reached reinforcements, a mile in their rear.

While Beatty was holding the rebels in check on the left, Fyffe had taken position on his right on a ridge, and was making a vigorous fight against the obstinate efforts of the enemy to turn his own right. Harker already had his hands full, and his gallant fellows were almost staggering under the swift blows of the enemy. Fyffe looked anxiously for Harker's Sixty-Fifth Ohio to help him on his right, but Harker had enough work cut out for them. Fyffe's Fifty-Ninth Ohio and Forty-Fourth Indiana, meantime, were struggling against heavy odds with batteries in position playing upon them effectively, and there was no opening for a charge. There was no alternative but to stand and take the destructive storm. The enemy finally succeeded in getting upon Fyffe's flank, and he withdrew a short distance, under cover of Swallow's Battery. The Thirteenth Ohio, meantime, had been subjected to a fearful raking of musketry and artillery. Its gallant leader, Colonel Hawkins, had fallen, and it was now only a remnant, but was still fighting bitterly under Major Jarvis. At an order from Fyffe to move forward they responded with rousing cheers, and charged in glorious style, driving the enemy pell-mell through the woods. The noble fellows had first smelled powder at Carnifex Ferry. Their early training under "Old Rosy" was not now dishonored. They pressed the enemy home, almost side by side with their gallant Western Virginia comrades of old Sam. Beatty's Nineteenth Ohio. Fyffe's entire line dashed gallantly forward with shouts which soared above the uproar of battle. The enemy fled up the ridge, down the slope, across the fields, and halted only when secure behind their heavy reserves. Colonel Fyffe, in his official report commending the gallantry of the soldiers, said: "One of the skirmishers, William Brown, of Company B, Fifty-Ninth Ohio Infantry, met me on the crest of the ridge, marching back through the line at the head of twenty-eight prisoners, besides two lieutenants, he had captured." This responsibility-taking fellow, like Paddy, had "surrounded" the knaves.

Harker, like Fyffe and other gallant Brigadiers on that terrible morning, sometimes feared he was neglected. The Fifty-First Indiana, under Colonel Streight; the Sixty-Fourth Ohio, Harker's own admirable regiment, under Lieutenant Colonel McIlvaine; then the Thirteenth Michigan, under brave Shoemaker; and Hathaway's Seventy-Third Indiana regiment, in sharp succession, with Bradley's Battery covering all of them, withstood the shattering shock with the firmness of veterans. Each in turn was at front, but just before Beatty's charge they were constrained to fall back with the line on the left to cover their flank. Bradley's Battery had now lost so many horses that he was compelled to leave two of his guns in possession of the enemy. But Shoemaker, seeing the rebels waver under the hot musketry of the line, charged at the head of his Michiganders, and brought back fifty-eight prisoners and the guns in triumph. Meantime, Beatty and Fyffe had pursued the enemy too far. The latter rallied on their reserves behind some hastily-constructed breastworks, and rolled back again with increased numbers, but they had been so thoroughly whipped that they halted presently, and contented themselves by taking up position on a ridge, a half mile or more from the Murfreesboro pike.

ROUSSEAU AND THE REGULARS.

Rousseau's division had formed in the cedar-thickets as soon as the extent of the disaster to the Right Wing was ascertained. He was needed on Negley's right to protect that officer's flank, and to relieve the retiring divisions of the Right. The Regular Brigade, Lieutenant Colonel Shepherd, at the head of the column, moved steadily into the thickets, and formed with Colonel John Beatty's brigade on the left, Scribner's in close support. Directly a dropping fire, like the big drops which precede a storm, indicated the proximity of the enemy. Fugitives had embarrassed the formation of the line, and the throng increased. Johnson's reserve brigade, and the debris of several regiments, drifted back against his front, and Johnson forming in line, fought until his ammunition was expended. Sherridan, too, was relieved from immediate pressure. But the enemy pushed hard. The gallant Regulars resisted with the staunchness of their professional esprit, and refused to yield an inch. Rousseau had vainly attempted to get his artillery into position. Loomis and Guenther, after vehement effort, found it impossible to plant a battery where it would be serviceable. The enemy were falling upon him in swift tumult. The hordes who were flooding the forests in front of St. Clair Morton and Van Cleve, also swarmed around his right flank. The Regulars were suffering frightfully. Captain Bell, of the Fifteenth United States Infantry, as noble a soldier as ever wielded blade, was killed; Captain York and Lieutenant Occleston, of the same regiment, fell severely wounded while fighting bravely with their commands, and scores of brave privates were sinking at every volley.

Rousseau, discovering the unprofitableness of wasting life in the thickets, at once gave orders to fall back to the open ground where the batteries could operate. The movement was hazardous, but necessary. The conflict was raging upon all sides. Negley was falling back. The enemy had flowed in behind Palmer, and Grose's superb brigade was beating them back, preventing them from crossing a swamp, which, from the sanguinary combats that were fought over it, gave it the title of "Hell's Half-acre." The Sixth and Twenty-Fourth Ohio, under young Anderson and Jones, here appeared fighting heroically. The enemy were plunging through the timber, evidently to break off the Center and repeat the battle of Prague, which they had so well begun. Rousseau himself, sword and hat in hand, blazed like a meteor along the lines, inspiring his men. Loomis and Guenther, with young Ludlow, who for his heroism was kissed in the heat of battle by gallant Charles Anderson, had rushed their splendid batteries to a crest on the open ground commanding "Hell's Half-Acre," and retained their souls impatiently until the infantry escaped from the murderous cedar-brakes. But the Regulars, followed swiftly by the eager and ferocious enemy, who filled the forests with their infernal slogan, were compelled to fall back, loading while retiring, and turning to fire at their remorseless pursuers.

There was scarcely time to seek an available position for the entire division, but the Second Ohio, Colonel Kell, and the Thirty-Third Ohio, commanded by Captain Ellis, having been in the rear in support, had taken position in support of the batteries, and afforded good cover for the retiring troops. Thomas and Rousseau, by the exercise of skill, and through the steadiness of the men, finally posted them in a depression which commanded the debouch from the forest, and from which, after ferocious fighting, they were finally enabled to drive back the enemy with a loss which exceeded even their own horrible casualties. "In the execution of this last movement," said General Thomas, "the Regular Brigade, under Lieutenant Colonel Shepherd, came under a most murderous fire, losing twenty-two officers and five hundred and eight men in killed and wounded, but with the co-operation of Scribner's and John Beatty's brigades, and Guenther's and Loomis' batteries, gallantly held its ground against overwhelming odds." It was here that chivalrous Rousseau sent word to Rosecrans that he had taken his stand. "Tell him," he said, "that I will stay right *here*. I won't budge an inch!"

The rebels had spread through the forest and down the slight slope toward the depression in which Rousseau was formed, shouting like devils, and dashed forward as if the key of the position was at last in their grasp. But the batteries of Loomis and Guenther, vomiting double-shotted cannister into their masses with frightful rapidity, and the infantry aiming low and deliberately, literally consumed their battalions. The file firing of the Regulars at this point was fearfully destructive. The enemy flew back to the woods in haste. But new legions collected, and directly the enemy shot a column clean out into the open space in front. At this instant the battle was raging along the whole line. The rebels were yelling hideously in the thickets, our musketry was rolling in front in terrific volume, and the roar of artillery vied with the majesty of tropical thunder. It seemed as if the very elements were convulsed. Now the splendid charge, led by Rosecrans in person, was made. Our fellows raised a shrill clamor, which leaped from rank to rank, and thrilled along the lines in spirit-stirring harmony. Word was carried to Rousseau that the enemy were flying, and soliciting permission to charge, he, too, took the head of his valiant column, and led it, roaring with victorious rage, straight at the front of the enemy, drivng them wildly to the fastnesses of the cedars. His own gallant staff and orderlies captured seventeen prisoners, with a captain and lieutenant at their head, the remnant of the Thirtieth Arkansas Infantry, which had been blown to pieces by Loomis, Van Pelt, Guenther, and Ludlow. The desperadoes were taken within one hundred and thirty yards of the batteries. Loomis here lost twelve men killed and wounded, and thirteen horses. Here, too, the gallant Major Carpenter, of the Nineteenth Regulars, with six mortal wounds in his body, fell dead on the field; Major John H. King, of the Fifteenth, and Slemmer, of the Sixteenth, were disabled. Captain Dennison, of the Eighteenth, and George F. White, a heroic sergeant of the Third Battalion, lost their lives. Gallant Kell, Lieutenant Colonel commanding the Second Ohio, was also killed. The staunch Second Ohio, which at Chaplin Hills had won honorable fame, here had the good fortune to capture the colors of the regiment which the batteries tore to pieces. Among the heroic efforts of that sanguinary day none surpassed in grandeur the valorous deeds which immortalized the splendid regiments of the Center. They came up out of that awful struggle wrenched and shattered, but even the tattered remains were an unconquerable host.

THE LEFT WING.

From the moment of the order from the General Commanding to suspend the execution of the plan of battle, when General Crittenden under his direction, sent Van Cleve to the Right, General Crittenden had been constantly in the field, vigilantly watching the progress of battle on his own front. He exhibited perfect *sang froid*, and displayed just soldierly pride in the gallantry of his splendid corps. There had been a constant play of batteries on his wing, and Palmer's division was soon heavily engaged, Wagner and Hascall, of Wood's division, being assailed in rapid succession. The havoc among men and horses from small arms and artillery, and among officers from the murderous fire of sharp-shooters, was harrowing.

PALMER'S DIVISION.

Palmer's division had retained its original formation—Cruft's brigade on the right, joining the left of Negley, braced and covered by a piece of timbered land, his left stretching to the eastward, toward the Murfreesboro pike. His front line was composed of the Second Kentucky and the Thirty-First Indiana Infantry, under Colonel Thomas D. Sedgwick, supported by the First Kentucky and the Ninetieth Ohio, under Colonel David A. Enyart, with Standart's Ohio Battery in half battery on either flank.

Colonel W. B. Hazen, commanding Palmer's Second Brigade, with the Sixth Kentucky Infantry and Forty-First Ohio in front, and on the right and left of the road respectively, joined Cruft on the left, the Ninth Indiana and One Hundred and Tenth Illinois Infantry in the second line, on the right and left of the road respectively. Hazen occupied a cottonfield in front of Cowan's "Burnt House"—the Stone River Hugomont—a point of most furious conflict in the successive struggles of the day. His right rested against a skirt of woods, the left lying behind the crest of a wave in the surface, which offered very doubtful cover, though the best the plain afforded.

The enemy fought for the triangle which he defended, and which he was conscious should be held at all hazards.

Colonel Grose's brigade was in reserve in rear of the interval between Cruft and Hazen; the Sixth Ohio and Thirty-Sixth Indiana in front, the Eighty-Fourth Illinois, Twenty-Third Kentucky and Twenty-Fourth Ohio forming the second line, with Parsons' Battery of the Fourth United States Artillery, and Cockerell's Battery, in support of the lines near the Center.

CRUFT — HAZEN — GROSE.

Soon after eight o'clock General Palmer, receiving information that Negley was about to advance, ordered Cruft to move up, and Hazen to seize some commanding positions in his front, together with the "Burnt House." Before the order was executed the enemy had moved upon Negley, after driving back the Right Wing, and compelled him to retire his right, so that it was now oblique to Cruft's front. The panic on the Right had also cropped out in the timber skirting the Murfreesboro pike, so that the order for Palmer to advance was quickly countermanded. Hazen had not advanced over twenty yards, when, in obedience to orders, he fell back. The enemy having appeared in the rear of the Left, the necessity for a retrogade movement was apparent. Hazen had barely got his two right regiments into position in the wood, when he begun to engage the enemy, who had broken cover over the crest in front in two lines, and dashed swiftly down to the "Burnt House." The two left regiments were retired about fifty yards, to a thinly-timbered elevation near the railroad. The enemy evinced great desperation in their efforts to cross the cottonfield and break Hazen's front, but the splendid firmness of his regiments repeatedly foiled them. The fighting was sharp and decisive, Hazen firmly holding his post of honor.

General Cruft had hardly advanced a hundred yards when he was halted, and Palmer, riding toward the pike, discovered a mass of rebels swarming in the rear of his right. Grose skillfully changed front to rear, and was instantly engaged with the enemy in a bitter contest, and, after great mutual slaughter, drove them back.

Meanwhile Cruft's skirmishers spread out, engaged the rebel skirmishers with fine spirit, and drove them, while his line gained a fence in his front. Directly a massive charging column of the enemy bore down upon him, and a tremendous combat ensued. The rebels charged with desperate abandon, but were constantly hurled backward. The infantry fire of our line was awful, while the battery play of Standart seemed to swallow up whole ranks of the foe. Flesh and blood could not endure it. The enemy fell back rapidly to cover. Before Cruft's line was fairly readjusted for an advance, he discovered indications of another onset. Ordering his men to hold their fire, he waited until the enemy moved up within point blank range, and poured a terrific volley into their masses. The blow was staggering, but the ferocious rebels were determined to carry their point. Our own battalions had been hurled into other weak points with such masterly skill that they saw no hope of victory, unless they could break each line successively. At this hour they were flushed with success on the Right, and were driving in the Center. Bragg, sanguine of victory, had recalled some of his victorious legions from his extreme left, and was precipitating them, together with Breckinridge's large division, and portions of reserve commands, upon our Left.

After a terrible engagement of nearly a half hour, the enemy were again rolled back upon their own position. The two gallant regiments in front, after a second display of almost unparalleled heroism, were relieved. General Cruft took advantage of a brief respite to effect a passage of his lines—the First Kentucky, Colonel Enyart, and Ninetieth Ohio, Colonel Ross, going to the front. These two gallant regiments, under Enyart, advanced to charge, but the Ninetieth Ohio, was recalled, and the First Kentucky charged alone, routing the enemy, and pursuing them clean beyond the "Burnt House," and to a point within fifty yards of their line of intrenchments. It was the most daring charge of the day, and but for the general conflict which raged all over that sanguinary field, would have been conspicuously distinguished. Enyart gathered up his little command, and began to fall back to his position. But the enemy, reinforcing from his reserves in the woods, burst upon the regiment and beat it back, with severe loss, to its position in line. The remainder of the line, with Standart's, Parsons', and Cockerell's admirably-worked batteries, and the heavy infantry fire from the line, checked the enemy in their career.

But the capricious changes of battle had left Cruft's right flank exposed to a cross-fire from the enemy in the woods. To retire was obviously a necessity. Retreat was impeded by confusion, caused by repulsion of brigades from other lines back upon his line of recedence, and artillery carriages retiring from his right obstructed the field. Standart's ammunition was decreased to an alarmingly short supply, and he was compelled to shift position to fight off the enemy. The men also had almost expended their ammunition. They had fired an average of fifty rounds each, or more. Cruft needed reinforcements, but did not receive them. They could not then be spared from other points. The enemy's fire seemed to envelop his whole line. Still he fought stubbornly, and held his ground long against fearful odds, but finally withdrew fighting. The Second Kentucky brought off three pieces, and the Thirty-First Indiana, one piece of artillery, of another division, by hand, which the gunners had been compelled to abandon, their horses having been killed. Miller's infantry, although their ammunition had about failed, had brought off two pieces of the same battery, so that none of it was sacrificed to the enemy. Standart saved his battery, with a loss of three men and seven horses, coming out with only sixteen rounds of ammunition. Cruft fell back to the pike, which he reached with about five hundred men, the Second Kentucky, in falling back, having been ordered to take a position on the left of the new line on the Right. After replenishing his cartridge-boxes, Cruft took a position in support of a battery on the left of the pike.

Meantime, the enemy persisted in his efforts to advance from the "Burnt House" across the cottonfield which Hazen had vacated. Wagner had shifted so far over to the left to guard the ford, that a gap was open between the two brigades, and Hazen, until Hascall filled the interval, was practically on the extreme left of the army. The fighting here had been so incessant that the cartridge-boxes of the Forty-First Ohio had been emptied. Hazen dared not withdraw a regiment from his front, and had fruitlessly endeavored to procure ammunition. He sent for relief. The One Hundred and Tenth Illinois fixed bayonets, and the Forty-First Ohio defiantly clubbed their muskets in desperate determination to hold their ground at all hazards until reinforcements should arrive. The Ninth Indiana, commanded by gallant W. H. Blake, dashed over from the Right with a shout, to relieve the Forty-First Ohio. "In advancing to this position," said Colonel Hazen, "under a galling fire, a cannon shot passed through the ranks of the Ninth Indiana, carrying death with it, and the ranks were closed without checking a step." Again: "The Forty-First Ohio now retired with its thinned ranks in as perfect order as on parade, cheering for the cause, and crying for ammunition." A few well-directed volleys from the Ninth Indiana drove the rebels back to their cover, and the soldiers had a brief respite.

A half hour later the enemy renewed their attack with increased vigor and bitterness, and succeeded in pushing a column in front of the "Burnt House" to the right in front of Cruft, whose brigade was then withdrawn. In this attack, it was the fortune of the Sixth Kentucky Union regiment to meet the Sixth Kentucky rebel regiment, and demolish them in the open field. Meantime, when Grose, in reserve, had changed front to rear to clear Palmer's right flank, his front line pushed forward about two hundred and fifty yards, and met an almost overpowering mass of the enemy. Both sides had opened fire upon observing each other, and were suffering dreadfully. Major Kinley, commanding Thirty-Sixth Indiana, soon fell badly wounded, and Captain Shultz, of the same regiment, was killed, while dozens of men had fallen around them. Captain Woodbury immediately assumed command of the regiment, and fought it skillfully thereafter. Colonel Nick Anderson received a wound in his thigh, but did not leave his regiment until after the enemy retreated from Murfreesboro. His Adjutant, Lieutenant Williams, and Lieutenant Foster, of the same regiment, were soon stricken to rise no more, and it seemed that none of the brave Sixth would survive to bury its dead. The Thirty-Sixth Indiana, fighting stubbornly by its side, was bleeding at every pore. After a resistance of the most obstinate character, the gallant fellows were compelled to recede from the cedars. Parsons, Huntington, and Cushing, with their big battery and the supports, now took a leading part in the tragedy. After a terrible contest, they broke the enemy's ranks, and drove him, in confusion, to cover. A half or three-quarters of an hour later the rebels renewed their assault, but were driven back with severe punishment.

The fighting at this point was frightful. The enemy were more numerous than the trees of the dense forest which covered them, and it did not seem possible to check their fierce advance. But our troops fought firmly, and were so effectually sustained by

Parsons' Battery that the masses of the enemy, unable to stand such slaughter, resentfully gave way and retired to cover.

The withdrawal of Cruft intensified the assault upon Hazen, and in compliance with General Palmer's orders, Grose's brigade, which had beaten the enemy in their own front, changed front to rear again, and moved over to assist Hazen near the railroad. The Twenty-Fourth Ohio, Colonel Fred. Jones, and the Thirty-Sixth Indiana, Captain Woodbury, with the Forty-First Ohio, were posted on the left of the Ninth Indiana. The enemy rushed to this point ferociously, and a sanguinary conflict ensued. The mettle of Nelson's "man-of-war" division never shone more conspicuously. The lines refused to budge an inch. The men aimed low and fired deliberately. Gallant Fred. Jones soon fell, cheering his men, and was borne from the field gasping his last sigh. A little later and his brave successor, Major Terry, received a fatal wound. Captain Enoch Weller assumed command of the Twenty-Fourth. Parsons' Battery again settled the fray. The enemy fell back to cover in a wood, but kept up such a sharp fire that Hazen was compelled to swing his right behind the railroad embankment. From this time onward until the partial lull near noon, this staunch brigade was constantly engaged, the enemy fighting from the wood in which they had taken refuge.

HASCALL AND WAGNER.

General Hascall's brigade was ordered from the Left to the Right by General Rosecrans in person, soon after Harker started, but owing to obstructions caused by the panic on the Right, which overflowed the road and the camp on the east side of it, he was compelled to halt. His brigade was moved from point to point, to render assistance, until General Palmer appealed to him for aid. Responding promptly, he sent down the Third Kentucky Infantry, and not ten minutes later, its gallant commander, Colonel McKee, was killed, and the regiment was badly cut up. They, however, maintained their ground unflinchingly. General Hascall moved at once, and took position on Hazen's left, on the east side of the Murfreesboro pike. Wagner had occupied that position early in the morning, but when the Left was transferred to the Right, General Wood caused him to shift to the Left, to cover a ford of Stone River. Cox's Tenth Indiana Battery was posted in half battery on either flank. The brigade was in front of Breckinridge's main position, where it was vigorously assaulted, but the enemy were promptly repulsed.

CHAPTER XXVII.

PREPARATIONS for Decisive Battle—Readjustment of the Lines—The Grand Battle Scene—"Battle's Magnificently Stern Array"—A Spectacle of Dreadful Splendor—Destruction of Human Life—Garesché's Death—Hazen in the Trial Battle—Hascall and Wagner—The Field's our own.

IN the middle of the day there was a comparative cessation of firing. The batteries ceased their thunder, and the sharp crepitating thrill of musketry was stilled, excepting the harassing bicker of the rebel sharpshooters, who, posted in trees with their long-range rifles, maintained a deadly fire. The enemy made a strong demonstration upon the Right, but it was a feint. They had developed numbers superior to our own—"five or six thousand," said plain-spoken Thomas. It seemed, from the latest developments of battle, that unless they exceeded us numerically in a much greater proportion, their next attack would be directed at the Left. General Rosecrans adjusted his forces for the shock which was to determine the fate of the day. We again retrace our steps a little to discover the situation.

Rousseau and Van Cleve's advance having relieved Sherridan's division from the pressure, Negley's division and Cruft's brigade from Palmer's division, withdrew from their original position in front of the cedars, and crossed the open field to the east of the Murfreesboro pike, about four hundred yards in rear of our front line, where Negley was ordered to replenish his ammunition and form in close column in reserve.

The Right and Center of our line now extended from Hazen to the Murfreesboro pike, in a northwesterly direction, Hascall supporting Hazen, Rousseau filling the interval to the Pioneer Brigade.

Negley in reserve, Van Cleve west of the Pioneer Brigade; McCook's corps refused on his right, and slightly to the rear on the Murfreesboro pike; the cavalry being still further to the rear, on the Murfreesboro pike and beyond Overall's Creek.

Walker's brigade of the Center, consisting of the Seventeenth, Thirty-First and Thirty-Eighth Ohio, and Eighty-Second Indiana, which had been protecting the rear at Stewartsboro until they were ordered to the front, came up about eleven o'clock, and were temporarily assigned to General Sherridan, who posted them on the left of McCook's new line, in the forest which had been occupied by Van Cleve. Rude barricades were constructed on the right. Excepting sharp skirmishing, nothing more of importance occurred on that front, although batteries of the enemy interfered with communication on the pike south of Overall's Creek. The enemy also contented himself, during the afternoon, in making his Left secure by throwing up counter-defenses. Kirk's brigade, under Colonel Dodge, was moved down the river during the afternoon, to check an attempt of the enemy's cavalry to cut up our trains.

After these dispositions were made, General Rosecrans was fully prepared for another assault. He waited not long. Bragg had withdrawn the heaviest portion of his Left Wing, and, together with his reserves, now rolled them with mighty momentum upon the staunch Left Wing of Crittenden.

THE GRAND BATTLE SCENE.

Several heavy assaults made by the enemy to feel our lines, were successively repulsed; but about the middle of the afternoon a storm of appalling fury burst upon the Left. The majesty of great battle was in it. Disciplined hosts rolled upon disciplined hosts with hideous momentum. The crash was like the collision of two planets—fire and smoke visible, and crushing systems frightfully audible—a spectacle of dreadful splendor. Each feature was sharply traced and clearly defined. The day was surpassingly beautiful. Occasionally a shallow cloud soared away softly over the convulsion below, but the blazing sun glared through the vapory smoke which expanded over the shocking field like a thin gauze, wafting lazily toward the South. The pomp of battalions in "battle's magnificently stern array," would have compelled the severe enthusiasm of Napoleon. Long, deep lines of soldiers in blue uniforms, ranks piled upon ranks in dense masses, prostrate upon the undulating field and in the woods, intersected and diversified the surface in martial mosaic of matchless pageantry. From the funereal cedars on the Right, to the swelling brink of Stone River, it seemed as if the acres had been ruled out in long blue parallels. The "banner of beauty and glory," marking the place of regiments far as vision could stretch, waved proudly and defiantly above them, not a star dimmed or a stripe erased. Hardly had it soared so grandly before, and every great patriot heart that throbbed under it was "ever mindful what it cost." At intervals bold figures of solitary horsemen, who now seemed magnified to heroic proportions, stood grimly and silent at tactical distance in the rear of their commands—faithful guardians of the soldiers—resisting the shock unmoved. Shining targets, they, for the ruthless marksmen of the foe! O! vain, sad sacrifice! It thrills the soul with anguish to scan the record of that gory day. Garesché, and Sill, and Roberts, and Shaeffer, Drake, and Williams, Forman, and McKee, Harrington, Hawkins, Kell, Stem, Wooster, Millikin, Cotton, the two Carpenters, gallant Fred. Jones, Terry, Pinney, brave Richmond, and so many nameless heroes—where are they all? The fallow fields and gloomy thickets of Stone River swallowed up their lives.

> "There shall weep for those who bled
> Many a loving heart and dear;
> For every drop of blood that's shed,
> There shall fall a Nation's tear!"

Behind this magnificent panoply, our batteries, grouped in mass in the Center upon the crest of the knoll, or distributed over the field in unstudied picturesqueness, were enveloped in wreaths of smoke and spouting flames. Here and there striking clusters of Generals and their staffs stood steadily under the withering battle blast. For a little while, Rosecrans and his staff, Thomas and his staff, McCook and his staff, Crittenden and his staff, met in splendid grouping—the four commanders together, their field escorts radiating in semi-circle behind them—a precious target for the enemy—upon a wave in the field, in easy range of riflemen and shells. McCook discovered the imprudence, and rather sharply ejaculated, "This is a nice mark for shells. They will come in here and kill half of us. Can't you thin out, men?" Directly a flight of bullets, and a whizzing shell, chirruping like a gigantic cricket, impressed the admonition upon them all. Thomas glanced upon either side, and then turning to the front, soliloquized, with a sort of fine scorn, "I guess it's about as safe one place as another." Thomas and his *alter ego*, phlegmatic and soldierly Von Schrader, Flint, Mackay, Landrum, and others of his staff; Crittenden, with veteran Lyne Starling, Buford, Knox, Case, Brown, and Kniffin, took post on the flow of the ridge to the right of the pike, obliquely to the rear of the batteries of Guenther and Loomis. McCook, with Campbell, Langdon, Nodine, Bates, Williams, Fisher, and Blake, were in the rear of the left flank of the Right Wing, behind Thomas and Crittenden—Palmer and Wood careering over the field in the flame of conflict—the latter sick and wounded, but sternly at his post.

The hostile array in front imparted awful sublimity to the pageant. But for its tragedy, that gory field would have been wonderfully magnificent. It was a wild, tumultuous tournament—a spectacle of martial art, as of carnage, whose lineaments were marvelously regular and perfect, as if it had been a pageant prepared for the eye of happy beauty and chivalry. But it was a fierce delirium, which swept thousands of human souls into eternity.

The legions of the enemy poured out upon the plain in countless multitudes, firm, compact, and powerful. They resembled a mass of dense gray clouds moving along the surface, as you may see great banks of mist rolling through the valleys, or upon mountain declivities. Their polished muskets gleamed like burnished brass, and their parti-colored battle-flags fluttered haughtily in the breeze. Their batteries wheeled swiftly into position, and the gunners plied their hellish art. It seemed as if a wall of iron could hardly resist those somber columns. They marched to slaughter with magnificent daring, and met a wall of brave hearts that iron, and lead, and steel could not move.

A hundred cannon now belched forth their thunder. The atmosphere was tremulous with the terrific vibration. The roar of artillery and the treble rattle of musketry, thrilling along the lines as if innumerable keys of some harsh instrument trembled under the agency of terrible power; crash of solid shot and shell, whirl of grape and cannister, thick volumes of smoke which enveloped the combatants, and dispersed in a thin canopy of bluish vapor; dying men and mangled horses, dismounted cannon and shattered caissons, disabled in shocking diversity over the field; the frantic career of riderless steeds; the splendid sweep of Generals and their staff officers over the fearful plain, conspired to create a scene of indescribable and horrific sublimity. No human language is fit to depict it. It was all under the scope of vision—the marching hosts, the magnificent tactical display, the dreadful panoply, the appalling destruction of human beings.

The rattle of musketry tearing along the lines sounded like the noise of ripping canvas, when the black squall suddenly strikes the unprepared ship. In our own lines there was no voice but the voice of command. Men went down with fearful wounds, but made no outcry—for men do not shriek on the field of battle. Dumb brutes neighed in their agony. A horse with leg torn away moaned with more than human pathos. Solid shot crashed through the bones of men and horses, and it seemed as if glass was being shivered. Steeds, riderless, frantic with anguish, wild with the furious tumult, were bounding over the field with desperate energy, seeking to fly from peril. Hundreds were torn to shreds. A single shell crushed through three noble beasts, and piled them in dreadful confusion under a shattered timber. A solid shot rebounded from a gun with a clang like a brazen bell, and carried away the head of a charger. Eighty horses were killed at a single battery.

Excepting in the front line, where the men stood up with almost superhuman firmness, the troops were hugging the soil, prone upon their bellies. But even here the round shot of the enemy plowed through the ranks, tearing one to shreds here, another there; yonder a man riven and scattered by six pounds of iron, so that scarce a bone was left to testify that there had been a man—some blood, some gory strips of flesh, a few patches of sky-blue cloth! Twenty men in a single brigade were thus annihilated. But scarce a man stirred from his position. Our heroic soldiers, steadfast and true, clung to their posts with almost unequalled fortitude and devotion.

The slaughter of the foe was still more frightful. Hideous gaps were rent in their massive columns. You could track the course of a shell or round shot in the withering ranks. Still they careered to the front with a determination only matched by our own. A line of lurid flame incessantly leaped from their terrible front, and carried destruction before it. On the skirt of the thicket on the right they swarmed like legions of fiends. Now a column shot to the edge of the cedars on the right. Volumes of cannister and musketry were poured into them. Then plunging back into cover, they rallied and surged again like great billows, vainly striving to reach our lines, until it seemed none would be left to charge. It was as if they were meeting the consuming flames of hell. In the cause of liberty and right, the daring courage of those desperadoes would have won immortal fame. The brunt of this horrible assault fell upon Palmer and Wood. Hazen held the center of this front, and its key. Thoms, Thompson, and Bond were sent down repeatedly by the General to encourage those heroic soldiers in that destroying conflict.

GARESCHE'S DEATH.

In the midst of the horrid carnival, the General himself galloped to the left of the railroad to reinforce a struggling line by the moral power of his own splendid example. Garesché, who had never left him since they had mounted in the morning, save to execute orders, was at his side. They were galloping through a tumult of iron missiles. An unexploded shell whizzed close by his leader, and the head of Garesché vanished with it. Sickening gouts of his blood were spattered upon his comrades, who turned in horror from the ghastly spectacle. The mutilated form of the hero careened gently over the saddle, and fell upon the field. The little prayer-book was in his pocket. Men would have imagined that this, at least, would have touched the mind of the Chief. He did not seem to observe it. His whole mind was intensely absorbed with the thought of conquering. Almost simultaneously another shell exploded in the midst of the staff, and brave Richmond, sergeant of the Fourth Regular Cavalry, fell. Then two of the escort. Then a fragment of a shell ripped across the side of youthful Willie Porter. The General, totally unmoved by danger, still careered through the field. Garesché had been blown away from his elbow; Kirby had been shot; Benton's horse was smarting with a wound; Hubbard's snorted with the sting of a ball in his neck; Taylor's was killed; Porter's horse and then himself were struck; poor Richmond was mortally hurt; four or five of his escort and orderlies were stretched upon the field. No wonder Bond said to him, "General, do you think it right to expose yourself so much?" And the response! A regiment was lying down upon the field before him waiting to be called into action. Shot and shell were whizzing furiously over them. The Chief dashed up to the line and addressed them: "Men, do you wish to know how to be safe? Shoot low. Give them a blizzard at their shins! But do you wish to know how to be safest of all? Give them a blizzard, and then charge with cold steel! Forward, now, and show what you are made of!" Bond had announced Garesché's death. It seemed to occur to the General as a half-remembered dream. "I am *very* sorry," he said; "we can not help it." A report that McCook was killed was communicated to him. He said, "We can not help it—this battle must be won."

Apparently unconscious of personal hazard and the shocking havoc around him, General Rosecrans moved about unscathed, calm, and absorbed by the intensity of his own thought, with inflexible fixedness of purpose deeply graven in his firm lips and brow. The field of battle where he rode that day is thickly sprinkled with the useless and exhausted implements of slaughter which vainly cluttered around him. Men can not look upon that plain to-day without a shudder at his fearful escapes.

Lessons in the art of battle were learned by veterans on that field. The troops were handled with matchless skill. Lines upon lines were piled upon each other so compactly that even the awful momentum and the ferocity of the rebel onslaughts did not shake them. Columns were hurled in solid ranks from one side of the field to the other extreme as if they were toys; or were flung into the face of the enemy as if it were a game playing. It is no grasp at rhetoric to describe the swift and steady evolutions of our brigades as perfect as the movements of a grand review. Thousands acquired an idea of the art of "handling masses," of which they never had dreamed before. It was a masterpiece of mental manipulation.

HAZEN IN THE TRIAL BATTLE.

To resume the thread of battle narrative. Hazen, Grose, Shaeffer, Hascall, and Wagner's brigades constituted the real battle front in the afternoon. Hazen had the key of the position. Shaeffer's brigade, by order of General Rosecrans, was put into action by General Sherridan on the right of General Wood's and left of Palmer's divisions, on Hazen's left. The Second and Fifteenth Missouri in the front line. The One Hundredth Illinois, Colonel Bartleson, had been sent to Hazen by General Rosecrans, and was posted in line with the One Hundred and Tenth Illinois and Ninth Indiana to the front, with the right resting on the railroad; the Second Missouri in the same line, with the remainder of Shaeffer's and Hascall's brigades immediately on the left.

"At about four o'clock in the afternoon," said Hazen with graphic eloquence, "the enemy again advanced upon my front in two lines. The battle had hushed, and the dreadful splendor of this advance can only be conceived, as all description must fall vastly short. His right was even with my left, and his left was lost in distance. He advanced steadily, and as it seemed, to certain victory. I sent back all of my remaining staff, successively, to ask for support, and braced up my own lines as perfectly as possible. The Sixth Kentucky had joined me from the other side some time previously, and was posted just over the embankment of the railroad. They were strengthened by such fragments of troops as I could pick up, until a good line was formed along the track. * * * * The fire of the troops was held until the enemy's right flank came in close range, when a single fire from my men was sufficient to disperse this portion of his lines, his left passing far around to our right." At the termination of that terrible fight, Hazen's brigade "rested where it had fought—not a stone's throw from where it was posted in the morning." Gallant brigade! and gallant leader! the "Old Guard" would have been proud to hail you comrades! "Such heroic service rendered their country this day," said eloquent Hazen, "such heroic and daring valor, justly entitles these men to the profound respect of the people and of the country." The regiments of that proud brigade, let it be not forgotten, are the Indiana Ninth, the Illinois One Hundred and Tenth, the Kentucky Sixth, and Ohio Forty-First. And side by side with them, Grose's unfaltering regiments—Nick Anderson's Sixth Ohio, gallant Fred. Jones' Ohio Twenty-Fourth, Kinley's Thirty-Sixth Indiana, Hamrick's Twenty-Third Kentucky, Waters' Eighty-Fourth Illinois—an aggregate of one thousand seven hundred and eighty-eight men when they marched from Nashville—a thousand now. The rest bled upon the field. Over on the left the gallant Missourians fought until their cartridge-boxes were emptied again. Gallant Shaeffer fell at their head—the last of the brilliant trio of which dauntless Phil. Sherridan that frightful morning had been so justly proud.

HASCALL AND WAGNER.

Wood, with the solicitude of a gallant leader who knows his troops, had watched his brigade with the keen eye of a soldier from morning's dawn. Suffering from illness, and smarting with a wound, he yet firmly kept his saddle, and proudly witnessed the effects of his own sharp discipline. Harker had been posted on the right, but that gallant and skillful officer was now resting in comparative security. He had assisted in repelling the enemy repeatedly, and his shattered ranks rested while they watched the vigilant foe. Wagner had held his position "at all hazards," and Cox, with his battery, supported by the Fifty-Seventh Indiana, had emptied his caissons, and was making a second draft upon them. Hascall had moved down upon his right after he had repelled the enemy early in the morning, and was sustaining an almost overpowering shock when Wagner sent Lane's Ninety-Seventh Ohio to his assistance. Breckinridge's troops, meantime, had crossed the river and advanced in masses upon Wagner. They were charging in full career, when Wagner, relying upon the pluck of his noble fellows, sent the Fifteenth Indiana, supported by the Seventeenth Indiana, to meet them in counter-charge. Meantime Cox's Battery, supported by the Fortieth Indiana, opened upon them with cannister. The steel of the Hoosiers and the iron hail of Cox was too much for the rebels. They fell back in confusion.

After Hascall had sent the Third Kentucky to Palmer's assistance, the Twenty-Sixth Ohio, under Major Squires, was also sent forward, and took position on the right in support of the former, Estep's Eighth Indiana Battery coming up soon after. The Third Kentucky had already lost its gallant Colonel, and the Twenty-Sixth Ohio was almost instantly brought into violent collision with the enemy. The Third Kentucky was reduced one-half, and its brave Major, D. R. Collier, soon received two severe wounds, but refused to quit the field. Adjutant Bullitt's horse was killed, and ten out of fourteen of the remaining officers of the gallant Third Kentucky were wounded. The Twenty-Sixth Ohio, fighting stubbornly, was also losing heavily. The enemy disregarded our artillery, and having pushed up in range of the small arms, their superior numbers proved destructive. But they were unable to advance further, and after nearly an hour of sanguinary combat, Hascall had the satisfaction to see the enemy recoil, and almost simultaneously they staggered from Wagner's front. Colonel Buell, at the head of the Fifty-Eighth Indiana, meantime, had been sent by Wood to Palmer's assistance, where they materially aided in repelling the enemy, and subsequently relieved the Third Kentucky. Hascall now threw forward the right of the Sixth Ohio regiment, which was on the right of the Twenty-Sixth, so that its fire would sweep the front of the Twenty-Sixth Ohio and Fifty-Eighth Indiana, and brought up Lane's Ninety-Seventh Ohio to strengthen the right still more; Estep's Battery supporting the Sixth Ohio.

Hascall galloped back and called the attention of General Rosecrans to the importance of his position, and the necessity of keeping it well supported. "He rode to the front with me," said Hascall, "approved the dispositions I had made, spoke a few words of encouragement to the men, cautioning them to hold their fire until the enemy got well up, and had no sooner retired than the enemy emerged from the woods and over the hill, and were moving upon us in splendid style and immense force. As soon as they came in sight the Sixth and Twenty-Sixth Ohio, and Estep's Battery opened upon them, and did splendid execution, but on they came until within one hundred yards of our line, and Colonel Buell, of the Fifty-Eighth Indiana, who had lost three men but had not fired a shot, ordered his men to fire. The effect was indescribable. The enemy fell in winrows, and went staggering back from the effect of this unexpected volley. Soon, however, they came up again, and assaulted furiously for about an hour and a half, but the men all stood their ground nobly, and at the end of that time compelled the enemy to retire. * * * The regiments all behaved splendidly again, and the Fifty-Eighth Indiana won immortal honors. * * * The Sixth, Twenty-Fourth, and Ninety-Seventh Ohio did noble service. * * * The One Hundredth Illinois fought splendidly in all the actions which took place on the left of the railroad." This last advance ended the third assault upon Hascall, and left him master of the position. "To the fearless spirits who hazarded and lost their lives upon this consecrated spot, the country owes a deep debt of gratitude."

While the third assault upon Hascall was progressing, the enemy's skirmishers were discovered slipping down the opposite slope of Stone River, and working their way down stream for the purpose of gaining Wood's left flank and rear. Cox's cannister soon drove them back, but a brigade of the enemy crossed the river under cover of the woods three hundred yards from Wagner's front. He had only the Fifteenth and Fifty-Seventh Indiana with which to resist them, the Fortieth being hotly engaged near the railroad—the Nintey-Seventh Ohio supporting Hascall. Cox's artillery ammunition was nearly exhausted, and it was impossible to replenish. The enemy had cut up the trains in the rear, so that the situation was somewhat alarming. Wagner, relying on his infantry, determined to attack the enemy first. The stalwart

Fifteenth Indiana again in the lead, the Fifty-Seventh supporting, moved boldly onward and engaged the enemy in a bitter contest. Colonel Hines and Lieutenant Colonel Lennard, of the Fifty-Seventh, now went down, and were carried from the field severely wounded. Lieutenant Colonel Wood fixed bayonets, and the Fifteenth rushed forward with a yell. The enemy broke, but the brave Hoosiers killed scores of them, drove two other regiments in disorder from the field, and captured one hundred and seventy-five men of the Twentieth Louisiana regiment. Captain Cox sent the last shot in his locker into the routed foe. After the disabling of their field officers, the Fifty-Seventh continued to fight without their officers, and participated in the glory of the brilliant combat. The Fifteenth lost thirty men killed and one hundred wounded in this single conflict. The enemy, dissatisfied with their effort, rallied and made a second dash, but Cox had found ammunition by this time. Wagner's line fell back slowly, fighting, until the enemy had advanced within cannister range of the battery, when both Cox and Estep let drive. It was a dose too much. The enemy, repeatedly repulsed on all their positions, resentfully retired, leaving Hazen, Hascall, and Wagner in possession of the position for which they had so heroically fought. Wagner, in closing the record of the day, congratulates himself proudly that he found his command, at the termination of the battle, "as far to the front as they were in the morning, and the noble dead of this brigade lay nearer the enemy's position than that of any other." Had Wagner heard of the charge of Enyart's regiment, he might have made one honorable exception.

THE BATTLE DIES OUT.

The afternoon was now far advanced. The last bitter assaults obviously had shaken the confidence of the enemy. Still they exhibited a sullen, resentful aspect. Heavy masses were again assembled in front of the Center with a view to renew the onslaught. But our artillery played upon them so effectively that only a small force pushed to the range of our musketry, and they were speedily hurled back. A last expiring effort was made by their artillery, which opened upon our lines terrifically, but at sunset, with now and then a roar and a brazen sigh from howitzers, and the vicious crack of rebel rifles, the sound of battle died away into the silence of evening.

"The day closed," said General Rosecrans, "leaving us masters of the original ground on our left, and our new line advantageously posted, with open ground in front, swept at all points by our artillery. We had lost heavily in killed and wounded, and a considerable number in stragglers and prisoners; also, twenty-eight pieces of artillery, the horses having been slain, and our troops being unable to withdraw them, by hand, over the rough ground; but the enemy had been thoroughly handled, and badly damaged at all points, having had no success where we had open ground, and our troops were properly posted, none, which did not depend on the original crushing of our Right and the superior masses which were, in consequence, brought to bear upon the narrow front of Sherridan's and Negley's divisions, and a part of Palmer's, coupled with the scarcity of ammunition, caused by the circuitous road which the train had taken, and the inconvenience of getting it from a remote distance through the cedars."

Excepting the tranposition of regiments which had fought three and four hours each in the front line without intermission, there was little change in the positions of the troops that night. The noble fellows were too weary to be tortured by unnecessary labor. The battle which had begun at "six twenty-two o'clock in the morning," was suspended at about five o'clock in the evening.

The dauntless deportment of the troops and the fidelity of their officers was beyond all praise. The men exhibited unconquerable spirit, obeyed orders with alacrity and precision, withstood the appalling assaults of heavy masses of the enemy, and the fury of their destructive artillery with unflinching pluckiness and determination. When ordered to charge, they moved to obey with wild, cheerful clamor; when forced to recede, they gave ground slowly, and bitterly contested it inch by inch. But for the misfortune that befell the Right Wing—which was in no sense the fault of the soldiers, for they were as stubborn, as firm, and as thoroughly disciplined as those of the Center and Left Wing—Bragg's army would have been crushed as if between the upper and the nether mill-stone. The raw troops that day proved themselves worthy comrades of the veterans. They fought with a vehemence and staunchness that astonished the best soldiers. Illinois, Missouri, Ohio, Wisconsin, Indiana, Kentucky, Michigan, Minnesota, Pennsylvania, and the Regulars, vied with each other in deeds of noblest heroism. The fair fame of no State, no division, no brigade, no regiment, no company, distinctively, as such, was tarnished by disgraceful conduct.

True, there were cowards; but in such numbers there must be some who lack moral firmness to endure, more than they lack physical courage to fight. Many straggled to the rear because their officers were killed. Others in the rout of the Right lost sight of their regiments and officers, and after being thus separated were too much discouraged to seek them again. Perhaps three thousand straggled and went to the rear. Colonel Burke, with the noble Tenth Ohio, stretched a line of bayonets across the country at Stewart's Creek and intercepted the retreat of hundreds. But three thousand stragglers from a volunteer army of forty-three thousand men, one third of which were new troops, is not a large proportion. But when men lose sight of their officers involuntarily, straggling is a necessary and inevitable consequence, and they are hardly culpable for going to the rear.

CHAPTER XXVIII.

After the Conflict—Headquarters—Consultation of Generals—A Gloomy Night—Decision of the Commander-in-Chief—Our Losses—The Personal Influence of General Rosecrans in Battle—Orders for January 1st—The Heroism of the Soldiers—The Medical Staff.

"Come one, come all, this rock shall fly
From its firm base as soon as I."

While the battle was raging, the General Commanding, constantly followed by his faithful staff, was galloping to every part of the field. So when it had subsided, when his escorts were almost ready to drop from their saddles with fatigue, he again rode over the ground to make his observations for future dispositions. There were no indications going to impress his mind that Bragg contemplated withdrawal. On the contrary the partial success he had met during the day confirmed a general impression that the enemy would renew their efforts on the morrow. The advantage was with them. They had driven the Right and Center, and part of the Left from their positions, captured many guns and prisoners, and as it subsequently appeared, they inferred from this and from the equally important fact that they had cut off our trains and communication, that Rosecrans would endeavor to fall back upon Nashville. How little they comprehended the man!

Headquarters were finally established in a little

cabin on the right of the road, within six-pounder range of the rebel front. The Generals of the army assembled at night to confer with the General Commanding. Many of them were despondent. Some advised a withdrawal. "Communication is cut off," they said; "some of the troops have no subsistence." The General Commanding, looking up sharply, said caustically, "We may all have to eat parched corn before we get out of this." The views of each officer were not recorded. General Thomas did not advise retreat. General Crittenden pluckily insisted that "we could whip them," and desired to go on with the Left Wing movement into Murfreesboro. After learning the opinions of his Generals, the Chief mounted and rode to the rear.

After diligent examination of the country he concluded that if forced to fall back he could make a firm stand on the high south bank of Overall's Creek. But he entertained no thought of retiring. His constancy was unshaken. He was immovably firm. He put his trust in God, relied upon his stubborn battalions and resolved to conquer. Riding back to headquarters, he said, with startling emphasis: "Gentlemen, we fight or die right here."

To appreciate the dramatic effect of this grave consultation of heroes, the reader must enter deeply into the spirit of the occasion. No pen can portray the situation. The day had begun in dreadful disaster, and the sun declined upon a spectacle of dreadful splendor. Seven thousand gallant men had fallen during ten hours. Regiments had lost, some their Colonels, some all their field officers, and half or more of their company commanders. Some had lost three-fourths of their officers. Johnson's two best Brigadiers were gone, Sherridan's three were dead. Able Wood was disabled. So was skillful Van Cleve. Ten Colonels, ten Lieutenant Colonels, and six Majors were either dead, captured, or wounded. Sherridan alone had lost seventy-two officers. The Regular Brigade, fourteen hundred strong the morning of that frightful day, had lost twenty-two most valuable officers and five hundred and eight disciplined, valiant, trusty *soldiers.* Almost two-thirds of the battle-field, almost one-fifth of our artillery, were in the hands of the enemy. Communication was in a measure cut off from Nashville. Some of the subsistence trains had been destroyed, and the weary, hungry soldiers, who marched and fought on Friday, Saturday, Monday, Tuesday, bloody Wednesday, and who had slept or watched shivering in the bleak November atmosphere Monday and Tuesday nights without fires, were now without food, sleeping again without fires. Artillery ammunition was scant, and it was extremely doubtful if more could be forced through the clouds of rebel cavalry that hovered upon the single thread of communication with the base of supplies.

No wonder the hearts of men sunk under the oppressive weight of adverse fortune. It required sublime trust in Providence and in his own unconquerable will, for the inflexible Leader of that shattered army to say, with the self-reliant eloquence which only they who realized the gloom of that dreary night can appreciate, "we found that we had ammunition enough for another battle—the *only* question being where that battle was to be fought." There was no magnificence in the response which flowed from his

Generals. When he pronounced, "We fight or die right here," "every one of my officers," said he—and he raised upon his elbow in a bed of sickness, his eyes flashing and his pointed finger tremulous with the enthusiasm which roused his soul, "I will say this of all my officers—that however advisable some of them regarded retreat—every one of them expressed the greatest alacrity to carry out my purposes, and they obeyed my orders cheerfully—not a man of them objected or hesitated." "General," said one of them, after the decision had been pronounced, "I did not know you were so game a man." The soldiers had discovered it, and with quick instinct put their trust in him. "We saw you," they said; "We'll fight with you!"

It seems superfluous to record the judgment here, but the point may be justly made. The great indisputable feature of this day's battle, standing out clearly as the sun in the heavens, was that General Rosecrans, by his masterly skill, by his dauntless personal courage, by his perfect self-possession under the most trying circumstances, by his persistent and tenacious efforts, and finally, by the greatness of his moral example, saved the army from ruin, and converted disaster into final triumph.

The history of this memorable day is a history of his incessant exertions, personal example, and self-reliance. Men can not forget the great valor of the forty odd thousand nameless braves who stood manfully, with more than manly fortitude, shoulder to shoulder, through ten dreadful hours of havoc and death, but they can not be identified. But to him to whom defeat would have been endless misfortune, and who was imminently in danger of being victimized by want of skill in others, whom he was compelled to trust, men are in justice bound to pay fair tribute. There is not a soldier in his great army who does not bear testimony that he *personally* retrieved the fortunes of that disastrous day. Without his directing mind, without his personal example, without his inflexible persistence and tenacity, overwhelming catastrophe was inevitable. The lines had been broken at every point on the Right. The Center, under Negley, struggling fiercely, must be swallowed up, the Left and all would be gone, unless the destroying tide could be stayed. No man could do it save he, though all were fighting manfully. History will indorse this record, let the heroism and soldierly character of Thomas, McCook, Crittenden, Wood, Sherridan, Davis, Negley, Van Cleve, Johnson, Rousseau, Palmer, Hazen, Hascall, and the dead Sill, and Shaeffer, Roberts, and other brilliant names, shine with such glowing luster as they should, let their services be valued as highly as they ought.

This tribute of justice detracts not an iota from any of his commanders. Thomas is not diminished in the estimation of his countrymen, who proudly revere him as the "true and prudent, distinguished in council, and on many battle-fields." McCook is none the less esteemed because Rosecrans excels; Crittenden's fame is not tarnished because that of the Chieftain of the army is more conspicuous. Wood, and Sherridan, and Davis, and Johnson, and Negley, and Palmer, and Rousseau, and Van Cleve, are none the less skillful, not less admired, because the soldiers of the army, who decide for themselves, adjudge that Rosecrans is more than master of his profession.

ORDERS FOR JANUARY FIRST.

But that night's consultation resulted in arrangements for the morrow. "Orders were given," said the General, "for the issue of all the spare ammunition, and we found that we had enough for another battle, the only question being where that battle was to be fought.

"It was decided, in order to complete our present lines, that the Left should be retired some two hundred and fifty yards, to more advantageous ground, the extreme left resting on Stone River, above the lower ford, and extending to Stokes' Battery. Starkweather's brigade, arriving near the close of the evening, bivouacked in close column, in reserve, in the rear of McCook's left.

"After careful examination, and free consultation with corps commanders, followed by a personal examination of the ground in the rear, as far as Overall's Creek, it was determined to await the enemy's attack in that position, to send for the provision train, and order up fresh supplies of ammunition, on the arrival of which, should the enemy not attack, offensive operations should be resumed."

McCook's corps was already disposed—Davis on the right, Sherridan joining him on the left, Johnson in reserve; Walker's brigade constituting Sherridan's left, and ordered to relieve Van Cleve in the morning. Thomas was to remain *in statu quo*. Crittenden reunited his command, bringing them all together on the left of the turnpike, and took up a new line of battle, about five hundred yards to the rear of the former line; Hascall's division rested their right on the position occupied by Stokes' Battery, and his left on General Palmer's right; General Palmer rested his left on the ford, his right extending toward the railroad, and perpendicular to it, thus bringing the line at right angles to the railroad and turnpike, and extending from Stokes' Battery to the ford.

THE SOLDIERS.

The jaded troops lay down upon their arms that night, many of them where they had fought. It was cold and dreary, and no fires were permitted in front, but there was no murmur of discontent. The moral aspect of that cheerless bivouac was sublime. "When I witnessed the uncomplaining soldiers in their dreary bivouac; when I saw them parch corn over a few little coals into which they were permitted to blow a spark of life; when they carved steaks from the loins of a horse which had been killed in battle, and ate, not simply without murmuring, but made merry over their distress, tears," said heroic Rousseau, "involuntarily rolled from my eyes." Subsequently said Rousseau, "Day and night in the cold, wet, and mud, my men suffered severely; but during the whole time I did not hear one single murmur at their hardships, but all were cheerful, and ever ready to stand by their arms and fight. Such endurance I never saw elsewhere." This eloquent testimony applied to the whole army. Some of the divisions, however, were fully supplied; Wood's certainly, for that true soldier took care to replenish the haversacks of the men on the eve of battle.

THE MEDICAL STAFF.

The battle-field was strewn with the wounded. Doctor Swift, the able Medical Director of the army, most efficiently aided by Doctor Beebe, Doctor Phelps, Doctor McDermot, and Doctor James, his Chiefs of Corps, together with the noble division, brigade, and regimental Surgeons, exerted their utmost power to remove all the sufferers as quickly as possible from the field to the hospitals. Doctor Swift was often in the flame of battle. Doctor James was in the very forefront when the enemy bore down upon Stokes' Battery. But few flinched from duty—three in the entire staff of surgeons, who shall be nameless now. Said General Rosecrans officially:

"The ability, order, and method exhibited in the management of the wounded, elicited the warmest commendation from all our general officers, in which I most cordially join. Notwithstanding the numbers to be cared for, through the energy of Doctor Swift, Medical Director, ably assisted by Doctor Weeds and the senior Surgeons of the various commands, there was less suffering from delay than I have ever before witnessed."

There is not one word of exaggeration in this, and if the enemy had not destroyed the General Hospital, both our wounded and their's who fell into our hands, would have been still more comfortably provided. God knows there was great suffering. Let this suffice. "It is not needful to sound the stream of blood in all its horrid depths."

CHAPTER XXIX.

THE First Day of January, 1863—Rain—Change of Division and Brigade Commanders—Position of Divisions—Van Cleve's Division Crosses Stone River—Demonstrations by the Enemy—The Regulars Double-Quick to Stewart's Creek and back—The Brilliant Affair of Colonel Innis and his Michiganders at Lavergne—Colonel J. W. Burke and the "Bloody Tenth"—A Trying New Year's Day—Effect of Wednesday's Reverse at Nashville—A Rebel Woman on the House-Top.

AFTER midnight it rained upon the soldiers. They were thoroughly saturated, and in a few hours the bivouacs were masses of mud. Fortunately the army was not harassed by serious alarms on the picket lines. Long before daylight the new line was adjusted, and the troops stood at arms. General Rosecrans waited developments. It was not his policy to force a renewal of the engagement until his stores were replenished.

Generals Wood and Van Cleve, though wounded early in the battle of Wednesday, remained in the field until its close. They were now unfit for duty, and repaired to Nashville. Brigadier General Hascall succeeded the former, and Colonel Samuel Beatty relieved the latter; Colonel George P. Buell taking Hascall's brigade, Colonel Ben. C. Grider, of the Ninth Kentucky, assuming command of Beatty's brigade. Walker's brigade relieved Van Cleve's division, Starkweather's subsequently taking position on the left of the latter. General Crittenden, in pursuance of orders, sent Beatty across Stone River at three o'clock in the morning, to hold the hill overlooking the river at the upper ford, a mile below the railroad bridge in front of Murfreesboro; Colonel Price, commanding the Third Brigade, crossed in advance, followed by the Second Brigade, Colonel Fyffe commanding. The brigades formed in two lines, the right resting on high ground near the river, east of the ford, the left thrown forward. Grider's brigade was formed near the hospitals, to protect the left flank. Lieutenant Livingston's Third Wisconsin Battery crossed the river and took up position on the rising ground in front of Fyffe. The infantry were concealed by lying down. The enemy's skirmishers appeared in front, but Livingston dispersed them by flinging a few shells at them. Grose's brigade, however, crossed to support Beatty, but subsequently, with Livingston's Battery, was withdrawn.

Wood's division was withdrawn by Hascall to a line about five hundred yards in rear of the position occupied the previous day. The line was now nearly at right angles with the railroad, Buell's brigade on the right, Harker in the center, Wagner on the left. Excepting some sharp skirmishing on Harker's and Wagner's fronts, which was finally ended by Bradley and Cox freely using shell and spherical case shot, Hascall's division was comparatively quiet during the day. Palmer's division also rested in battle-order, excepting Grose's brigade, which was sent across the river to support Beatty's division. Repeated attempts were made by the enemy to advance upon the Center, but they were foiled by Guenther's and Van Pelt's Batteries. Morton's Pioneer Brigade once repulsed them severely. The Regular Brigade was ordered up to meet an attack on McCook's front, and subsequently was sent to Stewart's Creek. When nearly there it was ordered back at double-quick time, but upon its return it went into bivouac near headquarters. Scribner's brigade was withdrawn to the rear early in the morning to prepare their rations. Before the famishing fellows got ready, an alarm caused a stampede among some teamsters near their camp, and a skirmishing flurry on Stone River compelled them to take arms. A little later the disappointed troops were marched up to the front again to meet a threatened attack. Negley's division was hurried off to McCook's right in the afternoon to meet a strong demonstration on that front. His troops bivouacked there that night. Bradley's brigade made a dash and captured eighty-five prisoners. Walker's brigade was constantly harassed by pickets, and the enemy constantly menaced his front. Church's Battery signalized itself by its effective gunnery, but the gallant veteran brigade, which had been *at* many combats and several battles, did not have the fortune which it craved, of showing its mettle in a grand battle. At eight o'clock that evening they made a successful reconnoissance, exhibiting great gallantry. At about two o'clock a strong demonstration was made by the enemy at the extremity of a field, a mile and a half from the Murfreesboro pike, but the presence of Gibson's brigade with a battery, occupying the woods near Overall's Creek, and Negley's division, and a portion of Rousseau's, prevented a serious collision. The harassments of the day ended with a demonstration upon Walker's front. The casualties this day were not numerous.

BRILLIANT AFFAIR AT LAVERGNE.

The Michigan Regiment of Mechanics and Engineers, Colonel Innis commanding — three hundred and ninety-one officers and men—had been posted at Lavergne, midway between Nashville and Murfreesboro, to protect communication. Colonel Innis took position on the hights in rear of the hamlet, and constructed a flimsy barricade of cedar brush for the protection of his little garrison. Wheeler's rebel cavalry, after destroying several trains upon the road, appeared in front of Innis at two o'clock with a force of three thousand men and two pieces of artillery. A flag of truce was sent in, demanding a surrender. Innis replied with more vehemence than piety, "Tell General Wheeler I'll see him d—d first. We don't surrender much! Let him take us." Whereon the rebels essayed. A daring officer, galloping at full speed in front of the first column of attack, called upon the garrison to surrender. A bullet pierced his breast. His command charged gallantly. Wheeler opened his artillery. The little garrison defended themselves manfully. The rebel horsemen dashed against the flimsy barricades with admirable spirit. The trusty rifles of the Michiganders destroyed them. The column recoiled into the adjacent thickets. Their commander sent another flag of truce, demanding surrender. "See him d—d first," said Innis, curtly. The desperadoes rolled up again with thundering force. The steady Michiganders hurled them back again. A third assault was foiled; then a fourth; then a fifth. The rebel General sent another flag of truce, explaining that his numbers were overwhelming, and demanding surrender to spare useless effusion of blood. Innis lost his temper, told the flag officer to "go to the d—l," and requested him to warn General Wheeler to send no more flags. He "would fire upon them if he did." The enemy charged more vehemently than before, and were again beaten off. They organized a seventh attack in heavy force, and thundered up the hill in a fury of passion. The gallant little garrison sent them reeling back again. Wheeler withdrew out of musket range, and sent in his flag asking permission to collect his dead and wounded. "Tell General Wheeler," said Innis, "that he is welcome to everything he can take beyond the range of my muskets. We'll take care of the wounded and dead who are under our guns."

THE "BLOODY TENTH."

Meantime, Innis had sent a swift messenger to Colonel Burke at Stewartsboro, five miles south, to come and help him. Gallant Burke gathered part of his sturdy Irishmen—the "bloody Tenth"—and raced up the road with all the speed of eager soldiers. The fighting fellows whose wild clamor had startled the echoes of the Gauley Mountains at Carnifex, and whose comrades were thickly strewn over the green hills of Perryville, stretched out their brawny legs, and stalked along the pike with eager energy. They had held their own post defiantly, rescued captured trains, drove the enemy from their front, but could get no fight. They were after one now, swiftly and hotly. "I never," said the gallant Burke, "saw fellows so disappointed. When we got to Lavergne, Innis had whipped the enemy, and we had no fight!" The

General Commanding did not forget their spirit. Subsequently in his official report, he said: "The Tenth Regiment of Ohio Volunteers, at Stewart's Creek, Lieutenant Colonel J. W. Burke commanding, deserves especial praise for the ability and spirit with which they held their post, defended our trains, secured the rear, chased away Wheeler's rebel cavalry, saving a large wagon train, and arrested and retained in service some two thousand stragglers from the battle-field." So of the valiant Michiganders he said: "The First Regiment of Michigan Engineers and Mechanics, at Lavergne, under command of Colonel Innis, fighting behind a slight protection of wagons and brush, gallantly repulsed a charge from more than ten times their number, of Wheeler's Cavalry." Not the least pleasing feature of these developments of soldierly spirit, was the generous enthusiasm with which Innis expressed his admiring obligations to Burke and the "Bloody Tenth."

A TRYING NEW YEAR'S DAY.

The rebels, however, succeeded in harassing our rear to an embarrassing extent, destroying trains, capturing squads of troops whom they paroled and released, being unable to escort them to their own lines. Several wounded officers who were retiring to Nashville for surgical attention, were disgracefully maltreated. Major Slemmer, of the Sixteenth United States Infantry, was ejected from his ambulance, and other officers were compelled to give their parole, and halt by the highway until they were relieved by passing trains.

New Year's Day was trying upon the army, but its

constancy was unshaken. The troops went into bivouac as they had the previous nights, sleeping upon their arms without fires, and somewhat annoyed by picket flurries along the lines. The General Commanding was constantly in the field waiting developments, and making dispositions for future operations. The quiet of the enemy assured him that they had been worried by Wednesday's battle, and it gave him time to replenish his ammunition and subsistence stores. His headquarters that night and thereafter were in a little dilapidated log-cabin, within shell range of the enemy on either front, on the right of the Murfreesboro pike. He slept an hour or two in his tent at the gable end of the cabin, and his staff squeezed together as thick as figs in a drum on the dirty floor of the tenement. All misgivings had been dismissed from the minds of officers and soldiers. All men felt with the General—"we shall beat them!"

WOMEN ON THE HOUSE-TOPS.

But there was another feature of "Happy New Year" worthy of observation. Tidings of Wednesday's reverse had been carried to Nashville on the swift wings of cowardice. The few patriot residents of the city and the garrison were profoundly afflicted. They apprehended that a dreadful calamity was about to fall upon them. Stragglers, officers, private soldiers, camp followers, poured up the Murfreesboro pike toward the city in streams. The wife of a rebel officer clambered to the roof of her mansion, and looking southward, beheld the shameless messengers of evil. Cushi was running with evil tidings. There was no prudent Ahimaaz to run by the way of the plain to circumvent him. The woman clapped her hands with sudden joy, shouting triumphantly, "they are beaten back." Her friends of either sex took no care to repress their exultation. Some were overbearing and imprudent. Officers and soldiers silenced them savagely. Yet they poured forth into the streets in numbers, and with a gayety that had not been witnessed since the Union armies had occupied the city.

The stragglers were roughly handled by General Mitchell. He denounced them vigorously as infamous cowards, swore their stories of disaster were lies, directed Lieutenant Colonel Cahill to organize them and form them in front of the city. He laughed to scorn the notion that "Rosecrans was whipped," and then with menacing vehemence swore that "if Rosecrans *should* be driven back, not one stone of Nashville should be left upon another. I'll blow the d—d town to fragments," said he, "if I am compelled to leave it." All this rebel joy, and all this patriot gloom grew out of the exaggerations of cowardly officers, fugitive soldiers, and teamsters who fled from battle. A *mal adroit* incident happened to confirm the untoward rumors. The extreme front was an improper place for the important official papers of the department. The numerical superiority of the rebel cavalry rendered it dangerous to keep them with headquarters' camp at an intermediate point, and they were accordingly sent back to Nashville. The malcontents of the Rock City accepted the incident as confirmation of disaster to the federals. Later in the evening they became restive and somber. It was impossible to explain it, but the mystery no doubt was revealed in the back parlors of Nashville. But it was very clear that there was "a plague in all your houses." General Rains was killed, and Moody's men had destroyed the "Rock City Guards." And the women who ascended to the house-tops were much moved, and went up to their chambers and wept. New Year's Day of 1863 was not a "Happy New Year."

CHAPTER XXX.

FRIDAY, January 2—Heavy Artillery Battle—Movements of the Troops—Van Cleve's Division Across Stone River—Grose Supports Him—Onslaught upon Van Cleve's Division—It is Broken—The Batteries Massed—The Center and Right Wing Assisting the Left—Negley, Davis and Morton to the Rescue—A Banner and a Battery Captured—Awful Effect of Our Artillery—The Rebels Routed—Brigadier General Hanson Killed.

FRIDAY morning was raw and chilly, but the clouds soon dispersed, and the sun glowed pleasantly. The troops were cheerful. Some subsistence and ammunition had arrived during the night. At dawn the sharpshooters of the enemy introduced the exercises of the morning with the sharp firing of their rifles. Commanders were at their posts, expecting an attack from the enemy. The "eyes of the army" were on its flanks, and skirting the Murfreesboro pike, galloping over the hills after rebel marauders. McCook and Thomas remained *in statu quo*, part of their respective forces in reserve.

Somewhere about eight o'clock, while Morton's Pioneer Brigade were making crossings at the railroad, the enemy opened a furious cannonade from four batteries on the east side of Stone River. They ranged chiefly upon Harker's position. His men were subject to sore trial, but they hugged the ground closely, and escaped with one man killed and eleven wounded. Estep's battery, upon which the enemy had exact range, was forced to yield its position. Bradley worked his guns with visible effect, until one of our own batteries undertook to throw grape over his head. Whereon he was reluctantly compelled to withdraw to a safer position. Stokes', Loomis', Guenther's, and several other batteries, took part in the duello, and in a short time silenced the enemy. While this was going on, an infantry demonstration was made upon Wagner's skirmishers, but the enemy were easily driven back. The rebels also gave Walker's brigade a salute, but Church soon satisfied them.

DISPOSITIONS ON THE LEFT.

General Rosecrans still persisted in his scheme of wheeling into Murfreesboro with his Left, and with that view, directed his attention chiefly to the position occupied by Van Cleve. Livingston's Battery recrossed the river, and took up its position on the left, leaving Lieutenant Hubbard, with a section of the battery, on the eminence at the right of Price's brigade. Price was on the right of the line, with the Fifty-First Ohio, Eighth Kentucky, and Thirty-Fifth Indiana Regiments in front, the Twenty-First Kentucky and Ninety-Ninth Ohio Regiments forming the second line in reserve. Fyffe's brigade was on the left, and the Seventy-Eighth Indiana was posted in the front line to fill a gap.

A sharp clatter of musketry in front, early in the morning, increased at eleven o'clock to the proportions of a severe fight. The enemy seemed to be creeping up. Crittenden, therefore, sent Grose's brigade across the river to strengthen Beatty's left. About eight hundred yards below the right of

Beatty's division line, the river makes a detour of perhaps a half mile to the rear, and courses nearly parallel with the line taken up by Beatty. Grose formed his regiments in echelon in support of the left of Beatty; the Twenty-Third Kentucky about two hundred yards to the left and rear of Beatty's left, the Twenty-Fourth Ohio, Thirty-Sixth Indiana, Eighty-Fourth Illinois, and Sixth Ohio Regiments, forming respectively, from right to left, the right of the Eighty-Fourth Illinois resting upon a bluff at the river, with the Third Wisconsin Battery near its left. The brigade immediately collected logs, brush, rails, and stones, making a good barricade, and waited developments. Cruft was posted on the opposite side of the river, supporting a battery.

SYMPTOMS.

Meantime, Beatty's skirmishers reported the movement of artillery toward his left, and that sixteen regiments of infantry had appeared in his front. At about noon the enemy flung a few shells at Hubbard's guns. Directly a battery opens upon him. The angry rattle of musketry increases in front. Rebel skirmishers gradually approach, until it becomes too hot for Livingston's gunners, and they retire to a more secure position. Shells, now and then a solid shot, knock the dirt over Beatty's men, but they lie flat on their bellies. The enemy shoots blindly. Soon our skirmishers are so strongly pressed that two companies are sent to strengthen them. Men are hurt on either side.

At half-past two o'clock four more rebel guns are discovered moving to the left. At three o'clock rebel skirmishers are seen throwing down the fences in their front. Battle menacing, certainly! All these conditions are noted. When the fences go down, Beatty orders Price to retire his brigade behind the crest of the hill. The enemy are seen moving up in the distance. They advance in powerful masses—battalion front, three ranks, or six men deep, in mass, in the attacking column—a column of equal strength in support, and another mass, not at all inferior, in reserve. Splendid display of martial pageantry. Their banners are flying haughtily; their steel is dazzling. They march with superb solidity. Those three powerful columns seem to be three monstrous machines. Breckinridge is launching them at three little brigades, and one Wisconsin battery. Perhaps!

THE ONSET.

The head of that frowning mass suddenly shoots clean out from the timber into the front. Fearfully splendid. Their batteries have opened in stunning accord. Shot and shell, whizzing, whirring, shrieking, as if they were winged fiends. The firm sod flies into clouds of dust; trunks of trees are shivered into atoms; splintered boughs rain upon the hills, as if awkward and careless woodsmen were topping the forests; the flesh and bones of horses crush as if they were brittle ice; a man is suddenly tripped up—his leg flies from its base; a soldier's head vanishes—and you do not even sigh, until you bury what remains.

The machine called a column of attack in mass—a thousand men in front, six men deep, with two other machines just like it, pushing behind to sustain its momentum, emits a blaze and a fume with a crashing and thr-r-r-r-upping sound—as if Titans were tearing strong canvas. Then a counter-crash, quickly—perhaps two or three, from as many lines. Volley for volley—then symmetry of sound is lost. File firing ensues—that is, every man loads and fires for himself with all his might, mostly shooting high, so that the lead flies overhead, and twigs flutter—many shooting so low that the dirt is chipped up at the toes of men. If the heaviest battalion is disciplined, and well handled, it shoots most bullets and weight of lead decides, unless cold steel is thrust into the scale. Then lead loses momentum. Price did not fire until the enemy were within a hundred yards of him. His volley shatters the head of the mass. Why didn't he "give them a blizzard, and then at 'em with the steel?" His little brigade fights hard, struggle to keep their feet. Good soldiers!—they had proved it before. Too many bullets for them. A gray cloud suddenly sweeps toward their flank. They brace up an instant, but are doomed to break. Pity! On the 10th of December they won honest fame. Fyffe flings in a flank fire, which stings, but does not destroy. Price goes back, breaks, confuses the second line, so that it can not recover to resist the overpowering billow. Fyffe is forced to fall off to the rear.

The veteran Nineteenth Ohio, which settled the Rich Mountain affair under "Old (?) Rosey," and the Ninth and Eleventh Kentucky, march up. They advance eagerly, and meet the machine, whose head is tattered and torn, and it falls away to let the other machine, that pushed it forward, roll upon the three regiments. Six regiments to three are heavy. Meantime "Old Rosey" had appeared on the field. Fifty-eight iron and brazen battering rams had been gathered in a mass on the nether side of the river. He was holding them in hand like a cocked pistol. Mendenhall had gathered them, and was directing them truly. The immortal Eighth Division, under soldierly Negley, was moving up. Gallant Davis, eager to make a new exhibit of the mettle of his Salamanders, *solicits* the favor to advance his division, and it is rushing across from Right to Left to get in first. Johnson sends over Gibson, with the thirteen hundred soldiers who remained of two thousand four hundred and fifty-eight, who had begun the slaughter of Wednesday. Pioneer Morton, who wants to be "doing it about right," whenever and wherever he can, rushes up in that "Excelsior" way of his, with his "general utility" men—who diversify soldiers' life by building bridges or fighting, and do either admirably. Remember, they represent forty regiments — Michigan, Missouri, Indiana, Kentucky, Ohio, Illinois, Wisconsin, Ireland, Germany — the Union.

REVERSE.

Pity the noble Left Wing should meet with reverse at all—it resisted so victoriously Wednesday; but it can afford it. Nothing but fair that the Right should enjoy reciprocation of favors. The Left assisted the Right; the Right can now help the Left—only the Center is most lucky and crowds in first. The Nineteenth Buckeyes, and the gallant Ninth and Eleventh Kentucky fight staunchly, and the Indiana Thirty-Fifth, on the left, talk of the bayonet, but it won't do now. That gray bank, with a steel crest, lifting upon the right flank, is too much bone and metal. The regiments go back, slowly at first, and at length they take water, as the first and the second line did. The billow behind them rolls on fast, and a crest breaks off into the river.

VICTORY.

Now the power of cannon is cast into the balance. The shock of fifty-eight brazen and iron monsters shake the earth, and a tempest tears through the forest. Legions of devils seem riving the timber where the Left's Third Division was fighting. The Eighth leaps into the stream. The Second Division of the Right is coming—"Carlin," said the Captain of the host, "take your brigade to the left; form it in two lines, and should you find our forces repulsed, allow them to pass through your lines, and on the approach of the enemy, give a whoop and a yell and go at 'em!" Carlin's brigade was dreadfully reduced. He felt some apprehensions lest they should not respond properly. "Tell them," said the General Commanding, "tell them they *must* do it for us, and the country!" Gallant Carlin announced the appeal of their Chieftain. They yell like Stentors and plunge into the stream. Gibson's thirteen hundred charge, shouting like the clangor of trumpets.

Strange that you forget the noise of cannon in battle frenzy. The ear is deaf to its uproar. You hear shells flutter and you dodge. You hear bullets pict, pict, pict, pict, pict, and a sheet of them thr-r-r-up; but unless you deliberately look upon battle as a spectacle to enchant vision, and listen to thunderous artillery to admire the majesty of wonderful artificial sound, the eye is unaffected by pageantry, and the ear waxes insensible to brazen detonation. Heart and mind in unison, say, "we shall beat them!" That absorbs sights and sound. Lo! the mystery of war's callousness. Thus, you see your best friend vanish from your elbow with scarce an emotion. The first gun booms, as if it were a doom. The first crash of musketry thrills to the very marrow of your bones. Then the mighty effort! Then blood in your veins becomes lightning. Then you mutely cry, "we shall beat them!"

There were fifty-eight guns *en masse* in the Center, others on the river bank, and Livingston's across the stream. Mendenhall's, and Loomis', of which were Parson's, and Swallow's, and Bradley's, and Shultz's, and Estep's, and Van Pelt's, Standart's, Stevens', Nell's, Marshall's, Cox's and Stokes' Batteries—hurling solid shot, shell, grape, spherical case and cannister; and the forests seemed bursting with agony. All hell had broken loose. Then the machines which are called columns, in mass, three lines deep, without intervals, six men thick, were torn to fragments. Grose was on the left of them. The Ohio Sixth and Twenty-Fourth, the Indiana Thirty-Sixth, the Kentucky Twenty-Third, and the Illinois Eighty-Fourth, raise with crazy clamor and rip into them. Scott's Illinois Nineteenth, Stoughton's Michigan Eleventh, Given with the Eighteenth, and Elliott and Bingham with the Sixty-Ninth Ohio; Sirwell with the Pennsylvania Seventy-Eighth, Moody with his "boys," of the trusty Ohio Seventy-Fourth, Neibling's "Twenty-Onesters," the Thirty-Seventh Hoosiers, under Ward and Kimball, stalk across the stream and pour in volleys from the right and left. Hazen is rushing in with his Salamanders; Davis, Carlin, and Morton follow swiftly, eager for laurels. The "Twenty-Onesters" are sent off to the left. The Seventy-Eighth Pennsylvanians, the Nineteenth Illinoisans, the Seventy-Fourth Ohioans rush upon a battery, and the "Twenty-Onesters," on the left, swoop upon it. A rebel color-bearer, probed with a bayonet, sinks in a pool of blood. A Seventy-Eighth Pennsylvanian seizes the banner of the rebel Tennessee Twenty-Sixth; the Nineteenth, the Twenty-First, the Seventy-Fourth, the Seventy-Eighth—no matter which State—swallow up the guns, four of them for trophies, and a mass of prisoners—gallant Scott is down, yet he shouts. Davis thunders in pursuit of the fugitives, while the Eighth Division gathers again. The fifty-eight pieces of iron and bronze, in mass, roar with frightful concussion, and sweep the forests in flank, in front, in reverse. Hazen sharply follows the fugitives; Davis is onward; Hascall is coming; the enemy, torn to pieces, are flying in wild dismay over the riven forests, and through the cotton fields. Horsemen, frantic with delight, race far over the field, trailing the captured banner along the regiments. Now the cannon and the infantry are all plunging forward. Twilight, and the thin blue powder fumes dispersing in haze, intermingle. Joyful shouts swell in shrill harmony on the far bank of the river—leap across the stream, roll along the front, spring from rank to rank, stretch from left to right, until its magnificently triumphant volume dies away in pleasant echoes among the distant hills. Such overwhelming ecstacy of victory!

"We shall beat them!" The figure of the Commander-in-Chief was again conspicuous, when the might of his own good sword was needed. He hurled his batteries and his battalions together, at the monstrous machines of Breckinridge, and destroyed them in forty minutes. Two thousand men or more, who had marched upon that field in haughty defiance, at three o'clock and fifty minutes, were dead or mangled at four o'clock and thirty minutes. Breckinridge was a fugitive; General Hanson mortally hurt; General Adams crippled; Colonel Pres. Cunningham killed; Colonel McGeggor fatally struck; and scores more of the master class, who fell in parricidal conflict. It was an appalling calamity to rebel arms. Our loss was about one hundred killed; perhaps four hundred wounded—five hundred in all.

Beatty was in it with his own brigade, under Colonel Grider, Fyffe's brigade, and the brigade of Stanley Matthews, then commanded by Colonel Samuel W. Price. The latter bore the brunt of the disaster, losing seventy-eight men killed, three hundred and eleven wounded. The colors of the Eighth Kentucky Regiment were torn into fragments by a shell. Fyffe, on the left, was not violently assaulted, and was compelled to retire when Price gave way. Fyffe himself was hurt by a fall from his horse. Grider received the same shock, and it was too severe for him. There was much confusion, and a few eager rebels pursued our fugitives into the stream. On the other side some of the broken regiments rallied quickly. The Nineteenth Ohio, Ninth Kentucky, and Fifty-First Ohio, were among the first to cross in pursuit of the flying foe.

The enemy hardly expected a flank fire from Grose.

It was very bitter. The wild scream of his valiant regiments was as effective as their musketry. The Twenty-Fourth Ohio was again robbed of a jewel. Colonel Fred. Jones and Major Terry had fallen on Wednesday. Captain Enoch Weller, commanding the regiment after Terry's death, was killed this day. Among its many dauntless officers, Adjutant Henry Y. Graham shone conspicuously. Gibson's brigade was called upon to assist General Palmer in driving a strong force of the rebels out of the woods on the flanks. The Thirty-Second Indiana—Willich's Germans—charged and drove two rebel regiments clean across the river.

Negley's division and the Pioneer Brigade had been ordered up to meet the onset, while Crittenden directed Mendenhall to dispose the batteries on the hill on the west side of the river. Hazen's brigade also crossed, and the Forty-First Ohio Regiment was among the advanced pursuers of the rebels. General Davis crossed the river at a ford below to attack the left flank of the enemy, but they retreated too rapidly. Darkness put an end to pursuit. Davis, with Hascall's division on his left, Palmer in support, begun at once to throw up breastworks upon the line conquered from the enemy. The battle on Friday evening was an awful paroxysm. General Rosecrans most graphically said: "The firing was terrific, and the havoc terrible. The enemy retreated more rapidly than they had advanced. In forty minutes they lost two thousand men."

While this conflict was raging, Walker advanced in his front with his brigade—the Seventeenth Ohio, Colonel J. W. Connell, and Thirty-first Ohio, Lieutenant Colonel Lister, in front, supported by the Thirty-Eighth Ohio, Colonel Phelps, and the Eighty-Second Indiana, Colonel Hunter. The enemy opened upon them sharply, but the brigade advanced firmly to a point within eighty yards of them. The front line then delivered a volley deliberately, and dropped upon their bellies to reload, the second line following suit. Bayonets were fixed, but the rebels fled to their intrenchments.

Several howitzers, in front of the center of the line, continued to howl until after night fell, echoing most dismally; and at nearly eight o'clock, Lieutenant Colonel Choate, Lieutenant Colonel Davis, of the Eighty-Second Indiana, and Captain J. W. Stinchcomb, of Colonel Walker's brigade, with a detachment of that command, made a successful reconnoissance in front of the Right Wing, driving in the enemy's outposts. The firing, during a few moments, was as passionate as opening battle. Bullets flew about headquarters thickly, but the flurry was soon over. Somewhat later, Colonel Dodge, with eight companies of the Second and Third Brigades, Johnson's division, made a reconnoissance on the extreme right, and disturbed a large force of the enemy.

Somewhat later, General Rosecrans, deeming it possible that the enemy might again attack our Right and Center, "made a demonstration on our Right by a heavy division of camp fires, and by laying out a line of battle with torches, which answered the purpose." Lieutenant Colonel Bassett Langdon, and Captain Fisher, of McCook's Staff, and Captain Charles R. Thompson, Aid to the General Commanding, were selected, on account of their superior vocal powers, to marshal the division. A troop of orderlies escorted them, and constructed blazing fires along the extreme Right, while the commanders of the Light Division moved their forces by the right and left flanks with sonorous clamor. Not long afterward, the General Commanding supervised the new line of battle laid out with flambeaux, and left it for the serious contemplation of the enemy.

It was raining at dark, but the gallant soldiers were jocund. Their bivouac fires blazed like bonfires. Cedars were piled upon cedars, until the black clouds above seemed canopies of lambent flame. The warriors, inspired with the enthusiasm of victory, shouted in their wild joy till sleep overcame them. The future was opening into a glowing vista. No more talk now of retreat. But hundreds labored through the dreary night, intrenching the front of the army. General Rosecrans, standing near his "cabin'd, crib'd, confined" quarters, in mud half way to his boot-tops, rubbed his hands complacently, and repeated, "We shall beat them!"

CHAPTER XXXI.

SATURDAY'S Operations — Too Much Rain—The Front Harassed — Rousseau Annoyed—He Seeks Revenge—John Beatty and Rough-Handed Spears — East Tennesseeans Charge with a Slogan — The Last Hostile Guns in Battle—The Wounded—Rebel Prisoners Eating Parched Corn—A General Surprised—The Rebels Retreat—Sunday—Mass—Official Summary of the Battle.

SATURDAY morning dawned inauspiciously. The rain fell in torrents. The field of battle was a morass. The camps were wretched muck of water and slop. Military operations upon an important scale were impracticable. Quite early in the morning a brigade of the enemy, under cover of the woods, suddenly pounced upon the Indiana Forty-Second, Lieutenant Colonel Shanklin commanding. After a sharp fight, the brave Hoosiers were cut up severely, and many captured, including their commander. The plowed fields being impassable by artillery, no advance could be made profitably; besides, the ammunition train did not arrive until ten o'clock. Batteries were put in position on the left, by which the ground could be swept, and even Murfreesboro reached by the Parrott guns.

The enemy harassed the front on the Right and Center, extending to the Left. It finally became so annoying that General Rosecrans ordered the corps commanders to clear their fronts, which was done speedily. The sharpshooters in the woods on the left of the Murfreesboro pike and the "Burnt House," however, annoyed Rousseau's front all day, killing and wounding some men. General Thomas and he obtained permission to dislodge them and their supports which covered a ford. Four batteries, including Guenther's and Van Pelt's, were opened, under the direction of Colonel Loomis, and the "Burnt House" and adjacent woods were soon battered to fragments.

EAST TENNESSEEANS.

At dark Rousseau sent Colonel John Beatty, with the Third Ohio, Lieutenant Colonel Lawson commanding, and the Eighty-Eighth Indiana, under Colonel Humphreys, to drive the enemy from his cover. Brigadier General Spears, who had arrived from Nashville that day with a subsistence train, solicited and obtained permission to participate in the affair. Beatty advanced on the right with the First East Tennessee Volunteers, Colonel Byrd, the Second East Tennessee, Lieutenant Colonel Melton, three hundred of the Fourteenth Michigan, commanded by Lieutenant Colonel Phillips, of the First East Tennessee Infantry, and three hundred of the Eighty-Fifth Illinois, which were held in reserve.

The line advanced gallantly, the skirmishers meeting with heavy resistance at the start. A column in support appeared on the left of the enemy, upon which Loomis opened his batteries, and they disappeared. Our troops forced their way steadily under a heavy fire, until within charging distance. Then the Tennesseeans raised a wild slogan, and the whole line dashed upon the enemy with the bayonet. The effect was magical. The rebels fled in dismay. Many were killed. The onslaught upon their intrenchments was so swift and sudden that thirty of them were captured. The Colonel of the famous First Louisiana regiment was killed, and his command was almost destroyed. Colonel Humphreys, of the Eighty-Eighth Indiana, was wounded in the hand by a bayonet thrust, and Captain Bell, of the Third Ohio, was severely hurt by a musket ball. This brilliant affair reflected great credit on the officers and troops engaged. The East Tennesseeans were especially gratified. They had proved themselves trusty soldiers. General Rousseau reported the results in person to General Rosecrans, who congratulated him, but said, "Don't you let them drive you out." "I 'm —blessed if I do," was Rousseau's emphatic response. Rousseau's and Spears' troops fired the last shots that were directed at the enemy in the memorable Battle of Stone River.

THE WOUNDED.

The inclemency of this miserable day afflicted the wounded intolerably. Scores were shivering in the rain and mud. The rebel cavalry had destroyed so many hospital tents that it was impossible to shelter all the sufferers. Every possible effort that ingenuity and generous sympathy could devise was exerted to mitigate their condition. Our own gallant soldiers submitted uncomplainingly, regretting their wounds because they could not continue in the ranks. The rebel wounded sometimes growled savagely at Yankee inhumanity. To silence them it was necessary to point to patient victims of their murderous malice—our own mutilated men—spread all over the areas outside of the hospitals, chattering with cold in saturated garments and suffering torment, and to reproach them with the destruction of our hospitals by their own companions. The zeal and devoted efforts of our Surgeons to discharge their entire duty, was beyond all praise.

Near General Crittenden's hospital, Captain Wiles, Provost Marshal General, assembled about a thousand prisoners, and organized them into companies for their own benefit. Some of them were jovial, but many were depressed and discouraged. By Saturday morning they were half famished, having fasted nearly forty-eight hours. Our trains having been cut off by rebel cavalry, there was no subsistence for them. Wiles sent them a load of corn, which they ate voraciously, jocosely denouncing "our fellers"—Wheeler's Cavalry—for "cutting off their rations." At this time some of Rousseau's men were eating porter horse steaks carved from the loins of Colonel Starkweather's horse, which had been shot in the battle—together with parched corn for dessert. Every State engaged in the rebellion was represented in that motley collection of gray-backs.

SATURDAY NIGHT.

Saturday night was equally cheerless. It rained incessantly. The General Commanding, apprehending a freshet in Stone River, ordered the withdrawal of the troops from the east bank of Stone River. Notwithstanding the wretched discomfort of a bivouac in the mud, the troops were even hilarious. A cheerful tone prevailed at headquarters, which was increased by the arrival of Colonel Dan McCook with a large supply train, after having repulsed a sharp attack of the enemy below Stewartsboro.

That evening while General Rosecrans was dictating his official telegraphic report of the battle, to be forwarded to General Halleck, General Crittenden called at his marquee and casually remarked that he supposed there would be no offensive operations on Sunday. He "did not believe Old Master would smile upon any unnecessary violation of his laws." General Rosecrans replied, "I am just telegraphing to General Halleck that we shall probably be quiet on Sunday." It was not then known that the battle was ended. Conversation ran back to the advance from Nashville. General Crittenden, with his customary frankness, now disapproved of it in strong language. He thought it had been extremely imprudent to advance when so inadequately supplied. "How many rations do you suppose there are at Nashville?" said Rosecrans. "Well," said Crittenden, "I suppose you had seven or eight days ahead." General Rosecrans' eyes twinkled sharply. He then said, "I supposed I had informed you. I had Thomas, and probably McCook. I have rations at Nashville to last until the 25th of January, and they can be made to last to the 1st of February." General Crittenden was surprised. He regretted that all the Generals had not known it, because it would have relieved their minds of many misgivings. General Rosecrans is apt to be reticent in matters of vital moment.

SUNDAY.

At about midnight there were indications of a freshet in Stone River. Before daylight the Left Wing was withdrawn to the east side of Stone River. Sunday morning the sun rose clearly. A little later tidings were received that the enemy had fled. The General Commanding devoted himself an hour to High Mass that morning, his faithful and brave companion, Father Trecy, officiating. Who shall say that God did not hear his prayer: "*Non nobis! Dominie non nobis! Sed. nomie tui da Gloriam!*"

Burial parties were sent out to inter the dead, and General Stanley followed the enemy to reconnoiter. Headquarters were removed to the east side of the pike, and for the first time since the 26th of December—nine full days—the General Commanding and his staff, and the noble soldiers of the Fourteenth Army Corps, enjoyed respite from fatigue, hunger, exposure, and battle. An officer said to General Rosecrans, "The army is enthusiastic in its approval of your tenacity." His eyes sparkled an instant, then he said sharply, "I suppose they have learned that Bragg is a good dog, but Holdfast is better."

The enemy left several thousand of their own wounded in the town, and four hundred and four of our wounded soldiers, but we found no hospital stores there for the use of the rebel wounded.

OFFICIAL SUMMARY.

"Of the operations and results of the series of skirmishes, closing with the battle of Stone River and the occupation of Murfreesboro," said General Rosecrans, "we moved on the enemy with the following forces:

Infantry	41,421
Cavalry	3,296
Artillery	2,223
Total	46,940

We fought the battle with the following forces:

Infantry	37,977
Cavalry	3,200
Artillery	2,223
Total	43,400

We lost in killed:

Officers	92
Enlisted men	1,441
Total	1,533

We lost in wounded:

Officers	384
Enlisted men	6,861
Total	7,245
Total killed and wounded	8,778

Being 20.03 per cent. of the entire force in action.

If there are any more bloody battles on record, considering the newness and inexperience of the troops, both officers and men; or if there have been better fighting qualities displayed by any people, I should be pleased to know it.

"As to the condition of the fight, we may say that we operated over an unknown country, against a position which was fifteen per cent. better than our own, every foot of ground and approaches being well known to the enemy, and that these disadvantages were fatally exhumed by the faulty position of our Right Wing.

"The force we fought is estimated as follows: We have prisoners from one hundred and thirty-two regiments of infantry (consolidations counted as one), averaging from those in General Bushrod Johnson's division, four hundred and eleven each—say, for certain, three hundred and fifty men each, will give,

			No. men.
132	Regiments infantry, say 350 men each		46,200
12	Battalions sharpshooters, say 100 men each		1,200
23	Battalions of artillery, say 80 men each		1,840
29	Regiments cavalry, men each	400	13,280
	And 24 organizations of cavalry, men each	70	
220			62,520

"Their average loss, taken from the statistics of Cleborne, Breckinridge, and Withers' divisions, was about two thousand and eighty each. This, for six divisions of infantry and one of cavalry, will amount to fourteen thousand five hundred and sixty men; or to ours nearly as one hundred and sixty-five to one hundred.

"Of fourteen thousand five hundred and sixty rebels struck by our missiles, it is estimated that twenty thousand rounds of artillery hit seven hundred and twenty-eight men; two million rounds of musketry hit thirteen thousand eight hundred and thirty-two men; averaging twenty-seven cannon shots to hit one man; one hundred and forty-five musket shots to hit one man.

"Our relative loss was as follows:

					Per cent.
Right Wing	15,933.	Musketry and	artillery	loss	20.72
Center	10,866.	"	"	"	18.4
Left Wing	13,288.	"	"	"	24.6

"On the whole, it is evident that we fought superior numbers on unknown ground, inflicting much more injury than we suffered. We were always superior on equal grounds with equal numbers, and only failed of a most crushing victory on Wednesday by the extension and direction of our Right Wing."

Early on Monday morning, General Thomas advanced into Murfreesboro, Negley's division in front, driving the enemy's rear guard of cavalry before them. Spears' brigade of East Tennesseeans and General Stanley with the Fourth Regular Cavalry, Captain Otis, and other cavalry regiments, came up with the rear guard of the enemy at Lytle's Creek, on the Manchester pike, three miles and a half from Murfreesboro, and after sharp fighting in the cedar-brakes, drove them at sunset from their last position. Zahn's brigade of cavalry reconnoitered six miles on the Shelbyville pike, but found no opposition.

McCook's and Crittenden's corps, following Thomas, took position in front of the town, occupying Murfreesboro. It was ascertained that the enemy's infantry had reached Shelbyville by 12 M. on Sunday, but owing to the impracticability of bringing up supplies, and the loss of five hundred and fifty-seven artillery horses, further pursuit was deemed inadvisable.

CHAPTER XXXII.

Review of the Field—The Self-Reliance of the General Commanding—His Influence in the Battle—Moral Power—The Staff—Field Officers—Special Mention for Important Services — Addenda — Enlisted Men Distinguished—Consolidated Report of Casualties—Bragg's Army and his Grand Tactics.

Prostration always follows the fatigue and exhaustive passion of battle. Our gallant troops sorely needed rest; their officers needed it still more. The subsequent irritability of those in command, and of all in executive office, sufficiently indicated that nature had been outraged. The patient endurance and lofty spirit of the troops had been wonderful and most admirable. No suffering or privation had evoked complaint. They were ever ready to spring to arms and fight. This was attributable in very large measure to the moral influence and example of the General Commanding, and the spirited officers of his command. He was incessantly employed. At night he was riding over the field preparing for the morrow. In battle he was everywhere. The troops saw him and had confidence in him. They would stand as long as he stood.

An old soldier, remarking upon the battle of Wednesday, said that he could not doubt that "everybody but Rosecrans was whipped that day." Just where others would have begun to retreat he begun to fight.

Instead of looking around for gunboats or intrenchments behind which to shelter what remained of his army, he commenced at once to make new dispositions for the reception of the triumphant, advancing host. He had but a few minutes at his disposal; but he improved them to the utmost. With calm, cheerful, confident, assuring presence, he rode through his anxious, troubled, apprehensive ranks, the light of battle in his eye rekindling valor in their souls, posting his remaining cannon so as to sweep with deadly aim the field over which the exulting rebels were so soon to advance, placing his infantry so as to support the artillery with the least exposure possible; and making every one feel that retreat was not to be thought of—that there was no choice but to conquer or die. Hardly were the most necessary dispositions completed when the rebel columns came rushing on, with shouts that shook the earth, undoubting that they would repeat in a few minutes the lesson they had just given McCook's routed command. But a sheet of flame leaped to meet them, a roar of cannon and rattle of musketry drowned their frantic yells, a pall of smoke shrouded the field of conflict from view, and there was no cessation until silence on the other side suggested the inutility of further firing on ours. Soon the cloud lifted; the sun shone out bright and warm; our grim battalions stood to their arms in readiness for the word of command; but there was no foe within sight—nothing but a plain heaped with the writhing and the dead. Such was the first taste of his quality given to Bragg's bullies by Rosecrans; and, though often thereafter impelled to repeat the dash of Wednesday morning, they never did it so recklessly, nor with anything like the success of their first attempt. Battles had been well fought before; some in which the General Commanding did his work fairly; many in which our soldiers behaved nobly; but the Stone River fight was saved, and Tennessee, Kentucky, Ohio, and Indiana with it, by William S. Rosecrans. That he exposed himself recklessly, constantly, and influenced his officers to do likewise, was no idle bravado, but a stern necessity. After McCook's discomfiture, the fight was lost but for this. Rarely pushing an advantage too far—giving his routed men time to recover from their first panic before sending them into action again—cool, patient, steady, yet resolute, sanguine and watchful—General Rosecrans proved himself more than fortunate, and won a high place in the confidence and the affections of his countrymen. He will not be forgotten.

Men who knew General Rosecrans at home, socially, before he became a warrior, had inferred from his temperament some proneness to hasty judgment, deficiency in executive skill, and lack of coolness and deliberation. No doubt his military mind has developed with experience, but it is plain the original estimate of his character was incorrect. There can be no mistake that in coolness, readiness, fertility of resource, celerity of thought, rapid decision, and comprehensive grasp of mind in the midst of the most trying situations of peril, personal and military, he proved himself perfectly equal to the tremendous responsibility which devolved upon him. Practical skill, profound strategy, and executive faculty with a mind which grasps general principles, and eagerly inquires into, and handles minute details, are rarely embodied in one character, and yet General Rosecrans demonstrated that he combines all.

When his Right Wing was so astoundingly flung back into his face with frightful rapidity and violence, it was enough to have shaken any ordinary mind. It must have touched him exquisitely. His plans were so thoroughly prepared and digested, and so well approved by his best Generals—he relied so earnestly upon the staunchness of the trusty Right Wing, that the pang of disappointment, when it gave way, must have been almost crushing for the instant. A little color, perhaps, faded from his face, but he dashed away emotion with a gesture of impatience, and vehemently said, "Never mind—never mind—we will rectify it—we will make it all right!" From that instant no man discerned a glimmer of despondency, uncertainty, or vacillation in his deportment, but he bent the whole force of his will, and directed all the powers of his mind into that field, with an obvious determination to make it his own. These were the observations of many who watched him all day long, with the keenest and most painful solicitude. The faintest relaxation of his constancy would have unmanned all his army.

THE STAFF.

The gallantry and unflinching fidelity of the Staff was worthy of highest admiration. They were in the midst of the conflict constantly and discharged their duties with unsparing zeal. It was not surprising that there should have been so many casualties in the Staff and escort, but it was marvellous that most of them were not killed. The conduct of the Aids, Captain Thompson, Captain Thoms, Lieutenant Byron

Kirby, and Lieutenant Bond, who were incessantly carrying orders to all parts of the field, was conspicuously brilliant. But Barnet, Goddard, Wiles, Skinner, Curtis, Gilman, Michler, Hubbard, Merrill, Newberry, Quartermaster Taylor, Commissary Simmons, Royse, youthful Porter, and Reynolds, and gallant Father Trecy exhibited constancy, coolness, and courage in the highest soldierly degree. The General Commanding has publicly expressed his and the country's obligations to them.

HONORABLE MENTION.

Without an exception, the Commanders of Corps, Divisions and Brigades, behaved with distinguished bravery. Each officer was constantly in his place. General Thomas did not seem to be any more disturbed by the tempest of battle than if it had been a summer shower—always calm, cool, imperturbable, but vigilant and watchful of his command. Rousseau was fiery and enthusiastic. "Battle's magnificently stern array," had a splendid effect upon him. He rode through the storm erect, with radiant countenance and flashing eyes, seeming to enjoy the infernal carnival. Loomis, of the famous Michigan Battery, is not unlike him in battle. A more superb couple of heroes never fought together on any field. Negley was eager, clear, vigilant, and self-possessed. McCook was as brave as any soldier need be, and was with his troops in their deepest trouble. Braver men, and cooler than Davis and Johnson, do not live. Sherridan, fighting on the left of the Right Wing, proved himself a soldier of a high order of courage and skill.

Crittenden was perfectly calm, but an unusual stateliness in his deportment seemed to indicate that he was gravely conscious of the glories and horrors of a great battle. He displayed, conspicuously, one of the distinguishing qualities of a true soldier—a will to obey orders implicitly. He was fortunate in having such Generals as Wood, Van Cleve, Hazen, Hascall, Harker, Cruft, Grose, Wagner, Beatty and Fyffe. The general estimate of the army, touching division commanders, placed General Wood in the very front rank—and his dispositions on the day of his advance from Lavergne and until his wound compelled him to relinquish his command, justified that verdict. His official report is a model of soldierly composition—technical, severe in style and yet eloquently descriptive, while it breathes the spirit of a thorough soldier throughout. General Palmer, by his constancy, fidelity, and unflinching courage, won the applause of the army. It is doing no injustice to the remainder of the army to describe the battle of Wednesday afternoon, fought by Hazen and Grose, of the Second Division of the Left Wing, with Hascall, Shaefer and Wagner on his left, as one of the most splendid efforts in martial history. True the Left was grandly supported by the Center, but the dreadful fighting of that frightful afternoon was chiefly done by the brigades which have been designated. The skill and firmness of Hazen, when the tide was turning on the Right, holding the key of his position sternly; the desperate heroism of his two immortal regiments—the One Hundredth Illinois fixing bayonets, and the Forty-First Ohio without bayonets, grimly clubbing their muskets to hold their position until relief should arrive to enable them to retire for ammunition, and shouting with wild vehemence; the splendid spirit of the glorious Ninth Indiana, marching across that horrid front, swept as it was by cannon and awful volleys of musketry, cheering with grand defiance of death, was one of the most sublime examples of tragic devotion in the annals of warfare. No wonder the General Commanding said that "Hazen ought to be a Major General." But it was the dramatic situation of Hazen's noble regiments which made them stand out in such comparative conspicuity. Where every regiment on the field displayed the devotion and courage of veterans, it seems almost invidious to individualize any. Who are the cowards and traitors who can despair of the country while the God of Battles gives us such soldiers to fight in defense of the Republic?

Let the Republic rejoice that few field officers in all that great army were recreants. The Fourteenth Army Corps was a host of heroes led by heroes. Each took his life in his sword-hand and flung it with magnificent devotion upon the altar of his country. The soul swells with lofty pride in contemplating the great deeds of our countrymen upon that dreadful field—and it thrills with anguish when it bends over the graves of the noble dead—oh! such multitudes of the brightest spirits in all this wide land! It seemed as if the demon of destruction reveled with infernal joy among our most gallant officers. Death singled out too many shining marks, and made them all his own. The nation "mourns for her children and will not be comforted, because they are not." Was that noble sacrifice in vain? "Words of my own," said General Rosecrans, with eloquent and touching pathos, "can not add to the renown of our brave and patriotic officers and soldiers who fell on the field of honor, nor increase respect for memory in the hearts of our countrymen. The names of such men as Lieutenant Colonel J. P. Garesché, the pure and noble Christian gentleman and chivalric officer, who gave his life an early offering on the altar of his country's freedom; the gentle, true and accomplished General Sill; the brave, ingenious, and able Colonels Roberts, Millikin, Shaeffer, McKee, Reed, Forman, Fred. Jones, Hawkins, Kell, Harrington, Williams, Stem, and the gallant and faithful Major Carpenter, of the Nineteenth Regulars, and many other field officers, will live in our country's history, as well as those of many others of inferior rank, whose soldierly deeds on this memorable battle-field won for them the admiration of their companions, and will dwell in our memories in long future years after God, in his mercy, shall have given us peace and restored us to the bosom of our homes and families."

Of the surviving brigade commanders, no word was heard on the field or after battle but of praise. Each seemed to have established himself so thoroughly in the confidence of his special command that the troops of the respective brigades proudly boasted that their own was the truest and best commander in the army. Hazen, Carlin, James St. Clair Morton, Miller, Samuel Beatty, and John Beatty, Gibson, Grose, Harker, Wagner, Starkweather, and Stanley, are officers, said the General Commanding, in whom the "Government may well confide. They are the men from whom our troops should be at once supplied with Brigadier Generals; and justice to the brave men and officers of the regiments, equally demands their promotion, to give them and their regiments their proper leaders. And then," said General Rosecrans, with the enthusiam of a Chieftian, who appreciates and loves the good soldiers who have fought so well, "many captains and subalterns also showed great gallantry, and capacity for superior commands. But above all, the steady rank and file showed invincible fighting courage and stamina worthy of a great and free nation, requiring only good officers, discipline and instruction, to make them equal if not superior to any troops in ancient or modern times."

St. Clair Morton, Hazen, Carlin, and Miller—the latter, at the especial request of General Thomas, were at once recommended for promotion to Brigadier Generals. Hazen exhibited consummate skill, demonstrating his fitness for a large command. There was a spirit and gallantry about young Harker in the midst of action that excited the liveliest admiration. Beatty (Samuel) was as cool and pleasant as an October morning. He deported himself as if he had taken a responsibility which he must execute under all circumstances, and he proceeded in a methodical business sort of way that suggested anything but bullets and blood. Rousseau, Wood, St. Clair Morton, Colonel Loomis, were the splendid figures of the battle-field. They were no braver nor more devoted than others, but there was a sort of gloriousness in their deportment on the field that excited enthusiasm in all who saw them. "Quiet Phil. Sherridan" preserved his sobriquet under all conditions, but the nervy curtness of his orders showed that his spirit was moved. The President did a wise thing when he made Sherridan a Major General. He did not do so wisely when he overlooked Wood. But it is probable that his honesty and desire to do right is compelled to play the coquette in endeavoring to strike an even balance, numerically, between candidates from the volunteer and regular armies respectively. Perhaps it is well to maintain the principle of compensation by appointing two Major Generals who have not proved that they know their business, to adjust a mistake made in appointing two others who understand it thoroughly. But soldiers who have fought do not appreciate it.

The tribute paid by General Rosecrans to General Stanley (since promoted), was warmly approved by the army. Brigadier General Stanley, he said, "already distinguished for four successful battles, Island No. 10, May 27, before Corinth, Iuka, and the battle of Corinth, at this time in command of our ten regiments of cavalry, fought the enemy's forty regiments of cavalry, and held them at bay, and beat them wherever he could meet them. He ought to be made a Major General for his services, and also for the good of the service."

The gallantry and the fidelity of the staff officers of all the commanders was never surpassed. Among those of subordinate rank, Captain Gates P. Thruston, of McCook's Staff, attracted most attention, being complimented in the official reports of six General officers including that of General McCook, and finally by General Rosecrans. The official lists of "special mentions," which include some of those who were conspicuously distinguished for gallantry and good conduct, embrace the following names, viz.:

NAMES SPECIALLY MENTIONED OFFICIALLY FOR IMPORTANT SERVICES IN THE BATTLE OF STONE RIVER.

By Major General McCook.—Brigadier Generals R. W. Johnson, P. H. Sherridan, and Jeff. C. Davis, commanding divisions in the Right Wing; for gallant conduct during the battles, and for prompt and conscientious attention to duty during their service with the Right Wing.

Brigadier General D. S. Stanley, Chief of Cavalry, commanded advance of Right Wing during its advance from Nolensville; is especially mentioned for energy and skill.

Division Commander Wood—Brigadier General M. T. Hascall, commanding First Brigade; deserves commendation and gratitude of his country.

Division Commander Palmer.—Brigadier General C. Cruft, First Brigade; for holding an important position, and for extricating his command from the mass of confusion around him, caused by repulse of Right Wing.

Division Commander D. S. Stanley.—Colonel Minty, Fourth Michigan Cavalry, deserves credit for the management of his command on the march and in several engagements.

Colonel Murray, Third Kentucky Cavalry; rendered important and distinguished service, gallantly charging and dispersing the enemy's cavalry in their attack on our train, Wednesday, December 31st.

Colonel Zahn, Third Ohio Cavalry; contributed greatly, by his personal example, to the restoration of order and confidence in that portion of the Second Brigade stampeded by the enemy's attack on Wednesday, 31st.

Division Commander Johnson.—Colonel W. H. Gibson, Forty-Ninth Ohio; commanded Willich's brigade after the capture of Willich; has been several times heretofore recommended for promotion, and is again earnestly recommended by Major General McCook, and by General Johnson, for meritorious conduct.

Colonel Charles Anderson, Ninety-Third Ohio; honorable mention by Major General Rousseau, for gallant conduct.

Colonel Wallace, Fifteenth Ohio; Colonel Dodge, Thirtieth Indiana; Colonel P. C. Baldwin; recommended for promotion for coolness and courage on the field of battle.

Division Commander Wood.—Colonel George D. Wagner, Fifteenth Indiana, commanding brigade; has commanded brigade for a year; is recommended for promotion, for brave and skillful conduct during the late battles.

Colonel C. G. Harker, Sixty-Fifth Ohio ; has commanded brigade for a year ; is recommended for promotion, for brave and skillful conduct. He is also specially mentioned by Major General McCook, for valuable services on the Right Wing.

Division Commander Palmer.—Colonel W. B. Hazen, Forty-First Ohio, commanding brigade; commanded brigade, and is especially mentioned for courage and skill in handling his troops, and for maintaining an important position.

Colonel W. Grose, Thirty-Sixth Indiana, commanding brigade ; commanded brigade, and is recommended for coolness and bravery, in fighting his troops against a superior force.

Division Commander Palmer.—Colonel Sedgwick, Second Kentucky; Colonel D. A. Enyart, First Kentucky ; Colonel Ross, Ninety-Fourth Ohio; Colonel Osborne, Thirty-First Indiana ; displayed marked gallantry on the field, and handled their respective commands with skill and judgment.

Division Commander Van Cleve.—Colonel Samuel Beatty, Ninteenth Ohio, commanding brigade ; commanding brigade, for coolness, intrepidity and skill.

Colonel J. P. Fyffe, Fifty-Ninth Ohio, commanding brigade; is recommended for coolness, intrepidity and skill. Is also especially mentioned by Major General McCook, for valuable services with the Right Wing.

Colonel Grider, Ninth Kentucky; commanded brigade, and is especially mentioned for gallantry and coolness under trying circumstances.

Division Commander Rousseau.—Colonel O. A Loomis, First Michigan Artillery ; rendered most important services throughout the battle.

Colonel John Starkweather, First Wisconsin, commanding brigade ; especially mentioned for coolness, skill and courage.

Division Commander Negley.— Colonel William Sirwell, Seventy-Eighth Pennsylvania ; Colonel Granville Moody, Seventy-Fourth Ohio ; Colonel Hull, Thirty-Seventh Indiana; for the skill and ability with which they handled their respective commands.

Division Commander Sherridan.—Colonel Greusel, Thirty-Sixth Illinois; Colonel Bradley, Fifty-First Illinois; are specially commended for skill and courage.

Colonel Sherman, Eighty-Eighth Illinois; honorably mentioned for distinguished service.

Division Commander Johnson.—Lieutenant Colonel Hotchkiss, Eighty-

Ninth Illinois; Lieutenant Colonel Jones, Thirty-Ninth Indiana; recommended for promotion for meritorious conduct. Lieutenant Colonel W. W. Berry, Louisville Legion; specially mentioned for gallant and meritorious conduct; is also specially mentioned by Major General Rousseau for retreating in good order before an overwhelming force, and drawing off by hand a section of artillery he had been ordered to support.

Division Commander Negley.—Lieutenant Colonel Neibling, Twenty-First Ohio; for skill and ability during the battles.

Division Commander Sherridan.—Lieutenant Colonel Laibolt, Second Missouri; specially mentioned for skill and courage. Lieutenant Colonel McCreary, Second Michigan; honorably mentioned for distinguished service.

Division Commander D. S. Stanley.—Major Kline, Third Indiana Cavalry; on the 27th engaged the enemy on the Nolensville pike, and put them to flight. Captain E. Otis, Fourth United States Cavalry; with his regiment rendered important and distinguished service, gallantly charging and dispersing the enemy's cavalry in their attack upon our train, on Wednesday, December 31st, capturing seventy prisoners, and rescuing three hundred of our own men.

Staff of Major General Crittenden.—Major Lyne Starling, Assistant Adjutant General; specially mentioned by Major General Crittenden for gallantry in the battles, general efficiency, and eighteen months' faithful service.

Division Commander Rousseau.—Major John King, Fifteenth United States Infantry, Major Carpenter, Nineteenth United States Infantry, Major Slemmer, Sixteenth United States Infantry, Major Caldwell, Eighteenth United States Infantry, Major Fred. Townsend, Eighteenth United States Infantry, commanding their respective regiments, are specially mentioned for distinguished gallantry and ability. Major Carpenter was killed, and Majors King and Slemmer wounded.

Division Commander Sherridan—Major Miller, Thirty-Sixth Illinois, Major Chandler, Eighty-Eighth Illinois, Major Hibbard, Twenty-Fourth Wisconsin; honorably mentioned. Captain John Mendenhall, Fourth United States Artillery, Chief of Artillery and Topographical Engineer on Major General Crittenden's staff; recommended for promotion for general efficiency and personal bravery and good conduct in battle.

Division Commander Wood.—Captain Chambers, Fifty-First Indiana, Captain Gladwin, Seventy-Third Ohio; these brave officers, with one hundred and twenty men, drove a large force of the enemy from a covered position, and unmasked his battery.

Division Commander Palmer.—Captain Standart, Company F, First

Ohio Artillery; for the gallant manner in which he handled his guns, and brought them off the field.

Staff of Major General McCook.—Captain Gates P. Thruston, First Ohio; specially mentioned by Major General McCook, and others, for particular acts of gallantry, skill and good conduct. He is mentioned by Generals Negley, Johnson, Davis, Sherridan, and Carlin.

Division Commander Davis.—Captain Hale, Seventy-Fifth Illinois; Captain J. H. Litson, Twenty-Second Illinois; specially mentioned for gallant conduct in skirmishing.

Division Commander Rousseau.—Captain Crofton, Sixteenth United States Infantry; Captain Fulmer, Fifteenth United States Infantry; Captain Mulligan, Nineteenth United States Infantry; these three infantry Captains commanded their respective battalions after their Majors had been disabled, and behaved with great gallantry, although opposed by overwhelming numbers. Captain Guenther, Fifth United States Infantry, Company H; deserves great credit and special mention.

Division Commander Sherridan.—Captain Hescock, First Missouri Battery; specially mentioned for bravery and skill in the battles, and for general efficiency.

Pioneer Brigade.—Captain Bridges, Nineteenth Illinois; continued in command of his regiment after receiving a painful wound.

Division Commander Johnson.—Lieutenant Belding, First Ohio Artillery, Company A; recommended for promotion for saving three of his guns by his personal exertions.

Division Commander Sherridan.—Lieutenant Lambessard, Nineteenth Illinois; Lieutenant Wyman Murphy, Twenty-First Wisconsin, Inspectors of Pioneer Brigade; are specially mentioned in two reports for gallant conduct and energy.

Surgeon McDermot, Medical Director Right Wing; for gallant conduct in the field, and great care and consideration for the wounded. Surgeon G. D. Beebe, Medical Director Center; for zeal, energy and efficiency. Surgeon A. J. Phelps, Medical Director Left Wing; for prompt attention to the wounded, great energy and efficiency in the discharge of his duties.

By Major General Rosecrans.—Major General G. H. Thomas, true and prudent, distinguished in council and on many battle-fields for his courage; Major General McCook, a brave, faithful and loyal soldier, who bravely breasted battle at Shiloh and at Perryville, and as bravely on the bloody field of Stone River; and Major General Thomas L. Crittenden, whose heart is that of a true soldier and patriot, and whose gallantry, often attested by his companions in arms in other fields, witnessed many times in this army—never more conspicuously than in this combat; and the gallant, ever ready Major General Rousseau, maintained their high character throughout this action.

Brigadier Generals Negley, Jefferson C. Davis, Stanley, Johnson, Palmer, Hascall, Van Cleve, Wood, Mitchell, Cruft and Sherridan; ought to be made Major Generals in our service. Brigade commanders, Colonels Carlin, Miller, Hazen, Samuel Beatty, of the Nineteenth Ohio, Gibson, Grose, Wagner, John Beatty, of the Third Ohio, Harker, Starkweather, Stanley; recommended for promotion.

And the Staff, viz.: The noble and lamented Lieutenant Colonel Garesché, Chief of Staff; Lieutenant Colonel Taylor, Chief Quartermaster; Lieutenant Colonel Simmons, Chief Commissary; Major C. Goddárd, senior Aiddecamp; Major Ralston Skinner, Judge Advocate General; Lieutenant Frank S. Bond, Aiddecamp of General Tyler; Captain Charles R. Thompson, my Aiddecamp; Lieutenant Byron Kirby, Sixth United States Infantry, Aiddecamp, who was wounded on the 31st; R. S. Thoms, Esq., a member of the Cincinnati Bar, who acted as Volunteer Aiddecamp; behaved with distinguished gallantry Colonel Barnet, Chief of Artillery and Ordnance; Captain G. H. Gilman, Nineteenth United States Infantry, Inspector of Artillery; Captain James Curtis, Fifteenth United States Infantry, Assistant Inspector General; Captain Wiles, Twenty-Second Indiana, Provost Marshal General; Captain Michler, Topographical Engineer; Captain Jesse Merrill, Signal Corps, whose corps behaved well; Captain Elmer Otis, Fourth Regular Cavalry, who commanded the Courier Line, connected the various headquarters most successfully, and who made a most opportune and brilliant charge on Wheeler's Cavalry, routing the brigade, and recapturing three hundred of our prisoners; Lieutenant Edson, United States Ordnance Officer, who, during the Battle of Wednesday, distributed ammunition, under the fire of the enemy's batteries, and behaved bravely. Captain Hubbard and Lieutenant Newberry, who joined the staff on the field, acting as aids, rendered valuable service in carrying orders on the field; Lieutenant Royse, Fourth United States Cavalry, commanded the escort of the headquarter's train, and distinguished himself with gallantry and efficiency. All performed their appropriate duties to the entire satisfaction of the General Commanding—"accompanying me everywhere," said the General, carrying orders through the thickest of the fight, watched while others slept, and never weary when duty called, deserve my public thanks and the respect and gratitude of the army.

ADDENDA.

Lieutenant Colonel Houssam, Seventy-Seventh Pennsylvania Volunteers.

Captain Bingham, Sixty-Ninth Ohio Volunteers.

Captain Cox, Tenth Indiana Battery.

Captain James P. Meade, Thirty-Eighth Illinois Volunteers.

Lieutenant John L. Dillon, Thirty-Eighth Illinois Volunteers.

Lieutenant Jones, Post's Brigade.

Seventy-Eighth Pennsylvania Volunteers captured a rebel flag from Twenty-Sixth Tennessee, assisted by other regiments of Negley's division.

Lieutenant Guenther, United States Battery, and the Second Ohio Volunteers, captured the flag of the Thirtieth Arkansas Regiment.

The Fifteenth Regiment of Indiana Volunteers, Lieutenant Colonel Wood commanding, charged and captured one hundred and seventy-three prisoners from the Twentieth Louisiana Regiment.

The Thirteenth Michigan Volunteers gallantly recaptured two guns belonging to Captain Bradley's Battery.

Carlin's brigade lost half its field officers in killed and wounded.

The Fifth Kentucky Volunteers dragged from the field, by hand, a section of artillery, through deep mud and under heavy fire.

Four color-bearers of the Twenty-First Illinois were shot down, yet the colors were borne safely through the fight.

SPECIAL RECOMMENDATIONS FOR PROMOTION.

Brigadier General David S. Stanley, senior Brigadier General at the battle of Stone River. He commanded the force that did the fighting at New Madrid. On the 27th of May, 1862, he commanded division before Corinth, and repulsed a vigorous sortie of the enemy. At the battle of Iuka his division fought well, supporting General Hamilton's division, and pursuing the enemy. His troops bore a conspicuous part in the battle of Corinth—charged the enemy, routed Maury's division at the point of the bayonet, and followed the advance guard in the pursuit. As Chief of Cavalry, in the Department of the Cumberland, he organized an effective force out of our almost disorganized Cavalry, and successfully operated against the enemy double in numbers. At the battle of Stone River he won universal admiration for himself by acts of personal daring and skillful management of his troops. Distinguished in five great battles, he is entitled to rank commensurate with the command so long intrusted to him.

Brigadier General James S. Negley has commanded a division nearly a year, always maintaining strict discipline, and keeping his command in excellent condition. As commander of the post at Nashville, he fortified and protected the city in a most judicious manner, while cut off from communication, without support from our forces in Kentucky, and surrounded by a vigilant enemy, he subsisted upon their country, made several successful sorties against them, at one time routing a large force at Lavergne, Tennessee. At the battle of Stone River he fought his troops obstinately, and handled them with consummate skill, winning a high reputation for courage and generalship, and contributing largely to the success of our arms.

Brigadier General Thomas J. Wood, a thoroughly loyal soldier from Kentucky. When the war broke out, he assisted the Governor of Indiana in organizing the troops in that State, and, through his energy and experience, was instrumental in creating and systematizing the military department for which that State is so justly celebrated. He made a forced march to be present at the battle of Shiloh, reaching there with his command in time to join in the pursuit. He commanded a division before Corinth. At the battle of Stone River his division repulsed the repeated assaults of the enemy in a most brilliant manner, and the night of the 31st December found it occupying the same ground it held in the morning. Early that day he was severely wounded while nobly discharging his duty, but he did not leave the field till night ended the conflict.

Brigadier General Jefferson C. Davis won distinction at the commencement of the rebellion, for gallant service at Fort Sumter. Afterward conspicuous in the sanguinary struggle in South-Western Missouri. He captured nine hundred prisoners at Blackwater, and by the splendid fighting of his troops, and his skillful management, contributed largely to the success of our arms at Pea Ridge. His services at Shiloh and before Corinth deserve honorable mention. At Stone River he sustained his high reputation. His division was compelled to retire by being flanked, not by being driven. On the 2d of January, he crossed Stone River with a single brigade of his division, and gallantly led them against the enemy, and assisted in routing and pursuing the corps of General Breckinridge.

Brigadier General John M. Palmer has long held a responsible command with credit to himself and honor to his country. The official report of Major General Crittenden pays him a well-deserved compliment for important services performed at the battle of Stone River. His troops were posted in the extreme front of the line of battle in an exposed position, when they successfully resisted the massed assaults of a foe flushed with anticipated victory, and held their ground during the whole of that fearful conflict. He exposed himself freely to heavy fire, and in the heat of battle maneuvered his command with prudence and ability.

Brigadier General H. P. Van Cleve first achieved distinction at Mill Springs, Kentucky, where his command charged and routed the enemy with the bayonet, and did a large part of the splendid fighting that resulted in that most important and brilliant victory. He has always borne the character of an able, conscientious, and brave officer. At the battle of Stone River he managed his command with skill and vigor. When McCook's corps was driven back after his (Van Cleve's) division had crossed the river to advance on Murfreesboro, General Van Cleve hastened with a large part of his command to the Right of the army, and in an open field assisted in checking the advance of the enemy. Though wounded early in the action of the 31st, he remained on the field all day, animating, and obstinately and prudently fighting his well-disciplined troops.

Brigadier General Phil. H. Sherridan is a model officer, and possesses in an eminent degree qualities that promise for him a brilliant and useful career in the profession of arms. As commander of a large force of cavalry at Corinth, he proved himself enterprising, capable, and more than a match in generalship for the enemy's most noted officers. At Stone River he won universal admiration. He held his troops in hand, and fought them several hours, repulsing the enemy in his front with great slaughter. Upon being flanked and compelled to retire, he withdrew his command more than a mile under a terrible fire in remarkable order, at the same time inflicting the severest punishment upon the foe. The constancy and steadfastness of his troops on the 31st of December enabled the reserve to reach the Right of our army in time to turn the tide of battle, and changed a threatened rout into a victory. He has fairly won promotion.

Colonel John Beatty, Third Ohio. Early in the war he participated in the important military operations in Western Virginia, and was present at Rich Mountain and Elkwater. He bore an honorable part under General Mitchell in the engagement at Bridgeport, Tennessee. He commanded the regiment on the extreme right of McCook's corps at the battle of Chaplin Hills, and displayed coolness and courage in that exposed and fatal position. At Stone River, Colonel Beatty's brigade was in reserve, and when the Right of our army was driven back, was gallantly led to the rescue, and through such splendid fighting as it and others did, the army was saved. On January 3d, Colonel Beatty's brigade, under his skillful management, assisted in storming the enemy's rifle pits, and achieving the success that led the enemy to abandon the position before Murfreesboro.

Colonel Wm. H. Gibson, Forty-Ninth Ohio Volunteers, entered the service July 3, 1861, as Colonel of the Forty-Ninth Ohio Volunteers, a regiment, while under his charge, second to no other in drill, discipline, and efficiency. He long commanded a brigade, and at one time a division at Shiloh, before Corinth, and at Stone River; he has proved himself a working, wide-awake, determined, and able officer. During the latter engagement he moved his brigade under orders to various parts of the field with admirable promptness and ability.

Colonel Wm. B. Hazen, Forty-First Ohio Volunteers, has been intrusted with the responsibility of commanding a brigade perhaps as long as any officer in the service of similar rank. At Shiloh he displayed marked ability. At Stone River he proved himself a brave and able soldier by the courage and skill displayed in forming and sheltering his troops, and in organizing and fighting all the material around him, in order to hold his important position.

Colonel W. P. Carlin, Thirty-Eighth Illinois Volunteers. This thoroughly educated and efficient officer has attained honorable distinction at Pea Ridge, Corinth, Chaplin Hills, and Stone River, as well as by the perfect state of discipline in which he always kept his command. At Chaplin Hills he pushed his brigade into Perryville, threatened the enemy's rear, and captured an ammunition train, several caissons, and a considerable number of the enemy. In the advance on Murfreesboro, through his daring and skill, the brigade routed a rebel force and captured a cannon. At Stone River, December 30, he drove in the rebel skirmishers and advance guard in admirable style. December 31st he held his troops in hand, fighting desperately against fearful odds until the supports on both sides were driven back, and the fact that he lost half his field officers in killed and wounded, and thirty-four and three-fourths per cent. of his command, testifies to his stubborn fighting.

Colonel Samuel Beatty, Nineteenth Ohio Volunteers, distinguished himself early in the war by gallant conduct in Western Virginia, particularly at Rich Mountain. At Shiloh he again did good service. On the morning of the 31st of December, at Stone River, when our Right had been turned, he assisted by steady and unflinching fighting in checking the advance of the enemy. January 3d he commanded the Third Division, Left Wing, in the sanguinary conflict east of Stone River, and though forced to retire before overwhelming numbers, he rallied his troops, and aided in the brilliant repulse and pursuit that soon followed. The official report of his commanding officer commended him for his coolness, intrepidity, and skill on the field of battle.

Colonel George D. Wagner, Fifteenth Indiana Volunteers, served as Colonel of the Fifteenth Indiana on Cheat Mountain in Western Virginia, and aided effectually in repulsing the attack of the rebel General Lee at Elkwater. Distinguished for energy and efficiency as a regimental commander, he has commanded successfully and efficiently a brigade, and at the battle of Stone River his conduct was heroic. He is respectfully recommended for promotion to Brigadier General.

Colonel William Grose, Thirty-Sixth Indiana Volunteers, has long commanded a brigade with ability that would make his promotion but a simple act of justice to him and his command. At the battle of Stone River his troops, posted in the extreme front, fought against great odds, and the commander of his division reports that he conducted himself with great coolness and bravery, and managed his troops in such a manner that he could suggest no improvement. He is respectfully recommended for promotion to the rank of Brigadier General.

Lieutenant Colonel O. L. Shepherd, commanding Regular Brigade; commanded the brigade with bravery and skill at the battle of Stone River, and is specially mentioned in the reports of Major General Rousseau and of Major General Thomas, his division and corps commanders. The fearful loss of the brigade, being upward of thirty-five per cent., attests the obstinacy of the fighting. He is respectfully recommended for a "brevet."

Major Fred. Townsend, of the Eighteenth United States Infantry, commanding a battalion of Regulars in the battle of Stone River, behaved with great gallantry, and is especially mentioned in the report of his division commander. He is respectfully recommended for a "brevet."

Major Slemmer, commanding battalion of Sixteenth Regulars, fought bravely, was badly wounded, and fell into the hands of the enemy. While in a little cabin with six other wounded officers, the fire of our batteries struck the house, and some of them prepared to put out a white flag, but Major Slemmer sent his boy to say that there was no one but six desperately wounded officers who would probably die any way, and that if it was necessary to hold the ground to blaze away and knock the house to pieces.

Major Caldwell, commanding battalion of Regulars at the battle of Stone River, has been in service twenty years—is honorably mentioned by his brigade commander for gallantry. He is respectfully recommended for a "brevet."

Major John H. King, Fifteenth United States Infantry, has commanded a battalion of Regulars for more than a year in active service, and always praised by his superiors for order and efficiency. Was in the battle of Shiloh, where he had a horse shot from under him ; and was second in command in the battle of Stone River, where he fought bravely. He is respectfully recommended for "brevet."

Captain Crofton commanded a battalion of the Sixteenth United States Infantry after Major Slemmer was wounded, in the battle of Stone River, where he fought bravely. He is respectfully recommended for "brevet."

Captain Mulligan, who succeeded Major Carpenter in command of the Nineteenth Infantry Battalion in the battle of Stone River, is mentioned by his commander for gallantry. He is respectfully recommended for a "brevet."

Captain Fulmer, Fifteenth Regular Infantry, succceeded to the command of that battalion at the battle of Stone River, after Major King was wounded, and behaved with great bravery during the whole action.

First Lieutenant J. L. Guenther, Battery H, Fifth United States Artillery. Too much can not be said in praise of this brave and accomplished officer. His services in Western Virginia especially at the battle of Greenbriar, deserves the most honorable mention. At Shiloh his heroic conduct and skill in managing his guns won universal admiration, and Captain W. Terrill, his senior officer, was made Brigadier General for like brilliant services. At the engagement at Dog Walk he behaved with coolness and intrepidity. For his magnificent conduct at Stone River he fairly earned the "brevet" of Major. His battery almost annihilated the Thirty-Fifth Arkansas rebel regiment and cut down and captured its colors. His splendid Napoleons, double-shotted with grape, defended themselves frequently unaided by infantry, and gained for them the thanks and admiration of the army. Served in Western Virginia with great credit.

Lieutenant Parsons commanding Companies H and M, Fourth United States Artillery, in the battle of Stone River, has always managed to get under the heaviest fire. He was in the affair at Cotton Hill, in Western Virginia, and at Shiloh in Mendenhall's Battery, which was specially mentioned in General Crittenden's report. At Perryville he behaved like a hero. His battery was specially distinguished in the battle of Stone River on the day of the 31st of December, and on the morning of the 2d of January. He is respectfully recommended for a Major "brevet."

Colonel John Kennett, Fourth Ohio Voluteer Cavalry, who commanded the Second Brigade of the Cavalry Divisions, accompanying Crittenden's Corps, behaved with great gallantry and efficiency throughout the entire engagement, commencing on the 26th of December and terminating on the 3d of January last. His cavalry drove the rebel cavalry from near Lavergne and followed them during our advance. On the 30th, during all the day, the cavalry of his brigade was scattered, but with those parts he could command, from time to time during the battle, he behaved with distinguished gallantly, charging the rebel cavalry in person. He rallied some of our cavalry and stopped stragglers in the rear, and captured a number of rebel prisoners. His unwearied labors and conspicuous courage on former occasions, as well as during the battle of Stone River, have endeared him to the army, and it is a matter of deep regret that a functional disease compelled him to quit the service. He well deserves to be a Brigadier General in the cavalry service.

ENLISTED MEN SPECIALLY MENTIONED FOR GALLANT CONDUCT IN THE BATTLE OF STONE RIVER.

Quartermaster Sergeant Colburn, Thirty-Third Ohio.

Sergeant Ferguson, Co. G, Fifty-Ninth Illinois.

First Sergeant German, Eighth Wisconsin Battery.

Privates A. F. Freeman and Abijah Lee (Orderlies with Brigadier General Davis).

Private James Gray, Co. E, Thirty-Ninth Indiana.

Sergeant Holan, Co. G, Sixty-Fourth Ohio.

Corporal James Slater and Private William Hayman, Second Indiana Cavalry (escort General Palmer).

Sergeant McKay, Co. E, Forty-First Ohio; Sergeant McMahon, Co. H, Forty-First Ohio, and Corporal J. B. Patterson, Co. G, Forty-First Ohio (commanded their respective companies in the battle and behaved with great gallantry, recommended for promotion).

Sergeant R. B. Rhodes, First Ohio Cavalry (commanded escort of Brigadier General Van Cleve).

Sergeant Jason Hurd, Nineteenth Ohio.

Private William Brown, Fifty-Seventh Ohio (captured thirty prisoners).

Private Nelson Shields, Thirteenth Ohio (preserving regimental flag).

Private J. F. Mitchell, Co. B. Thirty-Third Ohio.

Sergeant H. A. Millar, Seventy-Eighth Pennsylvania.

Sergeant A. R. Weaver, Seventy-Eighth Pennsylvania.

Sergeant F. Mechlin, Seventy-Eighth Pennsylvania.

Corporal W. Hughes, Seventy-Eighth Pennsylvania.

Sergeant P. A. Weaver, Seventy-Fourth Ohio.

Orderlies Jaggers and Parish, Fourth Ohio Volunteer Cavalry.

CASUALTIES.

Our losses in the service of operations, beginning with the 26th day of December and ending with the battle of Stone River, were as follows:

RIGHT WING, MAJOR GENERAL McCOOK.

FIRST DIVISION, BRIGADIER GENERAL JEFF. C. DAVIS.

First Brigade, Colonel P. Sidney Post Commanding.

REGIMENTS.	Killed		Wounded		Missing.		Aggregate	
	Officers..	Men.....	Officers..	Men.....	Officers..	Men.....	Officers..	Men.....
22d Indiana Volunteers..........	...	7	5	34	...	18	5	59
59th Illinois Volunteers................	...	7	...	43	...	30	...	80
74th Illinois Volunteers................	...	8	1	34	...	42	1	84
75th Illinois Volunteers....	...	2	2	19	...	59	2	80
5th Wisconsin Battery..................	...	1	1	5	...	6	1	12
Total First Brigade.....	...	25	9	135	...	155	9	315

Second Brigade, Colonel W. P. Carlin Commanding.

REGIMENTS.	Killed Officers	Killed Men	Wounded Officers	Wounded Men	Missing Officers	Missing Men	Aggregate Officers	Aggregate Men
21st Illinois Volunteers................	2	55	7	180	...	59	9	294
15th Wisconsin Volunteers...........	2	13	5	65	1	33	8	111
101st Ohio Volunteers..................	4	19	2	121	...	66	6	206
38th Illinois Volunteers................	2	32	5	104	...	34	7	170
2d Minnesota Battery..................	...	3	1	5	...	1	1	9
Total Second Brigade..........	10	122	20	475	1	193	31	790

Third Brigade, Colonel W. E. Woodruff Commanding.

REGIMENTS.	Killed Officers	Killed Men	Wounded Officers	Wounded Men	Missing Officers	Missing Men	Aggregate Officers	Aggregate Men
25th Illinois Volunteers................	1	15	3	72	...	5	4	92
35th Illinois Volunteers................	1	10	1	49	...	25	2	84
81st Indiana Volunteers................	2	4	1	46	1	15	4	65
8th Wisconsin Battery..................	1	...	...	4	...	1	1	5
Co. B, 2d Indiana Cavalry............	...	...	...	2	...	......	...	2
2d Kentucky Cavalry, Co. G..........	1	...	...	2	...	6	1	8
Total Third Brigade.............	6	29	5	175	1	52	12	256
Total First Division..............	16	176	34	785	2	400	52	1361

SECOND DIVISION, BRIGADIER GENERAL R. W. JOHNSON.

First Brigade, Brigadier General A. Willich, succeeded by Colonel W. H. Gibson Commanding.

REGIMENTS.	Killed		Wounded		Missing.		Aggregate	
	Officers	Men	Officers	Men	Officers	Men	Officers	Men
Brigade officers	...	...	...	...	1	......	1	......
15th Ohio Volunteers	...	17	2	68	1	127	3	212
49th Ohio Volunteers	2	18	6	88	...	108	8	214
32d Indiana Volunteers	...	12	...	40	...	115	...	167
39th Indiana Volunteers	1	30	2	116	2	229	5	375
89th Illinois Volunteers	1	9	1	45	...	94	2	148
Battery A, 1st Ohio	...	1	...	4	...	24	...	29
Total First Brigade	4	87	11	361	4	697	19	1145

Second Brigade, Brigadier General E. N. Kirk Commanding.

REGIMENTS.	Killed Officers	Killed Men	Wounded Officers	Wounded Men	Missing Officers	Missing Men	Aggregate Officers	Aggregate Men
Brigade officers	...	...	1	...	...	...	1	......
34th Illinois Volunteers	2	19	2	98	2	72	6	189
79th Illinois Volunteers	1	23	3	68	3	121	7	212
29th Indiana Volunteers	1	14	2	66	1	51	4	131
30th Indiana Volunteers	1	30	2	108	2	70	5	208
77th Pennsylvania Volunteers	1	4	1	28	2	28	4	60
Battery E, 1st Ohio	...	10	...	5	2	...	2	15
Total Second Brigade	6	100	11	373	2	342	29	815

Third Brigade, Colonel P. P. Baldwin Commanding.

REGIMENTS.	Killed Officers	Killed Men	Wounded Officers	Wounded Men	Missing Officers	Missing Men	Aggregate Officers	Aggregate Men
1st Ohio Volunteers	...	8	1	46	...	81	1	135
93d Ohio Volunteers	...	12	1	45	...	64	1	121
6th Indiana Volunteers	...	17	...	50	1	36	1	103
5th Kentucky Volunteers	1	18	7	73	...	26	8	117
5th Indiana Battery	...	3	1	18	...	1	1	22
3d Indiana Cavalry	...	4	...	6	...	15	...	25
Total Third Brigade	1	62	10	238	1	223	12	523
Total Second Division	11	249	32	972	17	1262	60	2483

THIRD DIVISION, BRIGADIER GENERAL PHIL. H. SHERRIDAN.

First Brigade, Brigadier General J. W. Sill Commanding.

REGIMENTS.	Killed		Wounded		Missing.		Aggregate	
	Officers..	Men.....	Officers..	Men.....	Officers..	Men.....	Officers..	Men.....
Brigade officers	1	...	1	......	...	...	2	......
36th Illinois Volunteers	1	45	3	144	6	13	10	202
88th Illinois Volunteers	1	13	2	48	...	48	3	109
24th Wisconsin Volunteers	1	19	1	55	...	98	2	172
21st Michigan Volunteers	...	18	7	82	...	36	7	136
4th Indiana Battery	...	6	...	17	...	3	...	26
Total First Brigade	4	101	14	346	6	198	24	645

Second Brigade, Colonel F. Shaeffer Commanding.

REGIMENTS.	Killed Officers	Killed Men	Wounded Officers	Wounded Men	Missing Officers	Missing Men	Aggregate Officers	Aggregate Men
2d Brigade, officers	1	...	...	...	...	...	1	...
2d Missouri Volunteers	...	7	...	40	1	14	1	61
15th Missouri Volunteers	3	9	4	51	...	5	7	65
44th Illinois Volunteers	1	28	4	104	...	17	5	149
73d Illinois Volunteers	1	15	3	61	1	7	5	83
1st Missouri Battery	1	5	...	13	...	1	1	19
Total Second Brigade	7	64	11	269	2	44	20	377

Third Brigade, Colonel G. W. Roberts Commanding.

REGIMENTS.	Killed Officers	Killed Men	Wounded Officers	Wounded Men	Missing Officers	Missing Men	Aggregate Officers	Aggregate Men
3d Brigade, officers	1	...	...	......	...	...	1	......
22d Illinois Volunteers	...	21	5	109	2	54	7	184
27th Illinois Volunteers	1	8	2	67	...	25	3	100
42d Illinois Volunteers	1	18	...	96	1	45	2	159
51st Illinois Volunteers	1	6	4	37	...	9	5	52
1st Illinois Battery	...	5	2	19	...	25	2	49
Total Third Brigade	4	58	13	328	3	158	20	544
Total Third Division	15	223	38	943	11	400	64	1566
Grand Total	42	648	104	2700	30	2062	176	5410

CENTER, MAJOR GENERAL GEO. H. THOMAS.

FIRST DIVISION, MAJOR GENERAL ROUSSEAU.

REGIMENTS.	Offi'rs		Non-Com. Officers		Enlisted Men.		Total.	
	Killed.....	Wounded..	Killed.....	Wounded..	Killed.....	Wounded..	Killed.....	Wounded..
33d Ohio Volunteers	...	...	...	4	2	17	2	21
94th Ohio Volunteers	...	2	...	7	2	15	2	24
2d Ohio Volunteers	1	4	2	7	5	22	8	33
10th Wisconsin Volunteers	...	...	...	...	3	15	3	15
38th Indiana Volunteers	1	2	3	19	10	65	14	86
1st Wisconsin Volunteers	...	1	...	4	...	3	...	8
21st Wisconsin Volunteers	...	1	...	...	...	1	...	2
2d Kentucky Cavalry	...	...	...	2	...	2	...	4
79th Pennsylvania Volunteers	...	...	...	3	2	5	2	8
24th Illinois Volunteers	...	...	...	...	...	4	...	4
15th Kentucky Volunteers	2	1	1	4	5	24	8	29
88th Indiana Volunteers	...	3	2	11	6	34	8	48
3d Ohio Volunteers	...	1	4	13	13	53	17	67
42d Indiana Volunteers	...	6	3	13	14	68	17	87
15th United States Infantry	1	4	1	13	9	54	11	71
16th United States Infantry	...	7	1	22	15	104	16	133
18th United States Infantry	2	11	10	32	43	173	55	216
19th United States Infantry	1	1	...	11	6	35	7	47
Company H, 5th United States Artillery	...	...	...	1	...	4	...	5
Total	8	44	27	166	135	698	170	908

SECOND DIVISION, BRIGADIER GENERAL NEGLEY.

REGIMENTS.	Offi'rs Killed	Offi'rs Wounded	Non-Com. Killed	Non-Com. Wounded	Enlisted Killed	Enlisted Wounded	Total Killed	Total Wounded
18th Ohio Volunteers	1	8	8	21	17	86	26	115
19th Illinois Volunteers	1	7	4	21	9	55	14	83
11th Michigan Volunteers	2	6	5	12	23	66	30	84
69th Ohio Volunteers	1	6	3	15	1	32	5	53
21st Ohio Volunteers	1	4	7	14	16	85	24	103
74th Ohio Volunteers	...	5	4	21	5	66	9	92
37th Indiana Volunteers	2	5	4	27	19	74	25	106
78th Pennsylvania Volunteers	...	5	3	17	13	103	16	125
1st East Tennessee Volunteers	...	...	...	2	..	9	...	11
2d East Tennessee Volunteers	...	1	...	1	...	3	...	5
Battery G, 1st Ohio	...	...	1	2	2	7	3	9
Battery M, 1st Ohio	...	1	1	...	...	...	1	1
Battery M, 1st Kentucky	...	1	...	...	1	2	1	3
Total	8	49	40	153	106	588	154	790

RECAPITULATION.

COMMANDS.	Offi'rs Killed	Offi'rs Wounded	Non-Com. Officers Killed	Non-Com. Officers Wounded	Enlisted Men. Killed	Enlisted Men. Wounded	Total. Killed	Total. Wounded
First Division	8	44	27	166	135	698	170	908
Second Division	8	49	40	153	106	588	154	790
Walker's Brigade	...	1	...	2	...	12	...	15
Aggregate	16	94	67	321	241	1298	324	1713

Total killed and wounded..............................2,037

LEFT WING, MAJOR GENERAL T. L. CRITTENDEN.

FIRST DIVISION, BRIGADIER GENERAL T. J. WOOD.

CASUALTIES.	Officers.	Men.....	Total....
Killed	11	200	211
Wounded	56	859	915
Missing	...	167	167
Total	67	1226	1293

SECOND DIVISION, BRIGADIER GENERAL J. M. PALMER.

COMMANDS.	Killed. Officers.	Killed. Men.....	Killed. Total....	Wounded. Officers.	Wounded. Men.....	Wounded. Total....
1st Brigade, Cruft's	...	44	44	9	218	227
2d Brigade, Hazen's	5	41	46	17	318	335
3d Brigade, Grose's	10	97	107	22	456	478
Standart's Ohio Battery	...	5	5	...	12	12
Parsons' 4th United States Artillery	...	2	2	...	14	14
Cockerell's Indiana Battery	...	2	2	1	43	44
Total	15	191	206	49	1061	1110

Second Division—Continued.

COMMANDS.	Missing.			
	Officers....	Men........	Total......	Aggregate
1st Brigade, Cruft's	6	120	126	397
2d Brigade, Hazen's	...	52	52	433
3d Brigade, Grose's	..	74	74	659
Standart's Ohio Battery	...	3	3	20
Parsons' 4th United States Artillery	...	6	6	22
Cockerell's Indiana Battery	...	2	2	48
Total	6	257	263	1579

THIRD DIVISION, BRIGADIER GENERAL VAN CLEVE.

COMMANDS.	Killed.			Wounded.			Missing.			Aggregate....
	Officers.	Men.....	Total....	Officers.	Men.....	Total....	Officers.	Men.....	Total....	
Brigadier General Van Cleve	...	...	...	1	...	1	...	...	...	1
1st Brigade	7	59	66	16	303	319	...	81	81	466
2d Brigade	4	76	80	14	225	239	2	160	162	481
3d Brigade	6	75	81	21	307	328	2	146	148	557
Artillery	...	6	6	...	19	19	...	...	...	25
Total	17	216	233	52	854	906	4	387	391	1530

GRAND AGGREGATE.

Officers killed	92	Men killed	1441	Total killed	1,533
Officers wounded	384	Men wounded	6861	Total wounded	7,245
Total	476	Total	8302	Total	8,778
Prisoners					3,000
Grand aggregate of killed, wounded, and prisoners					11,778

Incongruous official reports make exactness in aggregates impossible; but it was finally discovered upon examination of all the data that the actual numerical casualties of the Left Wing exceeded those of the Right Wing. Its per centage of losses was correspondingly greater. We lost about three thousand prisoners.

The dead were buried in trenches, excepting in a few instances where regiments, with honorable *esprit de corps*, sought tenderly for their comrades and interred them carefully, distinguishing their places of burial with head-boards. The body of Colonel Garesché was interred in the little cemetery on the knoll where headquarters were established on the night of the 30th of December, but it was subsequently exhumed by his brother and conveyed to the North.

BRAGG'S ARMY AND HIS GRAND TACTICS.

In the absence of positive data it is necessary to rely upon circumstantial evidence in order to establish the numerical force of Bragg's army in that battle. The estimates of General Rosecrans are not only plausible but fair. The testimony of the rebels themselves confirms the general affirmation that Bragg's army was at least equal, numerically, in infantry and artillery to Rosecrans' force, while his cavalry and mounted infantry exceeded that of General Stanley, at least four to one. Colonel Truesdail's reports, touching the strength of Bragg's infantry force, were generally verified, but reinforcements joined his forces after Rosecrans moved from Nashville.

It appeared subsequently that Bragg, confident in the superb discipline of his army, had misconceived the fighting qualities of our men. He assumed that at least half of Rosecrans' forces were raw, and therefore unreliable. He, therefore, not only concluded to give battle at Stone River, but it is asserted that he was preparing to fall suddenly upon the divisions at Gallatin, menacing Nashville with a sufficient force to prevent Rosecrans from sending succor to the forces at the former points.

It is certain that he was sanguine of success, and his defeat, although compensated in some degree by his success of Monday, was a sore disappointment. Had he been satisfied to withdraw from Murfreesboro Monday night the prestige of victory would have remained with him for a little while, though he would have been bitterly pursued and at all hazards. Bragg's mode of fighting was characteristic of the Southern people. It was all dash, and the admirable discipline of his troops told fearfully at every onset. They charged with splendid daring. But it was evident that they were best in onset. They did not at any time display the staunch stand-up fighting pluckiness which distinguished our troops. Where two lines were confronted in the field, man for man, the superiority of our troops was at once made manifest. Northern phlegm was too much for Southern fire. Their troops fought ferociously, ours with bitter determination. Now and then some of our regiments galled to death by their marksmen, would rush infuriately forward and drive everything before them. The rebels never attempted to resist a charge, though our troops resisted mad charges by them repeatedly. They overwhelmed the Right Wing and the Third Division of the Left by avoirdupois—not by fighting.

Their grand tactics were conspicuous in this battle as they were at Gaines' Mills, where they defeated Fitz John Porter, who, if he had possessed the skill of Rosecrans, would have utterly defeated the enemy, though vastly outnumbered by them. The rebel artillery practice was very fine. They had exact range all over our position. It was often remarked in the midst of battle that their gunners were very skillful. Nevertheless the superiority of our artillery was established. Their sharpshooters were their most formidable arm. They swarmed in the forests, and during Wednesday there was not a point on the battle-field that was not within their range. Half our officers who were wounded were struck by them. In McCook's front they had constructed platforms among the branches of the trees, from which to practice their devilish arts. Their mounted infantry were also signally serviceable to them. Without them their cavalry would not have been able to cut our communications so successfully. In fine, the rebels again illustrated in this battle, the fact that they had thoroughly devoted themselves to war—that they had rejected all theories; that they had adopted the wisest maxims of warfare, and had accepted the admonitions of experience. It was curious, however, that Bragg, whose reputation as an artillery officer stood highest in that branch of the service, should have been so thoroughly beaten with his favorite arm.

CHAPTER XXXIII.

INCIDENTS and Anecdotes—Comedy of Battle—An Irish Rebel—A Brace of Wounded Soldiers—Colonel Granville Moody—His "Boys"—His Piety and Pugnacity—Singular Incidents—Distracted Birds and Rabbits—"All the Dinner 's Gone"—Ambulance Corps on the Field—The Generals, how they Appeared in Battle.

RARE comedy was intermingled with the tragedy of battle. The humorism of battle saturates you after carnage is ended, and when the dead are buried. The richest of the fun and drollery is not printable. But soldiers roar over awkward adventures of their comrades when they assemble in their bivouacs. There were some good things, however, that the reader can enjoy. One was of Irish parentage, of course. A Milesian member of the First Louisiana rebel regiment, who had been captured, was strolling around a hospital with a broken arm, which had been dressed by one of our surgeons. Said an officer, "Why, Pat, you an Irishman and a rebel? How 's that? What are you fighting us for?" "An' sure, yer honor," retorted Pat quickly, "an' did yees iver hear of the likes of an army an' there wasn't Irishmen in it?" "But, Pat," interposed Father Trecy, "you were *forced* into the service, were you not?" "Yer riverence," replied the incorrigible fellow, with a respectful salute, "I wint into it wid good will; the boys was all agoin'; there was a fight, an' sure Patrick wasn't the man to lit inny more go forninst him." Pat was decidedly obdurate, and no more inquisitive rhetoric was wasted upon him.

A group of mangled soldiers were sauntering around a field hospital, waiting for temporary bandages to be applied to their wounds. The surgeon was fully occupied, and some delay was unavoidable. A brawny trooper, with a bullet in his left leg and a ball in his right arm, hobbled up to the surgeon, holding his wounded arm with his left hand. Projecting his mutilated leg he said, with laughable grimace, "Well, doctor, the d—d rebs come pretty near hittin' me." Another fellow, who had lost the end of his nose, elbowed his way into the circle, spouting blood as a whale spouts water, and convulsed the group: "The d—d rascals"—sputter—"doctor"—sputter—"came d—d near"—sputter—"*missin'* me."

Colonel Granville Moody, commanding the Seventy-Fourth Ohio Volunteers, is a famous Methodist preacher. He relinquished the altar for the sword. Malicious people insinuated that the Gospel had lost the services of a good advocate, and that the army was not promoted by its accession from the pulpit. But the Colonel proved that he was a tremendous fighter as well as a good preacher. He is fifty, or more, perhaps, but well preserved, with magnificent port, and six feet two or three inches of stature. He has a fine genial face, fiery dark eyes, and vocal range that would have excited the envy of Roaring Ralph Stackpole. He carried into battle a spirit of enthusiasm which inflamed his "boys" to the highest pitch of daring, and won for him the admiration of thousands. Lieutenant Colonel Von Schrader

(Inspector General on the staff of General Thomas), than whom a braver or better soldier never resisted storm of battle, had not been on friendly terms with Moody for some months, but admiring his splendid gallantry, he approached him in the heat of desperate conflict, extended his hand, expressed his earnest approbation of the Colonel's heroism, and begged that ever after peace might exist between them.

A little later Moody's "boys," as he paternally addressed them, were obliged to withstand a terrific fire without enjoying opportunity to return it. Moody galloped to General Negley and protested. "This fire, General, is positively murderous; it will kill all my boys." But there was no help for it. His martial flock, imposing upon his benevolent nature, sometimes indulged a little sly humor at his expense. In the midst of battle, an Irishman in the regiment shouted, "His riverence, the Colonel, has bin fightin' Satan all his life; I reckon he thinks hell 's broke loose now." Not long after the battle, General Negley merrily accused him of having indulged heterodox expletives in the ardor of engagement. "Is it a fact, Colonel," inquired the General, "that you told the boys to give 'em hell?" "Now," replied the Colonel reproachfully, "there's some more of the boys' mischief. I told them to give the rebels Hail Columbia, and they have wickedly perverted my language." The fighting parson, however, explained with a sly twinkle in the corner of his eye, which had something of a tendency to cast a doubt upon the subject.

But there was no doubt that one of his injunctions to his regiment sounded marvelously like a fervent ejaculation swelling up from the depths of the "Amen corner" in an old fashioned Methodist Church. This fact must be imagined that the anecdote may be appreciated. The Colonel's mind was saturated with piety and pugnacity. He praised God and pitched into the rebels alternately. He had been struck by bullets four times already. He had given the enemy "Hail Columbia" once, and they had reeled back to cover. Now they were swarming back to renew the contest. Moody's regiment were lying on their bellies waiting for them to come up. He had a moment to spare, and thought he would exhort them. The rebels were advancing swiftly, and probably cut him short. But as they approached he said quietly, "Now, boys, fight for your country and your God." "And," said one of his boys, "we all surely thought he was going to say 'Amen,' but at that instant the rebels let fly, and the old hero roared with the voice of a Stentor, 'AIM LOW!'" Weeks afterward, when the Colonel passed through his camp, the mischievous rascals would shout behind him, "Fight for your country and your God—AIM LOW!"

A singular incident occurred among the "Twenty-Onesters" (Twenty-First Ohio). Battle was raging with terrific fury on the Right, but had not yet involved Negley's line. The men were lying behind a crest waiting. A brace of frantic wild turkeys, so paralyzed with fright that they were incapable of flying, ran between the lines and endeavored to hide among the men. One of the "Twenty-Onesters" caught one, and cutting off its head began to strip it of feathers, boasting complacently that he would have fresh fowl after the fight. The wave of battle had surged alarmingly near the front of the "Twenty-

Onesters" before the soldier had plucked his game. But while he was inserting it in his haversack, an officer riding through the lines espied him and offered him a dollar for it. The soldier hesitated a moment, but accepted. The officer bagged the turkey, but neither he nor the soldier could make change. The "Twenty-Onesters" were ordered forward, and the soldier shouted, "Never mind. Take it along. I'll collect after the fight!"

But the frenzy of the turkeys was not so touching as the exquisite fright of the birds and rabbits. When the roar of battle rushed through the cedar-thickets, flocks of little birds fluttered and circled above the field in a state of utter bewilderment, and scores of rabbits fled for protection to our men lying down in line on the left, nestling under their coats and creeping under their legs in a state of utter distraction. They hopped over the field like toads, and as perfectly tamed by fright as household pets. Many officers witnessed it, remarking it as one of the most curious spectacles ever seen upon a battle-field.

An Irish soldier was hit by a bullet, and turned to his commander. "Captain," said Pat, "shure an' I'm hit!" "What the d—l are you doing there, then?" roared the Captain; "get out of that and give a better man your place." "Be jabers," retorted Pat, "I'll do no such thing. I want revinge, an' be dad I'll get it."

Lieutenant Willie Porter, detailed to the Adjutant General's office, and *ex officio* member of the staff, afforded a laugh in the midst of a shower of shells. Willie, a staunch youth of some eighteen or nineteen summers, had been weathering the storm all day at the heels of the General's horse. When he mounted in the morning he prudently filled the General's haversack with luncheon, and slung it over his shoulder. During the afternoon a fragment of a shell tore away part of his pantaloons near his waist, lacerated his body, and cut away the side of his haversack, letting the bread and meat fall to the ground. "There, now!" said Willie with admirable *sang froid*, a ludicrous grimace expanding his countenance, "all the dinner 's gone." Lieutenant Willie Porter and Lieutenant James Reynolds, his companion, about the same age, deserved honorable official mention for their gallantry.

Another member of the staff had a narrow escape from a shell which whizzed very closely to a portion of his body that is ordinarily protected by coat tails. He objected decidedly—"it would be so d—d ridiculous to be killed in that manner." The staff fairly roared over it, but the Captain "couldn't see it."

The operations of ambulance corps on the field during the fight furnished a curious battle picture. Dozens of those somber-looking vehicles were visible in the woods and on the plain streaming incessantly between the front and the hospitals, and often under fire. When the vail of smoke lifted occasionally, squads of men, in fours, with stretchers, were descried between the lines—when the conflict was partially suspended at one point, although it was raging to the right or left—bearing the wounded to the rear. Late in the evening of Wednesday an ambulance party on the right was fiercely hailed by the rebel pickets. "What the h—l are you doing here?" "Picking up wounded men!" "Well pick 'em up quick and get out of this?" Our men replied, "Send over and get your wounded." "All right!"

HOW THE GENERALS APPEARED IN BATTLE.

The rebel sharpshooters were sorely annoying. They picked off scores of our soldiers and officers. One of them permanently disabled Colonel Frizelle of the Ninety-Fourth Ohio. General Rosecrans probably owed his escape from them to the fact that his rank was not distinguishable. His uniform was mostly covered by an ample cavalry overcoat fastened by a single button under his chin, so that only a few buttons on the breast of his uniform were visible. This was merely the accident of weather. It was a chill morning, and overcoats were essential to comfort. It was fortunate also that "Toby," his gray charger, had not been brought to the front. It is altogether probable he would have mounted him that day to spare "Boney," his magnificent bay—a steed of unusual size and spirit, whose fire, symmetry, and proud style fully realized youthful imagination's conception of a war horse with "neck clothed in thunder, and smelling battle."

The General is an inveterate smoker. When he mounted in the morning he had a cigar in his mouth. The absorption of battle caused him to forget it, and the light expired, but the force of habit was triumphant. He retained the stump in his mouth during hours, removing it mechanically when he gave orders. The cigar, the sky-blue cavalry overcoat with standing collar, a low-crowned black felt hat pushed back upon his head until the back rim tipped down upon his neck at a sharp angle, concealing the coat collar, and his chin elevated more than ordinarily, "Boney" prancing gently and bowing his head with stately pride, was a picture of the General Commanding which his staff will readily recognize in this plain sketch.

Rousseau, in full uniform, rode a superb thoroughbred chestnut. He met a friend on the field just after his division had driven the enemy back into the woods. He was just about to send after Starkweather's brigade. At that moment his countenance was aglow with the enthusiasm of triumph—such a face as men love to meet in battle, for it was inspiriting. Drawing rein he accosted his friend cheerily, and shook a canteen at him. "You look dry and exhausted—let me refresh you." It was manna in the wilderness, said his friend, subsequently. The latter admired the chestnut. Rousseau, turning in his saddle, pointed to an ugly bullet laceration on the rump of his charger. "I wouldn't mind it," he said, "but it's a —— fine hoss—a Kentucky hoss." A shell whizzing in close proximity concluded the colloquy.

Crittenden rode a fine bay horse, and was clad in a dark overcoat, with a regulation cap covered with oilcloth. Crittenden at review is more moved than Crittenden in battle. McCook's fine chestnut was killed in the morning, and he rode a "plug" in the afternoon. Major Bates, of his staff, had also lost his horse, but compensated himself by "jayhawking," as he said, "somebody's big yaller stud hoss." This was while the awful battle of the Left Wing was going on Wednesday afternoon. McCook and his staff were in a shallow basin at the left of his line. He looked a little flushed and worried by fatigue, but did not seem in the least disturbed by battle. The misfortune of the Right probably affected him. The infantry fought in their overcoats, but the cannoniers stripped to the buff. It was interesting to observe that horses which at review are generally wild and rampant, were not at all difficult to manage in the midst of the stunning uproar of battle. They exhibited splendid spirit, but ordinarily they were perfectly tractable and gentle. You would have said they appreciated the spirit of the occasion. But when their riders were dismounted they were seized with frenzy, and plunged across the field in uncontrollable agony of fright.

After the battle, Major Goddard, for his services and gallantry, was promoted to the office of Adjutant General and Chief of Staff, with rank of Lieutenant Colonel. Lieutenant Bond was promoted to the Senior Aidship, with rank of Major. Lieutenant Kirby was recommended for promotion to a Captaincy, and for a brevet as Major. The gallant officers of staff of the Corps Generals were also promoted, Thomas, McCook, and Crittenden being designated commanders of the Fourteenth, Twentieth, and Twenty-First Army Corps, respectively, thus increasing the numerical force of their staffs, and elevating the grades of rank of officers.

CONGRATULATORY.

Upon the reception at Washington of the tidings of the success of Major General Rosecrans, the President of the United States sent him the following telegraphic acknowledgment of his personal and official gratitude.

WASHINGTON, *January* 5th.

To Major General Rosecrans:

Your dispatch, announcing the retreat of the enemy, has just reached here. God bless you and all with you. Please tender to all, and accept for yourself, the nation's gratitude for your and their skill, endurance, and dauntless courage.

A. LINCOLN.

The Secretary of War forwarded a similar congratulation, and Major General Halleck also sent a telegram, of which the following is a copy, viz.:

WASHINGTON, *January* 9, 1863.

Major General Rosecrans, Commanding Army of the Cumberland:

GENERAL—Rebel telegrams fully confirm your telegrams from the battle-field. The victory was well earned, and one of the most brilliant of the war. You and your brave army have won the gratitude of your country, and the admiration of the world. The field of Murfreesboro is made historical, and future generations will point out the place where so many heroes fell gloriously in defense of the Constitution and the Union. All honor to the Army of the Cumberland. Thanks to the living, and tears for the lamented dead.

H. W. HALLECK.

The victory electrified the nation, and the people heaped their grateful thanks upon the General and his splendid army. It was the most momentous battle of the war up to that period. It saved Tennessee and Kentucky, and there can be little doubt that Ohio and Indiana owe their present exemption from invasion to it.

AT MURFREESBORO.

General headquarters were established in Murfreesboro on Monday the 5th of January. The army took up a line in front and settled down to rest. Captain Morton and the Pioneer Brigade at once proceeded to reconstruct the railroad bridge across Stone River, and to fortify the town in order to make it an intermediate magazine of supplies. Details were dispatched to the surrounding country to collect all the forage and stock that could be found. The flouring mill at the post was put into operation and the troops were supplied with meal. The rainy season now interposed to obstruct offensive operations upon an extensive scale, though preparations were vigorously pressed. Bad weather was compensated for by a freshet in the Cumberland, which reopened navigation and gave assurance of supplies. The War Department caused the army to be remodeled, by constituting its three grand divisions *Corps de Armee*—the Fourteenth, Twentieth, and Twenty-First, under Thomas, McCook, and Crittenden, Major General Rosecrans commanding the grand army, and thus concluded the history of the original Fourteenth Army Corps.

APPENDIX.

OFFICIAL REPORTS

OF THE

BATTLE OF STONE RIVER.

GENERAL ROSECRANS' OFFICIAL REPORT.

HEADQUARTERS DEPARTMENT OF THE CUMBERLAND,
MURFREESBORO, TENNESSEE,
February 12, 1863.

GENERAL—As the sub-reports are now nearly all in, I have the honor to submit, for the information of the General-in-Chief, the subjoined report, with accompanying sub-reports, maps, and statistical rolls of the battle of Stone River.

To a proper understanding of this battle, it will be necessary to state the

PRELIMINARY MOVEMENTS AND PREPARATIONS.

Assuming command of the army, at Louisville, on the 27th day of October, it was found concentrated at Bowling Green and Glasgow, distant about one hundred and thirty miles from Louisville; from whence, after replenishing with ammunition, supplies, and clothing, they moved on to Nashville, the advance corps reaching that place on the morning of the 7th of November, a distance of one hundred and eighty-three miles from Louisville.

At this distance from my base of supplies, the first thing to be done was to provide for the subsistence of the troops, and open the Louisville and Nashville Railroad. The cars commenced running through on the 26th of November, previous to which time our supplies had been brought by rail to Mitchelville, thirty-five miles north of Nashville, and from thence, by constant labor, we had been able to haul enough to replenish the exhausted stores for the garrison at Nashville, and subsist the troops of the moving army.

From the 26th of November to the 26th of December, every effort was bent to complete the clothing of the army, to provide it with ammunition, and replenish the depot at Nashville with needful supplies to insure us against want from the largest possible detention likely to occur by the breaking of the Louisville and Nashville Railroad; and to insure this work, the road was guarded by a heavy force posted at Gallatin.

The enormous superiority in numbers of the rebel cavalry, kept our little cavalry force almost within the infantry lines, and gave the enemy control of the entire country around us. It was obvious, from the beginning, that we should be confronted by Bragg's army, recruited by an inexorable conscription, and aided by clouds of mounted men, formed into a guerrilla-like cavalry, to avoid the hardships of conscription and infantry service. The evident difficulties and labors of an advance into this country, and against such a force, and at such distance from our base of operations, with which we connected by a single precarious thread, made it manifest that our policy was to induce the enemy to travel over as much as possible of the space that separated us—thus avoiding for us the wear and tear, and diminution of our forces, and subjecting the enemy to all these inconveniences, beside increasing for him, and diminishing for us, the dangerous consequences of a retreat.

The means taken to obtain this end were eminently successful. The enemy, expecting us to go into winter quarters at Nashville, had prepared his own winter quarters at Murfreesboro, with the hope of possibly making them at Nashville, and had sent a large cavalry force into West Tennessee to annoy Grant, and another large force into Kentucky to break up the railroad. In the absence of these forces, and with adequate supplies in Nashville, the movement was judged opportune for an advance on the rebels. Polk's and Kirby Smith's forces were at Murfreesboro, and Hardee's corps on the Shelbyville and Nolensville pike, between Triune and Eaglesville, while our troops lay in front of Nashville, on the Franklin, Nolensville, and Murfreesboro turnpikes.

THE PLAN OF THE MOVEMENTS

Was as follows:

McCook, with three divisions, to advance by the Nolensville pike to Triune.

Thomas, with two divisions (Negley's and Rousseau's), to advance on his right, by the Franklin and Wilson pikes, threatening Hardee's right, and then to fall in by the cross-roads to Nolensville.

Crittenden, with Wood's, Palmer's, and Van Cleve's divisions, to advance by the Murfreesboro pike to Lavergne.

With Thomas' two divisions at Nolensville, McCook was to attack Hardee at Triune, and if the enemy reinforced Hardee, Thomas was to support McCook.

If McCook beat Hardee, or Hardee retreated, and the enemy met us at Stewart's Creek, five miles south of Lavergne, Crittenden was to attack him; Thomas was to come in on his left flank, and McCook, after detaching a division to pursue or observe Hardee, if retreating south, was to move, with the remainder of his force, on their rear.

THE MOVEMENT

Began on the morning of the 26th of December. McCook advanced on the Nolensville pike, skirmishing his way all day, meeting with stiff resistance from cavalry and artillery, and closing the day by a brisk fight, which gave him possession of Nolensville and the hills one and a half miles in front, capturing one gun, by the One Hundred and First Ohio and Fifteenth Wisconsin Regiments, his loss this day being about seventy-five killed and wounded.

Thomas followed on the right, and closed Negley's division on Nolensville, leaving the other (Rousseau's) division on the right flank.

Crittenden advanced to Lavergne, skirmishing heavily on his front, over a rough country, intersected by forests and cedar-brakes, with but slight loss.

On the 26th, General McCook advanced on Triune, but his movement was retarded by a dense fog.

Crittenden had orders to delay his movements until McCook had reached Triune, and developed the intentions of the enemy at that point, so that it could be determined which Thomas was to support.

McCook arrived at Triune, and reported that Hardee had retreated, and that he had sent a division in pursuit.

Crittenden began his advance about eleven o'clock A. M., driving before him a brigade of cavalry, supported by Maney's brigade of rebel infantry, and reached Stewart's Creek, the Third Kentucky gallantly charging the rear guard of the enemy, and saving the bridge, on which had been placed a pile of rails that had been set on fire. This was Saturday night.

McCook having settled the fact of Hardee's retreat, Thomas moved Negley's division on to join Crittenden at Stewart's Creek, and moved Rousseau's to Nolensville.

On Sunday the troops rested, except Rousseau's division, which was ordered to move on to Stewartston ; and Willich's brigade, which had pursued Hardee as far as Riggs' Cross-roads, and had determined the fact that Hardee had gone to Murfreesboro, when they returned to Triune.

On Monday morning McCook was ordered to move from Triune to Wilkinson's Cross-roads, six miles from Murfreesboro, leaving a brigade at Triune.

Crittenden crossed Stewart's Creek by the Smyrna bridge, on the main Murfreesboro pike, and Negley by the ford, two miles above ; their whole force to advance on Murfreesboro, distant eleven miles.

Rousseau was to remain at Stewart's Creek until his train came up, and prepare himself to follow.

McCook reached Wilkinson's Cross-roads by evening, with an advance brigade at Overall's Creek, saving and holding the bridge, meeting with but little resistance.

Crittenden's corps advanced, Palmer leading, on the Murfreesboro pike, followed by Negley, of Thomas' corps, to within three miles of Murfreesboro, having had several brisk skirmishes, driving the enemy rapidly, saving two bridges on the route, and forcing the enemy back to his intrenchments.

About three o'clock P. M., a signal message coming from the front, from General Palmer, said that he was in sight of Murfreesboro, and the enemy were running. An order was sent to General Crittenden to send a division to occupy Murfreesboro.

This led General Crittenden, on reaching the enemy's front, to order Harker's brigade to cross the river at a ford on his left, where he surprised a regiment of Breckinridge's division, and drove it back on its main lines, not more than five hundred yards distant, in considerable confusion; and he held this position until General Crittenden was advised, by prisoners captured by Harker's brigade, that Breckinridge was in force on his front, when, it being dark, he ordered the brigade back across the river, and reported the circumstances to the Commanding General, on his arrival, to whom he apologized for not having carried out the order to occupy Murfreesboro. The General approved of his action, of course, the order to occupy Murfreesboro having been based on the information received from General Crittenden's advance division, that the enemy were retreating from Murfreesboro.

Crittenden's corps, with Negley's division, bivouacked in order of battle, distant seven hundred yards from the enemy's intrenchments, our left extending down the river some five hundred yards. The Pioneer Brigade, bivouacking still lower down, prepared three fords, and covered one of them, while Wood's division covered the other two.

Van Cleve's division being in reserve, on the morning of the 30th Rousseau, with two brigades, was ordered down early from Stewart's Creek, leaving one brigade there, and sending another to Smyrna to cover our left and rear, and took his place in reserve in rear of Palmer's right, while General Negley moved on through the cedar-brakes until his right rested on the Wilkinson pike. The Pioneer Corps cut roads through the cedars for his ambulances and ammunition wagons.

The Commanding General remained with the Left and Center, examining the ground, while General McCook moved forward from Wilkinson's Cross-roads, slowly and steadily, meeting with heavy resistance, fighting his way from Overall's Creek until he got into position, with a loss of one hundred and thirty-five killed and wounded.

Our small division of cavalry, say three thousand men, had been divided into three parts, of which General Stanley took two, and accompanied General McCook, fighting his way across from the Wilkinson to the Franklin pike, and below it, Colonel Zahn's brigade leading gallantly, and meeting with such heavy resistance that McCook sent two brigades from Johnson's division, which succeeded in fighting their way into position, while the Third Brigade, which had been left at Triune, moved forward from that place, and arrived at nightfall near General McCook's headquarters. Thus on the close of the 30th, the troops had all got into position.

At four o'clock in the afternoon, General McCook announced his arrival on the Wilkinson pike, joining Thomas—the result of the combat in the afternoon, near Grieson's house, and the fact that Sherridan was in position there, that his right was advancing to support the cavalry; also, that Hardee's corps, with two divisions of Polk's, was on his front, extending down toward the Salem pike.

Without any map of the ground, which was to us *terra incognita*, when General McCook informed the General Commanding that his corps was facing strongly to the east, the General Commanding told him that such a direction to his line did not appear to him a proper one, but that it ought, with the exception of his left, to face much more nearly south, with Johnson's division in reserve; but that this matter must be confided to him, who knew the ground over which he had fought.

At nine o'clock P. M., the corps commanders met at the headquarters of the General Commanding, who explained to them the following

PLAN OF THE BATTLE.

McCook was to occupy the most advantageous position, refusing his right as much as practicable and necessary to secure it; to receive the attack of the enemy, or, if that did not come, to attack himself, sufficient to hold all the force on his front.

Thomas and Palmer to open with skirmishing, and gain the enemy's center and left as far as the river.

Crittenden to cross Van Cleve's division at the lower ford, covered and supported by the Sappers and Miners, and to advance on Breckinridge.

Wood's division to follow by brigades, crossing at the upper ford, and moving on Van Cleve's right, to carry everything into Murfreesboro.

This would have given us two divisions against one, and as soon as Breckinridge had been dislodged from his position, the batteries of Wood's division, taking position on the hights east of Stone River, in advance, would see the enemy's works in reverse, would dislodge them, and enable Palmer's division to press them back, and drive them westward across the river, or through the woods, while Thomas, sustaining the movement on the Center, would advance on the right of Palmer, crushing their right; and Crittenden's corps, advancing, would take Murfreesboro, and then moving westward on the Franklin road, get in their flank and rear, and drive them into the country, toward Salem, with the prospect of cutting off their retreat, and probably destroying their army.

It was explained to them that this combination, ensuring us a vast superiority on our left, required for its success, that General McCook should be able to hold his position for three hours; that if necessary to recede at all, he should recede as he had advanced on the preceding day, slowly, as steadily, refusing his right, thereby rendering our success certain.

Having thus explained the plan, the General Commanding addressed General McCook as follows:

"You know the ground—you have fought over its difficulties. Can you hold your present position for three hours?"

To which General McCook responded:

"Yes, I think I can."

The General Commanding then said:

"I don't like the facing so much to the east, but must confide that to you, who know the ground. If you don't think your present the best position, change it."

The officers then returned to their commands.

At daylight on the morning of the 31st, the troops breakfasted, and stood to their arms, and by seven o'clock were preparing for the

BATTLE.

The movement was begun on the Left by Van Cleve, who crossed at the lower fords. Wood prepared to sustain and follow him. The enemy meanwhile had prepared to attack General McCook, and by six and a half o'clock advanced in heavy columns regimental front, his left attacking Willich's and Kirk's brigades, of Johnson's division, and were, after a sharp, but fruitless contest, crumbled to pieces and driven back, leaving Edgarton's and part of Goodspeed's Batteries in the hands of the enemy.

The enemy following up, attacked Davis' division, and speedily dislodged Post's brigade. Carlin's brigade was compelled to follow, as Woodruff's brigade, from the weight of testimony, had previously left its position on his left. Johnson's brigades, in retiring, inclined too far to the west, and were too much scattered to make a combined resistance, though they fought bravely at one or two points before reaching Wilkinson's pike. The reserve brigade of Johnson's division, advancing from its bivouac near Wilkinson's pike toward the Right, took a good position, and made a gallant but ineffectual stand, as the whole rebel left was moving up on the ground abandoned by our troops.

Within an hour from the time of the opening of the battle, a staff officer from General McCook arrived, announcing to me that the Right Wing was heavily pressed, and needed assistance; but I was not advised of the rout of Willich's and Kirby's brigades, nor of the rapid withdrawal of Davis' division, necessitated thereby. Moreover, having supposed his wing posted more compactly, and his right more refused than it really was, the direction of the noise of battle did not indicate to me the true state of affairs. I consequently directed him to return and direct General McCook to dispose his troops to the best advantage, and to hold his ground obstinately. Soon after, a second officer from General McCook arrived, and stated that the Right Wing was being driven—a fact that was but too manifest, by the rapid movement of the noise of battle toward the north.

General Thomas was immediately dispatched to order Rousseau—then in reserve—into the cedar-brakes to the right and rear of Sherridan. General Crittenden was ordered to suspend Van Cleve's movement across the river on the left, and to cover the crossing with one brigade and move the other two brigades westward, across the fields toward the railroad, for a reserve. Wood was also directed to suspend his preparations for crossing and to hold Hascall in reserve.

At this moment fugitives and stragglers from McCook's corps began to make their appearance through the cedar-brakes in such numbers that I became satisfied that McCook's corps was routed. I therefore directed General Crittenden to send Van Cleve in to the right of Rousseau, Wood to lead Colonel Harker's brigade further down the Murfreesboro pike, to go in and attack the enemy on the right of Van Cleve, the Pioneer Brigade meanwhile occupying the knoll of ground west of the Murfreesboro pike, and about four hundred or five hundred yards in the rear of Palmer's center, supporting Stokes' Battery (see accompanying drawing). Sherridan, after sustaining four successive attacks, gradually swung his right round south-easterly to a north-western direction, repulsing the enemy four times, losing the gallant General Sill, of his right, and Colonel Roberts, of his left brigade, when, having exhausted his ammunition, Negley's division being in the same predicament, and heavily pressed, after desperate fighting they fell back from the position held at the commencement, through the cedar woods in which Rousseau's division, with a portion of Negley's and Sherridan's met the advancing enemy, and checked his movements.

The ammunition train of the Right Wing, endangered by its sudden discomfiture, was taken charge of by Captain Thruston, of the First Ohio Regiment; an ordnance officer, who, by his energy and gallantry, aided by a charge of cavalry, and such troops as he could pick up, carried it through the woods to the Murfreesboro pike, around to the rear of the Left Wing; thus enabling the troops of Sherridan's division to replenish their empty cartridge-boxes. During all this time, Palmer's front had likewise been in action, the enemy having made several attempts to advance upon it. At this stage, it became necessary to readjust the line of battle to the new state of affairs. Rousseau and Van Cleve's advance having relieved Sherridan's division from the pressure, Negley's division and Cruft's brigade from Palmer's division, withdrew from their original position in front of the cedars, and crossed the open field to the east of the Murfreesboro pike, about four hundred yards in rear of our front line, where Negley was ordered to replenish his ammunition and form in close column in reserve.

The Right and Center of our line, now extended from Hazen to Murfreesboro pike, in a north-westerly direction, Hascall supporting Hazen, Rousseau filling the interval to the Pioneer Brigade.

Negley in reserve, Van Cleve west of the Pioneer Brigade; McCook's corps refused on his right, and slightly to the rear, on Murfreesboro pike; the cavalry being still further to the rear on Murfreesboro pike and beyond Overall's Creek.

The enemy's infantry and cavalry attack on our extreme Right, was repulsed by Van Cleve's division, with Harker's brigade and the cavalry. After several attempts of the enemy to advance on this new line, they were thoroughly repulsed, as were also the attempts on the Left. The day closed leaving us masters of the original ground on our Left, and our line advantageously posted, with open ground, in front, swept at all points by our artillery. We had lost heavily in killed and wounded, and a considerable number in stragglers and prisoners; also, twenty-eight pieces of artillery, the horses having been slain, and our troops being unable to withdraw them, by hand, over the rough ground; but the enemy had been roughly handled, and badly damaged at all points, having had no success where we had open ground, and our troops properly posted, none, which did not depend on the original crushing of our Right and the superior masses which were, in consequence, brought to bear upon the narrow front of Sherridan's and Negley's divisions, and a part of Palmer's coupled with the scarcity of ammunition, caused by the circuitous road which the train had taken, and the inconvenience of getting it from a remote distance through the cedars. Orders were given for the issue of all the spare ammunition, and we found that we had enough for another battle, the only question being where that battle was to be fought.

It was decided, in order to complete our present lines, that the Left should be retired some two hundred and fifty yards, to more advantageous ground the extreme Left resting on Stone River, above the lower ford, and extending to Stokes' Battery. Starkweather's and Walker's brigades arriving near the close of the evening, the former bivouacked in close column, in reserve, in the rear of McCook's left, and the latter was posted on the left of Sherridan, near the Murfreesboro pike, and, next morning, relieved Van Cleve, who returned to his position in the Left Wing.

DISPOSITION FOR JANUARY 1, 1863.

After careful examination, and free consultation with corps commanders, followed by a personal examination of the ground in the rear, as far as Overall's Creek, it was determined to await the enemy's attack in that position, to send for the provision train, and order up fresh supplies of ammunition, on the arrival of which, should the enemy not attack, offensive operations should be resumed.

No demonstration on the morning of the 1st of January; Crittenden was ordered to occupy the points opposite the ford on his left, with a brigade.

About two o'clock in the afternoon, the enemy, who had shown signs of movement and massing on our Right, appeared at the extremity of a field a mile and a half from the Murfreesboro pike, but the presence of Gibson's brigade, with a battery, occupying the woods near Overall's Creek, and Negley's division and a portion of Rousseau's on the Murfreesboro pike, opposite the field, put an end to this demonstration, and the day closed with another demonstration by the enemy, on Walker's brigade, which ended in the same manner.

On Friday morning, the enemy opened four heavy batteries on our Center, and a strong demonstration of an attack a little further to the right; but a well-directed fire of artillery soon silenced his batteries, while the guns of Walker and Sherridan put an end to his effort there.

About three o'clock P. M., while the Commanding General was examining the position of Crittenden's Left, across the river, which was now held by Van Cleve's division, supported by a brigade from Palmer's, a double line of skirmishers was seen to emerge from the woods in a south-easterly direction, advancing down the fields, and were soon followed by heavy columns of infantry, battalion front, with three batteries of artillery.

Our only battery on this side of the river had been withdrawn from an eligible point, but the most available spot was pointed out, and it soon opened here upon the enemy. The line, however, advanced steadily to within one hundred yards of the front of Van Cleve's division, when a short and fierce contest ensued. Van Cleve's division giving way, retired in considerable confusion across the river, followed closely by the enemy.

General Crittenden immediately directed his Chief of Artillery to dispose the batteries on the hill, on the west side of the river, so as to open on them, while two brigades of Negley's division, from the reserve, and the Pioneer Brigade were ordered up to meet the onset.

The firing was terrific, and the havoc terrible. The enemy retreated more rapidly than they had advanced; in forty minutes they lost two thousand men.

General Davis, seeing some stragglers from Van Cleve's division, took one of his brigades and crossed at a ford below, to attack the enemy on his left flank, and, by General McCook's order, the rest of his division was permitted to follow; but when he arrived, two brigades of Negley's division, and Hazen's brigade, of Palmer's division, had pursued the flying enemy well across the field, capturing four pieces of artillery and a stand of colors.

It was now after dark, and raining, or we should have pursued the enemy into Murfreesboro. As it was, Crittenden's corps passed over, and with Davis, occupied the crests, which were intrenched in a few hours.

Deeming it possible that the enemy might again attack our Right and Center, thus weakened, I thought it advisable to make a demonstration on our Right by a heavy division of camp fires, and by laying out a line of battle with torches, which answered the purpose.

SATURDAY, 3D DAY OF JANUARY.

It rained heavily from three o'clock in the morning; the plowed ground over which our Left would be obliged to advance, was impassable for artillery. The ammunition train did not arrive until ten o'clock; it was, therefore, deemed unadvisable to advance, but batteries were put in position on the left, by which the ground could be swept, and even Murfreesboro reached, by the Parrott guns.

A heavy and constant picket firing had been kept up on our Right and Center, and extending to our Left, which at last became so annoying, that in the afternoon I directed the corps commanders to clear their fronts.

Occupying the woods to the left of Murfreesboro pike with sharpshooters, the enemy had annoyed Rousseau all day, and General Thomas and himself requested permission to dislodge them and their supports which covered a ford. This was granted, and a sharp fire from four batteries was opened for ten or fifteen minutes, when Rousseau sent two of his regiments, which, with Spears' Tennesseeans and the Eighty-Fifth Illinois Volunteers, that had come out with the wagon train, charged upon the enemy, and after a sharp contest cleared the woods, and drove the enemy from his trenches, capturing from seventy to eighty prisoners.

Sunday morning, the 4th of January, it was not deemed advisable to commence offensive movements, and news soon reached us that the enemy had fled from Murfreesboro. Burial parties were sent out to bury the dead, and the cavalry was sent to reconnoiter.

Early Monday morning General Thomas advanced, driving the rear guard of the rebel cavalry before him six or seven miles, toward Manchester.

McCook's and Crittenden's corps following, took position in front of the town, occupying Murfreesboro.

We learned that the enemy's infantry had reached Shelbyville by 12 M. on Sunday, but owing to the impracticability of bringing up supplies, and the loss of five hundred and fifty-seven artillery horses, further pursuit was deemed inadvisable.

It may be of interest to give the following

GENERAL SUMMARY

Of the operations and results of the series of skirmishes, closing with the battle of Stone River and the occupation of Murfreesboro. We moved on the enemy with the following forces:

Infantry	41,421
Cavalry	3,296
Artillery	2,223
Total	46,940

We fought the battle with the following forces:

Infantry	37,977
Cavalry	3,200
Artillery	2,223
Total	43,400

We lost in killed:

Officers	92
Enlisted men	1,441
Total	1,533

We lost in wounded:

Officers	384
Enlisted men	6,861
Total	7,245
Total killed and wounded	8,778

Being 20.03 per cent. of the entire force in action.

OUR LOSS IN PRISONERS

Is not fully made out; but the Provost Marshal General says, from present information, they will fall short of two thousand eight hundred.

If there are any more bloody battles on record, considering the newness and inexperience of the troops, both officers and men, or if there have been more fighting qualities displayed by any people, I should be pleased to know it.

AS TO THE CONDITION OF THE FIGHT,

We may say that we operated over an unknown country, against a position which was fifteen per cent. better than our own, every foot of ground and approaches being well known to the enemy, and that these disadvantages were fatally exhumed by the faulty position of our Right Wing.

The force we fought is estimated as follows: We have prisoners from one hundred and thirty-two regiments of infantry (consolidations counted as one), averaging from those in General Bushrod Johnson's division four hundred and eleven each—say, for certain, three hundred and fifty men each, will give

			No. men.
132	Regiments infantry, say 350 men each		46,200
12	Battalions sharpshooters, say 100 men each		1,200
23	Battalions of artillery, say 80 men each		1,840
29	Regiments cavalry, men each	400	13,280
	And 24 organizations of cavalry, men each	70	
220			62,520

Their average loss, taken from the statistics of Cleborne, Breckinridge and Withers' divisions, was about two thousand and eighty each. This, for six divisions of infantry and one of cavalry, will amount to fourteen thousand five hundred and sixty men; or to ours nearly as one hundred and sixty-five to one hundred.

Of fourteen thousand five hundred and sixty rebels struck by our missiles, it is estimated that twenty thousand rounds of artillery hit seven hundred and twenty-eight men ; two million rounds of musketry hit thirteen thousand eight hundred and thirty-two men; averaging twenty-seven cannon shots to hit one man ; one hundred and forty-five musket shots to hit one man.

Our relative loss was as follows :

			Per cent.
Right Wing	15,933.	Musketry and artillery loss	20.72
Center	10,866.	" " "	18.4
Left Wing	13,288.	" " "	24.6

On the whole, it is evident that we fought superior numbers on unknown ground, inflicting much more injury than we suffered. We were always superior on equal ground with equal numbers, and only failed of a most crushing victory on Wednesday by the extension and direction of our Right Wing.

This closes the narrative of the movements and seven days' fighting which terminated with the occupation of Murfreesboro. For a detailed history of the parts taken in the battles of the different commands, their obstinate bravery and patient endurance, in which the new regiments vied with those of more experience, I must refer to the accompanying sub-reports of the corps, division, cavalry and artillery commanders.

Besides the mention which has been already made of the service of *our artillery* by the brigade, division, and corps commanders, I deem it a duty to say that such a marked evidence of skill in handling the batteries, and in firing low with such effect, appears in this battle to deserve special commendation.

Among the lesser commands which deserve special mention for distinguished service in the battle, is the Pioneer Corps, a body of seventeen hundred (1,700) men, composed of details from the companies of each infantry regiment, organized and instructed by Captain James St. Clair Morton, Corps of Engineers, Chief Engineer of this army, which marched as an infantry brigade to the Left Wing, making bridges at Stewart's Creek, prepared and guarded the fort at Stone River on the nights of the 29th and 30th, supported Stokes' Battery, and fought with valor and determination on the 31st, holding its position until relieved; on the morning of the 2d advancing with the greatest promptitude and gallantry to support Van Cleve's division against the attack on our Left; on the evening of the same day, constructing a bridge and batteries between that time and Saturday evening; and the efficiency and *esprit de corps* suddenly developed in this command, its gallant behavior in action, the eminent service it is continually rendering the army, entitle both officers and men to special public notice and thanks, while they reflect the highest credit on the distinguished ability and capacity of Captain Morton, who will do honor to his promotion to a Brigadier General, which the President has promised him.

The ability, order, and method exhibited in the management of the wounded, elicited the warmest commendation from all our general officers, in which I most cordially join.

Notwithstanding the numbers to be cared for, through the energy of Doctor Swift, Medical Director, ably assisted by Doctor Weeds and the senior Surgeons of the various commands, there was less suffering from delay than I have ever before witnessed.

The Tenth Regiment of Ohio Volunteers, at Stewart's Creek, Lieutenant Colonel J. W. Burke commanding, deserves especial praise for the ability and spirit with which they held their post, defended our trains, secured their cars, chased away Wheeler's rebel cavalry, saving a large wagon train, and arrested and retained in service some two thousand stragglers from the battle-field.

The First Regiment of Michigan Engineers and Mechanics, at Lavergne, under command of Colonel Innis, fighting behind a slight protection of wagons and brush, gallantly repulsed a charge from more than ten times their numbers of Wheeler's cavalry.

For distinguished acts of individual zeal, heroism, gallantry, and good conduct, I refer to the accompanying "*List of Special Mentions and Recommendations for Promotion*," wherein are named some of the many noble men who have distinguished themselves and done honor to their country and the starry symbol of its unity. But those named there are by no means all whose names will be inscribed on the rolls of honor we are preparing, and hope to have held in grateful remembrance by our countrymen. To say that such men as Major General G. H. Thomas, true and prudent, distinguished in council and on many battle-fields, for his courage; or Major General McCook, a brave, faithful, and loyal soldier, who bravely breasted battle at Shiloh and at Perryville, and as bravely on the bloody field of Stone River; and Major General Thomas L. Crittenden, whose heart is that of a true soldier and patriot, and whose gallantry, often attested by his companions in arms in other fields, witnessed many times in this army long before I had the honor to command it, never more conspicuously than in this combat, maintained their high character throughout this action, but feebly express my feeling of obligation to them for counsel and support from the time of my arrival to the present hour. I doubly thank them, as well as the gallant, ever-ready Major General Rousseau, for their support in this battle.

Brigadier General Stanley, already distinguished for four successful battles, Island No. 10, May 27, before Corinth, Iuka, and the battle of Corinth, at this time in command of our ten regiments of cavalry, fought the enemy's forty regiments of cavalry, and held them at bay, and beat them wherever he could meet them. He ought to be made a Major General for his services, and also for the good of the service.

As for such Brigadiers as Negley, Jefferson C. Davis, Johnson, Palmer, Hascall, Van Cleve, Wood, Mitchell, Cruft, and Sherridan, they ought to be made Major Generals in our service. In such brigade commanders as Colonels Carlin, Miller, Hazen, Samuel Beatty of the Nineteenth Ohio, Gibson, Grose, Wagner, John Beatty of the Third Ohio, Harker, Starkweather, Stanley, and others, whose names are mentioned in the accompanying report, the Government may well confide. They are the men from whom our troops should be at once supplied with Brigadier Generals; and justice to the brave men and officers of the regiments, equally demands their promotion, to give them and their regiments their proper leaders. Many captains and subalterns also showed great gallantry and capacity for superior commands. But above all, the steady rank and file showed invincible fighting courage and stamina worthy of a great and free nation, requiring only good officers, discipline, and instruction, to make them equal if not superior to any troops in ancient or modern times. To them I offer my most heartfelt thanks and good wishes.

Words of my own can not add to the renown of our brave and patriotic officers and soldiers who fell on the field of honor, nor increase respect for their memory in the hearts of our countrymen. The names of such men as Lieutenant Colonel J. P. Garesché, the pure and noble Christian gentleman and chivalric officer, who gave his life an early offering on the altar of his country's freedom; the gentle, true, and accomplished General Sill; the brave, ingenious, and able Colonels Roberts, Millikin, Shaeffer, McKee, Reed, Forman, Fred. Jones, Hawkins, Kell, and the gallant and faithful Major Carpenter, of the Nineteenth Regulars, and many other field officers, will live in our country's history, as well as those of many others of inferior rank, whose soldierly deeds on this memorable battle-field won for them the admiration of their companions, and will dwell in our memories in long future years after God, in his mercy, shall have given us peace and restored us to the bosom of our homes and families. Simple justice to the officers of my Staff, the noble and lamented Lieutenant Colonel Garesché, Chief of Staff; Lieutenant Colonel Taylor, Chief Quartermaster; Lieutenant Colonel Simmons, Chief Commissary; Major C. Goddard, senior Aiddecamp; Major Ralston Skinner, Judge Advocate General; Lieutenant Frank S. Bond, Aiddecamp of General Tyler; Captain Charles R. Thompson, my Aiddecamp; Lieutenant Byron Kirby, Sixth United States Infantry, Aiddecamp, who was wounded on December 31st; R. S. Thoms, Esq., a member of the Cincinnati bar, who acted as volunteer Aiddecamp, behaved with distinguished gallantry; Colonel Barnet, Chief of Artillery and Ordnance; Captain G. H. Gilman, Nineteenth United States Infantry, Inspector of Artillery; Captain James Curtis, Fifteenth United States Infantry, Assistant Inspector General; Captain Wiles, Twenty-Second Indiana, Provost Marshal General; Captain Michler, Topographical Engineer; Captain Jesse Merrill, Signal Corps, whose corps behaved well; Captain Elmer Otis, Fourth Regular Cavalry, who commanded the Second Courier Line, connected the various headquarters most successfully, and who made a most opportune and brilliant charge on Wheeler's cavalry, routing the brigade, and recapturing three hundred of our prisoners.

Lieutenant Edson, United States Ordnance officer who, during the battle of Wednesday, distributed ammunition under the fire of the enemy's batteries and behaved bravely; Captain Hubbard and Lieutenant Newberry, who joined my staff on the field, acting as aids, rendered valuable service in carrying orders on the field. Lieutenant Royse, Fourth United States Cavalry, commanded the escort of the headquarters' train, and distinguished himself with gallantry and efficiency. All performed their appropriate duties to my entire satisfaction, accompanying me everywhere, and carrying orders through the thickest of the fight, watched while others slept, never weary when duty called, deserve my public thanks, and the respect and gratitude of the army.

With all the facts of the battle fully before me, the relative numbers and positions of our troops and those of the rebels, the gallantry and obstinacy of the contest and the final result, I say, from conviction, and as public acknowledgment due to Almighty God, in closing this report, "*non nobis! Dominie, non nobis. Sed nomie tui da Glorium.*"

[Signed,] WM. S. ROSECRANS,

Major General Commanding.

BRIGADIER GENERAL THOMAS, *Adjutant General United States Army.*

MAJ. GEN. McCOOK'S OFFICIAL REPORT.

Headquarters Right Wing Fourteenth Army Corps,
In Camp 2½ Miles South of Murfreesboro, Tennessee,
January 8, 1863.

Major C. Goddard, Chief of Staff:

Major—In compliance with telegraphic orders from the General Commanding, received at my camp on Mill Creek, five miles south of Nashville, at half-past four o'clock, A. M., on the morning of the 26th of December, 1862, I put the Right Wing of the Fourteenth Army Corps in motion toward Nolensville, Tennessee.

The First Division, Brigadier General Jeff. C. Davis commanding, marched at six A. M., upon the Edmonson pike, with orders to move upon that road to Prim's blacksmith's shop, whence it was to march direct, by a country road, to Nolensville.

The Third Division, Brigadier General Philip H. Sherridan commanding, also marched at six A. M., and upon the direct road to Nolensville.

The Second Division, Brigadier General R. W. Johnson commanding (the reserve of the Right Wing), followed the Third Division upon the direct road.

The advance guard of Generals Davis' and Sherridan's columns, encountered the enemy's cavalry about two miles beyond our picket line. There was continuous skirmishing with the enemy until the heads of these columns reached Nolensville.

About a mile beyond the town, the enemy made a determined stand in a defile and upon a range of hills that cross the turnpike at this point, lining the slopes with skirmishers and placing a six-gun battery on a commanding position, endeavoring to repel our advance.

They were attacked in front and their position handsomely turned, by General (Colonel) Carlin's brigade of Davis' division, capturing one piece of their artillery and several prisoners. After taking possession of the defile and hills, the command was encamped.

On the night of this day, I was visited by the General Commanding, who gave me verbal orders to move forward in the morning to Triune, seven miles distant, and attack Hardee's corps, supposed to be quartered at that place. At this place I was joined by Brigadier General D. S. Stanley, Chief of Cavalry, with the First and Second Tennessee Regiments and Fifteenth Pennsylvania Cavalry.

Preparations were made to move forward at daylight, the cavalry under General Stanley in advance, followed by the Second Division under General Johnson.

It having rained all the day previous and the entire night, there was a deep fog, which prevented our seeing one hundred and fifty yards in any direction.

The columns having moved about two miles to the front, they again encountered the enemy, consisting of cavalry, infantry, and artillery. The fog at this time being so thick that friend could not be distinguished from foe, and our cavalry being fired upon by our infantry skirmishers on the flanks—the enemy being conversant with the ground, my troops strangers to it, and, from prisoners captured, having learned that Hardee's corps had been in line of battle since night before, I did not deem it prudent to advance until the fog lifted. I ordered the command to halt until the work could be done understandingly. The fog having lifted at one o'clock P. M., an advance was immediately ordered, driving the enemy's cavalry before us.

On nearing Triune, we found that the main portion of the forces had retired, leaving a battery of six pieces, supported by cavalry, to contest the crossing of Wilson's Creek, which has steep and bluff banks.

The enemy having destroyed the bridge, it was with difficulty that it could be crossed. On the approach of our skirmishers, the battery, with the cavalry, took flight down the Eaglesville road. It now being nearly dark, and a severe and driving rain-storm blowing, they were pursued no further.

Johnson's division crossed, and camped beyond Wilson's Creek, repairing the destroyed bridge.

On the morning of the 28th, I ordered out a strong reconnoissance, under command of Brigadier General Willich, to learn whether the enemy had retired to Shelbyville or Murfreesboro. Pursuing seven miles down the Shelbyville road, it was found that the enemy had turned to the left, having taken a dirt road which led to the Salem pike, thence to Murfreesboro.

Leaving the Second Brigade of Johnson's division at Triune, I marched on the 29th, with my command, on the Balle Jack road, toward Murfreesboro, the road being very bad, and the command did not reach Wilkinson's Cross-roads (five miles from Murfreesboro) until late in the evening.

My command was encamped in line of battle, Sherridan's on the left of Wilkinson's pike, Davis' division on the right of the same road, Woodruff's brigade guarding the bridge over Overall's Creek, and the two brigades of Johnson's division watching the right.

On that evening, believing that the enemy intended giving our army battle at or near Murfreesboro, I ordered the brigade left at Triune to join the command without delay, which it did on the 30th.

At one o'clock A. M., on the 30th, I received an order from General Rosecrans to report in person at his headquarters, on the Murfreesboro pike, and arrived there at three and a half o'clock A. M., received my instructions, which were that the left of my line should rest on the right of General Negley's division, and my right was to be thrown forward until it became parallel, or nearly so, with Stone River, the extreme right to rest on or near the Franklin road.

My entire command advanced at nine and a half o'clock, and Sherridan's division moving down the Wilkinson turnpike, until its advance encountered the enemy's pickets.

The line of battle was then formed, the left of Sherridan's division resting upon the Wilkinson pike, immediately upon General Negley's right. The remainder of Sherridan's division was deployed to the right, the line running in a south-easterly direction. Davis' division, which had already been deployed, moved up, his left resting upon Sherridan's right, Johnson's division being held in reserve. Our front was covered with a strong line of skirmishers, who soon became sharply engaged with the enemy's sharpshooters and skirmishers.

The line moved forward, but slowly, as the enemy contested stubbornly every inch of ground gained by us. The ground was very favorable to them. They were under cover of heavy woods and cedar thickets. At twelve o'clock M. on the 30th, the house of a Mr. Harding came within our lines. From that point I ascertained where the enemy's line of battle was—our skirmishers being then about five hundred yards distant from it.

The right, under General Davis, moved handsomely, but slowly into position, as the ground over which he had to march was hotly contested by the enemy's skirmishers.

At one o'clock P. M., word was sent to General D. S. Stanley, Chief of Cavalry, that Colonel Zahn, commanding three regiments of cavalry on my right flank, was hard pressed by a superior force. I ordered one brigade of my reserve division to report to General Stanley, who conducted it to the Franklin road. On his approach the enemy pressing Colonel Zahn retired, and the brigade was ordered back to its former position.

At two o'clock P. M., a citizen, residing on the Franklin road, and about half a mile in front of the enemy's line of battle, was put under guard by General Stanley. He reported as follows :

"I was up to the enemy's line of battle twice yesterday, and once this morning, to get some stock taken from me. The enemy's troops are posted in the following manner: The right of Cheatham's division rests on the Wilkinson pike. Withers is on Cheatham's left, with his left resting on the Franklin road. Hardee's corps is entirely beyond that road, his right resting on that road, and his left extending toward the Salem pike."

This man was immediately sent to the General Commanding, and subsequently returned to me with the report that his information had been received.

I also sent a report to the General Commanding, by my Aiddecamp, Horace N. Fisher, that the right of my line rested directly in front of the enemy's center. This made me anxious for my right. All my division commanders were immediately informed of this fact, and two brigades of the reserve division, commanded respectively by Generals Willich and Kirk, two of the best and most experienced Brigadiers in the army, were ordered to the right of the line, to protect the right flank, and guard against surprise there.

At six o'clock P. M., I received an order from the General Commanding to have large and extended camp-fires built on my right, to deceive the enemy, making them believe we were massing troops there. This order was communicated to General Stanley, commanding cavalry, and carried into execution by Major R. H. Nodine, Twenty-Fifth Illinois, Engineer Officer on my staff.

On the morning of the 30th, the order of battle was nearly parallel with that of the enemy, my right slightly refused, and my line of battle in two lines.

Two brigades of the reserve reinforced the right of the line, and the Third Brigade of the reserve was posted in column about eight hundred yards in rear of the right. On the evening of the 30th, Sherridan's left rested on the Wilkinson road, and on the right of Negley's divison, and the line then ran in a south-easterly direction, through a cedar thicket, until General Davis' right rested near the Franklin road. Kirk's brigade was on Davis' right. Willich's brigade flanked on a line nearly perpendicular to the main line, forming a crochet to the rear, to avoid the possibilities of my right being turned by anything like an equal force. My line was a strong one, open ground in front for a short distance. My instructions for the following day were received at about six and a half o'clock P. M. on the 30th, which were as follows:

"Take strong position; if the enemy attack you, fall back slowly, refusing your right, contesting the ground inch by inch. If the enemy do not attack you, you will attack them, not vigorously, but warmly. The time of attack by you to be designated by the General Commanding."

I was also informed that Crittenden's corps would move, simultaneously with my attack, into Murfreesboro.

Written instructions were sent by me to each division commander, on the night of the 30th, explaining to each what would be required of them on the 31st.

At about six and a half o'clock on the 31st, a determined, heavy attack was made on Kirk's and Willich's brigades, on the extreme right. They were attacked by such an overwhelming force, that they were compelled to fall back.

General Kirk being seriously wounded at the first fire upon his main line, General Willich having his horse killed early in the action, and he falling into the hands of the enemy, the two brigades were deprived of their immediate commanders, and gave way in confusion. Colonel Post's brigade, on the right of Davis' division, and, in fact, my entire line to Sherridan's left, was, almost simultaneously, attacked by a heavy force of the enemy. The attack in front of Davis and Sherridan was repulsed several times; and had not the heavy attacking columns of the enemy on my right succeeded so well, my line could have been maintained, and the enemy driven back to his barricades, which extended from the Wilkinson pike, with but a short interval, three-fourths of a mile beyond the Franklin road. General Sherridan's division was ably maneuvered by him, under my own eye.

As soon as it became evident that my lines would be compelled to give way, orders were given to re-form my line in the first skirt of timber, in the rear of my first position. The enemy advancing so rapidly on my right, I found this impossible, and changed the point of re-forming my line to the high ground in the rear of the Wilkinson pike.

Moving to the left of my line, and in rear of Sherridan's division, I here met General Rousseau in a cedar-wood, posting his division to repel the attack. I then ordered my line to fall still further back, and form on the right of Rousseau. I gave General Johnson orders, in person, to form his division in rear of Rousseau; Rousseau's division having been withdrawn to the open ground in rear of the cedar-woods, the last position became untenable, and my troops were retired to the Nashville pike, where my wing, except Shaeffer's brigade of Sherridan's division, was reassembled and replenished with ammunition On arriving at the pike, I found Colonel Harker's brigade, of Wood's division, retiring before a heavy force of the enemy. I immediately ordered Robert's brigade, of Sherridan's division, to advance into a cedar-wood, and charge the enemy and drive him back. Although this brigade was reduced in numbers, and having but two rounds of cartridges, it advanced to the charge, under the gallant Colonel Bradley, driving the enemy back with the bayonet, capturing two guns and forty prisoners, and securing our communication on the Murfreesboro pike at this point. This brigade is composed of the Twenty-Second, Forty-Second, Twenty-Seventh, and Fifty-First Illinois. The Twenty-Seventh particularly distinguished itself.

About eleven o'clock A. M., Colonel Moses B. Walker's brigade arrived upon the field, and reported to me for duty. They were assigned to General Sherridan's command, to whose report I refer for the good conduct of this brigade.

On the afternoon of the 31st, the Right Wing assumed a strong position; its left, composed of Walker's brigade, resting near a commanding knoll, the line running nearly north-west along the slope of a ridge, covered with cedar growth, the right resting on the Murfreesboro pike. On the slope strong barricades were erected, which could have been well defended by single lines. The second line, Gibson's brigade (late Willich's) was used as a reserve. The Right Wing, excepting Davis' division and Gibson's brigade, did not participate in any general engagements after the 31st. There was constant skirmishing in my front till the night of the 3d.

On the 4th, the enemy left his position in front of the Right, and evacuated Murfreesbore the night of the same day. On the 6th the Right Wing marched to its present camp, two miles and a half south of Murfreesboro, on the Shelbyville pike.

The reports of Generals Johnson, Davis, and Sherridan, division commanders, are herewith enclosed. Accompanying General Johnson's report, you will find the reports of the brigade, regimental and battery commanders carefully prepared.

I have been thus particular on account of the Commanding General's dispatch to the General-in-Chief, and also from erroneous reports sent to the public by newspaper correspondents. The attention of the General Commanding is particularly called to the reports of Colonels Gibson and Dodge; also, to Lieutenant Colonel Jones' report, who commanded the pickets in front of Willich's brigade.

Captain Edgarton, commanding battery of Kirk's brigade, certainly was guilty of a great error in taking even a part of his horses to water at such an hour. He is in the hands of the enemy, and therefore no report can be had from him at present.

In a strict compliance with my orders, and the knowledge I possessed of the position of the enemy, which was communicated to my superior and the Generals under my command, I could not have made a better disposition of my troops.

On subsequent examination of the field, I found the statements of the citizen referred to in my report correct, as the barricades extended fully three-fourths of a mile beyond the Franklin road. I am well satisfied that Hardee's corps, supported by McCown's division (late of Kirby Smith's corps), attacked Kirk's and Willich's brigade about the same time Withers' division attacked Davis, and Cheatham's division attacked Sherridan. Cheatham's and Withers' divisions compose Polk's corps.

I was in the rear of the center of my line when this attack commenced; therefore I did not see all of the columns that attacked and turned my right; but it may be safely estimated that the rebel force outnumbered ours three to one.

After leaving my line of battle, the ground in the rear was, first, open fields; second, woods, then a dense cedar-thicket; and over such ground it was almost impossible for troops to retire in good order, particularly when assailed by superior numbers.

My ammunition train, under charge of my efficient Ordnance Officer, Captain Gates P. Thruston, First Ohio, was at an early hour ordered to take a position in the rear of the center of my line. It was then attacked by the cavalry, which was handsomely repulsed by a detachment of cavalry under the direction of Captain H. Pease, of General Davis' staff, and Captain G. P. Thruston, Ordnance Officer.

The train was conducted safely to the Nashville pike by Captain Thruston, cutting a road through the cedar-wood for the passage of the train.

To Brigadiers R. W. Johnson, Philip H. Sherridan, and Jeff. C. Davis, I return my thanks, for their gallant conduct upon the day of the battle, and for their prompt support and conscientious attention to duty during their service in the Right Wing. I commend them to my superiors and my country.

To Brigadier General D. S. Stanley my thanks are particularly due. He commanded my advance from Nolensville, and directed the cavalry on my right flank. A report of the valuable services of our cavalry will be furnished by General Stanley. I commend him to my superiors and my country.

For the particular instances of good conduct of individuals, I refer you to the reports of division commanders.

I can not refrain from again calling the attention of my superiors to the conspicuous gallantry and untiring zeal of Colonel W. H. Gibson, of the Forty-Ninth Ohio Volunteers. He succeeded to the command of Willich's brigade, and was ever prompt to dash upon the enemy with his gallant brigade when opportunity permitted. I have repeatedly recommended him for promotion. He has again won additional claims to his reward.

Colonel Harker, commanding a brigade of Wood's division, performed gallant service under my supervision, as also did Colonel Fyffe, of the Fifty-Ninth Ohio. They are commended to my superiors.

To my staff—Lieutenant Colonel E. Bassett Langdon, Inspector General; Major R. H. Nodine, Engineer Officer; Major J. A. Campbell, Assistant Adjutant General; Captain Gates P. Thruston, Ordnance Officer; Captain B. D. Williams, Aiddecamp; Captain J. F. Boyd, Assistant Quartermaster; Captain O. F. Blake, Provost Marshal; Major Caleb Bates, Volunteer Aiddecamp; Captain Horace N. Fisher, Volunteer Aiddecamp and Topographical Engineer—my thanks are due for their conspicuous gallantry and intelligence on the field.

My escort, under command of Lieutenant Huckston, Second Kentucky Cavalry, and my orderlies, behaved gallantly. When my horse was shot, Orderly Cook, of the Second Indiana Cavalry, replaced him with his own.

The officers of the Signal Corps were ever ready to perform any service in their line, or as aids.

The report of Surgeon C. McDermot, the Medical Director of the Right Wing, is also submitted. Surgeon McDermot's gallantry on the field, and his great care of the wounded, is worthy of great praise. My entire Medical Corps behaved nobly, except Assistant Surgeon W. S. Fish, of the Third Indiana Cavalry, who fled to Nashville. He is recommended for dismissal.

The casualties of my wing are 542 killed, and 2,234 wounded.

The nation is again called upon to mourn the loss of gallant spirits who fell upon the sanguinary field.

First of these, Brigadier General J. W. Sill, commanding First Brigade, Third Division. He was noble, conscientious in the discharge of every duty, brave to a fault. He had no ambition save to serve his country. He died a Christian soldier, and in the act of repulsing the enemy.

Such names as Roberts, Shaeffer, Harrison, Stem, Williams, Reed, Houssam, Drake, Wooster, and McKee, all field officers, and many other commissioned officers, of the Right Wing, who fell vindicating their flag, will never be forgotten by a grateful country.

All of which is respectfully submitted,

A. McD. McCOOK,
Major General United States Volunteers.

MAJ. GEN. THOMAS' OFFICIAL REPORT.

HEADQUARTERS CENTER FOURTEENTH ARMY CORPS,
DEPARTMENT OF THE CUMBERLAND,
MURFREESBORO, *January* 15, 1863.

Major C. Goddard, Adjutant General and Chief of Staff:

MAJOR—I have the honor to submit to the Major General commanding the Department of the Cumberland, the following report of the operations of that part of my command, which was engaged in the battle of Stone River, in front of Murfreesboro. It is proper to state here, that two brigades of Fry's division, and Reynold's entire division were detained near Gallatin and along the Louisville and Nashville Railroad, to watch the movements of the rebel leader, Morgan, who had been, for a long time, on the watch for an opportunity to destroy the railroad.

Rousseau's, Negley's, and Mitchell's divisions, and Walker's brigade, of Fry's division, were concentrated at Nashville; but Mitchell's division being required to garrison Nashville, my only available force was Rousseau's and Negley's divisions, and Walker's brigade, of Fry's division, about thirteen thousand three hundred and ninety-five (13,395) effective men.

December 26.—Negley's division, followed by Rousseau's division and Walker's brigade, marched by the Franklin pike to Brentwood, at that point taking the Wilson pike. Negley and Rousseau were to have encamped for the night at Owen's store. On reaching the latter place, Negley hearing heavy firing in the direction of Nolensville, left his train with a guard to follow, and pushed forward with his troops to the support of Brigadier General J. C. Davis' command, the advance division of McCook's corps, Davis having become hotly engaged with the enemy posted in Nolensville and in the pass through the hills south of that village. Rousseau encamped, with his division, at Owen's store, and Walker, with his brigade, at Brentwood. During the night a very heavy rain fell, making the cross-road almost impassable, and it was not until the night of the 27th that Rousseau reached Nolensville with his troops and train. Negley remained at Nolensville until ten A. M., on the 27th, when having brought his train across from Wilson's pike, he moved to the east, over an exceedingly rough by-road, to the right of Crittenden, at Stewartsboro, on the Murfreesboro pike. Walker, by my orders, retraced his steps from Brentwood and crossed over to the Nolensville pike.

December 28.—Negley remained in camp at Stewartsboro, bringing his train from the rear. Rousseau reached Stewartsboro on the night of the 28th. His train arrived early next day.

December 29.—Negley's division crossed Stewart's Creek, two miles south-west and above the turnpike bridge, and marched in support of the head and right flank of Crittenden's corps, which moved, by the Murfreesboro pike, to a point within two miles of Murfreesboro. The enemy fell back before our advance, contesting the ground obstinately with their cavalry rear-guard.

Rousseau remained in camp at Stewartsboro, detaching Starkweather's brigade, with a section of artillery, to the Jefferson pike crossing of Stone River, to observe the movements of the enemy in that direction. Walker reached Stewartsboro, from the Nolensville pike, about dark.

December 30.—A cavalry force of the enemy, something over four hundred strong, with two pieces of artillery, attacked Starkweather about nine A. M., but were soon driven off. The enemy opened a brisk fire on Crittenden's advance, doing but little execution, however, about seven A. M. During the morning, Negley's division was obliqued to the right, and took up a position on the right of Palmer's division of Crittenden's corps, and was then advanced through a dense cedar thicket, several hundred yards in width, to the Wilkinson Cross-road, driving the enemy's skirmishers steadily, and with considerable loss. Our loss comparatively small. About noon, Sherridan's division of McCook's corps, approached by the Wilkinson Cross-road, joined Negley's right, McCook's two other divisions coming up on Sherridan's right, thus forming a continuous line, the left resting on Stone River, the right stretching in a westerly direction, and resting on high wooded ground, a short distance to the south of the Wilkinson Cross-road, and has since been ascertained, nearly parallel with the enemy's intrenchments, thrown up on the sloping land bordering the north-west bank of Stone River. Rousseau's division (with the exception of Starkweather's brigade) being ordered up from Stewartsboro, reached the position occupied by the army about four P. M., and bivouacked on the Murfreesboro pike, in the rear of the center. During the night of the 30th, I sent orders to Walker to take up a strong position near the turnpike bridge over Stewart's Creek, and defend the position against any attempts of the enemy's cavalry to destroy it. Rousseau was ordered to move by six A. M., on the 31st, to a position in rear of Negley. This position placed his division with its left on the Murfreesboro pike, and its right extending into the cedar thicket, through which Negley had marched on the 30th.

In front of Negley's position, bordering a large open field, reaching to the Murfreesboro pike, a heavy growth of timber extended in a southerly direction toward the river. Across the field, running in an easterly direction, the enemy had thrown up rifle-pits at intervals from the timber to the river bank to the east side of the turnpike. Along this line of intrenchments, on an eminence about eight hundred yards from Negley's position, and nearly in front of his left, some cannon had been placed, affording the enemy great advantage in covering an attack on our center. However, Palmer, Negley, and Sherridan held the position their troops had so manfully won the morning of the 30th, against every attempt to drive them back, and remained in line of battle during the night.

December 31.—Between six and seven A. M., the enemy having massed a heavy force on McCook's right during the night of the 30th, attacked and drove it back, pushing his divisions in pursuit in echelon, and in supporting distance, until he had gained sufficient ground in our rear to wheel his masses to the right, and throw them upon the right flank of the Center, at the same moment attacking Negley and Palmer in front with a greatly superior force. To counteract this movement, I had ordered Rousseau to place two brigades, with a battery, to the right and rear of Sherridan's division, facing toward the west, so as to support Sherridan, should he be able to hold his ground, or to cover him, should he be compelled to fall back. About eleven o'clock, General Sherridan reported to me that his ammunition was entirely out, and he would be compelled to fall back to get more. As it became necessary for General Sherridan to fall back, the enemy pressed on still further to our rear, and soon took up a position, which gave them a concentrated cross-fire of musketry and cannon, on Negley's and Rousseau's troops, at short range. This compelled me to fall back out of the cedar-woods, and take up a line along a depression in the open ground, within good musket range of the edge of the woods, while the artillery was retired to the high ground to the right of the turnpike. From this last position, we were enabled to drive back the enemy, and cover the formation of our troops and secure the Center on the high ground. In the execution of this last movement, the Regular Brigade, under Lieutenant Colonel Shepard, Eighteenth United States Infantry, came under a most murderous fire, losing twenty-two officers and five hundred and eight men in killed and wounded; but, with the co-operation of Scribner's and Beatty's (John) brigades, and Guenther's and Loomis' Batteries, gallantly held its ground against overwhelming odds. The Center having succeeded in driving back the enemy from its front, and our artillery concentrating its fire on the cedar-thicket on our right, drove him back far under cover, from which, though attempting it, he could not make any advance.

January 1, 1863.—Repeated attempts were made by the enemy to advance on our position, during the morning, but they were driven back before emerging from the woods. Colonel Starkweather's brigade, of Rousseau's division, and Walker's brigade, of Fry's division, having reinforced us during the night, took post on the right of Rousseau, and left of Sherridan, and bore their share in repelling the attempts of the enemy on the morning of the 1st instant.

Negley's division was ordered, early in the day, to the support of McCook's right, in which position it remained during the night.

January 2.—About 7 A. M., the enemy opened a direct and cross-fire from his batteries in our front, and from a position on the east bank of Stone River, to our left and front, at the same time making a strong demonstration with infantry, resulting, however, in no serious attack. Our artillery, Loomis', Guenther's, Stokes', and another battery, the commander's name I can not now recall, soon drove back their infantry. Negley was withdrawn from the extreme right, and placed in reserve behind Crittenden's right. About 4 P. M., a division of Crittenden's command, which had crossed Stone River to reconnoiter, was attacked by an overwhelming force of the enemy, and, after a gallant resistance, compelled to fall back. The movements of the enemy having been observed and reported by some of my troops in the Center, I sent orders to Negley to advance to the support of Crittenden's troops, should they want help. This order was obeyed in most gallant style, and resulted in the complete annihilation of the Twenty-Sixth Tennessee (rebel) Regiment and the capture of their flag. Also, in the capture of a battery, which the enemy had been forced to abandon at the point of the bayonet. (See Negley's report.)

January 3.—Soon after daylight, the Forty-Second Indiana, on picket in a clump of woods about eight hundred yards in front of our lines, was attacked by a brigade of the enemy, evidently by superior numbers, and driven in, with considerable loss. Lieutenant Colonel Shanklin, commanding the regiment, was surrounded and taken prisoner, while gallantly endeavoring to draw off his men, under the fire of such superior numbers. From these woods, the enemy's sharpshooters continued to fire occasionally during the day, on our pickets.

About 6 P. M., two regiments from Colonel John Beatty's brigade, Rousseau's division, co-operating with two regiments of Spears' (Tennessee) brigade, of Negley's division, covered by the skillful and well-directed fire of Guenther's Fifth United States Artillery, and Loomis' First Michigan Battery, advanced on the woods and drove the enemy, not only from its cover, but from the intrenchments, a short distance beyond.

The enemy having retreated during the night of the 3d, our troops were occupied during the night of the 4th in burying the dead left on the field. In the afternoon, one brigade of Negley's division was advanced to the crossing of Stone River, with a brigade of Rousseau's division in supporting distance, in reserve.

January 5.—My entire command, preceeded by Stanley's cavalry, marched into Murfreesboro and took up the position which we now hold. The enemy's rear guard of cavalry was overtaken on the Shelbyville and Manchester roads, about five miles from Murfreesboro, and after sharp skirmishing for two or three hours, was driven from our immediate front.

The conduct of my command, from the time the army left Nashville to its entry into Murfreesboro, is deserving of the highest praise, both for their patient endurance of the fatigues and discomforts of a five days' battle and for the manly spirit exhibited by them in the various phases in this memorable contest. I refer you to the detailed reports of division commanders, for special mention of those officers and men of their commands whose conduct they thought worthy of particular notice.

All the members of my staff, Major G. E. Flynt, Assistant Adjutant General; Lieutenant Colonel A. Von Schrader, Seventy-Fourth Ohio; Acting Inspector General, Captain O. A. Mack, Thirteenth United States Infantry, Acting Chief Commissary; and Captain A. J. Mackay, Chief Quartermaster, were actively employed in carrying orders to various parts of my command, and in the execution of the appropriate duties of their office. Captain O. A. Mack was dangerously wounded in the right hip and abdomen, while conveying orders from me to Major General Rousseau. The officers of the Signal Corps, attached to my headquarters, did excellent service in their appropriate sphere, when possible; and as aidsdecamp, carrying orders. My escort, composed of a select detail from the First Ohio Cavalry, commanded by Lieutenant Barker, of the same regiment, have been on duty with me for nearly a year, deserve commendation for the faithful performance of their appropriate duties. Private Gusteam was killed by a cannon shot, on the morning of January 2. Surgeon C. D. Beebe deserves special mention, for his efficient arrangements for moving the wounded from the field, and giving them immediate attention.

The details will be seen in the accompanying reports of division commanders.

Very respectfully, your obedient servant,

GEORGE H. THOMAS,

Major General United States Volunteers.

MAJOR GENERAL CRITTENDEN'S REPORT.

HEADQUARTERS LEFT WING,
MURFREESBORO, *January* 20, 1863.

Lieutenant Colonel C. Goddard, Chief of Staff:

COLONEL—In obedience to orders, I left camp near Nashville on the 26th of December, and reached the point where the battle of Stone River was fought, before dusk on the morning of the 29th. The march from Nashville was accompanied by the skirmishing usual when an army moves toward an enemy, posted near by and in force. The gallant and handsome things done by several different portions of my command during this march, have been mentioned in detail by the immediate commanders conducting the advance and leading the skirmishers. The seizure of two bridges, one by General Hascall, and the other by Colonel Hazen ; the gallant charge of the troops of Hascall's brigade, at Lavergne ; and the counter-charge and capture of twenty-five of the enemy by a company of the new regiment, One Hundredth Illinois, when charged by the enemy's cavalry, are worthy of special notice.

It was about dusk, and just at the moment when Generals Wood and Palmer had halted to gather up their troops, that I reached the head of my command. These two Generals had their divisions in line of battle. General Wood on the left, and General Palmer on the right, the enemy in sight, and evidently in heavier force than we had yet encountered them; it was evident they intended to dispute the passage of the river and to fight a battle at or near Murfreesboro.

At this moment I received an order to occupy Murfreesboro with one division, camping the other two outside.

I immediately gave the order to advance, and the movement was commenced. General Wood was ordered to occupy the place, General Palmer being ordered, at General Wood's suggestion, to keep in line with Wood's division, and advance with him, until he had forced the passage of the river. At this time it was dark. General Wood had declared, when he received the order, that it was hazarding a great deal for very little, to move over unknown ground in the night, instead of awaiting for daylight, and that I ought to take the responsibility of disobeying the order. I thought the movement hazardous, but as the success of the whole army might depend on the prompt execution of orders by every officer, it was my duty to advance. After General Wood had issued the order to advance, and General Palmer had received his also, they both came to see me, and insisted that the order should not be carried out. I refused to rescind the order, but consented to suspend it for one hour, as General Rosecrans could be heard from in that time. During the interval the General himself came to the front, and approved of what I had done.

In the meantime, Colonel Harker, after a sharp skirmish, gallantly crossed the river with his brigade and Bradley's Battery, and Hascall was already in the river advancing, when the order to suspend the movement was received. As soon as possible I recalled Harker, and, to my great satisfaction, this able officer, with consummate address, withdrew from the actual presence of a vastly superior force his artillery and troops, and recrossed the river without any serious loss. During the night General McCook came over to see the Commanding General, and reported that he was on the Wilkinson pike, about three miles in the rear of our line, and that he should advance in the morning.

The next morning (the 30th) early, my line of battle was formed. Palmer's division occupied the ground to the right of the turnpike, his right resting on Negley's left, Negley having advanced into the woods and taken a position in the center, to take a position with General McCook when he should come into line. General Wood was to occupy that part of our front to the left of the turnpike, extending down the river. General Van Cleve was held in reserve to the rear and left. This position of our forces was, without material change, maintained all day, though the skirmishing during part of the day was very heavy, particularly on our extreme right, where McCook was coming up. Then, when it apparently assumed the proportion of a battle, I proposed to cross the river with my corps, and attack Murfreesboro from the left, by way of the Lebanon pike, but the General, though approving the plan of attack, would not consent that I should move until McCook was more seriously engaged.

On the morning of the 31st, when the battle begun, I occupied the front near the turnpike, General Palmer's division on the right, General Wood on the left, General Van Cleve in reserve to the rear and left. About 8 o'clock, when my troops under Van Cleve were crossing the river, as ordered, and when all was ready for an advance movement, it became evident that our Right was being driven back; orders were received and immediately issued recalling Van Cleve and stopping the advance; Van Cleve was ordered to leave a brigade to guard the ford, Matthews' brigade, Colonel Price commanding in Colonel Matthews' absence, was left, and to hurry with all possible dispatch to try and check the enemy to the right and rear. One brigade of his division, Colonel Fyffe's, had already been ordered to protect the train then threatened near the hospital, and General Van Cleve moved at once and quickly to the right with Beatty's brigade. He arrived most opportunely, as his own and Colonel Beatty's reports show, and checked the enemy. The confusion of our own troops, who were being driven from the woods at this point, hindered him, for some time, from forming his men in line of battle. This difficulty, however, was soon overcome, his line rapidly formed, and one small brigade, commanded by the gallant Colonel Beatty, of the Nineteenth Ohio, under the direction of General Van Cleve, boldly attacked vastly superior forces of the enemy, then advancing in full career, checked their advance and drove them back. Being soon reinforced by Fyffe's brigade and Harker's brigade, of Wood's division, the enemy were pressed vigorously, and too far. They came upon the enemy massed to receive them, who, outnumbering them and outflanking them, compelled them to fall back in turn. This they did in good order, and fighting with such effect that the enemy drew off and left them, and they were able to hold their position during the remainder of the day. From this time the great object of the enemy seemed to be to break our left and front, where, under great disadvantages, my two divisions, under Generals Wood and Palmer, maintained their ground.

When the troops composing the Center and Right Wing of our army had been driven by the enemy from our original line of battle to a line almost perpendicular to it, the First and Second Divisions of the Left Wing still nobly maintained their position. Though several times assaulted by the enemy in great force, it was evident that it was vital to us that this position should be held, at least until our troops, who had been driven back, could establish themselves on their new line. The country is deeply indebted to Generals Wood and Palmer for the sound judgment, skill, and courage with which they managed their commands at this important crisis in the battle. The reports of my Division Commanders show how nobly and how ably they were supported by their officers; and the most melancholy and convincing proof of the bravery of all who fought in this part of the field is their terrible list of killed and wounded, for with them was no rout, no confusion; the men who fell, fell fighting in the ranks.

Generals Wood and Van Cleve being wounded on the 31st, their commands devolved, of course, on other officers—General Hascall taking command of Wood's division, and Colonel Beatty of Van Cleve's on the 1st day of January. It was a fortunate thing that competent and gallant officers took command of these two noble divisions.

On the night of the 31st, with the consent of the General Commanding, I reunited my command, bringing them all together on the left of the turnpike, and before daylight, by orders from the General Commanding,, we took up a new line of battle, about five hundred yards to the rear of our former line; Hascall's division was ordered to rest their right on the position occupied by Stokes' Battery, and his left on General Palmer's right; General Palmer was to rest his left on the ford, his right extending toward the railroad, and perpendicular to it, thus bringing the line at right angles to the railroad and turnpike, and extending from Stokes' Battery to the ford. On the morning of the 1st of January, Van Cleve's division again crossed the river, and took position on ground the General considered it important we should hold, extending from the ford about half a mile from the river, the right resting on high ground near the river, and the left thrown forward, so that the direction of the line should be nearly perpendicular to it. These changes in position having been accomplished, the day passed quietly, except continued skirmishing and occasional artillery firing. The next day (January 2) large forces of the enemy's infantry and artillery were seen to pass to the right, apparently contemplating an attack. Lieutenant Livingston, with Drury's Battery, was ordered over the river, and Colonel Grose's brigade, of Palmer's division, was also crossed over, taking post on the hill near the hospital, so as to protect the left and rear of Beatty's position.

About four o'clock on the evening of the 2d, a sudden and concentrated attack was made on the Third Division, now commanded by Colonel Beatty; several batteries opened at the same time on their division.

The overwhelming numbers of the enemy directed upon two brigades, forced them, after a bloody but short conflict, back to the river. The object of the enemy (it is since ascertained) was to take the battery which we had on that side of the river. In this attempt it is most likely they would have succeeded, but for the sound judgment and wise precaution of Colonel Beatty, in changing the position of his battery. It was so late when the attack was made, that the enemy, failing in their enterprise to capture our battery, were sure of not suffering any great disaster in case of a repulse, because night would protect them. They not only failed to capture our battery, but lost four of their guns in their repulse and flight. As soon as it became evident that the enemy were driving Colonel Beatty, I turned to my Chief of Artillery, Captain John Mendenhall, and said, "Now, Mendenhall, you must cover my men with your cannon." Without any show of excitement or haste, almost as soon as the order was given, the batteries began to open, so perfectly had he placed them. In twenty minutes from the time the order was received, fifty-two guns were firing upon the enemy. They can not be said to have been checked in their advance; from a rapid advance they broke at once into a rapid retreat. Reinforcements soon began to arrive; our troops crossed the river and pursued the flying enemy until dark.

It is a pleasant thing to report that the officers and men from the Center and Right Wing hurried to the support of the Left Wing, when it was known to be hard pressed. General J. C. Davis sent a brigade at once without orders, then applied for and obtained orders to follow immediately with his division. General Negley, from the Center, crossed with a part of his division. General McCook, to whom I applied for a brigade, not knowing of Davis' movement, ordered immediately Colonel Gibson to go with his brigade, and the Colonel and the brigade passed at double-quick in less than five minutes after the request was made. Honor is due to such men. On the night of the 2d, General Hascall, with his division, and General Davis with his, camped a little in advance of the position which Beatty had occupied. General Palmer, commanding the Second Division, camped with two brigades in reserve to Hascall and Davis' divisions, and the remaining brigade on this side of the river. In this position these troops remained until Saturday night, when the river beginning to rise, and the rain continuing to fall, it was feared we might be separated from the rest of the army, and all recrossed the river except Palmer's two brigades, which remained, and did not come back until it was ascertained the next day (Sunday) that the enemy had evacuated Murfreesboro.

I feel that this report of the part taken by my command in the battle of Stone River is very imperfect. I have only endeavored to give a general outline of the most important features of the battle. The reports, however, of the division commanders, and the report of the Chief of Artillery, give a detailed and good account of the memorable incidents which occurred in this particular fight.

Reports of the division commanders show how nobly they were sustained by their subordinate officers, and all reports show how nobly the troops behaved. Generals Wood and Van Cleve, though wounded early in the battle of the 31st, remained in the saddle and on the field throughout the day, and at night were ordered to the rear; General Palmer exposing himself everywhere and freely, escaped unhurt, and commanded the Second Division throughout the battle. To these division commanders, I return my most earnest and heartfelt thanks, for the brave, prompt, and able manner in which they executed every order, and I most urgently present their names to the Commanding General and to the Government, as having fairly earned promotion.

After the 31st, General Hascall commanded Wood's division, the First, and Colonel Beatty the Second, Van Cleve's. To these officers I am indebted for the same cheerful and prompt obedience to orders, the same brave support which I received from their predecessors in command; and I also respectfully present their names to the Commanding General and the Government, as having earned promotion on the field of battle.

There are numerous cases of distinguished conduct in the brigade as well as regimental commanders, mentioned by my division commanders as meriting promotion. I respectfully refer the General Commanding to division, brigade, and regimental reports, and solicit for the gallant officers and men who have distinguished themselves for conduct and bravery in battle, the honors they have won. We have officers who have commanded brigades for almost a year, though they have but the rank of Colonel; in such cases, and in all like cases, as where a Lieutenant commands a company, it seems if the officers have capacity for their commands on the field, that they should have the rank the command is entitled to. The report of Captain Mendenhall, Chief of Artillery to the Left Wing, shows the efficiency, skill, and daring with which our artillery officers handled their batteries. Division and brigade commanders vie with each other in commendation upon different batteries. Some of the batteries, fighting as they did in all parts of the field, won praises from all. To these officers, also, attention is called, with a sincere hope that they may be rewarded as their valor and bearing deserves.

Major Lyne Starling, Assistant Adjutant General to the Left Wing, has been, for nearly eighteen months, the most indefatigable officer I ever knew, in his department. His services to me are invaluable. On the field here, as at Shiloh, he was distinguished, even among so many brave men, for his daring and efficiency. Captain R. Loder, Inspector General for the Left Wing, has entitled himself to my lasting gratitude, by his constant and able management of his department. It is sufficient to say that the gallant and lamented Colonel Garesché told him, in my presence, but a short time before the battle, that he had proved himself to be the best Inspector General in the army. On the field of battle bravery was added to the same efficiency and activity which marked his conduct in the camp.

Captain John Mendenhall, who has been mentioned already as Chief of Artillery to my command, but of whom too much can not be said, is also Topographical Engineer on my staff. In this capacity, as in all where he works, the work is well and faithfully done. His services at Shiloh, of which I was an eye-witness; his splendid conduct as Chief of Artillery to the Left Wing; his uniform soldierly bearing, point him out as eminently qualified for promotion.

To the Medical Director of the Left Wing, Doctor A. J. Phelps, the thanks of the army and the country are due, not only for his prompt attention to the wounded, but for his arrangements for their immediate accommodation. He took good care not only of the wounded of my command, but of more than two thousand wounded from other corps and from the enemy. Since the battle, I have visited his hospitals, and can bear testimony to the efficiency of the Medical Department of the Left Wing.

Captain Louis M. Buford and Lieutenant George Knox, my Aidsde-camp, were brave, active, and efficient helps to me all through the battle. Captain Buford was struck just over the heart, fortunately, by a ball too far spent to penetrate, and which only bruised. The Captain and Lieutenant Knox were frequently exposed to the heaviest firing, as they fearlessly carried my orders to all parts of the field.

Captain Case, of the Signal Corps, tendered his services as a volunteer aid, and proved himself a bold soldier and an efficient aid. Two other officers of the same corps, Lieutenants ———— tendered their services as aids, and were placed on my staff during the battle, and I thank them sincerely for their services.

Lieutenant Brown, of the Third Kentucky Cavalry, who commanded my escort, was as quietly brave on the battle-field as he is mild and gentlemanly in the camp.

Before concluding this report, it will be proper to add, that when I speak of a quiet day, I mean to speak comparatively. We had no quiet days; no rest from the time we reached the battle-field until the enemy fled, skirmishing constantly, and sometimes terrible cannonading. On the 2d, which we call a quiet day, until about four o'clock P. M., the First Division, under Hascall, laid for half an hour, in the early part of the day, under the heaviest cannonading we endured. Many men were killed, but he and his brave soldiers would not flinch.

The number of killed and wounded, demonstrates with what fearful energy and earnestness the battle was contested in my command.

Most respectfully, your obedient servant,

T. L. CRITTENDEN,

Major General Commanding.

THE CAVALRY.

GEN. D. S. STANLEY'S OFFICIAL REPORT.

HEADQUARTERS CAVALRY FOURTEENTH ARMY CORPS,
DEPARTMENT OF THE CUMBERLAND,
NEAR MURFREESBORO, *January* 9, 1863.

MAJOR—I have the honor to submit for the information of the General commanding the army, the following statement of the part taken by the cavalry under my command in the advance upon and battle of Murfreesboro :

Upon the 26th day of December I divided the cavalry into three columns, putting the First Brigade, commanded by Colonel Minty, Fourth Michigan Cavalry, upon the Murfreesboro pike, in advance of General Crittenden's corps. The Second Brigade, commanded by Colonel Zahn, Third Ohio Cavalry, was ordered on Franklin to dislodge the enemy's cavalry, and move parallel to General McCook's corps, protecting his right flank. The reserve cavalry, consisting of the new regiments, viz.: Anderson Troop, First Middle Tennessee, Second East Tennessee Cavalry, and four companies of the Third Indiana, I commanded in person, and preceded General McCook's corps on the Nolensville pike.

Colonel John Kennett, commanding cavalry division, commanded the cavalry on the Murfreesboro pike. For the operations of this column and also the movements of Colonel Zahn up to the 31st of December, I would refer you to the inclosed reports of Colonel Kennett, and Colonels Zahn and Minty.

On the morning of the 26th our cavalry first encountered the enemy on the Nolensville pike, one mile in advance of Balle Jack Pass ; their cavalry was in large force and accompanied by a battery of artillery, the fighting continued from ten o'clock until evening, during which time we had driven the enemy two miles beyond Lavergne. The Third Indiana and Anderson Troop behaved gallantly, charging the enemy twice, and bringing them to hand and hand encounters. The conduct of Majors Rosengarten and Ward, the former now deceased, was most heroic. On the 28th we made a reconnoissance to College Grove, and found that Hardee's rebel corps had marched to Murfreesboro.

On the 29th, Colonel Zahn's brigade having formed, was directed to march upon Murfreesboro by the Franklin road. The reserve cavalry moving on the Balle Jack road, the column communicating at the crossing of Stewart's Creek. We encountered the enemy's cavalry and found them in strong force at Wilkinson's Cross-roads. Our cavalry drove them rapidly aci oss Overall's Creek, and within one-half mile of the enemy's line of battle. The Anderson Cavalry behaved most gallantly this day, pushing at full charge upon the enemy for six miles; unfortunately their advance fronted too recklessly; having dispersed their cavalry, the troops fell upon two regiments of rebel infantry in ambush, and after a gallant struggle were compelled to retire, with the loss of Major Rosengarten and six men killed, and the brave Major Ward and five men desperately wounded. With the loss of these two most gallant officers the spirit of the "Anderson Troop," which gave such full promise, seems to have died out, and I have not been able to get any duty out of them since.

On the 30th the entire cavalry force was engaged in guarding the flanks of the army in position. Some small cavalry skirmishing occurred, but nothing of importance. At eleven o'clock P. M., the 30th, I marched for Lavergne, with the First Tennessee and the Anderson Cavalry. Near that place I was joined by detachments of the Fourth Michigan and Seventh Pennsylvania Cavalry. At half-past nine o'clock on the 31st, I received an order from the General Commanding, directing me to hasten to the Right. I made all possible speed, leaving a strong detachment to protect the trains crossing the road at Stewartsboro, and to pick up stragglers. Upon arriving upon the right flank of the army, I found order restored, and took position on General McCook's right, my right extending toward Wilkinson's Cross-roads, occupying the woods about the meeting-house and Overall's Creek. In this position we were attacked, about four o'clock P. M., by a long line of foot-skirmishers. My first impression was that these were covered infantry, but I soon learned that they were dismounted cavalry. We successfully held them at bay for half an hour with the Fourth Michigan and Seventh Pennsylvania dismounted, when, being outflanked, I ordered our line to mount and fall back to the open field. The enemy followed here, and, being reinforced by detachments of the Anderson and Third Kentucky Cavalry, and by the First Tennessee, we charged the enemy and put him to rout. The cavalry held the same position this night they had taken upon my arrival upon the field. About nine o'clock New Year's morning, the enemy showed a line of skirmishers in the woods to our front, and soon after brought a six-gun battery to bear upon my cavalry. As we could not reach the enemy's skirmishers nor reply to his artillery, I ordered my cavalry to fall back. A part of Zahn's brigade marched this day to Nashville, to protect our trains. Colonel Zahn's report is inclosed.

The 2d and 3d of January the cavalry was engaged in watching the flanks of our position. On the 4th it became evident that the enemy had fled; the cavalry was collected and moved to the fords of Stone River. Upon the 5th we entered Murfreesboro. Zahn's brigade marched in pursuit of the enemy on the Shelbyville pike six miles, finding no opposition. With the remainder of the cavalry, I marched on the Manchester pike, and encountered the enemy in heavy force at Lytle's Creek, three and a half miles from town. We fought with this force till near sundown, pushing them from one cedar-brake to another, when, being reinforced by General Spears' brigade of East Tennesseeans, we drove the enemy out of his last stand in disorder. We returned after dusk and encamped on Lytle's Creek. Our troops all behaved well. The skirmishing was of a very severe character.

The Fourth United States Cavalry, which was this day first under my control, behaved very handsomely. Captain Otis' command acted independently until the 5th instant, when they came under my command.

The duty of the cavalry was very arduous. From the 26th of December till the 4th of January, the saddles were only taken off to groom, and were immediately replaced.

Respectfully submitted,

D. S. STANLEY,

Brigadier General and Chief of Cavalry.

OFFICIAL REPORT OF COL. JOHN KENNETT.

HEADQUARTERS FIRST CAVALRY DIVISION,
CAMP STANLEY, *January* 8, 1863.

Captain W. H. Sinclair:

SIR—I have the honor to submit to you the reports of the part taken in the fighting of the two brigades composing the First Cavalry Division from December 26, 1862, up to the night of January 5, 1863, from Nashville to Murfreesboro, and six miles beyond Murfreesboro, on the Manchester and Shelbyville pikes.

On leaving Nashville the Second Brigade, under Colonel Zahn, took the road to Franklin; Brigadier General D. S. Stanley, with the First and Second Tennessee Cavalry and Anderson Troop, taking the Nolensville pike. The First Brigade, Colonel Minty commanding, under my charge, took the Murfreesboro pike. I reported my command to General Palmer, who placed us in advance. Our skirmishers drove the enemy some five miles. The afternoon was well spent when General Palmer relieved us with infantry skirmishers. The cavalry forming the reserve on the right and left flanks, the First Brigade marched directly as a reserve to the advance skirmishers of the army composing the Left Wing, on their flanks, up to December 30, 1862.

On December 31, 1862, we were posted as reserves on the flanks, throwing out our skirmishers and vedettes, watching the movements of the enemy. We performed a variety of duty as scouts on the different avenues leading to our camp and connecting with the roads centering upon Nashville, Tennessee—flankers, vedettes, couriers—engaging the enemy daily on the right flank.

Some few incidents which could not have fallen under the eye of the brigade commanders, having occurred under my immediate notice, I beg leave to append.

When the enemy charged upon our wing, scattering a few regiments, who stampeded to the rear, I received orders from General

Rosecrans in person, to collect all the cavalry at my command, and proceed to rally the Right Wing and drive the enemy away. I found Colonel Murray, of the Third Kentucky, in command of about a squadron of men. With that we made our way to the right. We found a complete stampede—infantry, cavalry, and artillery, rushing to the rear, and the rebel cavalry charging upon our retiring forces on the Murfreesboro pike. Colonel Murray, with great intrepidity, engaged the enemy toward the skirts of the wood, and drove them in three charges. His men behaved like old veterans. Between his command and the field, was filled with rushing rebel cavalry charging upon our retreating cavalry and infantry, holding many of our soldiers as prisoners.

I rallied the Third Ohio, some two companies, who were falling back, and formed them in the rear of a fence, where volley after volley had the effect of driving back the rebels on the run, the Third Ohio charging upon them effectually, thereby relieving the pike of their presence, saving the train, one piece of artillery, and rescuing from their grasp many of our men taken as prisoners. One of my staff, Lieutenant Reilly, being a prisoner in their hands was released. Lieutenant Murray, of the Third Ohio, displayed energy, courage, and coolness upon this occasion, in executing my orders. I also take great pride in mentioning the prompt manner with which my staff conveyed my orders in all these engagements.

Two of my orderlies displayed high order of chivalry. Jaggers charged upon two rebel cavalry, rescuing two men of the Fourth Ohio Volunteer Cavalry, who were being taken off as prisoners. The other, Farrish, shot two of the rebels, and came to my rescue in a personal encounter with a rebel, who was in the act of leveling his pistol at my head, but he found a carbine leveled into his own face, and at my order to surrender, he delivered his pistols, carbine, and horse to me. They both deserve promotion, and would make good officers.

The able and undaunted spirit and ability which Colonel Minty has displayed whenever coming under my eye, I take great satisfaction in noticing. The officers and men all displayed great self-sacrifice. Major Wynkoop, of the Seventh Pennsylvania commanding, and Lieutenant Wooley, Adjutant General of the First Brigade, carried out every order with unhesitating energy and will, displaying the highest order of gallantry.

Captain E. Otis, of the Fourth Regular Cavalry, although he does not belong to my division, but being posted on the Left Wing of our skirmishers on the march on the Manchester road, I feel it my duty as well as take great pleasure in stating he is is an able and efficient officer.

Brigadier General D. S. Stanley being in command of the forces pursuing the retiring rebels on the march, it fell to my lot to convey and see his orders executed. Before closing this report it is my duty to make honorable mention of the meritorious conduct of Lieutenant Newell, commanding a section of artillery attached to my division. During the first day's engagement near Lavergne, he placed his two pieces on well-selected ground, and did great execution, killing three horses, dismounting seven, and scattering the rebel cavalry by his well and timely aimed shots. He has on several occasions displayed talents of first order as an artillerist.

It would not be amiss at this time to state that my entire command were short of rations, performing duty, night and day, in the wet field without shelter, exposed to the wet, cold, and hunger, without a murmur. Major Paransom, of the Third Ohio, displayed great presence of mind and determination in maintaining his position on the right flank with his battalion, to cover an ammunition train, long after the cavalry on his right had been driven away by the enemy's shells.

Your obedient servant,

JOHN KENNETT,

Commanding Division.

OFFICIAL REPORT OF CAPT. ELMER OTIS.

HEADQUARTERS FOURTH UNITED STATES CAVALRY,
IN CAMP NEAR MURFREESBORO, TENNESSEE,
January 7, 1863.

Major C. Goddard, Acting Assistant Adjutant General:

SIR—I have the honor to make the following report of the operations of the Fourth United States Cavalry, in the battle in front of Murfreesboro:

On December 30, the Fourth United States Cavalry left camp at Stewart's Creek, leaving the train and baggage under a strong guard, commanded by Lieutenant Randlebrook. The regiment proceeded to join General Rosecrans on the field of battle, and was drawn up in line of battle in rear of the General's headquarters, but took no immediate part in the action that day. Company L, commanded by Lieutenant Royse, was General Rosecrans' immediate escort, and so remains at the present time. Company M, strengthened by fifty men detailed from Companies B, C, D, G, I, and K, commanded by Lieutenant L'Hommedieu, proceeded to establish a courier line from General Rosecrans' headquarters to Lavergne, and so remained doing good service until relieved, January 4, 1863. These details left me with only six small companies, numbering in aggregate two hundred and sixty men, rank and file.

On the morning of the 31st, Colonel Garesché informed me that rebel cavalry was appearing on the right flank of the line of battle, and ordered me to proceed with the Fourth United States Cavalry to look after them. This must have been between seven and eight o'clock in the morning. I crossed the Murfreesboro pike and drew up the six companies in line of battle in the following manner: each company was in a column of fours led by the company commanders, the companies on a line parallel to each other, company distance apart, leading the center myself. This was done owing to the wooded country and fences that were obstructions to the ordinary line of battle.

Proceeding to the right of the line, I found our entire right flank had given way. Learning from some men of General Davis' division the position of the enemy's cavalry, I made a turn to the right, moving about one-fourth of a mile, and discovered the enemy. I came out of a piece of timber I was in, and getting over a fence, rapidly charged the enemy with my entire command, completely routing them with the exception of two pieces of artillery, supported by about one hundred and twenty-five cavalry, stationed between my right and the Murfreesboro and Nashville pike, who were not at first discovered. I rallied my men again, and while rallying I saw about three hundred of volunteer cavalry on my right; I rode over to them and asked them to charge the artillery with me and the few men I had rallied to take the pieces. The officer replied that he was placed there to guard a train, and would not charge with me. I have no doubt I could have taken the artillery. Before I could get my men rallied the artillery moved off. About the time I got my command rallied, I received an order from General Rosecrans to proceed to the Nashville and Murfreesboro pike as soon as possible. I did so immediately. I have since thought the General did not know my position, or he would have allowed me to follow up the enemy. I was much nearer the pike than I thought I was. I saw no more of the enemy's cavalry on the pike that morning.

In this charge I can not speak in too high terms of the officers and men. Every man charged and kept in position, taking over a hundred prisoners of the enemy and releasing a large number of our own captured men. More redounds to their credit, considering that a large majority were recruits from volunteer infantry, and only some five days drilled mounted.

Two companies of infantry were released in a body. The train on the pike was, I have since learned, in the possession of the enemy with a large number of stragglers, who were being disarmed at the time. These stragglers did nothing to protect the train, scarcely firing a shot.

From prisoners taken I have learned that the Fourth United States Cavalry charged an entire brigade of cavalry, and routed them to such a degree that they disappeared from the field at this point entirely. Later in the day I sent seventy-nine prisoners in one body to the Tenth Ohio Infantry, stationed in our rear at Stewart's Creek. Another body of forty men started, but I regret to say were captured. Of the seventy-nine sent to the rear there was one captain and two lieutenants. I have no doubt there were other officers, but did not have an opportunity to examine them closely enough to find out.

Of the officers engaged it is almost impossible to particularize, they all did so well. Captain Eli Long led his company with the greatest gallantry, and was wounded by a ball through his left arm. Lieutenants Mouck, Kelly, Lee, and Healey could not have done better.

It was a matter of great surprise to me, considering the ground passed over, to find Dr. Comfort so soon on the field with his ambulance, caring for the wounded. He was in time to capture a prisoner himself. First Sergeant Murphy led Company G, and commanded it with great gallantry, the reports having counted eleven dead of the enemy on the ground over which his company charged. Sergeant Major John G. Webster behaved gallantly, capturing a lieutenant mounted on a fine mare. First Sergeant James McAlpin led Company K after Captain Long was wounded, and reports having killed two rebels with two successive shots of his pistol. First Sergeant John Dolan, Company B, captured a captain and received his sword. No one could have acted more bravely than First Sergeant McMaster, of Company I. First Sergeant Christian Haefling, in charge of courier line near headquarters, proceeded in the thickest of the fight and recovered the effects of Colonel Garesché on his body, killed in this day's fight. Our loss in this charge was small, Captain Eli Long and six privates wounded.

Proceeding on the Nashville pike, I was ordered to escort a train to the rear. I afterward got orders to return and report to General Rosecrans; I returned, and for two hours looked for the General with my command, but did not find him, although I found several of his staff. I proceeded to the right flank and formed my regiment in front of some rebel cavalry, who showed themselves in the distance, in order to protect our train. I returned to General Rosecrans' headquarters that night, and bivouacked near him. The next morning, January 1st, I was ordered to make a reconnoissance on the right flank which I did, making my reports frequently to Major Goddard, Acting Assistant Adjutant General; that night bivouacking near Overall's Creek, where my command remained watching the movements of the enemy until the 4th of January, when it was moved to Wilkinson's Cross-roads. On January 5th my command proceeded under command of General Stanley to engage the enemy's rear guard, on the Manchester pike, driving them some two or three miles.

Private Snow, of Company L, orderly to General Rosecrans, was ordered on January 2d, to pick up fifteen stragglers, march them to the front, and turn them over to some commissioned officer. Failing to find one he assumed command, formed them in line, telling them that he would shoot the first one that should run. He reports that they fought bravely.

Twelve men were taken prisoners while performing courier duty. Lieutenant Randlebrook was exceedingly vigilant guarding the train, and of great service in sending forward supplies.

I am, sir, very respectfully, your obedient servant,

ELMER OTIS,

Captain Commanding Fourth United States Cavalry in Field.

REPORT OF COLONEL R. H. G. MINTY.

HEADQUARTERS FIRST CAVALRY BRIGADE,
CAMP BEFORE MURFREESBORO, *January* 7, 1863.

Lieutenant Chamberlain, Acting Assistant Adjutant General, First Cavalry Division :

SIR—I have the honor to hand you the following report of the part taken by the First Brigade, First Division Cavalry Reserve, in the operations from the advance of the army from Nashville to, and including the battle before, Murfreesboro.

I marched from Camp Rosecrans, near Nashville, on the morning of the 26th ult., with the Third Kentucky, Fourth Michigan, Seventh Pennsylvania, and one company of the Second Indiana, and reported to General Palmer on the Murfreesboro road. In accordance with orders received from him, through the Colonel commanding the division, I placed the Third Kentucky on the left, and the Seventh Pennsylvania on the right of the road, keeping the Fourth Michigan on the pike, with a strong advance guard thrown out.

Ten miles from Nashville I met the enemy's pickets, who, as they fell back before us, were continually reinforced, until arriving at Lavergne they disputed our progress with a force of two thousand five hundred cavalry and mounted infantry, with four pieces of artillery, under General Wheeler. After some sharp skirmishing in which we suffered some loss, and did the enemy considerable damage, I moved under cover of a slight eminence on which Lieutenant Newell, of Battery D, First Ohio, had his section planted, leaving two companies of the Fourth Michigan dismounted, and in ambush behind a fence, to support the artillery. I must here mention that Lieutenant Newell did splendid service with his two three-inch Rodmans. Every shot was well planted, and he nobly fought the four guns of the enemy for over half an hour, when a battery from General Palmer's division came up to his assistance. One of the gunners was killed by a shell from the enemy while serving his gun.

Saturday, December 27.—The Seventh Pennsylvania, under Major Wynkoop, made a reconnoissance in front of General Palmer's division, which occupied a position on the left of the line. One battalion, Fourth Michigan, under Captain Mix, was sent out on the Jefferson pike, and did not rejoin the brigade until the following day.

The army advanced at about eleven o'clock A. M., the Third Kentucky and one company of the Second Indiana, under Colonel Murray, on the left flank, and the Fourth Michigan, under my immediate direction, covering the right flank.

Camped near Stewart's Creek this night.

Sunday, December 28.—I sent one battalion Seventh Pennsylvania, under Captain Jennings, to relieve the battalion Fourth Michigan on the Jefferson pike.

Monday, December 29.—The army again advanced—the Seventh

Pennsylvania, under Major Wynkoop, on the left flank; the Third Kentucky, under Colonel Murray, on the right flank; the Fourth Michigan, under Lieutenant Colonel Dickinson, in reserve; Second Indiana on courier duty. Light skirmishing with the enemy all day. Found the enemy in position in front of Murfreesboro at about three o'clock P. M. Bivouacked immediately in rear of our line of battle.

Tuesday, December 30.—One battalion of the Seventh Pennsylvania and one battalion of the Third Kentucky formed a chain of vedettes in rear of line of battle, with orders to drive up all stragglers.

Under orders from the Colonel commanding the division, I took the Fourth Michigan, and one battalion of the Seventh Pennsylvania, back on the Nashville road to operate against Wheeler's Cavalry, who, a few hours before, had captured the train of the Twenty-Eighth Brigade on the Jefferson pike. Between Stewart's Creek and Lavergne I met the enemy, who were chiefly dressed in our uniforms. The Seventh Pennsylvania drove them until after dark. I joined Colonel Walker's brigade, and camped with them near Lavergne for the night.

Wednesday, December 31.—Under orders from General Rosecrans I reported to Brigadier General Stanley, Chief of Cavalry, who came up the same morning with the First Middle Tennessee, and a part of the Fifteenth Pennsylvania, and in accordance with his orders we moved rapidly across the country toward the right flank of General McCook's position, leaving Lieutenant Colonel Dickinson with one hundred and twenty men to protect Lieutenant Newell's section of artillery at the Cross-roads, north-west from Stewart's Creek. The enemy's cavalry fell back rapidly before us for some miles. When close to Overall's Creek our own artillery, in position to our left, opened on us with shell, and wounded severely one man of the Fifteenth Pennsylvania.

Crossing Overall's Creek, I took up position parallel to and about three-quarters of a mile from the Murfreesboro and Nashville pike; the Fourth Michigan, under command of Captain Mix, forming a line of dismounted skirmishers close to the edge of the woods, out of which they had driven a large force of the enemy's cavalry. They were supported by a portion of the First Middle Tennessee Cavalry, also dismounted.

Captain Jennings' battalion of the Seventh Pennsylvania, and two companies of the Third Kentucky, under Captain Davis, were posted in the woods near and to the right of the Fourth Michigan, with the Fifteenth Pennsylvania (the Anderson Troop) in their rear.

My entire force at this time numbered nine hundred and fifty men.

The enemy advanced rapidly with two thousand five hundred cavalry, mounted and dismounted, and three pieces of artillery, all under the command of Generals Wheeler, Wharton, and Buford. They drove back the Fourth Michigan to the line of the First Tennessee skirmishers, and then attacked the Seventh Pennsylvania with great fury, but met with a determined resistance. I went forward to the line of dismounted skirmishers and endeavored to move them to the right to strengthen the Seventh Pennsylvania, but the moment the right of the line showed itself from behind the fence where they were posted, the whole of the enemy's fire was directed on it, turning it completely round.

At this moment the Fifteenth Pennsylvania gave way and retreated rapidly, leaving the battalion of the Seventh Pennsylvania and the dismounted men entirely unsupported, and no alternative but to retreat. I fell back a short distance and reformed in the rear of a rising ground, which protected us from the enemy's artillery.

The rebel cavalry followed us up sharply into the open ground, and now menaced us with three strong lines, two directly in front of our position, and one opposite our left flank, with its right thrown well forward, and a strong body of skirmishers in the woods on our right, threatening that flank.

General Stanley ordered a charge, and he himself led two companies of the Fourth Michigan (H and K), with about fifty men of the Fifteenth Pennsylvania, against the line in front of our left. He routed the enemy and captured one stand of colors, which was brought in by a sergeant of the Fifteenth Pennsylvania.

Captain Jennings, of the Seventh Pennsylvania, with his battalion, supported this movement. At the same time I charged the first line in our front with the Fourth Michigan and First Tennessee, and drove them from the field. The second line was formed on the far side of a lane, with a partially destroyed fence on each side, and still stood their ground. I reformed my men and again charged. The enemy again broke, and were driven from the field in the wildest confusion.

I held the ground that night, with the First Tennessee, Fifteenth Pennsylvania, and Fourth Michigan, picketing all of my first position.

A sergeant of the Seventh Pennsylvania, who was taken prisoner by the enemy when we were driven back, states that before we charged we had killed twenty-seven, including many officers.

January 1, 2, and 3.—Had the brigade under arms all day, with two regiments on picket and skirmishing with the enemy's pickets.

January 4.—I moved the brigade to Wilkinson's Cross-roads and bivouacked there for the night, with the Fourth Cavalry.

January 5.—I marched through Murfreesboro and took the Manchester pike. One mile out I met the enemy's pickets and reported the fact to General Stanley, who ordered an advance and took the lead with the Fourth Cavalry.

After crossing a small creek, about two miles from Murfreesboro, the bridge over which had been destroyed, the rebels commenced shelling us.

I sent the Third Kentucky well to the right and front and the Seventh Pennsylvania to the left, keeping the Fourth Michigan and First and Second Tennessee in reserve. After some little delay we again advanced. The Fourth Michigan, being next to and on the right of the road with one company, advanced as skirmishers; the Third Kentucky on the right of the Fourth Michigan, the First Tennessee on the right of the Third Kentucky, and the Second Tennessee in reserve. In this formation we moved through a cedar-thicket, with a dense undergrowth, rendering it almost impossible to force our way through. We had occasional heavy skirmishing with the enemy, who continued to shell us as we advanced.

About six miles out we met the enemy in force. A sharp skirmish ensued, the Fourth Cavalry, First Tennessee Infantry, and the Seventh Pennsylvania Cavalry having to bear the brunt of the fight on our side.

The enemy were driven from the field with heavy loss, and we returned to within a mile and a half of Murfreesboro and went into camp.

CASUALTIES.

REGIMENTS.	Killed		Wounded		Missing.		Aggregate	
	Officers..	Men......	Officers..	Men......	Officers..	Men......	Officers..	Men......
2d Indiana Cavalry	...	1	...	......	1	13	1	14
7th Pennsylvania Cavalry	...	2	...	9	...	50	...	61
3d Kentucky Cavalry	...	1	1	7	...	1	1	9
4th Michigan Cavalry	...	1	1	6	...	12	1	19
1st Middle Tennessee Cavalry	...	...	1	5	1	8	2	13
2d East Tennessee Cavalry	1	2	...	10	...	5	1	17
Total	1	7	3	37	2	89	6	133

Horses killed, 61 ; wounded, 65.

Colonel Murray with a handful of men, performed services that would do honor to a full regiment.

Captain Mix, with about fifty men, not only drove two hundred of the enemy for over two miles, but he there held his position against an entire regiment of rebel cavalry.

Lieutenant Eldridge, with eighteen men, and dismounted, attacked the enemy, routed them, and recaptured a wagon full of ammunition.

In the engagement of Wednesday, the 31st, while leading his company in a charge, Captain Mix's horse was shot under him, and, in the same charge, Lieutenant Woolley, my Acting Assistant Adjutant General, was thrown from his horse, severely hurting his leg, notwithstanding which he remounted and continued to perform all his duties.

In explanation of the large number of "missing" reported by the Seventh Pennsylvania, I would call your attention to the fact that the entire force of one battalion was deployed as a chain of vedettes in rear of our line of battle, when the Right Wing was driven back, and many of the men must have been captured by the enemy while endeavoring to drive forward the struggling infantry.

In reporting such officers and men who deserve special mention, I must confine myself to those who came under my personal observation.

First Sergeant Bedtelyon, of Company K, Fourth Michigan Cavalry, rode by my side during both charges against the enemy in the engagement of Wednesday evening, December 31st, and displayed great gallantry and coolness. I have recommended him to his Excellency, the Governor of Michigan, for promotion. Bugler Ben Depenbrock, Second Indiana Cavalry, and Quartermaster Sergeant Edward Owen, Fourth Michigan Cavalry—when we were driven back in the early part of the evening of December 31st, I was on foot and in rear of the dismounted skirmishers who were running for their horses—when these two gallant soldiers galloped to the front, bringing up my horse. Lieutenant John Woolley, Second Indiana Cavalry, Acting Assistant Adjutant General, First Cavalry Brigade, was thrown from his horse and so severely hurt that he could not walk without great difficulty, continued to press to the front on foot until he got another horse, and remained on the field until long after the engagement was over. Captain Frank W. Mix, Fourth Michigan Cavalry, had his horse shot under him during the first charge; he pressed forward on foot, caught a stray horse, and led his company in the second charge. Many others undoubtedly did as well as those I have mentioned, but the above are the cases that came under my immediate notice.

The brigade has captured and turned over one hundred and ninety-two prisoners.

I am, respectfully, your obedient servant,

R. H. G. MINTY,
Colonel Commanding.

THE RIGHT WING.

OFFICIAL REPORT OF GEN. R. W. JOHNSON.

HEADQUARTERS SECOND DIVISION,
RIGHT WING, *January* 6, 1863.

Major J. A. Campbell, Assistant Adjutant General:

I have the honor to submit the following report of the operations of the Second Division, under my command, beginning December 26, 1862, the day upon which it left Nashville, and terminating on January 6, 1863:

Agreeably to orders, the divisions of the Right Wing of the Fourteenth Army Corps marched from their camps near Nashville, taking the Nolensville pike, and arrived in that village the same day, at four o'clock P. M. On the following day the same divisions, with mine in advance, marched to Triune. The rebel rear guard contested the ground inch by inch, and the day was passed constantly skirmishing with them, with no loss on our side, but several casualties on their part. Triune was occupied by my division about four P. M. The following day (December 28), the command remained in Triune. A reconnoissance, to ascertain the direction the enemy had retreated, was made by a brigade of my command, commanded by Brigadier General A. Willich. It having ascertained that the enemy had retreated toward Murfreesboro, I was ordered to leave a brigade at

Triune, and on the 29th to march on Murfreesboro on what is known as the Balle Jack road. Colonel P. P. Baldwin, Third Brigade, was left at Triune. The command arrived at Wilkinson's Cross-roads about eight P. M., on the 29th, and an order sent at once to Colonel Baldwin to move forward his brigade, which arrived early on the afternoon of the 30th. My division was in reserve on the 29th. On the following morning, December 30, General Sherridan's division was ordered to advance in line of battle, covering the Wilkinson pike, while General Davis' division marched in the same order, on the right of General Sherridan. My division, being held in reserve, was marched in column on the pike. There being no troops on General Davis' right, and General Sherridan's left being guarded by General Crittenden's left wing (N. B.—Negley's division of Center), I was ordered to oblique to the right, covering the right of General Davis' division. About two o'clock P. M. I received an order from Major General McCook to look well to my right, as General Hardee (rebel), with his corps, was on the right flank of our column. I ordered the Second Brigade, Brigadier General E. N. Kirk commanding, to take position with his brigade, his left resting against the right of General Davis, his right refused so as to cover our right flank. About dark I placed General Willich's on the right of Kirk's, refusing his right, and directed a heavy line of skirmishers to be thrown forward, connecting on the left with those of General Davis, and extending to the right and rear, near the Wilkinson pike. This line of skirmishers was thrown forward about six hundred yards, and near those of the enemy. My Third Brigade, Colonel Baldwin commanding, was held in reserve. In consultation with General McCook, late in the afternoon of the 30th, he informed me that he had reliable information to the effect that the center of the rebel line of battle was opposite to our extreme right, and that we would probably be attacked by the entire rebel army early on the following morning. His prediction proved true. He also informed me that he had communicated this information to the Commanding General. I expected a change in the programme for the following day, but none was made. My brigade commanders were called together, and the operations of the following day fully explained to them. Every arrangement was made for an attack. Two gallant and experienced officers commanded my two advance brigades, and every precaution was taken against surprise.

At twenty-two minutes past six o'clock on the morning of the 31st, the outposts in front of my division were driven in by an overwhelming force of infantry, outnumbering my forces greatly, and known to contain about thirty-five thousand men. At the same time my extreme right was attacked by the enemy's cavalry. The gallant Kirk and Willich soon opened up a heavy fire of musketry and artillery on the advancing columns, causing wavering in the ranks, but fresh columns would soon replace them, and it was apparent that to fall back was a "military necessity." Edgarton's Battery, after firing three rounds, had so many of his horses killed as to render it unmanageable. He, however, remained with it, and continued so fire, until he fell by a severe wound, and he and his battery fell into the hands of the enemy. Before falling back, the horse of General Willich was killed, and he was wounded and taken prisoner. About the same time, General Kirk received a severe wound, which disabled him. Seeing the pressure upon my lines, I ordered up my reserve brigade, under the gallant Baldwin. The troops of his brigade advanced promptly, and delivered their fire, holding their ground for some time, but, they, too, were compelled to fall back. The troops of this division, for the first time, were compelled to yield the field temporarily, but the heroes of Shiloh and Perryville did not abandon their ground until forced to do so by the immense masses of the enemy hurled against them, and then inch by inch.

The ground over which the division passed, covered with the enemy's dead and those of our own men, shows that the field was warmly contested. Several times the lines were reformed and resistance offered, but the columns of the enemy were too heavy for a single line, and ours would have to yield. Finally the left flank of my division reached the line of General Rousseau's, when it was reformed and fought until out of ammunition, but my efficient ordnance officer, Lieutenant Murdoch, had a supply in readiness, which was soon issued, and the division assisted in driving the enemy from the field in their last desperate struggle of the day. Soon the curtain of darkness fell upon the scene of blood, and all was quiet, awaiting the coming of morn to renew hostilities.

Morning came but the enemy had withdrawn. January 1 was a day of comparative quiet in camp, few shots being fired, but many preparations made for a heavy battle on the following day. General Crittenden's wing was attacked in force on the 2d, and one of my brigades, Colonel Gibson's, was sent to reinforce them. For the gallant part taken by it reference is made to the report of Major General Crittenden. The enemy evacuated Murfreesboro on the night of the 3d. On the 6th I was ordered to move my camp to a point on the Shelbyville road, four miles south of Murfreesboro.

The conduct of the officers and men under my command was good. The Louisville Legion, under the command of the gallant Lieutenant Colonel Berry, brought off by hand one cannon, after the horses were killed. They yielded the ground only when overpowered, offering an obstinate resistance at every point. Some few in each regiment becoming panic-stricken, fled to Nashville for safety. Captain Simonson managed his battery with skill and courage, and with it did good execution. He lost two guns, but not until the horses had been killed and the guns disabled. Goodspeed's Battery lost three guns and quite a number of horses. This battery was handled well and did good execution, under Lieutenant Belden.

After the capture of General Willich, his brigade was commanded temporarily by Colonel Wallace of the Fifteenth Ohio, but was afterward commanded by Colonel W. H. Gibson, Forty-Ninth Ohio. General Kirk becoming disabled was replaced by Colonel Dodge, Thirtieth Indiana, while the Third Brigade was commanded by Colonel Baldwin. These four Colonels have demonstrated their fitness for command on several bloody fields, and are recommended to my superiors for promotion. Their coolness and courage rendered them conspicuous throughout the bloody engagement. Major Klein and his battalion of the Third Indiana Cavalry, deserve special mention under their gallant leader; the battalion was always in front, and rendered efficient service.

To Captains Barker, Hooker, Thruston, and McLeland: Lieutenants Taft, Hills, and Sheets of my staff, many thanks are due for their efficiency and promptness in carrying orders to all parts of the field. My Medical Director, Surgeon Marks, and the medical officers of the division, were untiring in their exertions to alleviate the sufferings of the wounded, and to them my thanks are due. My escort, composed of the following named men of the Third Kentucky Cavalry, who accompanied me throughout the engagement, deserves special mention for their good conduct:

Sergeant Wm. C. Miles; privates Geo. Long, Thos. Salyers, John Christian, John Whitten, James Bowen, B. Hammerslein, R. A. Novah.

Private Bowen's horse was killed by a cannon ball.

The loss of the division was as follows: Killed, 260; wounded, 1,005; missing, 1,280; total, 2,545.

The missing are supposed to have been captured.

Very respectfully your obedient servant,

R. W. JOHNSON,
Brigadier General Commanding.

GENERAL JEFF. C. DAVIS' REPORT.

HEADQUARTERS FIRST DIVISION, RIGHT WING,
January 8, 1863.

Major J. A. Campbell, Acting Adjutant General:

MAJOR—I have the honor to submit the following report of the part taken by the division under my command, in the recent operations against the enemy's forces in the vicinity of Triune and Murfreesboro:

On the morning of the 26th ult., in compliance with instructions received from the General commanding the Right Wing, I broke up camp at St. James' Chapel, on Mill Creek, and advanced upon Nolensville via the Edmonson pike, as far as Prim's blacksmith shop; from thence my advance was over a rugged country road, rendered almost impassable by the incessant rain which had been falling in torrents during the entire morning.

The enemy's pickets were discovered by my cavalry escort, composed of Company B, Thirty-Sixth Illinois Volunteers, under command of Captain Shirer, within a few miles of our camp. This small force of cavalry being the only mounted force under our command, I ordered them to the front, with instructions to drive in the enemy's pickets, and to attack him on his flanks at every opportunity. So effectually was this done that the infantry and artillery were enabled to move with little interruption to within a mile of Nolensville. By this time I had learned from reliable information, through citizens as well as cavalry scouts, that the enemy occupied the town in some force both of cavalry and artillery.

The First Brigade, consisting of the Twenty-Second Indiana, Seventy-Fourth, Seventy-Fifth, and Fifty-Ninth Illinois Regiments, and the Fifth Wisconsin Battery, commanded by Colonel P. Sidney Post, was immediately deployed for an advance upon the town. Pinney's Fifth Wisconsin Battery was posted so as to command the town and all approaches from the south-west. The enemy's cavalry was seen by this time taking position on a range of hills south-west of town, and was evidently attempting to flank our position. A few shells from Pinney's Battery soon caused them to fall back. A battery which by this time they had succeeded in getting into position, opened fire but was after a few rounds silenced by Pinney's guns.

The Second Brigade, consisting of the Twenty-First and Thirty-Eighth Illinois, Fifteenth Wisconsin, and One Hundred and First Ohio Regiments, and the Second Minnesota Battery, commanded by Colonel Carlin, had by this time formed a line of battle on Post's right, and moving rapidly forward soon engaged the enemy's dismounted cavalry in a sharp skirmish.

The Third Brigade, consisting of the Twenty-Fifth and Thirty-Fifth Illinois, Eighty-First Indiana, and the Eighth Wisconsin Battery, commanded by Colonel Woodruff, was deployed on the right so as to check any effort which might be made to attack my flank from this direction. Carlin advanced in excellent order, driving everything before him until ordered to halt, having dislodged the enemy from his position entirely.

By this time I ascertained that the enemy would probably make another effort to resist our advance about two miles further on, and notwithstanding it was late in the afternoon, and the men were much fatigued from a hard day's march through rain and mud, I could not forego the opportunity thus offered in giving them another chance to signalize their courage and endurance. Ascertaining the enemy's position as well as I could I ordered the advance. Their lines were soon discovered, occupying a range of high rocky hills, through which the Nolensville and Triune pike passes, known as "Knob's Gap." This was a favorable position to the enemy and well guarded by artillery, which opened fire at long range upon Carlin's lines.

Hotchkiss' and Pinney's Batteries were rapidly brought into action and opened fire, while Carlin's brigade charged the battery, carried the hights in his front and captured two guns. Post's brigade carried the hights on the left of the road with but little resistance, while Woodruff's brigade drove in the enemy's skirmishers on the extreme right.

The day had now closed and I ordered the troops to bivouac in accordance with instructions from the General Commanding, who arrived at this time upon the ground, followed by Generals Sherridan's and Johnson's divisions.

The steady courage and soldierly zeal displayed on this occasion by both officers and men, gave ample assurance of what could be expected of them in the coming struggle at Murfreesboro.

On the 27th, in accordance with the General's instructions, the division took position at the junction of the Balle Jack road with the Nolensville pike, one mile from Triune, where it remained in bivouac until the morning of the 29th, at which time the advance was resumed. In compliance with instructions, I moved forward on the Balle Jack as far as Stewart's Creek, a few miles beyond which it was reported by our cavalry the enemy had shown himself in considerable force. The General Commanding arriving at this time in person, at the head of the column, ordered a halt until the division in the rear could be brought up.

Brigadier General Stanley, commanding the cavalry in advance, soon reported the road clear and the march was resumed without obstruction, until the entire command reached the Wilkinson pike, six miles from Murfreesboro.

The division bivouacked during the night at Overall's Creek, three and a half miles from Murfreesboro, the left brigade resting on the Wilkinson pike. On the morning of the 30th the division moved forward and took position on General Sherridan's right, about three hundred yards south of and parallel to the Wilkinson pike, in which position it remained until two o'clock P. M. A few companies of skirmishers thrown to the front, in a skirt of timber land, soon found those of the enemy, and for several hours a brisk skirmish was kept up with varying results.

About two o' clock P. M., the General Commanding ordered a general advance of the whole line. This the enemy seemed at first disposed to resist only with his skirmishers; gradually, however, as both parties strengthened their lines of skirmishers, the contest became more animated. Our main lines steadily advanced, occupying and holding the ground gained by the skirmishers, until about half an hour before sunset, when the enemy's position was plainly discovered running diagonally across the old Murfreesboro and Franklin road. The enemy's batteries now announced our close proximity to their lines. Carpenter's and Hotchkiss' Batteries were soon brought into position and opened fire. Woodruff's and Carlin's brigades by this time felt the fire of the enemy's main lines and responded in the most gallant manner.

Post's brigade, moving steadily forward on the right, after a most obstinate resistance on the part of the enemy succeeded in driving his skirmishers from a strong position in our front, forcing them to retire upon their main lines. Night soon brought a close to the conflict. Receiving directions at this time, from General McCook, to desist from any further offensive demonstration further than what might be necessary to hold my position, I ordered the troops to rest for the night on their arms. Two brigades of General Johnson's division, heretofore held in reserve, arrived and took position on my right about sunset, thus extending our line of battle beyond the old Franklin and Murfreesboro road. These brigades were commanded by Generals Willich and Kirk.

The night passed off quietly until about daylight, when the enemy's forces were observed by our pickets to be in motion. Their object could not, however, with certainty be determined until near sunrise, when a vigorous attack was made upon Willich's and Kirk's brigades. These troops seemed not to have been fully prepared for the assault, and with little or no resistance retreated from their position leaving their artillery in the hands of the enemy. This left my right brigade exposed to a flank movement, which the enemy was now rapidly executing, and compelled me to order Post's brigade to fall back and partially change its front. Simultaneous with this movement the enemy commenced a heavy and very determined attack on both Carlin's and Woodruff's brigades.

These brigades were fully prepared for the attack, and received it with veteran courage. The conflict was fierce in the extreme on both sides. Our loss was heavy, and that of the enemy no less. It was according to my observations, the best contested point of the day, and would have been held but for the overwhelming force moving so persistently against my right. Carlin finding his right flank being severely pushed and threatened with being turned, ordered his troops to retire. Woodruff's brigade succeeded in repulsing the enemy, and holding its position until the withdrawal of the troops on both its flanks compelled it to retire.

Pinney's Battery, which had posted in an open field upon my extreme right, and ordered to be supported by a part of Post's brigade, now opened a destructive fire upon the enemy's advancing lines. This gallant and distinguished battery, supported by the Twenty-Second Indiana and Fifty-Ninth Illinois regiments, together with a brigade of General Johnson's division, commanded by Colonel Baldwin (Sixth Indiana Volunteers), for a short time brought the enemy to a check on our right. Hotchkiss' Battery, had also by this time taken an excellent position near the Wilkinson pike, so as to command the enemy's approach across a large cotton-field in his front, over which he was now advancing. The infantry, however, contrary to expectations, failed to support this battery, and after firing a few rounds was forced to retire. In accordance with instructions received during the night, announcing the plan of operations for the day, I desisted from any further attempts to engage the enemy except by skirmishers thrown to the rear for that purpose until my lines had reached within a few hundred yards of the Nashville and Murfreesboro pikes, when I again determined to reform my lines to resist his further advance. To this order but few of the regiments responded, their ranks being much thinned by killed and wounded, and not a few availed themselves of the favorable opportunity offered by the dense woods through which we were compelled to pass to skulk like cowards from the ranks.

The reserve force here moved to the front and relieved my command from any further participation. in the engagement until late in the afternoon when in compliance with instructions I took position on the right. My skirmishers were immediately thrown out and soon engaged the enemy's until night brought a close to hostilities for the day.

During the 1st and 2d of January, the division occupied this position in skirmishing with the enemy's pickets until late in the afternoon of the 2d, when I received orders from General Rosecrans to hasten to the support of a part of General Crittenden's command, who had been sometime hotly engaged with the enemy across the river on our extreme left.

Moving as rapidly as possible across the river to the field of battle, I found our gallant troops forcing the enemy back on his reserves. The brigade of Colonel Woodruff, being in the advance, only arrived in time to participate in the general engagement.

After relieving the troops of General Palmer and Colonel Beatty, and particularly the brigade of Colonel Hazen, which had so nobly vindicated their courage in the then closing conflict, I ordered a heavy line of skirmishers to be thrown out. The enemy's lines were soon encountered, and a renewal of the engagement seemed imminent. A few rounds of grape and cannister from one of our batteries, however, caused them to withdraw, and night again brought a cessation of hostilities.

During the night I disposed of my troops in such manner as would best enable me to repel an attack, and in compliance with instructions, I directed rifle pits and breastworks to be thrown up. This was done, and morning found us well prepared for any emergency, either offensive or defensive.

The following day (3d January), considerable skirmishing was kept up without abatement from early in the morning until dark. During the night, I received orders from General Crittenden to withdraw my command from the east bank of the river, and to report with it to General McCook.

This movement was executed between one and four o'clock in the morning, during which time the rain fell incessantly. The pickets about this time reported the enemy as having been very active in their movements during the latter part of the night, and their convictions that he was evacuating his position. Further observations made after daylight proved this to be the case.

The following list of casualties shows a loss in the division during the several engagements above described, as follows :

OFFICERS.		
Killed	16	
Wounded	34	
Missing	2—	52
ENLISTED MEN.		
Killed	176	
Wounded	784	
Missing	399—	1,359
Total		1,411

This division lost three pieces of artillery, and captured two. In the list of officers killed are the names of Colonel Stem, One Hundred and First Ohio ; Colonel Williams, Twenty-Fifth Illinois ; Lieutenant Colonel Wooster, One Hundred and First Ohio ; Lieutenant Colonel McKee, Fifteenth Wisconsin; Captain Carpenter, Eighth Wisconsin Battery, and Captain McCulloch, Second Kentucky Cavalry of my staff, whose noble deeds of valor on the field, had already placed their names on the list of brave men. The history of the war will record no brighter names, and the country will mourn the loss of no more devoted patriots than these.

Among the wounded are Colonel Alexander, Twenty-First Illinois; Lieutenant Colonel Tanner, Twenty-Second Indiana; Captain Pinney, Fifth Wisconsin Battery, and Captain Austin, Acting Assistant Adjutant General, on the staff of Colonel Woodruff, whose names it affords me special gratification to mention.

From the 26th of December, until the close of the engagement on the 4th of January, at Murfreesboro, no entire day elapsed that the division or some portion of it did not engage the enemy. During a great part of the time, the weather was excessively inclement and the troops suffered much from exposure. A heavy list of casualties and much suffering was unavoidable under the circumstances.

It affords me much pleasure to be able to report the cheerful and soldier-like manner in which these hardships and privations were endured by the troops throughout. History will record, and the country reward, their deeds.

My staff consisting of T. W. Morrison, Acting Assistant Adjutant General; Captain H. Pease, Inspector General; Captain McCulloch, Lieutenants Frank E. Reynolds, and Thomas H. Dailey, Aidsdecamp; Surgeon J. L. Judd, Medical Director; Captain Shriver, Ordnance Officer; Lieutenant R. Plunket, Provost Marshal; private Frank Clark, Clerk to the Assistant Adjutant General, and Acting Aiddecamp; deported themselves throughout the entire campaign, as well as on the battle-field, with distingushed zeal and conspicuous gallantry.

While expressing my high regard and approbation of the General Commanding, I desire to tender my thanks to yourself, Major, and to Colonel Langdon, Major Bates, Captains Thruston, Williams, and Fisher, of his staff, for the prompt and efficient manner in which the field duties were performed by them.

During the several engagements in which the division participated, my subaltern officers attracted my admiration by their conspicuous gallantry, and whose names, I regret, can not be mentioned in this report. They will be remembered in future recommendations for promotion.

I am, Major, very respectfully, your obedient servant,

JEFF. C. DAVIS,

Brigadier General Commanding.

GENERAL P. H. SHERRIDAN'S REPORT.

HEADQUARTERS THIRD DIVISION, RIGHT WING,
CAMP ON STONE RIVER, TENNESSEE,
January 9, 1863.

Major J. A. Campbell, Adjutant General and Chief of Staff:

MAJOR—In obedience to instructions from the headquarters of the Right Wing, I have the honor to report the following as the operations of my division, from the 26th day of December, 1862, to the 6th day of January, 1863.

On the 26th of December I moved from camp, near Nashville, on the Nolensville pike, in the direction of Nolensville. At the crossing of Mill Creek the enemy's cavalry made some resistance, but were soon routed, one private and one Lieutenant of the enemy being captured.

On approaching Nolensville, I received a message from General Davis, who had arrived at Nolensville, via the Edmonson pike, that the enemy were in considerable force on his front, and requesting me to support him.

On the arrival of the head of my division at Nolensville, General Davis advanced upon the enemy's position about two miles south of that place, supported by my division. The enemy had here made a stand in a gap of the mountains, but after a sharp conflict with General Davis' command, were routed and one piece of artillery captured.

On the next day (27th) I supported General Johnson's division in its advance on Triune, where the enemy were supposed to be in considerable force.

The town was taken possession of after a slight resistance, the main portion of their forces having evacuated the place.

On the 28th I encamped at Triune. On the 29th I supported General Davis' division, which had the advance from Triune on Murfreesboro, encamping that night at Wilkinson's Cross-roads, from which point there is a good turnpike to Murfreesboro.

On the next day (30th) I took the advance of the Right Wing on this turnpike, toward Murfreesboro, General Stanley with a regiment of cavalry having been thrown in advance.

After arriving at a point about three miles from Murfreesboro, the enemy's infantry pickets were encountered and driven back, their numbers constantly increasing until I had arrived within about two miles and a quarter of Murfreesboro. At this point the resistance was so strong as to require two regiments to drive them. I was here directed by Major General McCook to form my line of battle and place my artillery in position. My line was formed on the right of the pike and obliquely to it, four regiments to the front with a second line of four regiments, within short supporting distance, in the rear, with a reserve of one brigade, in column of regiments, to the rear and opposite the center. General Davis was then ordered to close in and form on my right, the enemy all this time keeping up a heavy artillery and musketry fire upon my skirmishers.

The enemy continued to occupy, with their skirmishers, a heavy belt of timber to the right and front of my line, and across some open fields, and near where the left of General Davis' division was intended to rest. General Davis was then directed by Major General McCook to swing his division, and I was directed to swing my right brigade with it until our continuous line would front nearly due east. This would give us possession of the timber above alluded to, and which was occupied by the enemy's skirmishers in considerable force. This movement was successfully executed, after a stubborn resistance on the part of the enemy, in which they used one battery of artillery. This battery was silenced in a very short time by Bush's and Hescock's Batteries, of my division, and two of the enemy's pieces disabled.

At sundown I had taken up my position, my right resting in the timber, my left on the Wilkinson pike, my reserve brigade of four regiments to the rear and opposite the center.

The killed and wounded during the day was seventy-five men. General Davis' left was closed in on my right, and his line thrown to the rear, so that it formed nearly a right angle with mine. General Negley's division, of Thomas' Corps, was immediately on my left, his right resting on the left hand side of the Wilkinson pike.

The enemy appeared to be in strong force in a heavy cedar-woods, across an open valley in my front and parallel to it, the cedar extending the whole length of the valley, the distance across the valley varying from three hundred to four hundred yards.

At two o'clock on the morning of the 31st, General Sill, who had command of my right brigade, reported great activity on the part of the enemy immediately in his front. This being the narrowest point in the valley, I was fearful that an attack might occur at that point. I therefore directed two regiments from the reserve to report to General Sill, who placed them in position in very short supporting distance of his lines.

At four o'clock in the morning the division was assembled under arms, and the cannoniers at their pieces. About fifteen minutes after seven o'clock in the morning, the enemy advanced to the attack across an open cottonfield on Sill's front. This column was opened on by Bush's Battery, of Sill's brigade, which had a direct fire on its front. Also by Hescock's and Houghtaling's Batteries, which had an oblique fire on their front, from a commanding position near the center of my line. The effect of this fire upon the enemy's columns was terrible. The enemy, however, continued to advance until they had reached nearly the edge of the timber, when they were opened upon by Sill's infantry at a range of not over fifty yards. The destruction to the enemy's column, which was closed in mass, being several regiments in depth, was terrible. For a short time they withstood the fire, wavered, then broke and ran. Sill directing his troops to charge, which was gallantly responded to, and the enemy driven back across the valley and behind their intrenchments. In this charge I had the misfortune to lose General Sill, who was killed.

The brigade then fell back in good order and renewed its original lines. The enemy soon rallied and advanced to the attack on my extreme right, and in front of Colonel Woodruff, of Davis' division. Here, unfortunately, the brigade of Colonel Woodruff gave way, also one regiment of Sill's brigade, which was in the second line. This regiment fell back some distance into the open field and then rallied, its place being occupied by a third regiment of my reserve. At this time the enemy, who had attacked on the extreme right of our wing, against Johnson, and also on Davis' front, had been successful, and the two divisions on my right were retiring in great confusion, closely followed by the enemy, completely turning my position, and exposing my line to a fire from the rear. I hastily withdrew the whole of Sill's brigade, and the three regiments sent to support it, at the same time directing Colonel Roberts, of the left brigade, who had changed front and formed in column of regiments, to charge the enemy in the timber from which I had withdrawn three regiments. This was very gallantly done by Colonel Roberts, who captured one piece of the enemy's artillery, which had to be abandoned.

In the meantime I had formed Sill's and Shaeffer's brigades on a line at right angles to my first line, and behind the three batteries of artillery, which were placed in a fine position, directing Colonel Roberts to return and form on the new line. I then made an unavailing attempt to form the troops on my right on this line, in front of which there were open fields through which the enemy was approaching under a heavy fire from Hescock's, Houghtaling's, and Bush's batteries.

After the attempt had proved to be entirely unsuccessful, and my right was again turned, General McCook directed me to advance to the front and form on the right of Negley. This movement was successfully accomplished, under a heavy fire of musketry and artillery, every regiment of mine remaining unbroken.

I took position on Negley's right, Roberts' brigade having been placed in position at right angles to Negley's line, facing to the south, the other two brigades being placed to the rear and at right angles with Roberts' and facing the west, covering the rear of Negley's lines. I then directed Houghtaling's Battery to take position at the angle of these two lines, Captain Hescock sending one section of his battery, under Lieutenant Taliaferro, and one section of Bush's Battery to the same point, the remaining pieces of Hescock's and Bush's Batteries were placed on the right of Negley's line, facing toward Murfreesboro. In this position I was immediately attacked, when one of the bitterest and most sanguinary contests of the whole day occurred.

General Cheatham's division advanced on Roberts' brigade, and heavy masses of the enemy with three batteries of artillery advanced over the open ground which I had occupied in the previous part of the engagement, at the same time the enemy opening from their intrenchments in the direction of Murfreesboro.

The contest then became terrible. The enemy made three attacks and were three times repulsed, the artillery range of the respective batteries being not over two hundred yards. In these attacks Roberts' brigade lost its gallant commander, who was killed.

There was no sign of faltering with the men, the only cry being for more ammunition, which, unfortunately, could not be supplied on account of the discomfiture of the troops on the right of our wing, which allowed the enemy to come in and capture our ammunition train.

Shaeffer's brigade being entirely out of ammunition, I directed them to fix bayonets and await the enemy. Roberts' brigade, which was nearly out of ammunition, I directed to fall back resisting the enemy. Captain Houghtaling having exhausted all his ammunition, and nearly all the horses of his battery having been killed, attempted, with the assistance of the men, to withdraw his pieces by hand.

Lieutenant Taliaferro, commanding the section of Hescock's Battery, having been killed, and several of his horses shot, his two pieces were brought off by his sergeant with the assistance of the men. The difficulty of withdrawing the artillery here became very great, the ground being rocky and covered with a dense growth of cedar. Houghtaling's Battery had to be abandoned, and also two pieces of Bush's Battery. The remaining pieces of artillery in the division were brought through the cedars with great difficulty, under a terrible fire from the enemy, on to the open space on the Murfreesboro pike, near the right of General Palmer's division. In coming through the cedars two regiments of Shaeffer's brigade succeeded in obtaining ammunition, and were immediately put in front to resist the enemy, who appeared to be driving in our entire lines.

On arriving at the open space I was directed by Major General Rosecrans to take those two regiments and put them into action on the right of Palmer's division, where the enemy were pressing heavily. The two regiments went in very gallantly, driving the enemy from the cedar timber and some distance to the front. At the same time I put four pieces of Hescock's Battery into action near by and on the same front. The other two regiments of Shaeffer's brigade, and the Thirty-Sixth Illinois of Sill's brigade, were directed to cross the railroad, where they could obtain ammunition. I then, by direction of Major General McCook, withdrew the two regiments that had been placed on the right of Palmer's division, also Captain Hescock's pieces, that point having been given up to the enemy in the rearrangement of our lines.

These regiments of Shaeffer's brigade having supplied themselves with ammunition, I put it into action, by direction of Major General Rosecrans, directly to the front and right of General Wood's division, on the left hand side of the railroad.

The brigade advanced through a clump of timber, and took position on the edge of a cottonfield, close upon the enemy's lines, relieving the division of General Wood, which was falling back under a heavy pressure from the enemy.

At this point I lost my third and last brigade commander, Colonel Shaeffer, who was killed. The brigade, remaining in this position until after it had expended its ammunition, was withdrawn to the rear of this timber, when it was again supplied and joined by the Thirty-Sixth Illinois. I was here directed by General Rosecrans to form a close column of attack and charge the enemy should they again come down on the open ground.

The remaining portion of the evening this gallant brigade remained in close column of regiments, and under fire of the enemy's batteries, which killed about twenty of the men by round shot. In the meantime, Colonel Roberts' brigade, which had come out of the cedars unbroken, was put into action by General McCook at a point a short distance to the rear, where the enemy threatened our communications on the Murfreesboro pike.

The brigade having but three or four rounds of ammunition, cheerfully went into action, gallantly charged the enemy, routing them, recapturing two pieces of artillery, and taking forty prisoners. The rout of the enemy at this point deserves special consideration, as they had here nearly reached the Murfreesboro pike.

On the night of the 31st I was placed in position on the Murfreesboro pike, facing south, and on the ground where Roberts' brigade had charged the enemy, General Davis being on my right.

On the 1st of January heavy skirmish fighting with occasional artillery shots on both sides was kept up till about three o'clock P. M., when a charge was made by a brigade of the enemy on my position. This was handsomely repulsed, and one officer and eighty-five men of the enemy captured. Colonel Walker's brigade, of Thomas' Corps, was also placed under my command temporarily, having a position on my left, where the same character of fighting was kept up.

On the 2d of January Colonel Walker sustained two heavy attacks, which he gallantly repulsed. On the 3d skirmishing took place throughout the day. On the 4th all was quiet in front, the enemy having disappeared. On the 5th nothing of importance occurred, and on the 6th I moved my camp to its present camp on Stone River, three miles south of Murfreesboro on the Shelbyville pike.

I trust that the General Commanding is satisfied with my division. It fought bravely and well. The loss of Houghtaling's Battery and one section of Bush's was unavoidable. All the horses were shot down or disabled, Captain Houghtaling wounded, and Lieutenant Taliaferro killed.

My division, alone and unbroken, made a gallant stand to protect the right flank of our army, being all that remained of the Right Wing. Had my ammunition held out I would not have fallen back, although such were my orders if hard pressed. As it was, this determined stand of my troops gave time for a rearrangement of our lines.

The division mourns the loss of Sill, Shaeffer, and Roberts. They were all instantly killed, and at the moment when their gallant brigades were charging the enemy. They were true soldiers—prompt and brave.

On the death of these officers, respectively, Colonel Greusel, Thirty-Sixth Illinois, took command of Sill's brigade, Lieutenant Colonel Laiboldt, Second Missouri, of Shaeffer's, and Colonel Bradley of Roberts' brigade. These officers behaved gallantly throughout the day.

It is also my sad duty to record the death of Colonel F. A. Harrington, of the Twenty-Seventh Illinois, who fell heroically leading his regiment to the charge.

I refer with pride to the splendid conduct, bravery, and efficiency of the following regimental commanders, and the officers and men of their respective commands:

Colonel F. T. Sherman, Eighty-Eighth Illinois.
Major F. Ehrler, Second Missouri.
Lieutenant Colonel John Weber, Fifteenth Missouri.
Captain W. W. Barrett, Forty-Fourth Illinois (wounded).
Major W. A. Presson, Seventy-Third Illinois (wounded).
Major Silas Miller, Thirty-Sixth Illinois (wounded and prisoner).
Captain P. C. Oleson, Thirty-Sixth Illinois.
Major E C. Hubbard, Twenty-Fourth Wisconsin.
Lieutenant Colonel McCreery, Twenty-First Michigan.
Lieutenant Colonel N. H. Walworth, Forty-Second Illinois.
Lieutenant Colonel F. Swannick, Twenty-Second Illinois (wounded and prisoner).
Captain Samuel Johnson, Twenty-Second Illinois.
Major W. A. Schmitt, Twenty-Seventh Illinois.
Captain Wescott, Fifty-First Illinois.

I respectfully bring to the notice of the General Commanding the good conduct of Captain Hescock, Chief of Artillery, whose services were almost invaluable. Also, Captains Houghtaling and Bush, and the officers and men of their batteries.

Surgeon D. J. Griffiths, Medical Director of my division, and Doctor McArthur of the Board of Medical Examiners of Illinois, were most assiduous in their care of the wounded.

Major H. F. Dietz, Provost Marshal, Captain Morhardt, Topographical Engineer, Lieutenant George Lee, Acting Assistant Adjutant General, Lieutenants A. M. Denning, Frank H. Allen, E. W. DeBruin, J. L. Forman, and Soward, Aidsdecamp, officers of my staff, were of the greatest service to me, delivering my orders faithfully, and promptly discharging the duties of their respective positions.

The ammunition train above alluded to as captured, was retaken from the enemy by the good conduct of Captain Thruston, ordnance officer of the corps, and Lieutenant Douglas, ordnance officer of my division, who, with Sergeant Cooper of my escort, rallied the stragglers and drove off the enemy's cavalry.

The following is the total of casualties in the division:

OFFICERS.		
Killed	15	
Wounded	38	
Missing	11—	64
ENLISTED MEN.		
Killed	223	
Wounded	943	
Missing	400—	1,566
Total		1,630

Of the eleven officers and four hundred enlisted men missing, many are known to be wounded and in the hands of the enemy.

Prisoners were captured from the enemy by my division as follows:

Majors	1
Captains	1
Lieutenants	3
Enlisted men	216
Total	221

I am, sir, very respectfully, your obedient servant,

P. H. SHERRIDAN,
Brigadier General Commanding.

THE CENTER.

GENERAL JAS. S. NEGLEY'S REPORT.

HEADQUARTERS EIGHTH DIVISION,
MURFREESBORO, *January* 8, 1863.

Major George E. Flynt, Chief of Staff:

SIR—I have the honor to submit the following report of the operations of the troops under my command, in the engagements with the enemy on Stone River:

On Tuesday morning, December 30, 1862, the Eighth Division, composed of the Seventh and Twenty-Ninth brigades, Schultz's, Marshall's and Wells' batteries, was posted on a rolling slope of the west bank of Stone River, in advance, but joining the extreme right of General Crittenden's line, and the left of General McCook's.

In the rear and on the right, was a dense cedar-wood with a broken, rocky surface. From one position, several roads were cut through the woods in our rear, by which to bring up the artillery and ammunition trains.

In front, a heavy growth of oak timber extended toward the river, which was about a mile distant. A narrow thicket, diagonally crossed our left, and skirted the base of a cultivated slope, expanding to the width of a mile, as it approached the Nashville pike.

This slope afforded the enemy his most commanding position (in the Center), on the crest of which his rifle pits extended (with intervals) from the oak timber immediately in my front, to the Nashville pike, with a battery of four Napoleon and two iron guns, placed in position, near the woods, and about eight hundred yards from my position.

Behind this timber, on the river bank, the enemy massed his columns, for the movements of the next day.

His skirmishers were driven from our immediate front after a sharp contest; in which the Nineteenth Illinois and Seventy-Eighth Pennsylvania Volunteers, displayed admirable efficiency. The position of my command was held, under a heavy fire, until darkness terminated the skirmishing in our front, by which time, we had inflicted considerable loss upon the enemy.

In the meantime, General Sherridan's division, came up and formed "line of battle" (his left resting on my right), and began to advance, driving the enemy, until he had passed the center of my brigade.

While General Sherridan was in this position, I changed my front slightly, bearing it more to the left, to avoid masking a portion of Sherridan's command.

The troops remained in this position and in "order of battle" all night, cheerfully enduring the cold and rain, awaiting the morrow's sun, to renew the contest.

Early the next morning, and before the heavy fog had drifted from our front, the enemy, in strong force, attacked General McCook's right, commencing a general engagement, which increased in intensity toward his left.

Sherridan's division stood its ground manfully, supported by the Eighth Division, repulsing and driving the enemy at every advance.

The enemy still gained ground on General McCook's right, and succeeded in placing several batteries in position, which covered my right; from these, and the battery on my left, which now opened, the troops were exposed to a converging fire, which was most destructive.

Houghtaling's, Schultz's, Marshall's, Bush's and Wells' Batteries, were all ordered into action in my front, pouring destructive volleys of grape and shell into the advancing columns of the enemy, mowing him down like swaths of grain.

For four hours, the Eighth Division, with a portion of Sherridan's and Palmer's divisions, maintained their position, amid a murderous storm of lead and iron, strewing the ground with their heroic dead.

The enemy, maddened to desperation, by the determined resistance, still pressed forward fresh troops, concentrating and forming them in a concentric line, on either flank.

By eleven o'clock, Sherridan's men, with their ammuniton exhausted, were falling back. General Rousseau's reserve and General Palmer's division, had retired in the rear of the cedars, to form a new line. The artillery ammunition was expended, that of the infantry reduced to a few rounds. The artillery horses were nearly all killed or wounded; my ammunition train had been sent back, to avoid capture; a heavy column of the enemy was marching directly to our rear, through the cedars. Communication with Generals Rosecrans and Thomas, was entirely cut off, and it was manifestly impossible for my command to hold the position, without eventually making a hopeless, fruitless sacrifice of the whole division.

To retire, was but to cut our way through the ranks of the enemy. The order was given and manfully executed; driving back the enemy in front, and checking his approaching columns in our rear.

All the regiments in my command, distinguished themselves for their coolness and daring, frequently halting and charging the enemy, under a withering fire of musketry.

On approaching General Rousseau's line, the battalion of regulars, under command of Major King, at my request, gallantly charged forward to our assistance, sustaining a severe loss in officers and men in the effort.

Colonels Stanley and Miller now promptly reformed their brigades, with the remaining portions of the batteries, and took position on the new line, as designated by Major General Thomas.

Shortly afterward the Twenty-Ninth Brigade was ordered to the left, to repel an attack from the enemy's cavalry upon the trains.

The troops remained in line all night, and the next day in "order of battle" until noon, when the division was ordered to the right of General McCook's line, in expectation of an attack upon his front.

The next day (January 2) at one o'clock P. M., my command was ordered to the support of General Crittenden, on the left, and took position in the rear of the batteries, on the west bank of Stone River.

About three P. M. a strong force of the enemy, with artillery, advanced rapidly upon General Van Cleve's division; which, after sustaining a severe fire for twenty or thirty minutes, fell back in considerable disorder; the enemy pressing vigorously forward to the river bank.

At this important moment, the Eighth Division was ordered to advance, which it did promptly; the men crossing the river and charging up the steep bank with unflinching bravery. The Twenty-First, Eighteenth, Sixty-Ninth, and Seventy-Fourth Ohio, Nineteenth Illinois, Eleventh Michigan, Thirty-Seventh Indiana, and Seventy-Eighth Pennsylvania Volunteers, displaying their usual promptness and gallantry. Four pieces of artillery and a stand of colors belonging to the Twenty-Sixth (rebel) Tennessee, were captured at the point of the bayonet, also a large number of prisoners; the enemy retreating in disorder.

It is proper to mention here, that the artillery practice of Schultz's, Mendenhall's, Standart's, Wells', Marshall's, and Stokes' batteries, which were acting temporarily under my orders, in this engagement, was highly satisfactory; giving the enemy great tribulation.

The promptness displayed by Captain Stokes, in bringing his battery into action by my orders, and the efficient manner with which it was served, affords additional evidence of his marked ability and bravery as an officer and patriot. In the same connection, I feel permitted to speak in complimentary terms of the gallant Morton, and his Pioneer Brigade, which marched forward under a scathing fire, to the support of my division.

The enemy having fallen back to his intrenchments, my division recrossed the river and resumed its former position.

On the evening of the 4th, the Twenty-Ninth Brigade was moved forward to the north bank of Stone River, near the railroad, as an advanced force. On the same day, General Spears' First Tennessee Brigade, was assigned to the Eighth Division. This brigade distinguished itself on the evening of the 2d, in a desperate charge on the enemy. On the morning of the 5th, I was ordered to take command of the advance and pursue the enemy toward Murfreesboro.

By nine A. M., the Eighth Division, Walker's brigade, Pioneer Brigade, and General Stanley's cavalry force had crossed the river and taken possession of Murfreesboro, without meeting any resistance; the rear guard of the enemy retreating on the Manchester and Shelbyville roads, our cavalry pursuing, supported by the Twenty-Ninth Brigade, on the Shelbyville pike, and by Colonel Byrd's First East Tennessee Regiment, on the Manchester pike.

The rear guard of the enemy (three regiments cavalry and one battery) was overtaken on the Manchester, five miles from Murfreesboro. Colonel Byrd fearlessly charged this unequal force of the enemy, driving him from his position, with a loss of four killed and twelve wounded; enemy's loss not ascertained.

Our army marched quietly into Murfreesboro, the chosen position of the enemy, which he was forced to abandon after a series of desperate engagements. The joyful hopes of traitors have been crushed; treason receiving another fatal blow.

My command enthusiastically join me in expression of admiration of the official conduct of Generals Rosecrans and Thomas. During the most eventful periods of the engagements their presence was at the point of danger, aiding with their counsels and animating the troops by their personal bravery and cool determination.

I refer to my command with feelings of national pride for the living, and personal sorrow for the dead. Without a murmur, they made forced marches over almost impassable roads, through drenching winter rains, without blankets or a change of clothing; deprived of sleep or repose, constantly on duty for eleven days; living three days on a pint of flour and parched corn. Ever vigilant, always ready, sacrificing their lives with a contempt of peril, displaying the coolness, determination, and high discipline of veterans, they are entitled to our country's gratitude. Pennsylvania, Ohio, Kentucky, Indiana, Illinois, Michigan, and Tennessee, may proudly inscribe upon their scrolls of fame the names of the Seventy-Eighth Pennsylvania Volunteers, Eighteenth, Twenty-First, Sixty-Ninth, and Seventy-Fourth Ohio, Schultz's and Marshall's (Ohio) Batteries, the Eleventh Michigan, Nineteenth Illinois, Thirty-Seventh Indiana, Wells' section (Kentucky) Battery, and Spears' Tennessee Brigade.

I wish to make honorable mention of the bravery and efficient services rendered by the following named officers and men, for whom I earnestly request promotion:

Brigadier General Spears, commanding First Tennessee Brigade.

Colonel T. R. Stanley, Eighteenth Ohio Volunteer Infantry, commanding Twenty-Ninth Brigade.

Colonel John T. Miller, Twenty-Ninth Indiana Volunteers, commanding Seventh Brigade.

Captain Jas. St. Clair Morton, commanding Pioneer Brigade.

Captain James H. Stokes, commanding Chicago Battery.

Major John H. King, commanding Fifteenth United States Infantry.

Captain Bush, commanding Fourth Indiana Battery.

Captain James A. Lowrie, Assistant Adjutant General.

Lieutenant Fred. H. Kennedy, Aiddecamp.

Captain Charles T. Wing, Assistant Quartermaster.

Major Fred. H. Gross, Medical Director.

Captain James R. Hayden, Ordnance Officer.

Lieutenant Wm. W. Barker, Aiddecamp.

Lieutenant Robert H. Cochran, Provost Marshal.

Lieutenant Francis Riddell, Acting Assistant Commissary of Subsistence.

Lieutenant Charles C. Cook, Acting Aiddecamp.

Lieutenant W. D. Ingraham, Topographical Engineers.

Captain Frederick Schultz and Lieutenant Joseph Hein, Battery M, First Ohio Artillery.

Lieutenants Alex. Marshall, John Crable, and Robert D. Whittlesey, Battery G, First Ohio Artillery.

Captain W. E. Standart, Battery B, First Ohio Artillery.

Lieutenant A. A. Ellsworth, Commanding Wells' Section Kentucky Artillery.

Lieutenant W. H. Spence, Wells' Section Kentucky Artillery.

Lieutenant H. Terry, Third Ohio Cavalry.

Secretaries—Sergeant H. B. Fletcher, Company K, Nineteenth Illinois Volunteers; Corporal Rufus Rice, Company K, First Wisconsin Volunteers; Private James A. Sangston, Company C, Seventy-Ninth Pennsylvania Volunteers, and Sergeant Charles Rambour, Company K, Seventy-Fourth Ohio Volunteers. Wm. Longwell, Orderly, Seventh Pennsylvania Cavalry.

Escort—Sergeant George C. Lee, Corporal E. H. Daugherty, Privates Henry Schwenk, Henry B. Zimmerman, John Higgins, Leon Starr, Daniel Walker, John McCorkle, Abraham Keppuly, George Gillem, John Cunningham.

CASUALTIES.

The following is an approximate report of the casualties in my command, during the battles before Murfreesboro, December 30th and 31st, 1862, and January 2d and 3d, 1863:

COMMAND.	WENT INTO ACTION.				LOST IN ACTION.										
					Killed.		Wounded.		Missing.		Horses.			Guns.	
Second Division—Center—Fourteenth Army Corps.	Officers	Men	Horses	Cannon	Officers	Men	Officers	Men	Officers	Men	Killed	Wound'd	Missing.	Lost	Disabled
First Tennessee Brigade	66	734	8	...	......	3	1	22	......	......	......	1	......	...	...
Twenty-Ninth Brigade	93	1719	37	...	8	78	25	259	......	94	5	3	5	...	...
Seventh Brigade	71	1948	......	...	3	79	20	415	1	193	......	......	......	...	...
Infantry	230	4401	45	...	11	160	46	696	1	287	5	4	5	...	...
Schultz's Battery	2	75	56	4	......	1	1	......	......	1	5	4	......	1	...
Marshall's Battery	3	110	116	6	......	5	......	5	......	14	34	12	......	4	...
Wells' Battery	2	47	40	3	......	1	......	3	......	6	18	6	4	1	1
Artillery	7	232	212	13	......	7	1	8	......	21	57	22	4	6	1
Total	237	4633	257	13	11	167	47	704	1	308	62	26	9	6	1

REMARKS.—My command captured upward of four hundred prisoners, four brass field pieces, and one stand of regimental colors.

I have the honor to remain, very respectfully,

Your obedient servant,

JAMES S. NEGLEY,

Brigadier General Commanding.

GENERAL L. H. ROUSSEAU'S REPORT.

NASHVILLE, TENN.,
January 11, 1863.

Major George E. Flynt, Chief of Staff:

SIR—I have the honor to report the part taken by my command, the Third Division of the army, in the battle of Murfreesboro, begun on the 31st ult., and ended on the 3d inst. :

Early on the morning of the 30th ult., in obedience to the order of Major General Thomas, my division moved forward toward Murfreesboro from Stewartsboro, on the Nashville and Murfreesboro turnpike, about nine miles from the latter place. On the march forward several dispatches from General Rosecrans reached me, asking exactly where my command was, and the hour and minute of the day. In consequence we moved rapidly forward, halted but once, and that for only five minutes. About half past ten o'clock, A. M., we reached a point three miles from Murfreesboro, where General Rosecrans and Thomas were, on the Nashville and Murfreesboro turnpike, and remained during the day, and bivouacked at night.

At about nine o'clock A. M. on the 31st, the report of artillery and the heavy firing of small arms on our right announced that the battle had begun by an attack on the Right Wing, commanded by Major General McCook. It was not long before the direction from which the firing came, indicated that General McCook's command had given way and was yielding ground to the enemy. His forces seemed to swing round toward our right and rear. At this time General Thomas ordered me to advance my division quickly to the front to the assistance of General McCook.

On reaching the right of General Negley's line of battle, General Thomas there directed me to let my left rest on his right, and to deploy my division off toward the right as far as I could, so as to resist the pressure on General McCook.

We consulted and agreed as to where the line should be formed. This was in a dense cedar-brake, through which my troops marched in quick time to get into position before the enemy reached us. He was then but a few hundred yards to the front, sweeping up in immense numbers, driving everything before him. This ground was new and unknown to us all. The woods were almost impassable to infantry, and artillery was perfectly useless, but the line was promptly formed. The Seventeenth Brigade, Colonel John Beatty commanding, on the left, the Regular Brigade, Lieutenant Colonel O. L. Shepard commanding, on the right; the Ninth Brigade, Colonel B. F. Scribner commanding, was placed perhaps a hundred yards in rear and opposite the center of the front line, so as to support either or both of the brigades in front as occasion might require. My recollection is that perhaps the Second and Thirty-Third Ohio regiments filled a gap between General Negley's right and the Seventeenth Brigade, occasioned by the effort to extend our lines far enough to the right to afford the desired aid to General McCook.

The Twenty-Eighth Brigade, Colonel John C. Starkweather commanding, and Stone's Battery of the First Kentucky Artillery, were at Jefferson crossing on Stone River, about eight miles below.

Our lines were hardly formed before a dropping fire from the enemy announced his approach. General McCook's troops, in a good deal of confusion, retired through our lines, and around our right under a most terrific fire. The enemy in pursuit furiously assailed our front, and greatly outflanking us, passed around to our right and rear.

By General Thomas' direction I had already ordered the artillery, Loomis' and Guenther's Batteries, to the open field in the rear. Seeing that my command was outflanked on the right, I sent orders to the brigade commanders to retire at once also to this field, and riding back myself, I posted the batteries on a ridge in the open ground parallel with our line of battle, and as my men emerged from the woods they were ordered to take position on the right and left, and in support of these batteries, which was promptly done. We had perhaps four or five hundred yards of open ground in our front. While the batteries were unlimbering, seeing General Van Cleve close by, I rode up and asked him if he would move his command to the right, and aid in checking up the enemy by forming on my left, and thus giving us a more extended line in that direction in the new position taken. In the promptest manner possible his line was put in motion, and in double-quick time reached the desired point in good season.

As the enemy emerged from the woods in great force shouting and cheering, the batteries of Loomis and Guenther, double-shotted with canister, opened upon them. They moved straight ahead for awhile, but were finally driven back with immense loss. In a little while they rallied again, and as it seemed, with fresh troops, again assailed our position, and were again, after a fierce struggle, driven back. Four deliberate and fiercely sustained assaults were made upon our position, and repulsed. During the last assault I was informed that our troops were advancing on our right, and saw troops, out of my division, led by General Rosecrans, moving in that direction. I informed General Thomas of the fact, and asked leave to advance my lines. He directed me to do so. We made a charge upon the enemy and drove him into the woods, my staff and orderlies capturing some seventeen prisoners, including a Captain and Lieutenant, who were within one hundred and thirty yards of the batteries. This ended the fighting of that day, the enemy in immense force hovering in the woods during the night, while we slept upon our arms on the field of battle. We occupied this position during the three following days and nights of the fight. Under General Thomas' direction I had it intrenched by rifle-pits, and believe the enemy could not have taken it at all.

During the day, the Twenty-Eighth Brigade, Colonel Starkweather, was attacked by Wheeler's Cavalry in force, and some of the wagons of his train were burned before they reached him, having started that morning from Stewartsboro to join him. The enemy were finally repulsed and driven off with loss. Starkweather's loss was small. In this affair the whole brigade behaved handsomely.

The burden of the fight fell upon the Second Wisconsin, Lieutenant Colonel Hobart commanding. This regiment, led by its efficient commander, behaved like veterans. From the evening of the 31st until Saturday night, no general battle occurred in front of my division, though firing of artillery and small arms was kept up during the day, and much of the small arms during the night. The rain on the night of the 31st, which continued at intervals until the Saturday night following, rendered the ground occupied by my command exceedingly sloppy and muddy, and during much of the time my men had neither shelter, food, nor fire. I procured corn, which they parched and ate, and some of them ate horse-steaks cut and broiled from horses on the battle-field. Day and night in the cold, wet, and mud, my men suffered severely, but during the whole time I did not hear one single murmur at their hardships, but all were cheerful and ever ready to stand by their arms and fight. Such endurance I never saw. In these severe trials of their patience and their strength, they were much encouraged by the constant presence and solicitous anxiety of General Thomas for their welfare.

On the evening of Saturday, 3d inst., I asked permission of General Thomas to drive the enemy from a wood on our left front, to which he gave his consent. Just before I directed the batteries of Guenther and Loomis to shell the woods with six rounds per gun, fired as rapidly as possible. This was very handsomely done, and ended just at dark, when the Third Ohio, Lieutenant Colonel O. H. Lawson, and Eighty-Eighth Indiana, Colonel George Humphreys, both under command of the brigade commander, Colonel John Beatty, moved promptly up to the woods. When near the woods they received a heavy fire from the enemy, but returned it vigorously and gallantly, and pressed forward. On reaching the woods a fresh body of the enemy, attracted by the fire, moved up on their left to support them. On that body of the enemy Loomis' Battery opened with shell. The fusilade was very rapid, and continued for perhaps three-quarters of an hour, when Beatty's command drove the enemy at the point of the bayonet, and held the woods. It turned out that the enemy were posted behind a stone breastwork in the woods, and when ousted about thirty men were taken prisoners behind the woods. This ended the battle of Murfreesboro.

On the morning of the 31st six companies of the Second Kentucky Cavalry, Major Thomas P. Nicholas commanding, were ordered down to watch and defend the fords of Stone River to our left and rear. The cavalry of the enemy several times, in force, attempted to cross these fords, but Nicholas very gallantly repulsed them with loss, and they did not cross the river.

I should have mentioned that Friday evening late I was directed by General Thomas to place a regiment in the woods on our left front as an outpost, and with the view to hold the woods, as they were near our lines, and the enemy could greatly annoy us if allowed to hold them. Our skirmishers were then just leaving the woods. I ordered the Forty-Second Indiana, Lieutenant Colonel Shanklin commanding, to take that position, which he did. But early the next morning the enemy, in large force, attacked Colonel Shanklin, first furiously shelling the woods, and drove the regiment back to our lines, taking

Shanklin prisoner. It was this wood that was retaken on Saturday night as before described.

The troops of the division behaved admirably. I could not wish them to behave more gallantly. The Ninth and Seventeenth Brigades, under the lead of their gallant commanders, Scribner and Beatty, were, as well as the Twenty-Eighth Brigade, Colonel Starkweather, veterans; they were with me at Chaplin Hills, and could not act badly.

The Twenty-Eighth Brigade held a position in our front after the first day's fighting, and did it bravely, doing all that was required of them like true soldiers.

The brigade of United States Infantry, Lieutenant Colonel O. L. Shepard commanding, was on the extreme right. On that body of brave men the shock of battle fell heaviest, and its loss was most severe. Over one-third of the command fell killed or wounded. But it stood up to the work and bravely breasted the storm, and though Major King, commanding the Fifteenth, and Major Slemmer ("Old Pickens"), the Sixteenth, fell severely wounded, and Major Carpenter, commanding the Nineteenth, fell dead in the last charge, together with many other brave officers and men, the brigade did not falter for a moment. These three battalions were a part of my old Fourth Brigade at the battle of Shiloh.

The Eighteenth Infantry, Majors Townsend and Caldwell commanding, were new troops to me, but I am proud now to say we know each other. If I could I would promote every officer and non-commissioned officer and private of this brigade of Regulars for gallantry and good service in this terrific battle. I make no distinction between these troops and my brave volunteer regiments, for in my judgment there were never better troops than these regiments in the world. But the troops of the line are soldiers by profession, and with a view to the future I feel it my duty to say what I have of them. The brigade was admirably and gallantly handled by Lieutenant Colonel Shepard.

I lost some of the bravest and best officers I had. Lieutenant Colonel Kell, commanding Second Ohio, was killed. After he fell his regiment was efficiently handled by Major Anson McCook, who ought to to be made Colonel of that regiment for gallantry on the field. Colonel Forman, my brave *boy* Colonel of the Fifteenth Kentucky, also fell. Major Carpenter, of the Nineteenth Infantry, fell in the last charge. His loss is irreparable. Many other gallant officers were lost.

Of the batteries of Guenther and Loomis I can not say too much. Loomis was Chief of Artillery for the Third Division, and I am much indebted to him. His battery was commanded by Lieutenant Van Pelt. Guenther is but a Lieutenant. Both of these men deserve to be promoted, and ought to be *at once*. Without them we could not have held our position.

I fell in with many gallant regiments and officers on the field not of my command. I wish I could name all of them here. While falling back to the line in the open field, I saw Colonel Charles Anderson gallantly and coolly rallying his men. Colonel Grider, of Kentucky, and his regiment, efficiently aided in repulsing the enemy. The Eighteenth Ohio, I think it was, though I do not know any of its officers, faced about, and charged the enemy in my presence, and I went along with it. The Eleventh Michigan and its gallant little Colonel (Stoughton) behaved well, and the Sixth Ohio Infantry, Colonel Nick Anderson, joined my command on the right of the Regular Brigade, and stood manfully up to the work.

I fell in with the Louisville Legion in retreat, Lieutenant Colonel Berry commanding. This regiment, though retreating before an overwhelming force, was dragging by hand a section of artillery which it had been ordered to support. A part of General McCook's wing of the army had fallen back with the rest, but through the woods and fields with great difficulty, bravely brought off the cannon it could no longer defend on the field. When I met it, it faced about and formed line of battle with cheers and shouts.

To Lieutenant McDowell, my Acting Assistant Adjutant General; Lieutenant Armstrong, Second Kentucky Cavalry; Lieutenant Millard, Nineteenth United States Infantry, Inspector General; Captain Taylor, Fifteenth Kentucky, and Lieutenant Alf. Pirtle, Ordnance officer, my regular aids, and to Captain John D. Wickliffe and Lieutenant W. G. Jenkins, both of Second Kentucky Cavalry, aids for that battle, I am much indebted for services on that field.

The wounded were kindly and tenderly cared for by the Third Division Medical Director, Surgeon Muscroft, and the other Surgeons of the command.

Lieutenant McDowell was wounded. My orderlies, James Emery and the rest, went through the whole fight behaving well. Emery was wounded. Lieutenant Carpenter, First Ohio Volunteer Infantry, one of my aids, was so badly injured by the fall of his horse that I would not permit him to go on the field. Lieutenant Hartman, Seventy-Ninth Pennsylvania Volunteer Infantry, a member of my staff, was ill with fever, and unable to leave his bed.

It should be mentioned that the Eighty-Eighth Indiana, Colonel Humphreys, being placed at one of the fords on Stone River where our forces were temporarily driven back, very opportunely rallied the stragglers, and promptly crossed the river and drove the enemy back. In this he was aided by the stragglers, who rallied and fought well. The Colonel was wounded by a bayonet thrust in the hand in the attack of Saturday night on the enemy in the woods in our front.

I have the honor to be, etc.,

LOVELL H. ROUSSEAU,

Major General.

THE LEFT WING.

BRIGADIER GENERAL PALMER'S REPORT.

HEADQUARTERS SECOND DIVISION LEFT WING,
CAMP NEAR MURFREESBORO, *January* 9, 1863.

Major L. Starling, Chief of Staff:

MAJOR—I have the honor to submit, for the information of the General Commanding, the following reports of the operations of this division, from and including the 27th of December up to, and including the 4th of January.

At 11.20 A. M., on the 27th of December, while in camp near Lavergne, I received orders to move forward, following the division of General Wood, and to detach a brigade to proceed by the Jefferson pike and seize the bridge across Stewart's Creek. The duty of conducting this operation was assigned to Colonel Hazen—which was well and skillfully done.

The brigades of Cruft and Grose reached the west bank of Stewart's Creek late in the afternoon of the 27th, and bivouacked there until the morning of the 29th.

During all the day, Sunday, the 28th, the enemy's pickets were in sight across the creek, firing upon us occasionally at long range, but did us no harm. On Monday morning, 29th of December, at nine o'clock, I was ordered to deploy one regiment as skirmishers; to dispose of my other troops so as to support it, and move forward at ten o'clock precisely and continue to advance until the enemy were found in position.

This disposition was made.

A few minutes before ten o'clock, Parsons was ordered to shell the woods to our front, and at ten o'clock Grose's brigade moved forward, skirmishing with the enemy, supported by the first brigade, Hazen not having yet joined me.

The command advanced steadily, driving the light force of rebel skirmishers before it to the top of the hill, some mile and a half this side of Stewart's Creek, and being under the impression that the divisions of Wood and Negley were to advance with me.

In a few moments Wood's advance came up on the left of the pike and the two divisions moved forward, constantly skirmishing (though much heavier on Wood's front than my own) to the ground occupied that night, afterward the theater of the battle of the 31st.

During the day the casualties were ten wounded in Grose's brigade, none severely.

On the morning of the 30th, my division was formed as follows: Third brigade (Grose's), in two lines, the left resting on the pike; first brigade (Cruft's), to the right, extending across the point of woods, his extreme right retired to connect with Negley's left; and Hazen's brigade in reserve.

There was considerable skirmishing during the day, the greater portion of which fell upon Cruft's brigade, which was in rather unpleasant proximity to a point of woods to his front and right, held by the enemy in strong force.

About four o'clock I was ordered to advance and open upon the enemy with all my artillery. This was not done, probably, as soon as the order contemplated. The ground occupied by the batteries at the time the order was received was low and confined; upon pushing forward the skirmishers of the first brigade to clear the way to a good artillery position, in the open field to the front, the rebels were found numerous and stubborn. Learning very soon that a mere demonstration was intended, all my batteries opened, and, I am satisfied, damaged the enemy considerably. The skirmish attending this movement was quite brisk; the troops engaged doing themselves great credit. This closed the operations of the day.

On the morning of the 31st, Cruft's brigade retained its position of the day before. Hazen's brigade had relieved Grose, who had fallen back to a point some two hundred yards to the rear, and was formed in two lines nearly opposite the interval between the First and Second Brigades; Standart's Battery on the extreme right, Parsons' near the center.

Early in the morning I rode to the right of my own command, and the battle had commenced on the extreme right of the line; soon afterward, near eight o'clock, General Negley, through one of his staff, informed me he was about to advance and requested me to advance to cover his left. I gave notice of this to the General Commanding, and a few moments later received orders to move forward. I at once ordered General Cruft to advance, keeping close up well toward Negley; Colonel Hazen to go forward, observing the movements of Wood's right; and Grose to steadily advance, supporting the advance brigades, and all to use their artillery freely.

My line had advanced hardly a hundred yards when, upon reaching my own right, I found that General Negley had, instead of advancing, thrown back his right, so that his line was almost perpendicular to that of Cruft and to his rear; and it was also apparent that the enemy were driving General McCook back, and were rapidly approaching our rear.

Cruft's line was halted by my order. I rode to the left to make some disposition to meet the coming storm, and by the time I reached the open ground to the south of the pike, the heads of the enemy's columns had forced their way to the open ground to my rear. To order Grose to change front to the rear was the work of a moment, and he obeyed the order almost as soon as given; retiring his new left so as to bring the enemy under the direct fire of his line; he opened upon them in fine style and with great effect, and held his ground until the enemy were driven back.

In the meantime General Negley's command had, to some extent, become compromised by the confusion on the right, and my first brigade was exposed in front and flank to a severe attack, which also now extended along my whole front. Orders were sent to Colonel Hazen to fall back from the open cottonfield into which he had moved He fell back a short distance, and a regiment from Wood's division which had occupied the crest of a low-wooded hill, between the pike and the railroad, having been removed, he took possession of that and there resisted the enemy. Hazen on the railroad, one or two regiments to the right, some troops in the point of woods south of the cottonfield and a short distance in advance of the general line, among whom I was only able to distinguish the gallant Colonel Whittaker and his Sixth Kentucky; still further to the right Cruft was fighting aided by Standart's guns, and to the rear Grose was fighting with apparently great odds against him. All were acquitting themselves nobly, and all were hard pressed. I could see that Grose was losing a great many men, but the importance of Hazen's position determined me, if necessary, to expend the last man in holding it. I gave my attention from that time chiefly to that point.

The One-Hundreth Illinois came up on the left of the railroad and fought steadily. As soon as Colonel Grose was relieved of the enemy in his rear, he again changed front, moved to the left and coöperated with Colonel Hazen. One regiment was sent to my support from General Wood's command, and which behaved splendidly. I regret my inability either to name the regiment or its officers. Again and again the attack was renewed by the enemy, and each time repulsed, and the gallant men who had so bravely struggled to hold the position occupied it during the night.

Brigadier General Cruft deserves great praise for so long holding the important position occupied on our right, and for skillfully extricating his command from the mass of confusion around it. Standart fought his guns until the enemy were upon him, and then brought them off safely ; while the Second Kentucky brought off by hand three guns abandoned by General Negley's division.

Colonel Hazen proved himself a brave and able soldier by the skill and courage exhibited in forming and sheltering his troops, and in organizing and fighting all the materials around him for the maintenance of his important position.

Colonel Grose exhibited great coolness and bravery, and fought against great odds. He was under my eye during the whole day, and I could see nothing to improve in the management of his command.

I shrink from the task of specially mentioning regiments or regimental officers. All did their duty, and from my imperfect acquaintance with regiments, I am apprehensive of injurious mistakes.

I recognized during the battle the Forty-First Ohio, which fought until it expended its last cartridge, and was then relieved by the noble Ninth Indiana, which came into line with a heavy shout, inspiring all with confidence. The Eighty-Fourth, One Hundred and Tenth, and One-Hundredth Illinois I knew; all new regiments, and all so fought that even the veterans of "Shiloh" and other bloody fields had no occasion to boast over them. The Eighty-Fourth stood its ground until more than one-third of its number were killed or wounded. The Sixth Ohio, the Twenty-Fourth Ohio, the Twenty-Third Kentucky, and the Thirty-Sixth Indiana were pointed out to me; and I recognized the brave Colonel Whittaker and his fighting men doing soldiers' duty. I only saw the regiments of Cruft's brigade fighting early in the day; I had no fears for them where valor could win. Indeed the whole division fought like soldiers trained under the rigid discipline of the lamented Nelson, and by their courage proved that they had caught a large portion of his heroic and unconquerable spirit.

During the whole day I regarded the battery under the command of Lieutenant Parsons, assisted by Lieutenants Cushing and Huntington, as my right arm, and well did the conduct of these courageous and skillful young officers justify my confidence. My orders to Parsons were simple: "Fight where you can do the most good." Never were orders better obeyed.

The reported conduct of the other batteries attached to the division is equally favorable. They were in other parts of the field.

My personal staff, Captain Norton, Acting Assistant Adjutant General; Lieutenants Simmons and Child; Lieutenant Croxton, Ordnance Officer; Lieutenant Hays, Division Topographical Engineer; Lieutenant Shaw, Seventh Illinois Cavalry, were with me all day on the field, and carried my orders everywhere with the greatest courage. Lieutenant Simmons was severely injured by a fragment of a shell.

I can not commend the conduct of Doctor Sherman, Ninth Indiana Volunteers, Medical Director, too highly. At all times from the commencement of the march from Nashville, and during the battles and skirmishes in which the division was engaged, up to the occupation of Murfreesboro, he was always at his post, and by his industry, humanity, and skill earned, not only my gratitude and that of this command, but that of the wounded of the enemy, many of whom were thrown upon his care.

On the 1st of January, this division was relieved and placed in reserve. On Friday the 2d, Grose's brigade was ordered over the river to the left to support the division of Colonel Beatty, and during the action the brigade of Colonel Hazen was also ordered over to coöperate with Grose, while the First Brigade (Cruft's) was posted to support a battery on the hill near the ford.

During the heavy cannonade the First Brigade maintained its position with perfect coolness.

While the engagement was going on across the river a rebel force of what seemed to be three small regiments, entered the clump of woods in front of the position of our batteries on the hill near the ford. These troops were in musket range of our right across the creek, and I determined at once to dislodge them. Seeing two regiments, one of which was commanded by Colonel Garrit, and the other by Colonel Attmire, I ordered them to advance to the edge of the wood and deploy some companies as skirmishers. They obeyed me cheerfully and pushed in. Not being willing to leave the repulse of the enemy a matter of doubt, or to expose these brave fellows to the danger of heavy loss, I ordered up two of Cruft's regiments, and upon approaching the edge of the woods halted them, and told them it was my purpose to clear the woods at the point of the bayonet. To inspire them with coolness and confidence, the preparation for the charge was made with great deliberation. To get the proper direction for the line, guides were thrown out and the proper changes were made. Bayonets fixed, and these two regiments, Thirty-First Indiana and Ninetieth Ohio, ordered to clear the woods. They went in splendidly. It was done so quickly that the rebels had hardly time to discharge their pieces. They fled with the utmost speed. All these regiments behaved handsomely.

The following is a list of the casualties of my command, and its fearful proportions demonstrate its hard service :

COMMANDS.	Killed.			Wounded.			Missing.			Aggregate...
	Officers.	Men.....	Total....	Officers.	Men.....	Total....	Officers.	Men.....	Total...	
1st Brigade......................	...	44	44	9	218	227	6	120	126	397
2d Brigade......................	5	41	46	17	318	335	...	52	52	433
3d Brigade......................	10	97	107	22	456	478	...	74	74	659
Standart's Battery............	...	5	5	...	12	12		3	3	20
Parsons' Battery..............	...	2	2	...	14	14		6	6	22
Cockerell's Battery..........	...	2	2	1	13	14		2	2	18
Total....................	15	191	206	49	1031	1080	6	257	263	1549

I have the honor to be very respectfully, yours,

J. M. PALMER,
Brigadier General Commanding.

GENERAL THOMAS J. WOOD'S REPORT.

NASHVILLE, TENN.,
January 6, 1863.

Major Lyne Starling, Chief of Staff:

On the morning of the 26th ult., the Left Wing of the Fourteenth Army Corps broke up its encampment in the vicinity of Nashville, and moved toward the enemy. Reliable information assured us that they were encamped in force at and in the vicinity of Murfreesboro ; but as their cavalry, supported occasionally by infantry, had extended its operations up to our outposts, and as we had been compelled, some days previous to the movement on the 26th ult., to fight for the greater part of the forage consumed by our animals, it was supposed we would meet with resistance as soon as our troops passed beyond the lines of our own outposts. Nor was this expectation disappointed. The order of march, on the first day of the movement, placed the Second Division (General Palmer's) in advance, followed by my own. Several miles northward of Lavergne, a small hamlet nearly equidistant between Nashville and Murfreesboro, portions of the enemy were encountered by our advance guard, a cavalry force, and a running fight at once commenced. The country occupied by these bodies of hostile troops, affords ground peculiarly favorable for a small force to retard the advance of a larger force. Large cultivated tracts occur at intervals, on either side of the turnpike road, but the country between the cultivated tracts is densely wooded, and much of the woodland is interspersed with cedar. The face of the country is undulating, presenting a succession of swells and depressions.

This brief description is applicable to the whole country between Nashville and Murfreseboro, and it will show to the most casual observer how favorable it was for covering the movements and designs of the enemy in resisting our progress. The resistance of the enemy prevented our troops from gaining possession of the commanding hights immediately south of Lavergne, during the first day's operation, and delayed the arrival of my division at the site selected for its encampment until some time after nightfall. The darkness of the evening and the lateness of the hour, prevented such a reconnoissance of the ground as is so necessary in close proximity to the enemy. But to guard effectually against surprise, a regiment from each brigade was thrown well forward as a grand guard, and the front and flanks of the division covered with a continuous line of skirmishers.

The troops were ordered to be roused at an hour and a half before dawn of the following morning, to get their breakfast as speedily as possible, and to be formed under arms and in order of battle before daylight. An occasional shell from the opposing hights, with which the enemy commenced to greet us shortly after the morning broke, showed these precautions were not lost. As it was understood from the Commanding General of the Corps, that the Right Wing was not so far advanced as the Left, the latter did not move forward until eleven o'clock A. M. on the 27th. At this hour the advance was ordered, and my division was directed to take the lead. The entire cavalry on duty with the Left Wing was ordered to report to me ; being satisfied, however, from the nature of the country that its position in the advance would be injudicious, and retard, rather than aid, the progress of the infantry, I directed it to take position in rear of the flanks of the leading brigade. I ordered Hascall's brigade to take the advance, and move forward in two lines, with the front and flanks well covered with skirmishers. The other two brigades, Wagner's and Harker's, were ordered to advance on either side of the turnpike road, prepared to sustain the leading brigade, and especially to protect its flanks. These two brigades were also ordered to protect their outer flanks by flankers. In this order the movement commenced. Possession of the hamlet of Lavergne was the first object to be attained. The enemy were strongly posted in the houses, and on the wooded hights in the rear, where they were enabled to oppose our advance by a direct and cross-fire of musketry. Hascall's brigade advanced nobly across an open field to the attack, and quickly routed the enemy from their stronghold. This was the work of only a few minutes, but more than twenty causalties in the two leading regiments proved how sharp was the fire of the enemy. The forward movement of Hascall's brigade was continued, supported by Estep's Eighth Indiana Battery. The enemy availed themselves of the numberless positions which occur along the entire road, to dispute our progress, but could not materially retard the advance of our troops so determined and enthusiastic. They continued to press forward through the densely-wooded country, in a drenching rain-storm, till the advance reached Stewart's Creek, distant some five miles from Lavergne. Stewart's Creek is a narrow, deep stream, flowing between high and precipitous banks. It is spanned by a wooden bridge, with a single arch. It was a matter of cardinal importance to secure possession of this bridge, as its destruction would entail difficulty and delay in crossing the river, and perhaps, involve the necessity of constructing a new bridge. The advance troops found, on their arrival, that the enemy had lighted a fire upon it, but had been pressed so warmly that there had been no time for the flames to be communicated to the bridge. The line of skirmishers and the Third Kentucky Volunteers, Colonel McKee, dashed bravely forward, though opposed to a fire from the opposing direction, threw the combustible materials into the stream, and saved the bridge. While this gallant feat was being performed, the left flank of the leading brigade was attacked by cavalry. The menaced regiments immediately changed front to left, repulsed the attack, and a company of the One-Hundredth Illinois, Colonel Bartleson, succeeded in cutting off and capturing twenty-five prisoners, with their arms, and twelve horses with their accouterments. The result of the day's operations was twenty casualties, wounded, in Hascall's brigade, and some twenty-five prisoners taken from the enemy. The enemy fell back in great disorder from Stewart's Creek. He left tents standing on the southern bank of the creek, and in this encampment the ground was strewn with arms.

Sunday, the 28th ult., we remained in camp waiting for the troops of the Right Wing and Center to get into position.

Monday, the 29th, the advance was resumed. Wagner's brigade, of my division, was deployed, in order of battle, on the left or eastern, and a brigade of General Palmer's division on the right or western, side of the road. Cox's Tenth Indiana Battery, supported Wagner's brigade. Moving *pari passu*, the two brigades advanced, clearing all opposition, till we arrived within two miles and a half of Murfreesboro. Harker's brigade was disposed on the left of Wagner's brigade, in the advance, and Hascall's held in reserve. On arriving within two miles and a half of Murfreesboro, the evidences were perfectly unmistakable that the enemy were in force immediately in our front, prepared to resist, seriously and determinedly, our further advance. The rebels, displayed in battle array, were plainly seen in our front.

Negley's division, which was to take position in the Center, to complete the communication between the Right and Left Wings, was not up, but several miles in the rear. Van Cleve's division, which was to support the left, was in the rear of Negley's. Consequently I halted the troops in advance, reported the fact to General Crittenden, commanding the Left Wing, and desired further orders. Up to this moment, the information received had indicated, with considerable probability, that the enemy would evacuate Murfreesboro, offering no serious opposition. But observations assured me, very soon after arriving so near the town, that we should meet with determined resistance, and I did not deem it proper to precipitate the force in advance—two divisions, my own and Palmer's—on the entire force of the enemy, with the remainder of our troops so far in the rear, as to make it entirely possible, perhaps probable, that a serious reverse would occur before they could support us. Furthermore, the afternoon was well nigh spent, and an attempt to advance would have involved us in the obscurity of the night, on unexamined ground, in the presence of an unseen foe, to whom our movements would have rendered us seriously vulnerable.

The halt being approved, my division was disposed in order of battle, and the front securely guarded by a continuous line of skirmishers, thrown out well in advance of their reserves. The right of the division, Wagner's brigade, rested on the turnpike, and occupied a piece of wooded ground, with an open field in front of it; the center, Harker's brigade, occupied, in part, the woods in which Wagner's brigade was posted, and extended leftward into an open field, covered in front by a low swell which it was to occupy in case of an attack, and General Hascall's brigade was posted on the left of the division, with the left flank resting nearly on Stone River. The entire division was drawn up in two lines. Stone River runs obliquely in front of the position occupied by the division leaving a triangular piece of ground of some hundreds of yards in breadth in front of the right, and narrowing to almost a point in front of the left.

Such was the position occupied by my division, Monday night. It remained in this position throughout Tuesday, the 30th—the skirmishers keeping up an active fire with the enemy. In this encounter, Lieutenant Elliott, Adjutant of the Fifty-Seventh Indiana, was badly wounded. In the afternoon, I had three days' subsistence issued to the men; and, near nightfall, by order, twenty additional rounds of cartridges were distributed to them. Commanders were directed to instruct the troops to be exceedingly vigilant, and to report promptly any indication in their fronts of a movement by the enemy. The artillery horses were kept attached to their pieces. Between midnight and daylight Wednesday morning, I received a message from Colonel Wagner, to the effect that the enemy seemed to be moving large bodies of troops from the right to the left. I immediately dispatched the information to the headquarters of the Left Wing, and I doubt not it was sent thence to the Commanding General, and by him distributed to the rest of the corps. The division was roused at five o'clock Wednesday morning; the men took their breakfasts, and, before daylight, were ready for action. Shortly after dawn, I repaired to the headquarters of the Left Wing for orders. I met the Commanding General there, and received orders from him to commence passing Stone River, immediately in front of the division, by brigades. I rode at once to my division, and directed Colonel Harker to commence the movement with his brigade, dispatching an order to General Hascall to follow Colonel Harker, and an order to Colonel Wagner to follow General Hascall. While Colonel Harker was preparing to move, I rode to the front to examine the ground. A long, wooded ridge, withdrawn a few hundred yards from the stream, extends along the southern and eastern side of Stone River. On the crest of this ridge the enemy appeared to be posted in force. During the morning some firing had been heard on the right, but not to a sufficient extent to indicate that the troops were seriously engaged. But the sudden and fierce roar and rattle of musketry, which burst upon us at this moment, indicated that the enemy had attacked the Right Wing in heavy force, and soon the arrival of messengers, riding in hot haste, confirmed the indications. I was ordered to stop the movement to cross the river, and to withdraw the brigades to the rear, for the purpose of reinforcing the Center and Right. General Hascall's and Col. Harker's brigades were withdrawn, and the latter, under orders from the Commanding General, moved to the right and rear. I ordered Colonel Wagner to hold his position in the woods at all hazards, as this was an important point, and so long as it was held, not only were our left front and flanks secured, but the command of the road leading to the rear preserved. The vigorous attack on our Right and Center, extended to our Left, and our whole line became seriously engaged. Not only was the extreme left exposed to the attack in the front, but was much harassed by the enemy's artillery, posted on the hights on the southern side of Stone River. But the troops nobly maintained their position, and gallantly repulsed the enemy. A slackening of the enemy's fire at this moment, in his attack on our Center and Left, and other indications that his forces were weakening in the Center, rendered the juncture apparently favorable for bringing additional and fresh troops into the engagement. Hascall's brigade was now brought forward, and put into position on the right of Wagner's brigade. But the abatement of the enemy's fire was but the lulling of the storm, to burst soon with greater fury. The attack was renewed on our Center and Left with redoubled violence. Hascall's brigade had got into position in good season, and aided in gallant style in driving back the enemy. Estep's Battery, generally associated with Hascall's brigade, had been detached early in the morning, and sent to the Right and rearward, to aid in driving back the enemy from our Center and Right. The falling back of the Right Wing had brought our lines into a crochet. This rendered the position of the troops on the extreme left particularly hazardous, for had the enemy succeeded in gaining the turnpike, in his attack on the Right, the Left would have been exposed to an attack in the reverse. This danger imposed on me the necessity of keeping a rigid watch to the right, to be prepared to change front in that direction, should it become necessary. Again the enemy were seen concentrating large masses of troops in the fields to the front and right, and soon these masses moved to the attack. Estep's Battery was now moved to the front to join Hascall's brigade. The artillery in the front lines, as well as those placed in the rear of the Center and Left, poured a destructive fire on the advancing foe, but on he came until within small-arm range, when he was repulsed and driven back. But our thinned ranks and dead and wounded officers told, in sad and unmistakable language, how seriously we were sufferers from these repeated assaults. Colonel McKee, of the Third Kentucky, had been killed; and Colonel Hines and Lieutenant Colonel Dennard, of the Fifty-Seventh Indiana, and Colonel Blake and Lieutenant Colonel Neff, of the Fortieth Indiana, with others, were wounded. During this attack, the Fifteenth Indiana, commanded by Lieutenant Colonel Wood, counter-charged on one of the enemy's regiments, and captured one hundred and seventy-five prisoners. The capture was from the Twentieth Louisiana. While this attack was in progress, I received a message from General Palmer, commanding the Second Division of the Left Wing, that he was sorely pressed, and desired I would send him a regiment, if I could possibly spare one. I sent an order to General Hascall, to send a regiment to General Palmer's assistance, if his own situation would warrant it. He dispatched the Fifty-Eighth Indiana, Colonel G. P. Buell's regiment, to report to General Palmer. The regiment got into position, reserved its fire until the enemy were in close range, and then poured in a withering discharge, from which the foe recoiled in disorder. Our extreme left next became the object of the enemy's attention. Skirmishers were seen descending the slope on the opposite side of the river, as also working their way down the stream for the purpose, apparently, of gaining our left flank and rear. A few well-directed charges of grape and canister from Cox's Battery, drove them back. This battery did most excellent service in counter-battering the enemy's artillery, posted on the hights on the southern side of the river. The afternoon was now well advanced, but the enemy did not seem disposed to relinquish the design of forcing us from our position. Heavy masses were again assembled in front of the center, with a view, evidently, of renewing the onset. But the well-directed fire of the artillery held them in check, and only a small force came within range of our small arms, which was readily repulsed. The enemy concluded his operations against the Left, as night approached, by opening on it with his artillery. Cox's and Estep's Batteries gallantly and effectually replied. But darkness soon put a conclusion to this artillery duel, and when the night descended brought a period to the long and bloody contest of this ever-memorable day, which found the First and Second Brigades, Hascall's and Wagner's, occupying, with some slight interchange in the position of particular regiments, the ground on which they had gone into the fight in the morning. Every effort of the enemy to dislodge them had failed; every attack was gallantly repulsed. I can not speak in too high terms of praise of the soldierly bearing and steadfast courage with which the officers and men of these two brigades maintained the battles throughout the day. Their good conduct deserves and will receive the highest commendations of their commanders and countrymen. The Commanding General of the enemy has borne testimony in his dispatch to the gallantry and success of their resistance. Cox's and Estep's Batteries were splendidly served throughout the day, and did the most effective service. They lost heavily in men and horses, and it was necessary for Estep to call on the One-Hundredth Illinois, for a detail to aid in working his guns. I have previously remarked that the Third Brigade, Colonel Harker's, was detached early in the morning and sent to reinforce the

Right. It remained on that part of the field during the entire day. I am not able, consequently, to speak of its service from personal observation. But its extremely heavy list of casualties shows how hotly it was engaged, and what valuable service it rendered. I am sure it met the expectation I had ever confidently entertained of what would be its bearing in presence of the foe. Bradley's Sixth Ohio Battery was associated with this brigade during the day, was skillfully handled, and did most effective service. It lost two of its guns, but they were spiked before they were abandoned. They were subsequently recaptured by the Thirteenth Michigan, attached to this brigade. From all I have learned of the service of the Third Brigade and Bradley's Battery, I am sure they deserve equal commendation with the other two brigades and batteries, which so stoutly held the left. An official report of events so thrilling as those of the battle of the 31st ult., made from personal observations amid the din and roar of the conflict, and unaided by the reports of the subordinate commanders, must necessarily present but a brief and meager outline of the part enacted by the troops whose services it professes to portray. A report so prepared may, entirely unintentionally on the part of the writer, do injustice to particular troops and officers. From the inability of reference to the reports of subordinate commanders, I can not give any detail of the heavy casualties of the battle of the 31st. I must leave them to be reported with the subsequent casualties by my successor in command. The absence of such reports prevents me from signalizing by names such regimental and company officers as particularly distinguished themselves. But where all did so well it would be difficult, perhaps invidious, to discriminate among them. To my brigade commanders, Brigadier General Hascall, commanding First Brigade, Colonel Wagner, Fifteenth Indiana, commanding Second Brigade, and Colonel Harker, Sixty-Fifth Ohio, commanding Third Brigade, my warmest thanks are due for their valuable assistance, their hearty co-operation, and intelligent performance of duty throughout the whole of that trying day. For these services and their gallant and manly bearing under the heaviest fire, they richly deserve the highest commendation, and the gratitude of their countrymen. Colonels Wagner and Harker have long and ably commanded brigades, and I respectfully submit it would be simply an act of justice to confer on them the actual and legal rank of the command they have so long exercised. To Major S. Race, Chief of Artillery; Surgeon W. W. Blair, Fifty-Eighth Indiana; Captain M. P. Bestow, Assistant Adjutant General; First Lieutenant J. L. Yargan, Fifty-Eighth Indiana, Aiddecamp; Captain Y. R. Palmer, Thirteenth Michigan, Inspector General, and Major Walker, Second Indiana Cavalry, Volunteer Aiddecamp, my thanks are due and cordially given. Captain L. D. Myers, Division Quartermaster; Captain Henderson, Commissary of Subsistence to the division, and First Lieutenant Martin, Twenty-First Ohio, Signal Officer, but for some time engaged in performing the duties of Acting Assistant Quartermaster, great credit is due for the intelligent and efficient performance of duty in their respective departments. Captain Bruce, Fifty-Eighth Indiana, Ordnance Officer of the First Virginia, deserves credit for valuable services rendered in the Ordnance Department for the entire division, during the absence of the Division Ordnance Officer.

My division is composed of regiments from the States of Illinois, Indiana, Ohio, Michigan, and Kentucky. To the relatives and personal friends of those who have fallen in defense of their country, I would respectfully offer my sympathy and condolence.

About ten o'clock Wednesday morning, during one of the heaviest attacks, I was struck by a Minnie ball on the inner side of the left heel. Fortunately, the ball struck obliquely, or the injury would have been much severer. My boot was torn open, the foot lacerated, and a severe contusion inflicted. I did not dismount from my horse till seven o'clock in the evening. The coldness of the night, combined with the injury, made my foot so painful and stiff as to render it evident I would not be effective for immediate service. I was ordered by the Commanding General of the corps to repair that night, by ambulance, with an escort, to this city. It was with extreme regret I found myself in a condition to make it necessary, on account of my injury, to leave the division I had formed and so long commanded ; but the regret was alleviated by the reflection that I had left the division under the command of an able and experienced officer, one who had long served with it, who knew it well, and in whom it had confidence—Brigadier General Hascall.

I am still confined to my room, but trust ere long to be able to resume my duties. I am, very respectfully, your obedient servant,

TH. J. WOOD,
Brigadier General Commanding.

GENERAL M. S. HASCALL'S REPORT.

HEADQUARTERS FIRST DIVISION,
MURFREESBORO, TENN., *January* 10, 1863.

Major Starling, Assistant Adjutant General :

I have the honor to submit the following report of the operations of this division during the recent battles, after the command devolved upon me, on the evening of December 31, 1862. At that time the division was considerably scattered, as Colonel Harker's brigade had been in action during the 31st, on the extreme right, and had not returned. Colonel Wagner was in position to the left of the railroad, where he had been in action during the day, and my brigade was to the right of the railroad. About eleven P. M., of that day, Colonel Harker retired with his brigade, and the division was once more together. At this time I received an order to send all the wagons of the division to the rear ; and shortly after this was executed, I received orders from General Crittenden to fall back, so that my right should rest on the position occupied by Stokes' Battery, and my left on the right of General Palmer's division. This brought the new line of the division about five hundred yards to the rear of the one of the day before. The line of the division was now nearly at right angles with the railroad, with the center of the line resting on it, the First Brigade, Colonel Buell, on the right of the Third, Colonel Harker in the center, and the Second, Colonel Wagner's, on the left. In this position we lay all the next day (January 1, 1863) with nothing more than picket firing and an occasional artillery duel, to break the silence. The division lost, however, several killed and wounded during the day. Each of my brigades was in line of battle, and I was occupying so much front that it kept the men constantly on the alert. Most of the other divisions had one or two brigades in reserve and could, therefore, relieve their men some. We maintained this position during the night of the 1st and till about eight A. M. on the morning of the 2d, the batteries occupying the intervals between the brigades. At this time the enemy opened upon us the most terrific fire of shot and shell that we sustained during the entire engagement. It appears that during the night before, they had massed several batteries in our front, so they opened upon us from a line of batteries one-fourth of a mile long, all at once. They had our range perfectly, so that their shot were terribly effective from the first. Estep's Battery, on the right of my line, being in an exposed situation and receiving a very heavy fire, had to retire at once, not, however, till so many horses had been killed, as to render it necessary for two of the pieces to be hauled to the rear by the infantry. Bradley's Battery, with Colonel Harker, in the center, having a better position, and longer-range guns, opened a brisk fire on the enemy in return, and had every probability of maintaining their position until Stokes' Battery, in their rear, undertook to open on the enemy with grape which took effect on Bradley's men, instead of the enemy, and compelled Bradley to retire. The infantry, however, along my entire line, although suffering severely from the effects of this fire, all maintained their position. In about half an hour this firing ceased, and nothing further, worthy of note, happened, until near four o'clock in the afternoon of that day. At this time General Van Cleve's division, which was stationed across Stone River, to our left, was suddenly attacked by a heavy force of the enemy, under Breckinridge, and so fierce was the onslaught that the division was compelled, almost immediately, to give way. General Jeff. C. Davis and General Negley were ordered to their relief with their divisions, and as soon as they had time to get over, the attack was checked, and the enemy began to retire. At this time I received an order from General Crittenden to cross with my division, and immediately put the different brigades in motion. While crossing at the ford one or two pieces of the enemy's artillery were playing upon us, but as it was then dusk, their firing was not accurate, and I think we sustained no loss in crossing. By the time we were over it was dark, and the firing had nearly ceased. Negley's division was returning, and Davis had taken up a position a little in advance of where Van Cleve was attacked, his right resting on the bank of the river. I moved up and went into position on the left of Davis, my left inclining somewhat to the rear, to prevent it from being turned. General Davis and myself then fortified our fronts as well as we could with the logs, stones, and rails at hand, and remained in this position that night, the next day (January 3), and till about twelve o'clock that night, without anything more than picket firing transpiring. I should remark that it rained very hard all day January 3d, and during the night, so that our men and officers suffered severely. By this time the rain had so swollen the river that General Crittenden became apprehensive that it would not be fordable by morning, and we might be cut off from communication with the main body of the army. He then ordered us back, and my division took up a position in reserve near General Rosecran's headquarters, arriving there about two o'clock in the morning, completely drenched with mud and rain. They had now been on duty four days and nights, some of the time with nothing to eat, and constantly in the front, where they had to be all the time on the alert. The next morning we heard that the enemy had evacuated. The battle was over. The conduct of the division, throughout, was admirable, and it can be truthfully said, concerning it, that it held its original position, and every other position assigned to it, during the whole four days.

I am under great obligations to my brigade commanders, Colonels Wagner, Harker, and Buell. Colonel Wagner had his horse shot under him on the 31st., and his clothes completely riddled with bullets. He, nevertheless, stood by throughout, and ably and gallantly performed his duty. The conduct of Colonel. Harker was equally brave and efficient. They have now each commanded brigades for nearly a year, and it seems to me that common justice demands that they now receive the promotion they have so gallantly earned. Colonel Buell came in command of the First Brigade in consequence of my taking command of the division; and, although comparatively inexperienced, he performed every duty gallantly and well. All the officers of the division, with a single exception, behaved gallantly and did well, therefore, I need not discriminate. The exception was Colonel John W. Blake, of the Fortieth Indiana; and I consider it my duty to draw the line of distinction broad and deep between those who do well and those who prove recreant. He became so drunk as to be unfit for duty, before going into action, on the 31st., and was sent to the rear, in arrest, by his immediate commander, Colonel Wagner. The next that was heard from him, he was in Nashville, claiming to be wounded and a paroled prisoner. For this bad conduct I recommend that he be dishonorably discharged from the service.

The casualties in the division were as follows:

The First Brigade went into action with seventy-four officers and one thousand four hundred and fifty-four enlisted men, and lost:

OFFICERS.		
Killed	4	
Wounded	21—	25
ENLISTED MEN.		
Killed	42	
Wounded	278	
Missing	34—	354
Total		379

The Second Brigade went into action with eighty-six officers and one thousand three hundred and eighty enlisted men, and lost:

OFFICERS.

Killed	2	
Wounded	18—	20

ENLISTED MEN.

Killed	54	
Wounded	269	
Missing	32—	355
Total		375

The Third Brigade went into action with ninety-seven officers and one thousand seven hundred and ninety enlisted men, including the Sixth Ohio Battery, and lost:

OFFICERS.

Killed	5	
Wounded	17—	22

ENLISTED MEN.

Killed	104	
Wounded	312	
Missing	101—	517
Total		539

RECAPITULATION.

The division went into action with two hundred and fifty-four officers and four thousand six hundred and eighty-three enlisted men, and lost:

OFFICERS.

Killed	11	
Wounded	56—	67

ENLISTED MEN.

Killed	200	
Wounded	859	
Missing	167—	1,226
Total		1,293

All of which is respectfully submitted.

M. S. HASCALL,

Brigadier General Commanding.

GENERAL H. P. VAN CLEVE'S REPORT.

HEADQUARTERS THIRD DIVISION,
ARMY OF THE CUMBERLAND.

Major Lyne Starling, Assistant Adjutant General:

MAJOR—I have the honor to submit the following report of the operations of my division on the 31st of December, 1862:

At seven o'clock on the morning of that day I received an order to cross Stone River, on which my left rested, and march toward Murfreesboro. The First Brigade, Colonel Beatty, Third Brigade, Colonel Price, and the batteries, Captain Swallow commanding, were promptly moved over and formed into line; the Second Brigade, Colonel Fyffe, being retained on the south side by a subsequent order.

My lines being formed and about to advance, by your order I recrossed the river, leaving the Third Brigade to guard the ford. With the First Brigade I marched rapidly to the support of General Rousseau, whose division was hard pressed by the enemy. We formed in a wood on the south side of the Murfreesboro and Nashville turnpike. Our lines were no sooner formed than the enemy were seen advancing, driving before them our scattered troops. Our ranks were opened to suffer them to pass, when they closed and opened on the enemy with a withering fire, who were soon brought to a halt. A murderous fire was kept up on both sides about twenty minutes, when the enemy began to recoil. Our second line now relieving the first with hearty cheer, the rebels broke and retreated. The Second Brigade coming up at this moment, formed on the right and joined in the pursuit. We pressed the enemy through this wood, then across an open field to another wood, where they appear to have met with reinforcements and reformed. The Seventh Indiana Battery, Captain Swallow, joined us on this open field, and rendered efficient aid. Here I received information from General Rosecrans that General Rousseau was driving the enemy, accompanied with an order for me to press them hard.

At the same moment I was notified by a messenger from Colonel Harker, whose brigade was to my right and rear, that the enemy were in force on my right in a wood, and were planting a battery there. I immediately sent a message to Colonel Harker to press the enemy hard, as I had no reserve to protect my right; to Captain Swallow, who was doing good service with his battery, not to suffer it to be captured; to Colonel Beatty to send two regiments, if they could possibly be spared, to the support of Colonel Fyffe, and a fourth to General Crittenden to inform him of my critical situation. The enemy now poured a galling fire of musketry, accompanied with grape and shell, on our right. Colonel Fyffe's brigade, supported by Captain Swallow's Battery, gallantly returned the fire, but being overpowered by numbers on front and flank, were soon compelled to retire, followed but a short distance by the enemy. Captain Swallow, to whom too much praise can not be awarded, brought off his battery safely.

Colonel Beatty, who had been pressing the enemy on the left, as soon as he learned the condition of affairs, retired in good order; with two of his regiments was ordered by General Rosecrans to protect a battery on the Murfreesboro road; the remaining two regiments of his brigade and Colonel Fyffe's brigade were reformed, and took a position on the left of General McCook's Corps, and to the right of the Pioneer, which position we occupied without further adventure till after dark.

I can not close this report without inviting your attention to the gallantry displayed by those under my command during this engagement. To both officers and men too much praise can not be awarded. I would particularly notice the coolness, intrepidity, and skill of my brigade commanders, Colonels Beatty and Fyffe, and of Captain Swallow, Chief of Artillery. To the members of my staff, Captain E. A. Otis, Assistant Adjutant General; Captain C. H. Wood, Inspector General; Captain William Starling, Topographical Engineer; Lieutenants T. F. Murdoch and H. M. Williams, Aidsdecamp, I owe much for the promptness, faithfulness, and gallantry with which they executed my orders, and conveyed intelligence on the field. Sergeant R. B. Rhodes, of the First Ohio Cavalry, in command of my escort, conducted himself like a true soldier, and deserves honorable mention.

A slight wound received early this day, becoming exceedingly painful, on the following morning I was compelled to turn over the command of the division to Colonel Beatty, and retire from the field.

Very respectfully, your obedient servant,

H. P. VAN CLEVE,
Brigadier General.

COLONEL SAMUEL BEATTY'S REPORT.

HEADQUARTERS THIRD DIVISION,
CAMP NEAR MURFREESBORO, *January*, 1863.

Major Lyne Starling, Assistant Adjutant General :

MAJOR—I have the honor to submit the following report of the operations of this division for the time embraced between the 1st and 3d days of January, 1863, inclusive:

I was called to the command of the division on the morning of January 1st, by General Van Cleve's disability from the wound received in the battle of the preceding day.

At three P. M. on that day, I received orders to cross Stone River with my command at the "upper ford," and hold the hill overlooking the river near the ford. Accordingly at daybreak the Third Brigade, Colonel Price commanding, crossed the river at the place indicated, throwing out skirmishers and flankers. Colonel Price was quickly followed by Colonel Fyffe's brigade; the force being formed in two lines, the right retiring on the high ground near the river and east of the ford, and the left thrown forward so that the direction of the line should be nearly perpendicular to the river.

In the meantime, the First Brigade, Colonel Grider commanding, had been disposed as follows: Two regiments were formed in the hollow near the hospital as a reserve, the other two remaining on the other side of the river to support a battery.

The enemy's skirmishers were now discovered in a wood, distant half a mile or so from our first line, and occasional firing took place on both sides.

Information of all these movements was sent to General Crittenden, who sent me word that if I needed artillery to order up a battery. The Third Wisconsin Battery, Lieutenant Livingston commanding, was accordingly, at about ten o'clock A. M., ordered to cross the river and remain in the hollow near the ford.

Small parties of the enemy's cavalry and infantry were occasionally seen, and at length a strong line was distinctly visible through the openings of the wood. Lieutenant Livingston was ordered to bring up his battery. It was accordingly placed in position on the rising ground in front of Colonel Fyffe's brigade. Several shells were thrown at the enemy's line, which caused its disappearance; it was supposed that they had laid down. One section, Lieutenant Hubbard commanding, was now moved to the hill on the right, whence also one or two shells were thrown at detached parties. Colonel Fyffe's brigade was moved to the left of the battery, where it was covered by a skirt of woods. Our whole force had been constantly concealed by making the men lie down.

About one o'clock the remaining two regiments of Colonel Grider's brigade, the Nineteenth Ohio and Ninth Kentucky, were ordered to cross the river, which they did, forming near the hospital on the left of the other two regiments of the same brigade, to protect our left flank. The enemy's force was occasionally seen moving to our left, and Generals Crittenden and Palmer were advised of the fact; Colonel Grose was consequently ordered to support me. His brigade formed so as to protect our left, relieving the Nineteenth Ohio and Ninth Kentucky. These two regiments were formed in rear of the right of the second line as a reserve, being posted in the hollow near the ford.

No other disturbance occurred during the day, except the occasional firing of the skirmishers, so Colonel Grose's brigade and Livingston's Battery recrossed the river. About midnight we were alarmed by sharp firing from the skirmishers; they reported that it was caused by the enemy's skirmishers advancing and firing upon us. One of our men was killed and one wounded. Nothing else occurred during the night. On the morning of Friday, January 2d, Livingston's Battery came across the river again, and was posted as before. There was light skirmishing during the earlier part of the day.

The Seventy-Ninth Indiana, Colonel Knifler, was ordered to take place in the first line, to close the gap between Colonel Fyffe's brigade and the others. Nothing of note occurred until about eleven o'clock, when the firing of the enemy's skirmishers became very constant and heavy, as they slowly crept up toward us. The skirmishers now reported a battery being planted in our front, and shortly afterward, that fifteen regiments of infantry and three pieces of artillery were moving to our left.

Notice of all these movements was given to Generals Crittenden and Palmer, and Colonel Grose's brigade again came over to our support. About noon the enemy's battery opened with occasional shells, directed at Lieutenant Hubbard's section of artillery on the hill. The enemy's artillery were now seen moving to our left, and soon another battery opened fire upon Lieutenant Hubbard's section.

As the enemy's skirmishers were so near that their firing was annoying and dangerous to the artillery, I ordered Lieutenant Livingston to retire and take a position on the hill near the hospital. A few shells were still thrown by the enemy's battery on our left, and occasional ones from an apparently heavy battery across the river. As the enemy's skirmishers pressed ours very closely, our lines were strengthened by throwing out two more companies. The firing was very sharp, and many of our men as well as theirs were wounded. At about half past two o'clock it was reported that four more of the enemy's guns were moving toward our left. Word was sent of this, as in case of all other movements, to General Crittenden. At about three o'clock our skirmishers reported that the enemy's skirmishers were throwing down the fence in front of our line. Orders were sent to Colonel Price to let his first line fall back behind the crest of the hill, but before he could receive them the enemy were advancing across the field to the charge. They were formed in column, with a front of apparently two regiments.

The first column was three regiments, or six ranks deep ; this was succeeded by a second of the same depth, and a third apparently greater.

At the same moment their artillery opened from three or four different points, throwing shot, shell, and canister directly into us.

As the enemy's columns approached to within a hundred yards or so, the first line rose up and delivered a heavy fire upon their column, which checked it for a moment ; they soon pressed on, however. The regiments of the first line, the Fifty-First Ohio, Eighth Kentucky, and Thirty-Fifth and Seventy-Ninth Indiana, fought gallantly until the enemy were within a few yards of them, when, overpowered by numbers, they were compelled to retire.

This movement confused and disorganized the second line, which also was ordered to fall back. The reserve, consisting of the Nineteenth Ohio, Ninth Kentucky, and Eleventh Kentucky, was now ordered up. They advanced most gallantly toward the crest of the hill, and poured a destructive fire upon the enemy, whose first column was by this time almost annihilated. Their supporting columns soon came up, however, and at the same time a force advanced along the river bank upon our right flank. Our men fought with most desperate courage, as will appear from their severe loss, until forced back by the actual pressure of the enemy. Even then they broke back from the right, file by file, stubbornly contesting their ground. At last, however, the right being forced back, the left was ordered to retire, which it slowly did until the bank of the river was reached.

Attempts were made to rally the men at several points, but it was impossible from the heavy fire and the close proximity of the enemy; most of them were, therefore, forced across the river, where many of them rallied and returned with the first supporting troops; and I am proud to say that the colors of the Nineteenth Ohio, Ninth Kentucky, and Fifty-First Ohio were the first to recross the stream after the enemy's check. The tremendous fire of our artillery on the south side of the river, with Livingston's Battery on the other, with the determined resistance they had met, had stopped the enemy at the river; and now, as our troops pressed forward, they fled in confusion, leaving four of their guns.

Several brave officers had rallied a great number of our men, and were the foremost in the advance.

Night now came on and closed the pursuit. The regiments were rapidly reorganized, and in a few hours were in a state of efficiency, and turned out promptly and cheerfully at an alarm.

The Second Brigade, Colonel Fyffe, was not attacked, the front of the enemy's column not extending to them. Seeing the right driven back, they also retired in good order. Lieutenant Livingston's Battery fired constantly and well from the first appearance of the enemy, until the very last moment he could remain safely. He then crossed the river without losing a piece.

I can not too much commend the gallant manner in which my men fought, and the promptness with which, when forced to give way, they rallied and reorganized.

The following is a report of the number of killed, wounded, and missing in the engagement before Murfreesboro, Tennessee:

COMMANDS.	Killed.			Wounded.			Missing.			Aggregate....
	Officers.	Men.....	Total...	Officers.	Men.....	Total...	Officers.	Men.....	Total...	
Brigadier General Van Cleve....	...	...	...	1	...	1	...	...	...	1
1st Brigade..............................	7	59	66	16	303	319	...	81	81	466
2d Brigade..............................	4	76	80	14	225	239	2	160	162	481
3d Brigade..............................	6	75	81	21	307	328	2	146	148	557
Artillery	...	6	6	...	19	19	...	...	...	25
Total..........................	17	216	233	52	854	906	4	387	391	1530

To the commanders of the different brigades, Colonels Grider, Price, and Fyffe, my thanks are due for the gallantry and coolness of their behavior under very trying circumstances. Lieutenant Livingston, of the Third Wisconsin Battery, did efficient service, and performed his duty ably and handsomely. Lieutenant Smoch, Third Kentucky Cavalry, who commanded a detachment of couriers, remained constantly on hand near me, and was of great use.

To the following officers, members of my staff, I tender my thanks for their assistance, and the manner in which it was rendered: Captain E. A. Otis, Assistant Adjutant General; Captain C. H. Wood, Acting Assistant Inspector General; Captain William Starling, Topographical Engineer, and Lieutenants T. F. Murdoch and H. M. Williams, Aidsdecamp.

Respectfully submitted,

SAMUEL BEATTY,

Colonel Commanding.

CAPTAIN J. ST. CLAIR MORTON'S REPORT.

The following is a full abstract of the Official Report of Captain James St. Clair Morton, Corps of Engineers, commanding Brigade of Pioneers:

The Pioneer Brigade of the Army of the Cumberland consists of three battalions of infantry, selected from forty different regiments, and the Chicago Board of Trade Battery, Captain Stokes. Captain Bridges, of the Nineteenth Illinois, commanded the First Battalion; Captain Hood, of the Eleventh Michigan, the Second, and Captain Clements, of the Sixty-Ninth Ohio, the Third Battalion.

On the march from Nashville the brigade constructed two bridges over Stewart's Creek, between the hours of four P. M. and four o'clock A. M., 29th and 30th December, arriving at the battle-field on the 30th.

On the morning of the 31st of December, the brigade was engaged in improving the fords of Stone River, in which the right battalion sustained the fire of some rebel cavalry. Captain (now Brigadier General) Morton was ordered, soon afterward, to take position in line of battle. The brigade was formed by order of General Rosecrans, in person, fronting toward the right. The enemy appeared on a rise of ground, in front, from which they had driven one of our batteries. Stokes' Battery immediately opened fire, with canister, and drove them back. Captain Morton, at the personal order of General Rosecrans, who, with his staff accompanied him, advanced to the eminence and held it, under a heavy fire from the rebel batteries and sharpshooters. Stokes' Battery was supported by the First Battalion, on the left, posted in a thicket; the Third Battalion on the right, its flank protected by the Second Battalion, posted in a wood, still further to the right.

Shortly after the line was formed the enemy appeared across the field, preparing to charge upon one of our retiring detachments, which had been rallied by the Commanding General. Stokes' Battery opened upon the foe, and the advance of the enemy was speedily arrested. The right battalion was attacked soon after, the enemy obviously intending to penetrate the line under cover of the forest. The battalion changed front to obtain a flanking fire, and by a single volley repulsed the enemy, composed of the Eleventh and Fourteenth Texas regiments. The Seventy-Ninth Indiana had rallied on the right of the battalion in the meantime, and assisted in the success. This was one of the most brilliant episodes of the battle. It followed quickly upon the charge made by the General in person, and was really the second act of the drama, which changed the tide of battle.

Toward sunset the enemy appeared on Morton's left. Two sections of Stokes' Battery were brought to the left of the First Battalion, and a brigade of the enemy which had attacked the battalion in the thicket, was bitterly repulsed. Their dead were left within fifty paces of Morton's lines. The troops behaved admirably.

The Pioneers slept on their arms that night. Early New Year's morning, the enemy again appeared on the left, apparently to advance through a gap between it and the Murfreesboro turnpike. Morton immediately changed front and occupied the gap. A hot engagement ensued, infantry and artillery being used so effectively that the enemy could not push beyond the edge of the wood, and they were finally driven back with severe loss. The position was held by the Pioneers until after nightfall, when they were relieved and formed in reserve.

On the morning of Friday, the second part of the Pioneers were engaged making road-crossings over the railroad, when the enemy opened a severe cannonade. Stokes' Battery returned the fire, and the battalions advanced, supporting it under a fire of solid shot and shell, until the rebel battery was silenced, when the Pioneers fell back to their position.

In the afternoon, when Breckinridge made his attack upon Van Cleve's small division, which had been thrown across the river on our left, General Rosecrans, in person, ordered the Pioneers to the left as reinforcements. Morton marched his command at double-quick, and arrived on the line occupying a gap in it, under the firing of a rebel battery, which was soon silenced by Stokes' Battery, which was worked with great skill and vigor.

General Negley's (Eighth) division was already tremendously engaged. The enemy had advanced in columns of brigades six deep without intervals, presenting a most formidable mass, and threatening to carry everything before them. Our batteries opened in magnificent concert, and the most obstinate combat of the whole series of engagements was culminating. General Negley now requested Morton to reinforce him, and the Pioneers were at once moved up at double-quick and formed, the Third Battalion in second line behind the division under command of General Jeff. C. Davis, the First extending beyond it, and throwing out its own advance, occupying the space between it and the river ; Stokes' Battery was posted on a knoll between the First and Second Battalions, the Second being in second line on the extreme right. The fighting, meantime, of the most violent description, was growing slack, and the enemy, finally defeated, were flying back to Murfreesboro, darkness preventing pursuit.

After nightfall the Pioneers recrossed the river, and again assumed position in the reserve, the Second Battalion being detailed to dig rifle-pits in the front, near the pike and on the extreme right. They labored all night in the rain. On January 3d, the Third Battalion relieved the First, then on duty in the trenches; on the 4th, the Second and Third Battalions began the construction of two lunettes on the north bank of the river, and the First Battalion began a trestle bridge across it; on the 5th the work continued, and the Third Battalion, with the advance of the army, went in pursuit of the enemy.

The loss of the brigade was as follows:

BATTALIONS.	OFFICERS.	MEN.		Total...
	Wounded.	Killed.	Wounded.	
First	3	4	5	12
Second	...	4	5	9
Third	...	4	10	14
Stokes' Battery	1	3	9	13
Total	4	15	29	48

The force of the brigade actually engaged was sixteen hundred men —ninety-five in Stokes' battery.

Throughout the engagement the Pioneers behaved nobly, and upon requisition worked zealously night and day, although insufficiently subsisted, and under vicissitudes of inclement weather and rebel fire.

Captain Morton euolgized the conduct of the artillerymen in the highest manner. They fought under the eye of the General, and won high encomiums from him. Captain Morton, in his report, says: "As the Commanding General was everywhere present on the field with his staff, he can not but have remarked the good service done by Captain Stokes, who manifested the greatest zeal, and managed his battery with the utmost decision and success."

Captain Morton most honorably mentions his Adjutant, Lieutenant Lambessen, of the Nineteenth Illinois; his Inspectors, Lieutenants Clark of the Sixteenth United States Infantry, and Murphy of the Twenty-First Wisconsin; his Aids, Lieutenant Reeve of the Thirty-Seventh Indiana, and Assistant Engineer Pearsall; "all of whom exhibited the utmost ardor and alacrity in the performance of their duty."

Captain Hood, Captain Clements and Captain Bridges, commanding the battalions, are highly extolled. The latter, though wounded on the 31st remained in command of his battalion.

CAPTAIN JOHN MENDENHALL'S REPORT.

HEADQUARTERS LEFT WING,
January 10, 1863.

Major L. Starling, Chief of Staff:

MAJOR—I have the honor to submit the following report of the operations of the artillery in the Left Wing from December 26, 1862, to January 2, 1863. This army marched from camp near Nashville, December 26th; the Left Wing marching on the Murfreesboro pike.

December 26.—About three P. M., our advance was brought to a stand-still near Lavergne, by a rebel battery. It was opposed by a section of artillery serving with the cavalry, which being unable to dislodge the enemy, our advance battery (Captain Standart, Battery B, First Ohio) was, after a little delay, put in position and opened fire, soon silencing the enemy.

December 27.—General Hascall took the advance with his brigade, and Lieutenant Estep's Eighth Indiana Battery. They marched steadily forward till the enemy were driven across Stewart's Creek; the battery halting only when it was necessary to fire; two pieces were posted near, covering the bridge.

December 28.—Some artillery was so disposed as to check the enemy, should they attempt to destroy or retake the bridge.

December 29.—Lieutenant Parsons, commanding Batteries H and M, Fourth Artillery, being in a commanding position, threw a few shells about nine A. M., driving the enemy's picket from the opposite woods. Our column advanced across the bridge at ten A. M., meeting with little resistance till within about three miles of Murfreesboro. Our troops were placed in line of battle as they came up, the artillery remaining with their divisions.

December 30.—About nine A. M., the enemy opened fire upon Captain Cox's Tenth Indiana Battery (which was between the pike and the railroad, and in front partially covered by woods). Captain Bradley's Sixth Ohio Battery, at once took a position to the left of the woods and in a cornfield. The two batteries soon silenced that of the enemy's. One shot killed a man near where a number of General and Staff officers were standing, and another passing through Battery H, Fourth Artillery, killing one man, wounding another, besides disabling a horse.

December 31.—The Left Wing started to cross Stone River, about eight A. M., but before a division had crossed, intelligence was received that the Right was falling back. Colonel Fyffe's brigade, which was about crossing, was ordered to counter-march and move at double-quick to the Right. Captain Swallow's Seventh Indiana Battery operated for a time with this brigade, shelling the rebel cavalry from the brick hospital. Colonel Beatty's brigade, having recrossed the river, advanced to the support of the Right Wing; but the Twenty-Sixth Pennsylvania Battery, Lieutenant Stevens commanding, being unable to follow the brigade through the woods, took a position near the pike, and received the enemy with shot and shell as they advanced after our retreating columns, and I think done his part in checking them. He advanced as they retreated, and took a position in a cornfield on the right of the pike near the three-mile post, and again opened upon the enemy. The position of this battery under went several changes during the rest of the day, but remained in the same immediate vicinity. The Third Wisconsin Battery, having recrossed the river with the brigade, took a position commanding the ford and about twelve M., opened upon the enemy's cavalry, while attempting to drive off some of our wagons which had crossed the river, and were near a hospital we had established on the other side, driving them away with very little booty. The batteries of General Wood's division (Cox's Tenth Indiana, Estep's Eighth Indiana, and Bradley's Sixth Ohio, all under command of Major Race, of the First Ohio Artillery) fought with the brigades with which they were serving. I had no occasion to give special orders to them during the day. The batteries of General Palmer's division served with it during the morning, rendering good service. Captain Standart's Battery fell back with General Cruft's brigade, and was not again engaged during the day. Captain Cockerell, during the afternoon, was ordered to the front, taking a position in the cornfield on the left of the woods where the enemy were making such desperate attempts to force back the Left. At this place, Captain Cockerell was severely wounded in the foot, and the command of his battery devolved upon Lieutenant Osburn. Two guns of this battery were disabled from their own firing, the axles being too weak. One of the limbers of this battery was blown up during the day. Lieutenant Parsons, commanding Batteries H and M, Fourth Artillery, was ordered up to support the Left, about four P. M., and took a position near the railroad. After he had expended all his ammunition, I sent Captain Swallow's Seventh Indiana Battery to replace him. These batteries did much to repel the enemy as they advanced with the evident determination to drive us back at all hazards if possible. During the night, the batteries were resupplied with ammunition, and I directed them to take positions, as follows, before daylight, viz.: Lieutenant Livingston, commanding ford on the extreme left; Captain Swallow, on his right, near the railroad; Lieutenant Stevens also near the railroad, but on the left of Captain Swallow. The batteries of the First Division between the railroad and the pike. Captain Bradley on the Left, Captain Cox on the Right, and Lieutenant Estep, in the Center. The Second Division batteries near the pike in reserve.

During the morning, Lieutenant Livingston was directed to cross the river (he was assigned a position by Colonel Beatty), and Captain Swallow took his place commanding the ford; Lieutenant Parsons was ordered to a position on General Rousseau's front by General Rosecrans, and Captain Cox was moved across the pike near Stokes' Battery, to support the right of his division, which had moved its right to that point. After dark, Captain Standart was ordered to relieve Stokes' Battery. No firing, except now and then a shell at the enemy's pickets, during the day.

January 2.—Early in the forenoon, the enemy opened fire first upon our Left, which was not responded to, their shot and shell doing no harm. They were opened more furiously upon the troops and batteries near the railroad and pike, several of our batteries replying and soon silencing them. When the enemy had nearly ceased firing, Stokes' Battery opened with canister upon Captain Bradley's Battery and Colonel Harker's brigade wounding several men and horses.

Captain Standart, with three pieces, Captain Bradley's and Lieutenant Estep's Batteries, retired a short distance to fit up, they having received more or less injury from the enemy. Captain Bradley fell back on account of being fired into by Captain Stokes. He returned to his former position, after a little while, but Captain Standart and Lieutenant Estep remained in reserve. I then ordered Lieutenant Parsons with Batteries H and M, Fourth Artillery, to a position on the ridge to the right of Captain Swallows (who was on the highest point-ridge, covering the ford) and Lieutenant Osburn, Battery F, First Ohio, to a position perhaps a hundred yards to the right of Lieutenant Parsons. During the afternoon Colonel Beatty changed the position of Lieutenant Livingston's Battery to near the the hospital (across the river).

About four P. M., while riding along the pike with General Crittenden, we heard heavy firing of artillery and musketry on the Left. We at once rode briskly over, and arriving upon the hill near the fords saw our infantry retiring before the enemy. The General asked me if I could not do something to relieve Colonel Beatty with my guns—Captain Swallow had already opened with his battery. I ordered Lieutenant Parsons to move a little forward with his guns; then rode back to bring up Lieutenant Estep with his Eight Indiana Battery; meeting Captain Morton with his brigade of Pioneers, he asked for advice and I told him to move briskly forward with his brigade, and send his battery to the crest of the hill near the batteries engaged; the Eighth Indiana Battery took position to the right of Lieutenant Parsons. Seeing that Lieutenant Osburn was in position (between Lieutenant Parsons and Estep) I rode to Lieutenant Stevens' Twenty-Sixth Pennsylvania Battery, and directed him to change front to fire to the left, and open fire; and then to Captain Standart's, and directed him to move to the left with his pieces, and take position covering the ford. I found that Captain Bradley had anticipated my wishes, and had changed front to fire to the left, and opened upon the enemy. This battery was near the railroad. Lieutenant Livingston's Battery (which was across the river) opened upon the advancing enemy and continued to fire until he thought he could no longer maintain his position when he crossed over, one section at a time, and opened fire again. The firing ceased about dark. During this terrible encounter of little more than an hour in duration, forty-three pieces of artillery belonging to the Left Wing, Captain Stokes' Battery of six guns and the batteries of General Negley's division about nine guns, making a total of about fifty-eight pieces, opened fire upon the enemy. The enemy soon retired; our troops following. Three batteries of the Left Wing, besides those of General Davis, crossed the river in pursuit. During this engagement, Lieutenant Parsons had one of his howitzers dismounted by a shot from the enemy, but it was almost immediately replaced by one captured from the enemy and brought over by the Nineteenth Illinois.

Captain Cockerell and Lieutenant Buckmar were both wounded on the 31st. The former commanded Battery F, First Ohio, and the latter belonged to the Seventh Indiana Battery. Major Race, First Ohio Artillery, Chief of Artillery, in the First Division, and the several battery commanders with their officers and men all, with *one exception*, deserves most grateful mention for their coolness and bravery throughout the battle. Lieutenant Parsons, commanding Batteries H and M, Fourth Artillery, and his officers, Lieutenants Cushing and Huntington, deserve great credit for their courage under the hottest of the enemy's fire. They were probably under closer fire and more of it than any other battery in the Left Wing, and perhaps in the army. I am more than pleased with the way they behaved, as well as the brave men under them. Captain Bradley, Sixth Ohio Battery, deserves particular notice for the manner in which he handled his battery. The *one exception* above referred to, is Lieutenant Richard Jervis, of the Eighth Indiana, who is represented to have acted in a very cowardly manner, by retiring a section of the battery at a critical moment without orders, or notifying his battery commander.

The following are the casualties, etc., in the several batteries:

BATTERIES AND COMMANDERS.	Officers wounded.	MEN.		
		Killed.......	Wounded.....	Missing.......
H and M, Fourth Artillery, Lieutenant Parsons...	......	2	14	6
B, First Ohio, Captain Standart..........	......	3	13	3
F, First Ohio, Captain Cockerell..........	1	2	12	......
Seventh Indiana, Captain Swallow..........	1	4	7	......
Third Wisconsin, Lieutenant Livingston..........	......	......	4	......
Twenty-Sixth Pennsylvania, Lieutenant Stevens..	......	2	7	......
Eighth Indiana, Lieutenant Estep..........	......	......	6	6
Tenth Indiana, Captain Cox..........	......	1	4	......
Sixth Ohio, Captain Bradley..........	......	2	2	1
Total..........	2	16	69	16

I am, Major, very respectfully,

Your most obedient servant,

JOHN MENDENHALL,

Chief of Artillery.

THE SCIENCE OF EDUCATION;

AND ART OF TEACHING. IN TWO PARTS. BY JOHN OGDEN, A. M.

1 Vol., 12mo. 480 pp. Price, $1.25.

It is proper to say that Mr. Ogden has, for the last six or seven years, been engaged almost exclusively with Teachers and in Normal Schools.

NOTICES.

From the Rev. Wm. Russell, State Educational Lecturer, Massachusetts.

The truly philosophical and thoroughly practical methods of early culture, suggested to the primary teacher, if faithfully acted on, would make our elementary schools scenes of the most attractive and delightful, as well as instructive, occupation for childhood.

From Wm. F. Phelps, A. M., Principal of the N. J. State Normal School.

MY DEAR SIR:—Allow me to say that, in my humble judgment, you have struck the right vein, both in the conception and execution of your ideas regarding the Philosophy ot Teaching. You afford a splendid contribution to our limited means for the training of Teachers. A good scholar merely has fulfilled only one of the conditions essential to a good educator. What we most need is a clear elucidation and a scientific classification of the principles of education, so that they may be mastered and applied to the rearing and training of rational and immortal beings. I need not assure you that this task you have, according to my notions, most happily executed. The application of diagrams to the work seems to me to be a happy thought, addressing the subject to that most perfect of all senses, the sense of sight.

From Cyrus Knowlton, Esq., Principal of Hughes High School, Cincinnati.

It is by far the best work of the kind with which I am acquainted.

From A. J. Rickoff, late Superintendent of Cincinnati Public Schools.

MESSRS. MOORE, WILSTACH, KEYS & CO.:

I have given attention to every work announced in England or this country, treating upon this subject; and I may say, without hesitation, that Mr. Ogden's treatise is, in its conception and arrangement, the *most scientific* among them all. It can not be read by the teacher without great practical advantage; it will prepare him for the business of the schoolroom; it will give new direction to his speculations; it will, I believe, greatly assist to establish the business of teaching as a profession.

Schoolmasters owe it to themselves and their profession, to give this book a circulation never yet reached by any of a similar character. Its use should not be confined to teachers alone. It should find a place in the library of every family, as the most valuable contribution yet made in our language for the advancement of education.

OGDEN ON EDUCATION,

Is a very full and systematic work on the general subject of education, full of suggestive thoughts, tersely expressed. They deserve and demand proper consideration, seasoned by that confidence in their author which his evident carefulness and experience beget.—*Rhode Island Schoolmaster.*

Is just the hand-book for teachers who intend to be thorough and foremost in their profession. Intelligent parents would find it an interesting and valuable aid in the hours when they "ponder in their hearts" how to bring up children.—*Toronto (C. W.) Colonist.*

A very elaborate, philosophical, and thorough work on a great subject, too much overlooked by thinking men. * * * Must be immensely valuable to every parent and teacher.—*N. Y. Observer.*

Contains, in a single volume, a great deal of valuable material. The whole subject of human culture is laid before the reader, and treated in simple yet comprehensive language. * * * Parents and teachers should be induced to study this excellent work.—*Mass. Teacher.*

Has many features, both novel and ingenious, which entitle it to consideration as an original work.—*New York Century.*

Enters very fully and closely into the Philosophy of teaching.—*Philadelphia Press.*

Is a sound, judicious and original work. It does not deal in commonly-received notions, but really enters into the profound themes, upon which it treats with great strength of thought, keenness of perception, and practical skill.—*Zion's Herald, Boston.*

It is the only work extant that can pretend to a full and complete system of instruction. Much has previously been written on the subject that is valuable, which has failed, however, in a great measure, to become available, because of the absence of system, and a failure even to recognize a systematic arrangement as a desideratum. Mr. Ogden approximates more nearly a scientific treatment of his subject than any author we have met.—*Iowa Instructor and School Journal.*

ART OF ELOCUTION:

EXEMPLIFIED IN A SYSTEMATIC COURSE OF EXERCISES.

BY H. N. DAY, A. M.,

Author of "Elements of the Art of Rhetoric," "Rhetorical Praxis," and formerly Professor of Rhetoric in "Western Reserve College."

This work is the fruit of much experience in teaching, and of long and earnest study. 1 Vol., 12mo., 384 pages. Price, $1.

From the late Professor Goodrich, of Yale College, Editor of the more recent editions of Webster's Unabridged Dictionary.

"Prof. Day has gone over the subject with much care, and endeavored to form an art where Dr. Rush had created a science. He has laid open briefly but clearly the great facts relating to the voice in connection with a series of exercises, designed to give the pupil a perfect command of the organs of speech, and a clear conception of what he actually does with his voice in expressing the various modifications of thought and feeling. Such a course of exercises is admirably adapted to break up the dull, inarticulate, mechanical mode of speaking formed by so many in early life, and perpetuated by the hurried and declamatory style of speaking prevalent in most schools.

"His explanations are far more clear and practical than those of any writer we know of, who has attempted to lay open the subject so fully; and we do trust that much good will result from a general circulation of this work among teachers. It will give definite views on many subjects which were wrapped in mystery till Dr. Rush commenced his investigations, and which are still very imperfectly understood by many who think themselves acquainted with the general principles of his treatise. Prof. Day, however, has examined for himself. He has not trusted to the *dicta* of any man. He has seen reason to differ from Dr. Rush on some minor points, and has given the subject a very thorough and searching examination in all its material parts."

A Professor of high standing in another of our best colleges, in a private note, thus speaks of it: "I know not how to do without it. I know of nothing which I could substitute for it."

From the Ohio Educational Monthly.

"This is a good book, prepared by a good man for a good purpose. The author was, some thirty years ago, valedictorian at Yale, and then tutor in that college. Subsequently, for some years, he was Professor of Rhetoric in Western Reserve College, and now he worthily fills the office of President of the Ohio Female College, at College Hill. A better text-book upon the art of Elocution we have never met."

From the R. I. Schoolmaster.

"Prof. Day's Rhetoric has a very high reputation; and this book is what might be expected from the author of that work. The treatise on the art of Elocution is simple, complete, systematic and scientific. The extracts are well chosen. We commend the work highly."

From Prof. SYLLA, *of the University of Chicago.*

"I have examined the work of H. N. Day, on 'The Art of Elocution,' with much pleasure. Having put parts of the work to a practical test, I would cheerfully commend it to the attention of teachers and public speakers."

---

1 Vol., 12mo., 68 pages.

THE SYSTEMATIC ACCOUNTANT

THE ART OF BOOK-KEEPING,

METHODICALLY UNFOLDED IN ITS PRINCIPLES, AND ILLUSTRATED BY COPIOUS EXERCISES, FOR USE IN SCHOOLS AND FOR PRIVATE STUDY.

BY HENRY N. DAY, A. M.

Author of "Elements of the Art of Rhetoric," "Rhetorical Praxis," and "The Art of Elocution."

BAYARD TAYLOR'S
CYCLOPEDIA OF MODERN TRAVEL.

A Record of Adventure, Exploration and discovery for the past fifty years. Comprising Narratives of the most distinguished Travelers since the beginning of this Century. Prepared and arranged by Bayard Taylor. 1 vol. royal 8vo. 1034 pp. Embellished with fine portraits on steel by Buttre, and illustrated by over sixty wood engravings by Orr, and thirteen authentic Maps by Schonberg. Sold by canvassing agents only.

A magnificent octavo volume, which for general interest and value, is worthy of the distinguished compiler, and equally worthy of universal patronage. The volume really contains the value of a whole library, reliable as a book of reference, and as interesting as a book of romance.—*Springfield (Mass.) Republican.*

The popular lectures and writings of Bayard Taylor, have awakened in the United States a thirst for information respecting foreign countries and nations. A striking proof of this is given in the fact that a publishing house in Cincinnati, have issued under the auspices of Bayard Taylor, a volume of nearly one thousand pp., devoted exclusively to records of travel. These Reports are perfectly reliable; the matters of fact of each explorer, often in his own language, are condensed into a consecutive narrative, by the most competent living author in the same department.—*N. Y. Independent.*

The reading public owes to Bayard Taylor many a debt for rare and valuable instruction, most agreeably conveyed; but we doubt if he ever performed a more useful service than in compiling this massive, varied and most valuable volume. The entire circle of books of which he has given the spirit and juice, would form a library; and many of them are now almost inaccessible. Mr. Taylor's part has been conscientiously done. It is not merely a work of selection and groupings; much of it is his own statement of the results more voluminously given, and written in a clear and elegant style. We can not but regard it as a very useful as well as entertaining work, well adapted to communicate accurate and comprehensive views of the world, and supplying for families an almost inexhaustible fund of pleasant reading.—*N. Y. Evangelist.*

No writer of the present age can be found so admirably qualified for such an undertaking.—*Louisville Journal.*

Such is the full title-page of a magnificent octavo volume of 1034 pages, just issued. * * * We said "a magnificent octavo." It is so whether we consider its contents, or the superb style in which the publishers have gotten it up. It is just the book for the family library; all classes will be interested in its perusal.—*Ladies Repository.*

The conception of this work is admirable; and its execution is what might be expected from one of the most accomplished and intelligent travelers of the age. * * * It is remarkable for compactness, condensation and symmetry; and whoever will take the time to read it through, will possess himself of an amount of information, in respect to the physical, intellectual, and moral condition of almost every portion of the globe, which he can scarcely expect to find elsewhere. The work is illustrated with a large number of maps and engravings, which are executed with great skill and care, and add much to the interest of the narratives to which they are prefixed.—*Puritan Recorder.*

Mr. Bayard Taylor is the very Ulysses of modern tourists, and Emperor Adrian of living ramblers—and so is qualified to edit, or compile from the works of other travelers. * * * It is but the merest justice to say, that Mr. Taylor has done all that even an uneasily satisfied reader could expect, to produce a capital book.—*Boston Chronicle.*

Apart from the confidence inspired by the name of the writer, it needs but a brief explanation of its contents to show that it forms a highly important addition to the family library. Its pages are crowded with interesting information.—*N. Y. Tribune.*

From Professor C. C. Felton of Harvard University.

A scholar, traveler and writer, having a reputation so deservedly high in this threefold relation as Bayard Taylor, may be presumed to give his name only to works worthy of it. The present volume I have examined carefully, and have read a considerable part of it; and I have found it prepared and arranged with excellent judgment, and filled with matter of the highest interest and value. Both the plan and execution are in my judgment marked by ability, extensive knowledge, good taste, and good sense.

From Oliver Wendell Holmes, M. D., Author of "The Autocrat of the Breakfast Table," etc.

Mr. Bayard Taylor has done the reading public a great favor in bringing together the most essential and interesting portions of so many narratives within a very moderate compass, and in such a form as to be accessible to multitudes whose libraries must take little room and cost but moderate expenditure. It is safe to say that no man's selection would be accepted so unhesitatingly in America as those of our own favorite travel story-teller.

From Hon. Robert C. Winthrop, of Boston, formerly Speaker House of Representatives, U. S

I have examined it with great interest. It contains a large amount of entertaining and instructive matter, very conveniently and carefully arranged; and I shall value it as a work both for present reading and future reference.

The Wheat Plant:

Its origin, culture, growth, development, composition, varieties, diseases, etc.; together with a chapter on Indian Corn, its culture, etc. By JOHN H. KLIPPART, *Corresponding Secretary of the Ohio State Board of Agriculture. One hundred Illustrations. One Vol., 12mo. pp.* 706. *Price*, $1.50.

From the Cincinnati Commercial.

No work in the language will be found to equal it in the complete, thorough discussion of the great cereal in its entire history. The book ought to be considered indispensable to every farmer, and will be an addition to the library of every intelligent merchant as well as devotee to science.

From the Milwaukie Daily Wisconsin.

We have read it with profit and interest. It should be placed in the hands of every farmer in Wisconsin. Ohio is one of the best wheat-growing States of the Union; yet the average of wheat to the acre has declined from twenty-five bushels to thirteen—all for the want of cultivation by artificial stimulants and manures. In England the crop has been more than doubled, until it now averages thirty-six bushels the acre. This has been accomplished by the closest attention to the wants of the soil.

From the New York Tribune.

The author of this instructive treatise has employed the labor of many years to a thorough investigation of the important plant to which it is devoted. A minnte and accurate knowledge of the subject is exhibited on every page, and its fullness of detail, clearness of illustration, and variety of information, must at once elevate it to the rank of a standard authority.

From the Iowa State Democrat.

It would occupy too much space to go into a general review of this truly valuable work, but we must content ourselves with a few brief sentences taken at random. * * It is highly important that it should be in the hands of every farmer in the Union.

From the Louisville Journal.

The above is a work of over seven hundred pages, comprehending all that is known as to the physiology, culture, varieties, diseases, etc., of the wheat plant. The first comprehensive treatise ever produced in this country on this subject, and perhaps the most thorough work on the subject ever published. * * * * * *

From the Cleveland Morning Leader.

The importance to farmers and all agriculturists of such a book as this, written with great care by such an author, can not be too highly estimated. The Wheat crop is the great crop of the West. * * * Mr. Klippart, from his widely-extended acquaintance with eminent and practical agriculturists, has abundant means for comparing notes and making practical observations, which his abilities as an author enable him to present, in the most beneficial manner, to those interested. * * * * Every farmer should have a copy of this invaluable work. It will amply repay its cost.

From the Davenport Daily Gazette.

This work has been prepared with great care by a man perhaps better qualified for the task than any other person in the country. He has produced a work which should be in the hands of every agriculturist, as it contains a vast amount of information which, if properly put into practice, must result in better and more certain wheat crops.

From the American Farmer, Baltimore.

We have examined this work with great interest, and have marked many of its pages for future reference and quotation in our magazine.

From Prof. Hoyt, in Wisconsin Farmer.

The most elaborate, but also the most valuable production hitherto published on that important subject in this country.

From L. V. Bierce, in Ohio Farmer.

To point out any particular portion as particularly excellent, where all is first-rate, is a difficult task. No farmer should be without it.

From the Country Gentleman.

It is the result of careful and untiring investigation, which, although conducted with special reference to this crop, its varieties, growth, etc., in Ohio, can not but be of great service to the farmers of other States.

PRACTICAL LANDSCAPE GARDENING.

By G. M. Kern. *Containing Twenty-two Illustrations and Plans for laying out Grounds, with full directions for Planting Shade Trees, Shrubbery and Flowers. Third Edition. One volume,* 12mo., *Muslin. Price,* $1 50.

Mr. Kern has produced the right book at the right moment.—Putnam's Magazine.

His suggestions are in an eminent degree valuable, and his opinions (which are expressed in clear, concise, and lucid diction), easily interpreted by even the most limited conception, fairly assert his claim to a station in the foremost rank of rural improvers.—N. Y. Horticulturist.

It abounds in useful and tasteful suggestions, and in practical instructions.—Northern Farmer.

It is a very timely and valuable book. . . . . Better adapted to the wants and circumstances of our people than any other upon the subject.—Ohio Cultivator.

No one can long walk hand in hand with Mr. Kern without being sensible that he is in the hands of one who is worthy of all confidence.—Louisville Courier.

Has so nobly succeeded as to render his volume an invaluable acquisition to all.—Boston Traveler.

It is plain in its details, and will be more valuable to the million than any work on the subject of Landscape Gardening yet published. The mechanical execution of the volume is the very perfection of printing and binding.—Ohio Farmer.

Admirably calculated to meet the wants of the public.—Boston Atlas.

By a careful perusal of this little volume, which will cost but $1 50, the purchaser will probably find that he has learned what he has been all his life wishing to know, and what will be worth to him more than ten times its cost.—Nashville Whig.

He descends to the minutest details of instruction, so that his book may be taken as a manual for the practical operator.—N. Y. Evangelist.

GRAPE AND STRAWBERRY CULTURE.

The Culture of the Grape and Wine Making. By Robert Buchanan. *With an Appendix, containing Directions for the Cultivation of the Strawberry. By* N. Longworth. *Sixth Edition. One volume,* 12mo., *Muslin. Price,* 63 *cents.*

It contains much opportune and instructive information relative to the cultivation of these two delicious fruits.—Michigan Farmer.

One of the books which pass current through the world on account of the great authority of the author's name.—Hoboken Gazette.

There are no men better qualified for the undertaking.—Louisville Journal.

It deals more with facts, with actual experience and observation, and less with speculation, supposition and belief, than any thing on this topic that has yet appeared in the United States. In other words, a man may take it and plant a vineyard, and raise grapes with success.—Horticulturist.

We can not too strongly recommend this little volume to the attention of all who have a vine or a strawberry bed.—Farm and Shop.

This book embodies the essential principles necessary to be observed in the successful management of these fruits.—Boston Cultivator.

We have on two or three occasions said of this little book, that it is the best we have ever seen on the subjects of which it treats. A man with ordinary judgment can not fail in grape or strawberry culture, if he tries to follow its advice.—Ohio Farmer.

HOOPER'S WESTERN FRUIT BOOK.

A Compendious Collection of Facts, from the Notes and Experience of Successful Fruit Culturists. Arranged for Practical use in Orchard and Garden. One vol., 12mo., *with Illustrations. Price,* $1 00.

Three thousand copies of this work have already been disposed of.

RENOUARD'S HISTORY OF MEDICINE.

A History of Medicine, from its Origin to the Nineteenth Century, with an Appendix, containing a series of Philosophic and Historic Letters on Medicine of the present Century, by Dr. Renouard, Paris. Translated from the French, by C. G. Comegys, Prof. Inst. Med. in Miami Medical College. One volume octavo. Sheep, Price, $3 50.

SYNOPTIC TABLE OF CONTENTS:

I. AGE OF FOUNDATION. 1. PRIMITIVE PERIOD: From the Origin of Society to the Destruction of Troy, 1184, B. C. 2. SACRED OR MYSTIC PERIOD: Ending with the Dispersion of the Pythagoreans, 500, B. C. 3. PHILOSOPHIC PERIOD: Ending at the Foundation of the Alexandrian Library, 320, B. C. 4. ANATOMICAL PERIOD: Ending at the Death of Galen, A. D. 200. II. AGE OF TRANSITION. 5. GREEK PERIOD: Ending at the Burning of the Alexandrian Library, A. D. 640. 6. ARABIC PERIOD: Ending at the Revival of Letters in Europe, A. D. 1400. III. AGE OF RENOVATION. 7. ERUDITE PERIOD: Comprising the Fifteenth and Sixteenth Centuries. 8. REFORM PERIOD: Comprising the Seventeenth and Eighteenth Centuries.

From Professor Jackson, of the University of Pennsylvania.

PHILADELPHIA, May 1.

My Dear Sir—The work you have translated, "Histoire de la Medecine," by Dr. P. V. Renouard, is a compendious, well-arranged treatise on the subject.

Every physician and student of medicine should be acquainted with the history of his science. It is not only interesting, but of advantage to know the views and the interpretations of the same pathological conditions investigated at the present day, in past ages. They were handled then with as much force and skill as now, but without the scientific light that assists so powerfully modern research. . . .

Very truly yours, SAMUEL JACKSON.

The best history of medicine extant, and one that will find a place in the library of every physician who aims at an acquaintance with the past history of his profession. . . . . . . There are many items in it we should like to offer for the instruction and amusement of our readers.—American Journal of Pharmacy.

From the pages of Dr. Renouard, a very accurate acquaintance may be obtained with the history of medicine—its relation to civilization, its progress compared with other sciences and arts, its more distinguished cultivators, with the several theories and systems proposed by them; and its relationship to the reigning philosophical dogmas of the several periods. His historical narrative is clear and concise—tracing the progress of medicine through its three ages or epochs—that of foundation or origin, that of tradition, and that of renovation.—American Journal of Medical Science.

Is a work of profound and curious research, and will fill a place in our English literature which has heretofore been vacant. It presents a compact view of the progress of medicine in different ages; a lucid exposition of the theories of rival sects; a clear delineation of the changes of different systems; together with the bearings of the whole on the progress of civilization. The work also abounds in amusing and instructive incidents relating to the medical profession. The biographical pictures of the great cultivators of the science, such as Hippocrates, Galen, Avicenna, Haller, Harvey, Jenner, and others, are skillfully drawn. *Dr. Comegys deserves the thanks of not only the members of the medical profession, but also of every American scholar, for the fidelity and success with which his task has been performed.*—Harper's Magazine.

From the British and Foreign Medico-Chirurgical Review, for July, 1857.

HISTORY OF MEDICINE.—It is expressly from the conviction of the deficiency of the English language in works on the History of Medicine, that we feel indebted to Dr. Comegys for the excellent translation of the comparatively recent work of Renouard, the title of which is placed at the head of this article. . . . . . We hope before long to find that in every important school of medicine in this country, opportunities will be offered to students whereby they may be enabled to attain some knowledge at least of the history of that profession to the practice of which their lives are to be devoted.

HUGH MILLER'S NEW BOOK.

SCENES AND LEGENDS OF THE NORTH OF SCOTLAND.

By Hugh Miller, author of "Footprints of the Creator." 1 vol. 12 mo. Pp. 436. Price $1.

"A delightful book by one of the most delightful of living authors."—*N. Y. Cour. and Enq.*

"In this book Hugh Miller appears as the simple dramatist, reproducing home stories and legends in their native costume, and in full life. The volume is rich in entertainment for all lovers of the genuine Scotch character." *N. Y. Independent.*

"Fascinating portraits of quaint original characters and charming tales of the old faded superstitions of Scotland, make up the 'Scenes and Legends.' Purity of diction and thoughtful earnestness, with a vein of easy, half-concealed humor pervading it, are the characteristics of the author's style. Added to these, in the present volume, are frequent touches of the most elegantly wrought fancy; passages of sorrowful tenderness that change the opening smile into a tear, and exalted sentiment that brings reflection to the heart." *Citizen.*

"This is a book which will be read by those who have read the other works of this distinguished author. His beautiful style, his powers of description, his pathos, his quiet humor and manly good sense would give interest to any subject. * * There is no part of the book that is not interesting."—*Louisville Journal.*

"This is one of the most unique and original books that has been written for many years, uniting in a singularly happy manner all the charms of fiction to the more substantial and enduring graces of truth. The author is a capital story teller, prefacing what he has to say with no learned circumlocutions. We cannot now call to mind any other style that so admirably combines every requisite for this kind of writing, with the exception of that of his more illustrious countryman, Scott, as the one Hugh Miller possesses."—*Columbian.*

"The contents of the book will be as instructive and entertaining, as the exterior is elegant and attractive. Hugh Miller writes like a living man, who has eyes, and ears, and intellect, and a heart of his own, and not like a galvanized skeleton, who inflicts his dull repetitions of what other men have seen and felt in stately stupidity upon their unfortunate readers. His observation is keen, and his powers of description unrivaled. His style is like a mountain-stream, that flows on in beauty and freshness, imparting enlivening influences all around. His reflections, when he indulges in them, are just and impressive."—*Christian Herald.*

"Tales so romantic, yet so natural, and told in a vein of unaffected simplicity and graphic delineation, rivaling Hogg and Scott, of the same land, will command a vast number of admiring readers."—*N. Y. Christ. Intel.*

"The interest of its facts far exceeds romance."—*N. Y. Evan.*

"This book is worthy of a place by the side of the world-renowned volumes which have already proceeded from the same pen."—*Phil. Chronicle.*

www.ingramcontent.com/pod-product-compliance
Lightning Source LLC
LaVergne TN
LVHW020927110826
845150LV00004B/789

9781425553777